DATE DUE

THE COMMONWEALTH AND INTERNATIONAL LIBRARY
Joint Chairmen of the Honorary Editorial Advisory Board
SIR ROBERT ROBINSON, O.M., F.R.S., LONDON
DEAN ATHELSTAN SPILHAUS, MINNESOTA
Publisher: ROBERT MAXWELL, M.C., M.P.

EDUCATION AND EDUCATIONAL RESEARCH
General Editors: DR. EDMUND KING

SOCIETY, SCHOOLS AND PROGRESS IN EASTERN EUROPE

SOCIETY, SCHOOLS AND PROGRESS IN EASTERN EUROPE

BY

NIGEL GRANT

PERGAMON PRESS

OXFORD · LONDON · EDINBURGH · NEW YORK
TORONTO · SYDNEY · PARIS · BRAUNSCHWEIG

1969

PERGAMON PRESS LTD.,
Headington Hill Hall, Oxford
4 & 5 Fitzroy Square, London W.1

PERGAMON PRESS (SCOTLAND) LTD.,
2 & 3 Teviot Place, Edinburgh 1

PERGAMON PRESS INC.,
Maxwell House, Fairview Park, Elmsford, New York 10523

PERGAMON OF CANADA LTD.,
207 Queen's Quay West, Toronto 1

PERGAMON PRESS (AUST.) PTY. LTD.,
19a Boundary Street, Rushcutters Bay, N.S.W. 2011, Australia

PERGAMON PRESS S.A.R.L.,
24 rue des Écoles, Paris 5ᵉ

VIEWEG & SOHN GMBH,
Burgplatz 1, Braunschweig

Copyright © 1969 Pergamon Press Ltd.

First edition 1969

Library of Congress Catalog Card No. 74–77637

Printed in Great Britain by A. Wheaton & Co., Exeter

This book is sold subject to the condition
that it shall not, by way of trade, be lent,
resold, hired out, or otherwise disposed
of without the publisher's consent,
in any form of binding or cover
other than that in which
it is published.

08 013321 5 (flexicover)
08 013322 3 (hard cover)

Contents

COMPARATIVE STUDIES	ix
LIST OF FIGURES AND TABLES	xix
ACKNOWLEDGEMENTS	xxiii
AUTHOR'S NOTE	xxv

PART I

1. Introduction	3
2. Lands and Peoples	11
3. The Making of Eastern Europe (I)—The Social and Historical Background	31
4. The Making of Eastern Europe (II)—The Political Background	46
5. Communist Education—Marxist Theory and Soviet Practice	59
6. Educational Patterns—The Old and the New	73
7. Eastern European Education Today: Some General Features	90
1. Education and Ideology	90
2. Discipline and Moral Education	102
3. Science and Technology	112
4. The Youth Organizations	123
5. Girls and Women	138
6. Administration and Control	147
8. Eastern European Education Today: The Pattern of Schooling	155
1. Pre-School Institutions	155
2. Basic Schools	157
3. Secondary Schools	164
4. Higher Education	167
5. Teacher Training	169

PART II

1. Poland — 175

1. Background to the System — 175
2. The Old System — 182
3. Post-war Developments — 184
4. The Present System — 185
5. Prospects — 201

2. East Germany — 203

1. Background to the System — 203
2. The Old System — 206
3. Post-war Developments — 207
4. The Present System — 212
5. Prospect — 230

3. Czechoslovakia — 232

1. Background to the System — 232
2. The Old System and Post-war Developments — 235
3. The Present System — 235

4. Hungary — 259

1. Background to the System — 259
2. The Old System and Post-war Developments — 262
3. The Present System — 263

5. Rumania — 282

1. Background to the System — 282
2. The Old System and Post-war Developments — 285
3. The Present System — 288
4. Prospects — 297

6. Yugoslavia — 300

1. Background to the System — 300
2. The Old System and Post-war Developments — 306
3. The Present System — 308

7. Bulgaria — 331

1. Background to the System — 331
2. The Old System and Post-war Developments — 333
3. The Present System — 334

8. Albania	345
GLOSSARY	350
INDEX	357

Comparative Studies

An introduction to the Series "Society, Schools and Progress"

by EDMUND KING

THIS volume is one of a mutually supporting series of books on SOCIETY, SCHOOLS AND PROGRESS in a number of important countries or regions. The series is intended to serve students of sociology, government and politics, as well as education. Investment in education, or satisfaction of the consumer demand for it, is now the biggest single item of non-military public expenditure in many countries and an increasing proportion in all the rest. The systematic use of education to achieve security, prosperity and social well-being makes it imperative to have up-to-date surveys realistically related to all these objectives; for it is impossible to study one effectively without reference to the others or to assess the objectives without reference to education as the chosen instrument.

Comparative studies of all kinds are in vogue. We find university departments of comparative government, law, religion, anthropology, literature and the like. Some comparison is taken for granted in a contracting world of closer relationships. But not all comparative studies are forward-looking or constructive. Comparisons based solely or mainly on backward-looking interests can have their own kind of respectability without necessarily drawing lessons for the present. However, some contemporary comparisons show utility as well as interest or respectability, particularly when observers are enabled to analyse social organization, formative customs, value systems and so forth.

More important still are area studies based upon a comprehensive survey of a whole culture, showing the interpenetration of its technology, government, social relationships, religion and arts; for here we see our neighbours making man—and making him in an idiom which challenges our own assumptions and practices. This concerted and conscious making of posterity by a multiplicity of interlocking influences is perhaps mankind's most astonishing feature—at least on a par with rationality and speech, and inseparable from them. As the last third of the twentieth century begins, however, we are witnessing the struggle of competing educational prescriptions for the whole future of mankind.

THE MAKING OF THE FUTURE

The most important studies of all in the world today are those undertaken with a view to modifying deliberately the formative conditions in which our children and their descendants will live —that is to say, their education. In the pre-industrial past there was plenty of time for the slow evolution of civilization and technology. Even in this century people used to think of societies and education as growing empirically and evolving. Today's world cannot wait upon the spontaneity that sufficed yesterday. It is often said that the Industrial Revolution is entering on its second and more important phase—the systematic application to *social* relationships of mechanized and urban-style abundance, with corresponding transformation of all learning opportunities.

Certainly that is the dream of the hitherto underprivileged majority of mankind. All countries are involved in this social stocktaking and reckoning for the future, no matter whether they are called socialistic or capitalistic. In any case, the pace of change is so fast everywhere that some co-ordination or phasing of development is accepted as a critical responsibility of statecraft in all countries.

THE TRANSFORMATION OF EDUCATION

In relation to education, this sequence of events has already been attended by remarkable changes. Education used to be undertaken largely at home, by society at large, by working relationships or by voluntary organizations. Now it is a publicly regulated, publicly financed activity for the most part. It is provided as a necessary service by an expanding range of public employees. Of course unofficial people and social groups continue to take a keen interest, especially in their own children; but increasingly it is the State which co-ordinates and directs the process for all children. In some countries the State claims a monopoly of education; in most others that claim is hotly resisted, though inevitably the State is conceded a growing share in the partnership.

In any case, the State or its professional subsidiaries will assume a mounting responsibility for the allocation of funds, for increasingly expensive instruments and premises, for ensuring fair distribution of opportunity, for preventing the waste of talent, for safeguarding economic and social well-being and for setting the national priorities into proper order. Therefore, no matter what education has been in the past, the logic of the Industrial Revolution has turned it into publicly regulated and publicly provided activities, directed towards the deliberate construction of a more satisfactory future.

That commitment is now implicitly indivisible within any one country. It is also accepted that internationally, too, everyone's education is likely to be to the advantage of everyone else in the long run. For this reason alone, international comparisons and assessments are of the utmost importance.

Whole countries are finding that their external context is changing in unprecedented ways. The emancipation of formerly subject peoples is a conspicuous example. Another instance is seen in the large regional developments whereby food production, commerce, and mutual protection are ensured in "developing countries"—usually with some notable reliance on educational improvements. Even quite powerful and well-established countries (like several in Western Europe) co-operate increasingly with their neighbours for commercial and political reasons; and all these changes necessitate some adjustment of school orientation and programmes, if only for the interchange of personnel. Apart from such specific instances, it is increasingly obvious that no education anywhere is worth the name unless it is viable in world terms.

Great though these adjustments are between sovereign nations, the changes that transcend all national boundaries and apply to all school systems alike are even more radically influential. In all countries, the area of education monopolized by the schools and other formally instructive institutions is diminishing in relation to educative forces outside. For example, the first public television programmes in the world began in 1936; yet within twenty-five years television and radio absorbed almost as much of children's time and interest (taking the year all round) as the formal school hours in a number of countries. The appeal of such external influences may be greater than the schools'. The universal teacher problem accentuates the change.

In any case, all instruction offered in school is largely conditional for its success on subsequent reinforcement. This it does not always get in a world of expanding opportunities and experiences for young people, which challenge schools' previous prerogatives and sometimes their precepts. A whole new range of "service occupations" provides alternative perspectives. Furthermore, technological and social change necessitate much professional retraining and personal reorientation in all advanced countries. There is far less idea of a once-for-all preparation for life. Learning the unknown is taking the place of teaching the certainties.

In all countries we share this uncertainty. Deeply rooted though we all are in our own ways of life, our scrutiny of the future becomes increasingly a comparison of our hypotheses and experiments. No really adequate answers to any educational or social problem can be determined within one country's confines any longer. Comparative Education is above all the discipline which systematizes our observations and conclusions in relation to the shaping of the future.

COMPARATIVE EDUCATION IN GENERAL

Comparative studies of education are necessarily based upon existing practices, institutions, and background influences which have shaped the present variety of educational idioms throughout the world. It is essential to acquaint ourselves with the most important systems, not as alien phenomena but as variations upon the preoccupations of every family and every school in our own country. To be both civilized and scientific we must try to "feel inside" the common human concerns of our neighbours. By this transference of sympathy we achieve some sort of detachment which will enable us to appreciate our own involvement in circumstances—quite as much as theirs.

What adds up to education in our own country is as confused a tangle as any to be found in those other countries where we more easily assume the role of critical advisers. Much of it is habituation, and much is emotionally bound rather than rational. Advice and rational planning that do not take account of these actual influences on education at any one place and time are unscientific as well as failing in humanity. From a practical point of view, too, they will fail, because they lack a sense of the local and topical dynamic. We must know the living present. It is this that gives momentum to the future and conditions it. Thus, even at this first or informative stage of Comparative Education, we are made analytically aware (not only descriptively) of today's climax of forces. We inevitably envisage some possibilities for the future—if only with reference to our own reactions and purposes.

Therefore, though Comparative Education must go on to study particular problems (such as control or university expansion), it must begin with area studies or dynamic analyses of concurrent influences such as this series provides. Without awareness of what "education" seems now to be to its participants, no student or planner can effectively share in the shaping of the future. He may have falsely identified his "problems". He will probably misjudge their topical significance. On the basis of unrealistic generalizations he will certainly fail to communicate acceptable advice. The climax of local culture which amounts to education in any one place is emotionally more sensitive even than language issues or religion, because it includes within itself these very influences and many others.

THE PURPOSE OF THIS SERIES

SOCIETY, SCHOOLS AND PROGRESS are here surveyed in the world's most significant countries—significant not simply for reasons of technological or political strength, but because of the widely relevant decisions in education now being taken. Since the end of the Second World War a ferment of reform has been going on. No reform takes place in the sterile conditions of a laboratory. In the social field not even research can be isolated and sterilized. Experiment in education involves all the untidiness and unpredictability of human responses, which are the source of all creative ingenuity. Every planner or theorist, every student of "problems" that seem abstract and general enough, needs an opportunity of studying again and again the forensic application of his theories.

Nevertheless, so that some general study may be made of frequently recurring tendencies and problems, the books in the SOCIETY, SCHOOLS AND PROGRESS series are arranged in a fairly uniform pattern. They all begin with the historical and institutional background. They then go on to describe administration, the school system, family influences, and background social forces in much the same order of progression. Thus it is easy to make cross-references from one volume to another. Cross-cultural analysis of particular problems or interests is facilitated, but always in relation to the living context which so often reveals unexpected pitfalls or opportunities.

After this second or "problem" level of cross-cultural analysis in detail, the serious student can go on to a third stage. He can assess as a dynamic whole the collective preparation for the future of each of the countries featured. The third level of assessing orientation, or of planning, is not always marked by logic alone within any one of the countries concerned; but an international survey of discernible trends can be of great practical importance. The evolving form of the future can at least be surmised, and continuing research can guide it.

Public investment in education (and consumer demand still more) has often been a precarious venture from the half-known into the unsuspected. Yet buildings, teachers and the children's lives may be committed for generations. For this third level of comparative analysis it is therefore necessary to work closely with specialists in other disciplines, such as economists and sociologists. But the specialist in Comparative Education gives insight and information to them, just as he receives from them. Making the future is no project for any one man, any one discipline, any one interpretation.[1]

This brings us to a last general point. It is more important than ever to have soundly based comparative studies of education, because the relevance of even the best of systems has limits imposed by time. Reorientation and retraining successively throughout life will be the experience of most people in advanced countries for generations to come. That trend is already evident at the most educated levels in the United States, Sweden, Britain and some other countries. All human roles are being transformed, too, not just subjects and occupations. Therefore it is useless to rely on what has been done, or is being done, in schools. We must try instead to think of what will be required, and to observe experiments now being undertaken on the very frontiers of education, where new matrices, new media, new elements and methods of learning are being revealed.

The less settled educational patterns of "developing countries" (where most of mankind live) make it easier for them to be radical. They can by-pass the institutions, methods and curricula of older-established school systems in their eager pursuit of unprecedented but valid objectives. This is all immediately important to us, because the whole world's educative relationships are being transformed, our own along with all the others. For that reason, one or more of the books in each batch of volumes published in the SOCIETY, SCHOOLS AND PROGRESS series will deal with a developing country, whose experience is particularly relevant in assessing education's contribution to the future.

[1] For major problems of decision-taking and implementation, see E. J. King, *Comparative Studies and Educational Decision*, Methuen and Bobbs-Merrill, 1968.

THE PARTICULAR CASE OF EASTERN EUROPEAN COUNTRIES

The countries considered in this volume all have communist governments. All communist governments emphasize that no real distinction can be made between education and politics, between education and industrial or social development. These characteristics alone would necessitate the closest examination of educational developments in Eastern European countries. But there are obvious reasons for a particular interest in those communist countries which, unlike the U.S.S.R. and China, have sought to follow the Marxist–Leninist path in ways which reflect either the wish to experiment or else the previous existence of strong cultural influences which in recent years have been reasserting themselves. Mr. Grant's insights, derived from linguistic and sociological skill no less than from his penetration of educational problems, throw a fascinating light on the divergences as well as the similarities of communist educational systems.

The divergences revealed in the present volume would alone justify the author's labours; but when they are collectively or individually contrasted with the characteristics of the two major communist prototypes they become doubly valuable. Therefore it is to be hoped that readers will also refer to the volume by Dean Chiu-Sam Tsang on *Society, Schools and Progress in China*, and also to Mr. Grant's excellent book on *Soviet Education* or to my own collection of essays on *Communist Education* to which Mr. Grant has kindly referred.

Several other valuable comparisons or contrasts can be made. Communist countries seem monolithic when viewed from outside, particularly when official dogmas or projects of reform are so prominently publicised that they divert attention from several kinds of distinctiveness. Besides the obvious fact that Poland is not Czechoslovakia and that neither of these is the German Democratic Republic (as the author's "inside view" brings out), there are regional and indeed partisan discrepancies. Thus we find not only a "Polishness" or a Czechoslovak character within communist administration, which has led to armed intervention, and to Soviet reproof for educational decisions; we also find regional and sometimes institutional variability of the same kinds that make comparative study so valuable elsewhere. So while we pursue the "theme interest" of communist education and analyse some of its particular problems, we are never allowed to lose sight of the strong contextual influences at work.

Some contextual influences could be described as topical and developmental, rather than environmental in a more geographical or cultural sense. The countries surveyed in this book were themselves at different levels of development (however reckoned) before the communist take-over, and progress has been varied since. Developmental considerations are increasingly important in educational comparisons. Moreover, a country like Yugoslavia still displays much internal diversity of attainment levels, which continues to vex planners and administrators who are sometimes inclined to theorize snags out of the way by referring to canonical texts or party example. Questions of decentralization or methodological experiment still cast doubt on unitary dogmatism, in time leading to demands for various kinds of adjustment and indeed dissonant interpretations.

Since about 1964 in particular, the recognition of some complementariness in communist countries (as distinct from orthodoxy and theoretical planning) has had encouraging aspects for the student of comparative education. Books have come off the official presses of some countries discussed in this volume which openly demand the complementary comparison of views and experiences from capitalist countries as an aid to educational decision, in place of reliance on an official line. Thus within communist systems we discern a developmental trend of the utmost consequence for future peace in the world, and specifically encouraging to comparative studies of many kinds.

Lastly, the objective detachment which is exemplified in the present volume enables the reader to admire and assess rather than simply suspect or condemn. There is so much to admire, and still more to evaluate sympathetically. But has the good achieved been gained by communist theory and domination? Or has it been won by systematic reorganization and the universalization of educational opportunity? If so, we should admire those human gains as triumphs of educational and social advance, not as vindication of a particular political form. We should not let communist doctrines be "proved" simply by good works, any more than all those different religious sects are proved right by the good works that all men praise everywhere. The good claimed for communism could often be achieved by simple socialism; and even that is inclined to claim credit for good works that are really attributable to the revolutionary reorganization of human resources, or the thoroughgoing utilization of widespread educational opportunity.

Figures and Tables

Fig.		*page*
1.	Map: Eastern Europe (political)	9
2.	Map: Peoples of Eastern Europe before World War II	21
3.	Poland: Study-plan for practical and technical instruction in classes V–VIII	140
4.	Diagrammatic representation of control and administration of education in most Eastern European countries	151
5.	Patterns of schooling in Eastern Europe: the typical system	168
6.	The Polish educational system	186
7.	Poland: Eight-year school curriculum	188
8.	Poland: General educational lyceum, 1965–6	193
9.	Poland: General educational lyceum, reformed curriculum	194
10.	Poland: Basic vocational school—electromechanic	197
11.	East Germany: School system 1959–65	210
12.	East Germany: School system (1965)	211
13.	East Germany: Curriculum of the ten-year polytechnical school (before 1965)	215
14.	East Germany: Extended secondary school curriculum before 1965	220
15.	East Germany: Curriculum for *Abitur* class in machine construction, *Berufsschulen* (before 1965)	222
16.	East Germany: Curriculum for two-year vocational schools (*Berufsschulen*)	223
17.	Czechoslovakia: School system	236
18.	Czechoslovakia: Basic nine-year school curriculum	240

19.	Czechoslovakia: General secondary school curriculum (1965–6)	244
20.	Czechoslovakia: Technical school curriculum. Mechanical engineering: special subject—engineering technology	246
21.	Czechoslovakia: Agricultural school curriculum. Special subjects—plant cultivation and animal husbandry	247
22.	Czechoslovakia: Apprentice school curriculum (for mechanics)	250
23.	Czechoslovakia: Apprentice school curriculum (for weavers)	251
24.	Czechoslovakia: Apprentice school curriculum (agricultural mechanization)	252
25.	Czechoslovakia: Secondary schools for workers	254
26.	Hungary: Educational system	264
27.	Hungary: Eight-year school curriculum	265
28.	Hungary: Secondary general school (*gimnázium*) curriculum 1965 ("5+1")	270
29.	Rumania: School system	287
30.	Rumania: Eight-year basic school curriculum	*facing* 288
31.	Rumania: Middle general school (*lycée*) curriculum	290–1
32.	Yugoslavia: School system	309
33.	Yugoslavia: Eight-year basic school draft curriculum (1960)	311
34.	Yugoslavia: Basic eight-year school curriculum (Serbia)	312
35.	Yugoslavia: Curriculum for eight-year schools (Serbia, 1952)	315
36.	Yugoslavia: *Gimnazija* curriculum	317
37.	Yugoslavia: Technical school curriculum: electro-energetics branch	319–20
38.	Yugoslavia: Agricultural technological school curriculum (arable farming)	321
39.	Yugoslavia: Technical school with practical instruction (metalwork)	322

40.	Bulgaria: School system	335
41.	Bulgaria: Eleven-year general school curriculum	336–7
42.	Albania: General secondary school curriculum	347

Acknowledgements

MY THANKS are due to many people who have helped, directly or indirectly, in the preparation of this book.

Firstly, I should like to thank the many pupils, teachers, school directors, professors, lecturers, students and education officials whom I watched at work and questioned, often at length, in Berlin, Warsaw, Prague, Budapest, Bucharest and Belgrade.

For arranging school visits, often with little or no notice, and for providing literature, documents, comments and information of all kinds, I am particularly indebted to the following:

Professor W. Okoń, Dr. Edward Fleming, and the staffs of Warsaw University Faculty of Pedagogy and the Instytut Pedagogiki, Warsaw;

The staff of the Deutsches Pädagogisches Zentralinstitut, Berlin;

Dr. František Singule and Dr. Kamil Škoda, Charles University, Prague;

Dr. Botos Tiborné and the Ministry of Cultural Affairs, Budapest;

Dr. Horváth and the Staff of the Országos Pedagógiai Intézet, Budapest;

Drs. Armașu, Ștefanescu and Popescu-Neveanu, and the staffs of the Ministry of Education and Institutul de Științe Pedagogice, Bucharest;

Dr. Nikola Potkonjak, Prof. D. Franković, and the staff of the Jugoslovenski Zavod za Proučavanje Školskih i Prosvetna Pitanja, Belgrade.

For comments, observations and much useful information I should also like to thank Prof. Ivan Nenov, Bulgarian Deputy Minister of Education, W. Kenneth Richmond of Glasgow

University Education Department, the Polish Cultural Institute, London, the East German Ministry of Public Education, the Polish, Czechoslovak, Rumanian, Hungarian, Yugoslav and Bulgarian Embassies, the U.S. Office of Education, Washington D.C., the Osteuropa-Institut an der Freien Universität Berlin, and in special measure to D. Matko, J. Gold and other members of Glasgow University Institute of Soviet and East European Studies.

Responsibility for the use to which any information has been put, as well as for any interpretations made and opinions expressed, is entirely my own.

N. G.

Author's Note

SINCE the manuscript of this book went to press the East European cauldron has continued to boil, and more furiously than was generally expected. Some of the developments have been fairly routine, but had better be mentioned to bring the account more up to date. In Poland, the Ministry of Education and the Ministry of Higher Education have been combined. In Rumania, the setting up of specialist lycées, adumbrated at the end of Part II, Chapter 5, has gone forward, so that Rumania now has secondary schools, of the type already well established elsewhere, offering both professional and general educational qualifications. In Rumania, too, the higher educational system is being reorganized; the details are complex, but broadly what is involved is the institution of a general first degree course of four years, suitable both for secondary teaching and as the first stage of more specialized work, with a further course of one or two years of postgraduate work for specialists in the various sciences; at the same time, the teacher-training colleges are being further amalgamated into the university structure. In East Germany a reform of the higher educational system, resembling in some ways the organization by "steps" in Yugoslavia, is under study. In the secondary schools the main change has been a general (if slight) reduction in the time for polytechnical and work study, except in East Germany, where there has been a slight increase. In teacher training, the abolition of secondary schools for the training of primary teachers has continued; there are still some in Serbia (as a temporary measure) and in Rumania.

All this, of course, is dwarfed by events in the political field. With the intervention of the Soviet Union and other Warsaw Pact countries in Czechoslovakia in the summer of 1968, many of the developments outlined in the text have been at least partially halted; relations between Yugoslavia and the other countries of the *bloc* have worsened again, the position of Rumania is less secure than it was (and armed intervention there, though it has not happened yet, is no longer inconceivable); there are signs of a refreeze in Poland and East Germany, as well as in the Soviet Union itself; and, of course, the unprecedented growth of "liberalism" in Czechoslovakia has been checked by open force. Altogether, the processes of "thaw" and increasing independence have received a severe setback.

But a setback is not necessarily an end. In spite of everything, the Czechoslovak version of communism is still a great deal more liberal than it was under Novotný—so far, at any rate. It is true that the USSR has reasserted its direct control over most of the *bloc*, but the very act of doing so has shown something of the limitations of force as an instrument of policy under present conditions; already it has been a catastrophically expensive action in political terms. The logic of the situation in Eastern Europe is still in the direction of further liberalization and independence; to halt it completely may be possible, but only at a price that the present leadership of the Soviet Union might well hesitate to pay.

I have thought it better, therefore, to let the text stand without alteration, rather than make piecemeal amendments. The events of 1968, meanwhile, can serve as a reminder of the speed with which things can change in that troubled part of the world. Only the future can tell how many more ups and downs will mark the development of the East European countries in their internal and external politics; but at least the commitment to the development of education remains constant—and in that, at least, there is some cause to hope for better times.

NIGEL GRANT

PART ONE

CHAPTER 1

Introduction

"EASTERN EUROPE" has become a political as well as a geographical expression. Like many terms in current use, it is convenient but often exasperatingly imprecise, and definitions can shift according to one's point of view. To the geographer, it can be relatively straightforward: one can draw a line from somewhere on the Baltic Coast (Rostock, say, or Szczecin) south to the Adriatic, and define as "Eastern Europe" everything between that and another line from the Urals to the Caspian Sea. Some flexibility is possible, as definitions of this kind are always arbitrary to some degree, but since geography has been confounded by geo-politics, this will not do. As the term is normally used at the moment, neutralist Finland is left out. So are Greece and Turkey, which are "Atlantic" powers in alignment if not in position. The European part of Russia is usually excluded too, being more conveniently dealt with in the larger unit of the U.S.S.R. Czechoslovakia, on the other hand, with a strong claim to be considered in Central Europe, is left in. The overriding criterion is political; East European countries are countries ruled by communist governments. Geographical overtones are largely coincidental, and must give way if they do not fit. But imprecise and inconsistent though the term often is, it has its uses. It is not easy to discuss dispassionately "countries behind the Iron Curtain" and "Soviet satellites"—or, alternatively, "people's democracies" and "socialist countries", according to taste. Emotionally loaded terms all too often cloud the issue; "Eastern Europe" is at least comparatively neutral, and thus useful if clearly enough defined.

But even as a political term it raises difficulties. Does it, for example, include Yugoslavia or not? Some prefer to leave it out, presumably because of Tito's break with the Cominform in 1948, and to regard it for most practical purposes as part of the "West". For a long time, this made good enough sense. Yugoslavia's brand of communism has long been established as a deviant form, and treated accordingly with blandishments from some quarters and denunciations from others. The other countries, by contrast, all had communist governments of similar structure, ran their economies in much the same way, were involved economically in COMECON—the communist Common Market—and militarily came under the umbrella of the Warsaw Treaty. Above all, they were effectively under the control of the Soviet Union, which they followed in domestic as in foreign policy, and tended to regard as the principal model for almost everything from agricultural planning to army uniforms. In this situation, Yugoslavia was obviously the heretic outside the fold. But it has become increasingly plain in the last few years that such a high degree of political uniformity can no longer be assumed. Yugoslavia's relations with the U.S.S.R. and the rest of the *bloc* are not always smooth, but usually civil and sometimes warm; it is Albania that now stands out in the cold. Looking now to China for leadership and moral support (and aid), she does not even maintain diplomatic relations with the Soviet Union, which she regards as totally lost to revisionism, backsliding and betrayal of the world communist movement.

But there are other breaks, more important if less drastic, in the former front of unanimity. Rumania has been striking out on an independent line ever since the early 1960's, resisting economic integration in COMECON, showing signs of growing impatience with the Warsaw Treaty, and busily building up cultural and trading links with the West. Poland, of all countries, has been flirting with West Germany, and most of the other countries are displaying divergent tendencies which make it more and more difficult to find any definition of "Eastern Europe" which will take them all in while leaving Yugoslavia outside on her own.

The monolithic character of the communist world began to crack even before it was properly consolidated. The rush of events since Khrushchov repudiated much of Stalin's legacy at the famous "secret speech" in 1956 has shown that nowadays Communism, like Christianity, means many different things to different people, nations and governments. This book, therefore, will deal with those countries in Europe which happen to be ruled by communist governments—whatever their complexion, whatever their relationship at the moment with the Soviet Union, and whether they are on speaking terms or not. For the sake of convenience, they can be grouped into the "northern tier"—East Germany, Poland, Czechoslavakia—and the "southern tier"—Hungary, Yugoslavia, Rumania, Bulgaria and Albania. Admittedly, this is a loose classification, politically and otherwise; the southern tier takes in Yugoslavia and Albania, the arch-revisionists and arch-dogmatists respectively, while the northern tier has to include Czechoslovakia, with her home-made revolution, along with East Germany, still under Soviet military occupation. Nor is political alignment all; there are many important differences in natural wealth and extent of industrialization, which are bound to have an effect on the structure of society, and on the educational system. Further, doctrinal similarities do not rule out tensions of other kinds, such as nationalist squabbles between Rumanians and Hungarians, Yugoslavs and Albanians, or mutual suspicions between Poles, Czechs and East Germans.

But important though the differences are, and even more important though they are liable to become in the future, it would be a mistake to let them obscure fundamental similarities which give the countries in question enough in common to justify their being treated together. Geographically, the area is compact if varied; historically, these countries share a great many experiences, mostly traumatic. Politically, they all subscribe to some form of Marxist–Leninist doctrine; and this, however diverse the interpretations placed on it, however great the expansion of contacts with the West, however high nationalism raises its head in their affairs, sets them apart from the other countries of Europe.

The "Iron Curtain" may be rusting or even crumbling in places, but in a more subtle sense there is still a basic cleavage between Eastern and Western Europe which is likely to remain for many years to come, for all the blurring at the edges that can be seen at the present time.

Educationally too, the East European countries have much in common. There were many similarities in their pre-war school systems, inspired mainly by German and French models, and in the attitudes that lay behind them. In many cases, they shared problems of backwardness, illiteracy, and general neglect of mass education and technical training, especially in the south. Practically all of them, whatever their level of pre-war development, were forced by the devastations of the Second World War to start almost from scratch in building up their educational systems again. All of them, for a time at least, came under the influence of the U.S.S.R., and as they reconstructed their school systems on communist lines drew heavily on the model of Soviet education; and even where there have been the greatest departures from this pattern, the influence of the same basic policies can still be seen at work.

When we are accustomed to thinking on the scale of vastness set by such contemporary giants as the U.S.A., the U.S.S.R. or China, Eastern Europe does not, perhaps, seem to be an area of major world importance. Even by comparison with the rest of Europe it is dwarfed in size. But it should not be dismissed too lightly, or too readily classified simply as an adjunct of its Soviet neighbour. Although it occupies less than half a million square miles (compare the U.S.S.R.'s nearly 9 million), and is strung out on a fairly narrow band from the Baltic to the Adriatic and Black Seas, it is negligible neither in population, with 118 millions—over half that of the U.S.S.R.—nor in industrial output, in spite of the backwardness of many of the countries immediately after the war. Politically, too, the countries of Eastern Europe are coming to wield an influence out of all proportion to size, population or gross national product. The days are gone when the words "communist" and "Soviet" were practically synonymous. Even the contemporary rivalry between Moscow and Peking, and the division of communist countries into pro-Soviet and pro-Chinese, provides too simple a picture of communism as a world phenomenon today, let alone tomorrow—as witness the Soviet Union's switch from coercion to persuasion when dealing with hitherto obedient client states, and the offers by formerly insignificant Rumania to mediate between the two giants. Yugoslavia, too, has for a long time acted as a bridge between the eastern and western *blocs* without (as in Stalin's time) incurring the full penalties of excommunication. During the controversies that went on between the various communist parties in the late 1950's and early 1960's, Palmiro Togliatti, leader of the Italian Communist Party, was the chief advocate of a policy of "polycentrism", a recognition of the right of every communist party to follow its own "road to socialism". Criticized though it was from many quarters at the time, this policy has been gaining ground steadily in the communist world for the past few years; and as this development proceeds, the various countries of Eastern Europe present interesting examples of differing interpretations in practice of Marxist–Leninist theory. It may well be that what began as Stalin's buffer-zone against the West, subject to almost imperially direct rule in all but name, is changing into some kind of communist "Commonwealth" (not without the splits, bickerings and shifts of alignment that such a process is liable to bring in its train). Flexible groupings of this kind are much more difficult to generalize about than more close-knit units, but they are much more interesting and liable to be more informative.

In education too, Eastern Europe is more important than is often recognized. There is no need to urge here the importance of communist theory and practice to the study of education in a world context; the central place given to education in communist policy, and the implications of this for countries adhering to other kinds of régime, has been widely recognized since the first Sputnik shattered many illusions as well as records. Comparative studies have tended to concentrate on the U.S.S.R. This is reasonable enough, up to a point; it is, after all, the only major country where communist policies can be observed in action for much more than a couple of decades, and has been widely regarded, in the East as well as the West, as the primary examplar of communist practice in education as in many other things. But this has often involved neglect of the other communist systems. Information has been more difficult to come by from China and her Asian allies, while the countries of Eastern Europe have often been treated as reflections, slightly modified, of what goes on in the U.S.S.R. Not that this has been altogether unjustified; Soviet models *were* imported wholesale into Bulgaria, Hungary, Czechoslovakia, etc.; modification was, frequently, the minimum made necessary by the brute facts of geography and economics; and as changes became necessary, the Soviet Union was often used, once again, as the model and master-plan—as witness the way in which many countries fell into line over polytechnical education as recently as the early 1960's. But diversity, never totally absent, is on the increase. National sentiment and tradition, as well as local conditions are reasserting themselves more and more, so that the systems of the various countries, while still communist, are also Rumanian, Polish, Hungarian and so on. Even in Europe, then, communist education is no longer quite the same thing as Soviet education. The basic affinities and links remain, but the present trend is towards diversity, experiment, reinterpretation. Polycentrism shows in the educational as well as the political and economic fields. Where once there was one model of communist education, there are now several, and they are growing more distinctive with every year that passes.

The U.S.S.R., after all, is not only the first laboratory of the communist experiment. It is also the successor to Holy Russia, the inheritor of a complex tradition going back to the days of early Muscovy and before. As Nicholas Hans puts it: "The fundamental fact of identity between historical Russia and the present international Marxist Soviet Union should be borne in mind in order to understand the theory and practice of Soviet education". The educational model, then, that the East European countries used after the war was Russian as well as communist; many of the

Fig. 1. Map: Eastern Europe (political)

developments of the present time stem from a desire to recognize more fully the fact that they are *not* Russian. No country, however revolutionary, is totally free of its past; no ideology has succeeded totally in wiping out national traditions, and this applies to Communism as much as any other. Thus, though the influence of Soviet educational policies cannot be denied, the schools of Czechoslovakia, Rumania, Hungary and Yugoslavia have, in their own way, as good a claim to be examplars of communist education as those of the Soviet Union. Family resemblances are often strong, but families do consist of individuals.

Educational systems do not exist in a vacuum nor do educational policies, however overriding their motive ideologies may be. Whatever the intentions of those who run them, they are deeply affected by the context—geographic, demographic, historical, social, economic, as well as political—in which they operate. It will be necessary then, to consider the most relevant of these factors as a background against which to examine the schools and the work they do, for these factors largely determine the problems that the schools have to face and the means by which they try to face them.

CHAPTER 2

Lands and Peoples

EASTERN EUROPE is a block of territory, pinched at the middle, strung out irregularly from the Baltic Sea to the northern frontiers of Greece, of approximately 1000 miles. It varies in depth from 500 miles in the north and rather more across the Balkans in the south to not much over 200 miles at its narrowest point, at the Czechoslovak–Hungarian frontier; it can be (and is) flown across in a matter of minutes. Thus the considerations of "defence in depth", whatever they may have been in 1945, have been rendered much less relevant in the 1960's.

The total area covers something less than half a million square miles, not a great expanse when measured against the rest of Europe, with or without European Russia. But, though small by such standards, it is remarkably varied. In the north, it forms part of the great plain that sweeps from the Urals to nothern France, much of it good agricultural land. Lacking natural barriers, it is open to the bitter winters of the East, though spared the worst rigours of the Russian heartland. Further south, past the mountains of Czechoslovakia, there are the lush plains of Hungary and the Yugoslav Vojvodina, yielding in turn to the bleaker highlands of Bosnia, Serbia, Macedonia and Albania, largely dry and barren; hot, sometimes oppressively so, in the summers, cold in the winters. Rumania and Bulgaria are similarly varied; bare mountains dropping to more hospitable plain country along the Danube valley and towards the Black Sea. In this relatively narrow strip of territory, then, we have almost every kind of climate that the continent can provide, and almost every variety of soil from the richest to the nearly totally barren.

On balance, though, the overall potential for agriculture is reasonably good. In spite of having some extremely unpromising areas, all of the countries except Albania are able to devote a substantial proportion of their land area to farming[1] (over 60 per cent in Hungary, over 50 per cent in Poland, down to a little over 30 per cent in Yugoslavia). Even poorly endowed Albania, incidentally, with about 13 per cent of the land under cultivation, is better off in this respect than the U.S.S.R. or China, with 10 and 12 per cent respectively. In most countries, too, much of the non-arable land can be used for grazing, or forestry—nearly 40 per cent in Poland, for instance.[2] Agriculture is not normally a strong-point of any communist country's economy; none the less, except for Czechoslovakia, they manage to be more or less self-supporting, and some of them export a good deal—as Bulgaria does fruit, for example.[3] That agriculture has often been mismanaged does not alter the basic fact that, potentially at least, most of these countries are well placed for food production, and that agriculture, for all the increased emphasis on heavy industry since the war, plays an important part in their economies.

This raises a number of educational problems. In the first place, a high proportion of the population remains on the land, in villages. The proportion varies a good deal from country to country and place to place, but over the area as a whole, less than half the population can be classed as urban (compare the United Kingdom, with over 80 per cent).[4] This, in turn, raises problems of schooling in rural areas. It is always easier, for example, to maintain a supply of teachers in the cities and the main towns, where living standards tend to be higher and amenities of all kinds—theatres, cinemas, hospitals and medical services, libraries, shopping facilities, and so forth—more abundant than in the countryside. Bucharest has a small surplus of teachers, while the village schools are often short staffed;[5] the Rumanian authorities

[1] J. P. Cole, *The Geography of World Affairs*, pp. 212, 215. (Penguin, 1963.)
[2] *Poland 1944–1964*, p. 98. (Polonia, Warsaw, 1964.)
[3] J. P. Cole, *op. cit.*, p. 212.
[4] *Ibid.*, p. 107.
[5] Oral communications in Bucharest, September 1965.

seek to solve this by setting up training institutions in provincial centres, by controlling the influx of population to the towns, and by directing teachers for periods of two years or so to places where they are most needed. But this is only a partial solution; it is not always easy to enforce, and in any case involves a higher rate of turnover of staff in the rural schools. Again, the Yugoslavs have no difficulty in getting teachers in Belgrade, Zagreb or Ljubljana; the surplus of teachers is great enough to make it common for them to be over-qualified for the level of class they are employed to teach. But in the more remote areas, especially in Bosnia, Montenegro or the southern parts of Serbia, many schools are 40 per cent (or even more) understaffed.[6] The Yugoslav authorities, unwilling or unable to resort to direction of labour, try a variety of expedients such as extra payments, the provision of housing, persuasion, and so on, but have not managed to close the gap between town and country. Thus the country areas have much more than their share of oversized classes and under-qualified teachers at best, and a higher level of illiteracy at worst. It is normal, almost everywhere, for the peasantry to form a class of second-grade citizens educationally, and in the communist countries there remains the danger of keeping them that way. This in turn is likely to hinder any ambitious plans for the improvement of agriculture, which is a difficult enough matter at the best of times.

The important role of agriculture in many of the East European countries affects education in other ways too. One of the cardinal principles of communist education is that it must be "closely related to life" (of which more later). This means, among other things, that the authorities take seriously the need to relate general education to the pupils' vocational needs, and to the needs of the economy of the country at large. This problem does not really arise in primitive peasant economies; except for (possibly) some basic elementary schooling, education passes the future peasant by, and those who do succeed in advancing their

[6] Oral communications in Belgrade, 1965.

schooling tend to leave the land, since the opportunities to make any use of their training and qualifications are certainly limited and usually nonexistent. This is what happened in most of the East European countries before the war, and to some extent still does. But if a country is committed to a programme of universal literacy and mass education, *and* to the improvement of agriculture, this will not do. Some way has to be found to make the whole range of primary, secondary and indeed higher education relevant to the conditions of rural life; and since the educational systems at present are town-based and biased towards the professions and industry (in practice if not in theory), some rethinking is necessary. It would be ironic if every improvement in the provision of educational facilities were to mean, automatically, a further drift from the land. Some drift is, of course, inevitable; as industrialization progresses, and as agriculture becomes less dependent on pairs of human hands, the proportion of the population devoted to agriculture dwindles; in Poland, for example, it has dropped from 60 per cent in 1931 to 47 per cent in 1950, and to 38 per cent in 1960.[7] In Yugoslavia it has fallen from 60 to 50 per cent in the last decade.[8] In East Germany it is down to 18 per cent.[9] Urban population, on a world scale, seems to be increasing at about twice the rate of population in general, and this trend is to be seen in Eastern Europe as elsewhere. But the fact remains that significant sections of the population in these countries will continue, for the foreseeable future, to live in the countryside and earn their living in agriculture—a fact that any educational system "closely related to life" will have to take account of.

At the same time, there is enormous room, even a pressing need, for the improvement of farming techniques. Agricultural efficiency, as measured by yield per acre, compares favourably with Greece, Spain, Portugal and many countries outside Europe, but is on the whole rather low when measured against Western

[7] *Poland 1944–1964*, p. 73.
[8] Stana Tomašević and Mustafa Begtić, *Vocational Training in Yugoslavia*, pp. 35–36. (Belgrade, 1961.)
[9] *Statistisches Jahrbuch der DDR 1964*. (Staatsverlag der DDR, Berlin, 1964.)

Europe or the United States.[10] Peasant farming is not usually highly productive, and the various forms of collectivization—usually unpopular and now abandoned in some countries—have not been particularly successful in improving this. But this is perhaps not the main issue; the pressing need is to produce more by applying the findings of science to practical farming, a task perhaps simple enough in principle but made difficult by (among other things) the deeply ingrained conservatism of peasant communities almost everywhere. Government advisors and agronomic teams are all very well, but they have often found it hard going to convince farmers that the familiar ways are not necessarily the best. On the longer term, the answer may lie in the schools, and much attention, therefore, is being being given to various types of agricultural trade schools, agricultural secondary schools, and the like. In some countries, attempts are being made to create new types of school, where a full-scale academic secondary education will be linked with agricultural training—the proposed *agricultural lycées* in Rumania are an example of this.[11] On the success of schools of this type may depend the chances of improving agriculture *and* eliminating what one Polish writer calls "the privileges of residence"[12] operating against rural pupils, by making both elementary and secondary schooling relevant to the needs not only of the future professional man and clerical worker, but the future peasant as well.

The East European countries vary, too, in their possession of mineral wealth and the extent to which they have exploited it and built up their own industries. Broadly, the "northern tier" is both richer in minerals and more highly industrialized than the southern, though there are many exceptions and the picture is changing. Czechoslovakia and Poland, the only countries producing a sizeable quantity of hard coal, had a head start on

[10] *Statistički Kalendar Jugoslavije 1965.* (Savenzi zavod za statistiku, Belgrade, 1965.)

[11] Nicolae Ceauşescu, "Raport la cel de-al IX Congres al Partidului Comunist Român." Quoted in Stanciu Stoian, "Un obiectiv important al politicii noastre" (*Revista de Pedagogie*, **8**, 1965, p. 9).

[12] Maria Paschalska, *Education in Poland*, p. 15. (Polonia, Warsaw, 1962.)

the others, and East Germany produces much more lignite than the rest. These three countries, alone in the area, are included in the "top twenty" for steel production, with between 7 and 3 million long tons of steel output per year. Iron ore deposits, though useful, are not large, but with the other advantages the northern countries have been able to build up important engineering industries; the biggest concentrations in Eastern Europe (apart from those gravitating around Berlin, Warsaw and Prague) are in the south of Poland and East Germany, particularly around Katowice and Leipzig, and in the Ostrava district of Czechoslovakia, in the neighbourhood of the Upper Silesian coalfield. Hungary, with an industrial concentration in the Miskolc area, is intermediate between the two groups.[13]

But the southern countries, though still predominantly agricultural, are changing. Albania, it is true, has practically no industry, but Yugoslavia has deposits of bauxite and zinc, Bulgaria has some iron, zinc, lead and other minerals; Rumania has a fair endowment of minerals, notably manganese and, above all, oil in the Ploieşti region—a fact gratefully acknowledged by the inclusion of an oil-derrick in the Republic's coat of arms. Heavy industry has been built up, such as Bulgaria's industrial town of Dimitrovgrad or the Kremikovtsi Industrial Complex near Sofia, or Rumania's giant iron and steel works at Galaţi. This last was built in the face of some Soviet opposition, since the U.S.S.R. would have preferred Rumania and Bulgaria to have concentrated on the production of food and raw materials as part of the proposed "Lower Danubian economic complex" within COMECON,[14] leaving the bulk of heavy industrial development to the northern countries, and, of course, the U.S.S.R. itself. But the trend of current policy, in Rumania as elsewhere, is to press ahead with industrial development and diversify the economy— and thus, incidentally, since broad-based economies are usually

---

[13] J. P. Cole, op. cit., pp. 212–15.
[14] Ghiţa Ionescu, *The Break-up of the Soviet Empire in Eastern Europe*, pp. 123–33. (Penguin, 1965.) George Schöpflin, "Rumania Strikes Out on her Own" (*New Society*).

more resilient than narrow-based ones, reinforcing tendencies towards greater political as well as economic independence.

The educational implications of these developments are profound. The more industry is built up, the greater are the demands on the educational system. Obviously, a country seeking to expand industry has a need for technologists, scientists, engineers, specialists of all kinds and, at a lower level, a greatly expanded corps of technicians and skilled workers—hence increased pressures on higher, secondary technical and adult education. But it was precisely in these fields that the educational systems were most deficient, notably in the southern countries. East Germany was better placed than most in this respect, since there had been *Berufsschulen*—part-time trade schools compulsory for all school leavers from 14 to 19—since the end of the First World War. But in Poland there were no vocational schools for adults, and only 207,500 students in vocational schools of any kind—less than a fifth of the present enrolment.[15] In Czechoslovakia there were 75,500 students in technical schools before the war, as against the present figure of over a quarter of a million.[16] In Yugoslavia there were fifty-three technical schools before the war, with about 10,000 students, compared with 257 at the end of the 1950's with over 76,000 students.[17] In Bulgaria there were only a few specialized schools and a handful of trade schools, and they were of poor quality in any case.[18] In the post-war expansion of educational facilities, therefore, the claims of the technical sector were urgent. But, as we shall see, backwardness in technical education in these countries was only part of a picture of general educational backwardness, from the elementary school up. Illiteracy was not a problem in Czechoslovakia, and in Hungary, at 8·8 per cent, it was low by the standards of the area—but less than half the children of school age completed even six years of elementary

[15] *Poland 1944–1964*, p. 158.
[16] Stanislav Vodinský, *Czechoslovakia: Education*, p. 50. (Orbis, Prague, 1963.)
[17] Stana Tomašević and Mustafa Begtić, *op. cit.*, p. 77.
[18] Nevena Geliazkova (ed.), *Prosperity and Culture in Bulgaria*, p. 102. (Foreign Languages Press, Sofia, 1964.)

schooling.[19] In Poland, barely 25 per cent completed the seven-year elementary school, and over a quarter of the population were illiterate.[20] In Rumania, too, 25 per cent were illiterate,[21] while in Yugoslavia the figure stood at 46 per cent in the 1930's; even this estimate was generous, since anyone who could sign his name was reckoned to be literate. In the 1961 census, a reading test was used to determine literacy more stringently; this yielded a figure of just under 20 per cent.[22] For this reason, then, a disproportionate amount of money and resources had to be found to make up the back-log of the previous decades; vastly improved literacy, as well as technical schooling on a higher level, was a necessary condition of industrial advance. There was (and is) also the problem of built-in attitudes to vocational schooling, for this was widely regarded as very much a second best to the academic school that led to higher education and the liberal professions. One Rumanian commentator[23] has mentioned the traditional discriminatory view of "theoretical schools for the élite", middle-grade professional schools for the "N.C.O.s" and vocational schools for the "other ranks". He adds that "in the socialist régime, the system is realized in the spirit of equality, by right and in fact, to education according to the needs of society and the apititudes of the individual". But traditional attitudes are hard to shift, such statements notwithstanding, and even the ambitious programmes of expansion in technical schooling have not entirely met the problem—the most able pupils still often prefer the more prestigious academic secondary schools. According to one Yugoslav student,[24] the qualifications gained in technical secondary schools are just as good for most purposes as those taken in an academic

[19] Márton Horváth, "Public and Higher Education", pp. 80–81. In: János Veres (ed.), *The Experiences of Building a New Society*. (Pannonia, Budapest, 1964.)
[20] Zygmunt Parnowski, *Education in Poland*. (Polonia, Warsaw, 1958.) *Poland 1944–1964*, p. 153.
[21] Herta Haase and Seymour Rosen, *Education in Rumania*, p. 2. (U.S. Office of Education, Washington D.C., 1960.)
[22] Tomašević and Begtić, *op. cit.*, p. 37.
[23] Stanciu Stoian, "Un obiectiv important al politicii noastre" (*Revista de Pedagogie*, **8**, 1965, p. 10).
[24] Oral communication, Belgrade, 1965.

school, and better in some cases where the student wishes to enter some scientific branch of higher education; none the less, his parents had dragooned him into going to a *gimnazija* "to fulfil their own ambitions at second-hand". This kind of reaction is common throughout the area, and although the bias at secondary level is shifting to courses of the technical type (41 per cent in Poland, for instance, as against 22 per cent pre-war),[25] technical schooling still often represents a second choice. Thus in industry, as in agriculture, the problem remains of making secondary education relevant to the needs of those entering employment, and here again there have been serious attempts to combine full-scale general education with training for work in industry, avoiding if possible the idea that such schooling is a poor relation of the traditional academic type. The technical schools of Czechoslovakia, Yugoslavia, Hungary, with their substantial element of academic subjects, the proposed technical *lycées* of Rumania, the East German *Berufsschulen mit Abitur*, and so on, are attempts to close this gap. This is no doubt one reason for the widespread introduction of some kind of technical or polytechnical training in the academic secondary schools as well.

The expansion of industry has other less direct effects, already touched on. In so far as any East European country relies for its living mainly on agricultural produce and raw materials, it is more dependent for its viability on COMECON—that is, in effect, the Soviet Union—and it is a political commonplace, in the West and in the East, that economic dependence usually means dependence in other fields. As industrialization progresses —as we have seen in the case of Rumania—economic independence grows too, and this is liable to extend to political matters. This, in turn, tends to make for assertions of independence in other areas, cultural, social and frequently educational, as the authorities seek to instil a sense of national individuality in the future as well as the present citizens. We should expect to find, in such circumstances, a greater degree of divergence from the Soviet educational model, and in the case of Rumania (the main

[25] Maria Paschalska, *op. cit.*, p. 57.

protagonist of independence within the *bloc* at the moment) this is precisely what we do find. This is not to say that industrialization, in itself, is the immediate cause of self-assertiveness in education. Other factors, such as national and cultural pride, are also at work. But it can bring such tendencies to a head, and by making a country such as Rumania relatively immune to economic pressures, open up the possibilities in striking out on one's own in education as in other areas of national life.[26]

It is no accident that the authors of Ruritanian fantasies frequently place their imaginary states—Slobodia, Valdania, Bosnivina, Concordia and a whole General Assembly more— somewhere in the Balkans. The population of Eastern Europe is as varied as its geography. In this comparatively small area there are substantial populations of Slavs—Poles, Czechoslovaks, Yugoslavs and Bulgarians, to mention only those with nation-states of their own—the remnants of a complex of tribes that began to spread in all directions from (probably) Poland in the early centuries of the present era. Germans, as well as forming the majority in East Germany, are represented by significant minorities elsewhere. The Rumanians, who trace their descent from Roman settlers in Dacia, speak a language still recognizably Latin in spite of many Slav borrowings. The Hungarians, descended from nomads who swept in from Asia during the Middle Ages, speak a language unrelated to anything except Finnish and Estonian, and that remotely. Finally there are the Albanians, the Gheg and Tosk tribes of the Epirotic mountain country, whose language forms a division all by itself of the Indo-European family, heavily impregnated with Turkish loan material.

But even this is an over-simplification. For one thing, there are many more Slav peoples than there are states. The Poles have a strong sense of national identity and a unified language, but even this exhibits a variety of forms, especially in the east where it blends into Byelorussian and Ukranian. The Czechoslovaks are, linguistically at least, two nations rather than one, and two forms

[26] George Schöpflin, *op. cit.*, and Ghiţa Ionescu, *loc. cit.*

Note: Principal changes in post-war period:

1. Expulsion of bulk of German population from Oder-Neisse Territories, East Prussia, Sudetenland, and heavy emigration from elsewhere.
2. Russian settlement (partial) in Baltic States, Bessarabia and Ukraine/Byelorussia generally, especially in towns.
3. Population exchanges between Hungary and Slovakia

In many areas the populations are still more mixed than the map shows; small groups are not shown, but are numerous.

FIG. 2. Map: Peoples of Eastern Europe before World War II

of the language are now recognized for official and educational purposes, namely Czech in Bohemia and Moravia, Slovak in Slovakia. There are also within East Germany the Sorbian or Wendish Slavs, who have been cut off by surrounding Germans since medieval times. Among the southern Slavs the picture is even more complicated. Linguistically, they form a crescent-shaped spectrum shifting from Slovene in the north of Yugoslavia, through Croat and Serbian in the greater part of the country, to Macedonian in the south, where it curves round into Bulgarian, finishing up on the Black Sea coast between Rumanians and Greeks. Within Yugoslavia, Serbian and Croat are similar enough to be treated almost as one language, but Slovene is distinct, and Macedonian is much closer to Bulgarian—itself developed from several dialects. The division of the southern Slavs into Yugoslavia and Bulgaria is not primarily a linguistic one; Macedonia and indeed Serbia have more in common with Bulgaria in some ways than with Slovenia. Religious and cultural differences complicate the picture further; Croats and Serbs are divided by the Latin and Cyrillic scripts, the legacy of Catholic and Orthodox influence respectively. The Bosnians, though Serbian by language for all practical purposes, have a claim to separate nationhood based on their Muslim background. Yugoslavia—"the land of the South Slavs"—is from this point of view an artificial creation and often an uneasy one at that.[27] The sense of separateness felt by most Slavs is apparent throughout the East European area. Many will make verbal concessions to pan-Slavic sentiment, a sentiment of long standing which Russian rulers from the Tsars to Stalin[28] have tried to exploit, without much success. The idea of pan-Slavic unity tempted, for a time, the Yugoslavs and the Bulgarians, but it made little impressions on the Poles, who associated it, in the light of long experience, with Russian domination. The Slavic nature of many of the East European countries does not,

[27] Jean-Marie Domenach and Alain Pontault, *Yugoslavia*. (Vista, London, 1962.) Vladimir Dedijer, *The Beloved Land*. (McGibbon & Kee, London, 1961.) Both works vividly convey the tensions that divide Yugoslavia's national groups.

[28] Milovan Djilas, *Conversations with Stalin*, pp. 24–26, 48. (Penguin, 1963.)

then, impose any great degree of unity on them; they continue to assert, often stridently, their separate nationhood.

This is even more true of the non-Slav peoples, the Rumanians, Hungarians and Albanians. Being more isolated, they are less liable to fragmentation than the Slavs, but even here the imposed separations of history, and the existence of geographical barriers, have produced some variation. The Albanians are divided into the Ghegs and the Tosks, who were on blood-feud terms until recently—indeed, the post-war quarrels within the Communist Party between Enver Hoxha and Koçi Xoce showed considerable correlation between political factions and tribal origins. Within Rumania there are several main divisions—Vlachs, Arumanians, Transylvanians, etc.—not to mention the population of the Moldavian S.S.R. across the Soviet Border, who are linguistically Rumanian in all but alphabet. Among the non-Slavs, the Germans are rather a special case. East Germany itself, with its population of about 17 millions, is a geographical anomaly, cut off from the 60 millions in West Germany by an artificial frontier based solely on the lines of military occupation. For obvious reasons, undue harping on German nationality is not encouraged, either by the Soviet Union or by the East German authorities themselves. Reunification is still official policy, of course, though one hears less about this than in the pre-Wall days of the 1950's when slogans like "Deutsche an einen Tisch"—German at one table— proliferated all over East Berlin; but it is reunification on terms that, at the moment, seem unlikely to be achieved. Before the war there were 3 million Germans in the Sudetenland are a of Czechoslovakia, but they were expelled after the war,[29] as were other Germans from areas annexed by Poland. There are also enclaves of Germans scattered over most of Eastern Europe. There are over 60,000 in Yugoslavia alone.[30] Rumania has 40,000[31]—the so-called Saxons of Transylvania and the Swabians of the Banat—

[29] Over 9 million Germans were expelled from or left Eastern Europe after the war. For a graphic representation, see Martin Gilbert, *Recent History Atlas*, p. 89. (Weidenfeld & Nicolson, London, 1966.)

[30] Jean-Marie Domenach and Alain Pontault, *op. cit.* p. 190.

[31] *Anuarul Statistic al RPR* 1963. (Direcţia Centrală de Statistică, Bucharest.)

most of whom have been there for centuries. They enjoyed, on the whole, a privileged position, but this, and the preferential treatment shown them by Hitler—he turned them into extra-territorial *Volksdeutsche*—did them no good in the long run. The East Germans are sensitive enough about the way their compatriots behaved during the war, and are therefore not in a position to act as a rallying-point for a minority groups outside their frontiers. Germans in the other countries, therefore, though normally allowed their own schools and newspapers, are not as a rule popular, especially in countries that suffered under German occupation, where many still tend to regard the distinction between "good" and "bad" Germans as rather academic. Increasingly, they tend either to assimilate or emigrate, and most of the countries where they live are glad enough to see them go. Most Germans from Rumania (like the Sudeten Germans from Czechoslovakia) tend to emigrate to *West* Germany, but this does not trouble the Rumanians in the least. As they see it, they are lightening one minority problem, and they have enough already. This, again, is true of much of the East European area.

On the map, political frontiers look definite enough[32]. To all appearances, the transition is abrupt, and even crossing frontiers on the ground seems to bear this out. At one station, the railway signs are all in German, at the next, Polish; in the same way, one seems to leap from Hungary to Rumania, Rumania to Yugoslavia, and so on. But population patterns have a habit of being much more untidy than they look. This is probably least obvious (though not absent) in relatively stable Western Europe, and most obvious in Africa, where the borders of colonies—and now states—were drawn on the map without regard for or knowledge of the people actually living there. In Eastern Europe a history of migrations, wars, invasions, conquests, right up to the end of the Second World War, has left a kaleidoscope of nationalities whose distribution has little bearing on the sharp lines drawn on a map that assigns Rumanians to one side, Bulgars to the other. In

[32] For good illustrations of this point, see Martin Gilbert, *Recent History Atlas*, pp. 6, 62, 89.

the present century, boundaries have been drawn and redrawn with bewildering frequency—bewildering often to the inhabitants as well as the observer. Poland and Czechoslovakia include large areas once ethnically German; Albanians spill over their northern frontier into the Kosmet area of Yugoslavia, as do Greeks into southern Albania; there are Hungarians in northern Serbia and central Rumania, Serbs in Hungary and Rumania, Rumanians in Bulgaria and vice versa. Examples could be multiplied indefinitely.

In the fixing of frontiers, political horse-trading has frequently ignored the complexion of populations. Poland got the areas east of the Oder–Neisse Line not because they were populated by Poles (only parts of them were) but to give Poland a sea-coast as well as a *quid pro quo* for the territories in the east ceded to the U.S.S.R., which were in any case mainly inhabited by Byelorussians and Ukrainians. The Polish state was thus in effect shifted some 200 miles to the west. Any reluctance on Yugoslavia's part to let the Albanians have the Kosmet[33] may have been due to fears that this might reinforce centrifugal tendencies further north, where coexistence between Serbs, Croats and Slovenes has often been, to put it midly, uneasy. Again, Czechoslovakia's retention of the Sudetenland owed more to considerations of "natural frontiers" than population, the Germans being expelled as a national security risk; the Czechs had all too good a reason to remember the use that was made of the "self-determination" issue there in 1938, when Hitler made this the first step in his total subjugation of Czechoslovakia.

But it should be pointed out that in many places the problem is virtually insoluble, and that even the most scrupulous concern for the principle of self-determination could not please everyone. The Hungarians of Transylvania, for example, form a fairly compact mass of over 1½ million, totally surrounded by Rumanians and

[33] There was in any case, after the war, the possibility of a federal union that would have included, among others, Yugoslavia and Albania. This, and the fact that Albania was at that time a protégé of Yugoslavia, damped down the national issue until the break of 1948—by which time any kind of accommodation had become impossible.

thus effectively cut off from Hungary itself. The whole area of Transylvania has changed hands several times since the break-up of the Austro-Hungarian Empire after the First World War. The Rumanians got it after the Treaty of Versailles, Hitler gave it to the Hungarians during the Second World War, and Stalin gave it back to the Rumanians after the war. Each change, of course, meant foreign rule for somebody—not a pleasant prospect in countries where national passions have always been quick to boil over. The history of the area is crammed with incidents of national conflict,[34] ranging from the slightly comic—as when the Hungarian police subjected a girl of 6 to questioning because she wore a red, yellow and blue ribbon in her hair (the Rumanian national colours)—to the bestial, such as the massacre of 150 Rumanian peasants by Hungarians in the village of Ip-Sabaj in 1943, or the public beheadings of Hungarians carried out in the village of Aita Seaca by gangs of Rumanian nationalists a couple of years later. National hatreds have not always taken such a violent course, nor are there many groups as sizeable as the Transylvanian Magyars in such a position; but there are plenty of smaller ones, and to some degree the story is repeated all over Eastern Europe.

There are other groups too, with no homelands to look to for moral support, at least not in any effective sense. The long Turkish occupation of the Balkans left little pools of Turks as the tide receded; there are Armenians in Rumania, Gipsies in Hungary, and many other groups, such as Ukrainians in Yugoslavia and Russians in Bulgaria, scattered too far from their homelands to make anything but minority status completely impossible. Wherever the frontiers are drawn, and whatever considerations govern their settlement, mixed populations are an inevitable fact of life in Eastern Europe. In theory, this should not matter all that much in a communist country; loyalty to class is considered much more important than loyalty to a nationality, and the international doctrine of Marxism–Leninism is supposed to override narrow

---

[34] These particular examples are from Jack Lindsay and Maurice Cornforth, *Rumanian Summer*, pp. 90–101. (Lawrence & Wishart, London, 1953.) There were plenty of others.

jingoistic feelings. The constitutions[35] of the East European countries make a great deal of national equality, and state firm guarantees of the rights of minorities to their own languages, books, newspapers, schools and so forth. But one of the legacies of a turbulent history has been an almost universally strong nationalism[36] from the Baltic to the Balkans, submerged at times but rarely far below the surface—doubtless a survival mechanism in a situation where practically everbody in this area has had lengthy experience of being ruled, often oppressively, by somebody else. It is one thing to enact toleration, another to achieve it; and there have been cases of governments making use of national sentiment as a means of increasing their support among the people as a whole—an appeal that has proved usually much more effective than appeals to political loyalty. Tito discovered this in 1948, as the Poles, Hungarians and Rumanians have since. But nationalist self-assertion rarely takes place in a vacuum; it may well take the form of self-assertion *against* some other national group, majority or minority. Thus Yugoslav self-assertion took on an anti-Russian tinge after the break with Stalin, as did Hungarian nationalism in 1956. Communist governments rarely let anti-Soviet feeling go too far, though; in Poland fear of German revanchism keeps it in check,[37] in Rumania some of it is channelled in the direction of the Hungarians.

Given even the best of intentions, the mixture of nationalities and babel of tongues is bound to be an educational headache. Basically, the alternatives are complete integration on the one

---

[35] e.g. *Constitution of the Socialist Republic of Rumania*, Article 22, pp. 123–4. (Bucharest, 1965.)

[36] Officially "nationalism" is condemned, along with its more extreme variant "chauvinism", as a negative phenomenon, incompatible with the idea of "proletarian internationalism". But all the régimes encourage what they call "socialist patriotism" (see Chapter 7, §§ 1 and 2). There is, of course, a difference, but in times of tension it is not always easy to detect.

[37] The fact that West Germany does not recognize the Oder–Neisse frontier, and that some of the wilder elements (never actually repudiated) call from time to time for action to recover the "lost territories" of Silesia, Prussia and Pomerania, convinces the Poles that the German menace did not die with the Third Reich.

hand, and educational autonomy, with separate schools and even higher institutes for the minorities, on the other. Of these, the first is not found, officially at least; complete denial of minority rights would be too flagrant a denial of the principles of any communist régime, as well as being too reminiscent of the old days. Besides, there are usually limits to the amount of offence that can be caused to a neighbour. But the provision of separate schools for minorities raises other problems, both for the minority peoples themselves and for the "host" country as a whole. To avoid complete separation (and this, in view of the structure of many of these countries, is no small matter) the majority language must be learned as well: Ukranians in Poland have to learn Polish, Slovaks and Italians in Yugoslavia, Serbo-Croat, Germans in Rumania, Rumanian, and so on. But, since it adds the burden of an additional language, this may put the minorities at an educational disadvantage, which may stay with them through further education and employment. Historically, many of the groups have held privileged positions (Hungarians in Rumania and Yugoslavia, Germans almost everywhere), and others have been underprivileged (Gipsies in Hungary and Rumania, Albanians in Yugoslavia, Serbs in Rumania). The provision of schooling in the mother tongue, coupled with the teaching of the national language, is an attempt to equalize in both directions, but by necessarily adding to the burden of learning may still retain some danger of turning the minorities into second-class citizens. There is no clear solution, but the possibility that bi-lingualism may be a lighter burden than some might expect may mitigate the difficulties, given good intentions on the part both of the authorities and the national minorities.

There is also the problem of size. Some groups are big enough and concentrated enough to make the provision of special schools a fairly simple matter—this is true of the Hungarians and Albanians in Yugoslavia, for example. But some of the communities are tiny, and scattered in villages that could barely support an elementary school, let alone anything beyond that. There tends, therefore, to be a falling-off in the provision of school places for minorities beyond the primary stage; for those wishing to continue especially in higher education, it is usually necessary to do so through the medium of the state language—another disincentive for those who might otherwise have gone beyond the compulsory stage. When the Rumanian Government merged the Hungarian "Bolyai" University at Cluj with the Rumanian "Victor Babeş" University in the same city,[38] thus effectively reducing the scope for studies in the Hungarian language, it was no doubt moved by a desire to gain popular support by cutting the Magyars—long regarded as a privileged group—down to size.[39] But this is something of a special case; there are not many concentrations of over a million of any minority in Eastern Europe, and there are limits to the extent to which special facilities can be provided. As educational facilities expand generally, therefore, there tends to be more assimilation, especially among peoples who have no prospect of being "sent home" under some future frontier arrangement. Where nationalist sentiment is being encouraged, government policy seeks to speed this process; but elsewhere it seems to happen anyway, and more for practical than sentimental reasons. Mobility of personnel, for one thing, tends to iron out linguistic differences. This has been found in the U.S.S.R., in many parts of Asia and Africa, and, in a small way, in the Celtic-speaking areas of Scotland and Wales. For reasons that have little to do with communist rule, and due only in part to nationalist pressures, the same process is taking place in Eastern Europe. But the process is neither smooth nor easy and involves many problems and dislocations while it lasts.

The part played by the geographical background to an educational system should not be exaggerated. In Eastern Europe they are spared the problems of distance and vastness that have played so important a part in the shaping of education in the U.S.A., or the problems that have been raised by these and often poor communications and sparse population in the U.S.S.R. They do not

[38] Herta Haase and Seymour Rosen, *Education in Rumania*, p. 16. (U.S. Office of Education, Washington D.C., 1960.)

[39] George Schöpflin, *op. cit.*

have to cope with economic backwardness on the scale of India or China, with the added complications of an alarming explosion of population; nor have they had to perform the leap of centuries in the space of decades, as many Africans, Asians and Latin Americans are having to do. Climate ranges from the benign to the unfriendly, but avoids the worst excesses at both ends of the scale that can so disrupt social living elsewhere. But the problems bequeathed by geography to the educators are real enough. The challenge of changing agriculture, the development of industry—especially in places where little existed before—makes heavy demands on the powers of the schools to supply the needs of society and its individual members. Particularly in the south, the pace itself, and the need to make up for lost time in education as in the economies, though adding impetus to the expansion of education, is also liable to strain it. Most trying of all, perhaps, is the problem of nationalities, the patchwork of peoples with their long history of mutual suspicion and hates. There is, of course, no intrinsic reason why mixtures of peoples should cause more than some complications and inconveniences—the Swiss, after all, have managed a similar situation not too badly. But the hates lie deeper; these, with other problems, are rather the contribution of historical factors, and it is to these that we now turn.

CHAPTER 3

The Making of Eastern Europe (I)—The Social and Historical Background

DIVERSE though they are, the peoples of Eastern Europe share a common experience, that of being subject races. Many of them have had the compensating experience of subjugating others; many have done both at once, or in rapid succession, switching roles rapidly as wars and conquests have rolled almost ceaselessly over this area from the beginning of recorded history until our own time.

Though it is Belgium that is usually known as the "cockpit of Europe", most of the East European countries could establish as good a claim to this unenviable title. One of the greatest misfortunes of their peoples has been to live in marchlands between greater forces pressing in from east and west. In the north, the lack of natural barriers has left the country wide open, and invasions have crossed and recrossed it. They came mainly from the east—Huns, Avars, Magyars, Mongols—but also from the west; the *Drang nach Osten* of the Germanic peoples began in early medieval times, continued with the penetrations of the Teutonic Knights, and ended only with the defeat of Hitler's Wehrmacht. Further south, barriers do exist in the form of a series of mountain ranges. These did not prove particularly effective against Turkish or Austrian expansion, but they did at least provide some refuge for many peoples who might otherwise have been wiped out completely, instead of merely being decimated at intervals. At the same time, they had the effect that has often been remarked on in the history of ancient Greece—they were politically divisive. By cutting off communities from each other, they weakened the cohesion of already weak peoples, and created a vacuum that attracted the unwelcome attentions of major powers. Outside intervention has been a constant fact of political life in Eastern Europe.

The history of this area, frequently put on one side under some vague heading like the "Eastern Question" of the textbooks, is so complicated that it would be quite inappropriate even to attempt to go into the details here. Broadly, though, in modern times at any rate, it has been the history of a much-fought-over frontier zone at the meeting-point of four great empires: Prussia (subsequently Germany), Austria, Russia and Turkey.

In the north, the pressures came mainly from Germany and Russia, with Austria intruding further south. Poland traditionally dates the founding of the nation from just over a thousand years ago; a small part of this millenium was spent in relative security, even following an expansionist policy (mainly at Russia's expense), and dealing effectively with German penetration by defeating the Teutonic Knights at Tannenberg in 1410. But when the Jagiellonian dynasty ended in 1572, a period of weakness began, with an elective monarchy and a Diet hamstrung by the right of any one member to veto any action at all. This time of paralysis culminated in a series of partitions in which Prussia, Russia and Austria engulfed Poland by stages, first biting pieces off then swallowing the remainder entire. Apart from a brief and shadowy resurrection (Napoleon's puppet "Grand Duchy of Warsaw") Poland ceased to exist as a state from the end of the eighteenth century until she re-emerged in 1918, only to be swallowed again in 1939. As for the Slavs who now form Czechoslovakia, their nationhood was one of the prime victims of the Thirty Years' War, and they remained subject to the Habsburgs (with periodic spasms of revolt) until the final collapse of the Austrian Empire at the end of The First World War.

The position in the south, was, as usual, more complicated. The Turks had surged up into the Balkans long before they finally destroyed the last remnants of the Byzantine Empire by taking Constantinople in 1453. They took Sofia in 1385, crushed Serbian resistance at Kossovo Polje four years later, destroyed Belgrade (it has been destroyed eleven times in all)[1] and moved on to the very gates of Vienna, where the tide finally stopped and turned. There were some breaks in the pattern; Venice managed to hold on to the Dalmatian coast, the mountaineers of Montenegro were never properly subdued, and many of the conquered peoples were under rather ineffective control. But when the Ottoman Sultanate was at the peak of its powers, South-eastern Europe formed part of an Empire that stretched from Algeria to the Caucasus, from the Red Sea to the Black Sea coast, from the Persian Gulf to the plains of Hungary. Thereafter began the slow decline. Some of the conquests were short-lived; the counter-expansion began almost immediately from Austria and Russia that was to continue fitfully into the twentieth century. Hungary was retaken by the end of the seventeenth century, Russia held the north coast of the Black Sea by the turn of the nineteenth. As the two empires pressed on, Turkey—"the sick man of Europe"—gradually crumbled. Russia took Bessarabia in 1812, Austria occupied Bosnia in 1878. At the same time, revolts among the subject peoples grew in intensity, and ferocious though the reaction was, they eventually bore fruit. Serbia broke free effectively in 1817; and throughout the century one country after another threw off the Turkish yoke—Rumania, Greece, Bulgaria—sometimes remaining nominally subject to the Sultan for a time, then breaking away completely. The great powers stood by, intervening when it suited their interests, which was often. By the end of the Second Balkan War in 1913, Turkey in Europe had been reduced to a rump of territory round Constantinople.

But this picture of Austrian and Russian penetration, coupled with national revolts against Ottoman rule, was further complicated by rivalries among the subject peoples themselves. Here too the powers jockeyed for position, playing off one against another,

[1] Vladimir Dedijer, *The Beloved Land* (McGibbon & Kee, London, 1961), gives fifty-four times. The difference between the figures may depend on how complete a destruction one counts.

operating through client states, and intervening at their convenience to impose settlements. There were many claims and counter-claims; Macedonia was claimed by Serbia and Bulgaria, for example, the Dobrudja by Rumania and Bulgaria, and so on, and large tracts of territory were exchanged at the conference tables. But sometimes the disputes boiled over into war; these conflicts sometimes seemed somewhat comic-opera to western bystanders; Bernard Shaw had great fun with the Balkan War of 1878 in *Arms and the Man*, but the Serbs and Bulgars who actually fought it (helped by Austria and Russia respectively) took it seriously enough. Balkan Wars may have been lacking in scale, but they made up for it in ferocity.

It is not difficult to trace a direct line from these past conflicts to the national tensions of the present day, noted earlier. The last Balkan War was as recent as 1913; and although all wars since have been primarily the affair of international heavyweights, the time-honoured traditions of dog-eat-dog had plenty of scope in these too. Hungary and Poland took a share of the spoil when Hitler dismembered Czechoslovakia; Bulgaria and Hungary seized parts of Yugoslavia when the Axis occupied the country, and we have already seen something of the changes of ownership that went on between Hungary and Rumania, and something of the consequences.[2] German occupation of Eastern Europe provided great opportunities to many of the smaller nations allied with the Third Reich to press claims and settle old scores, opportunities that were generally exploited to the full. It is perhaps small wonder that even in more settled times national hatreds remain so near the surface, and that pride in one's nationality—often all there was to sustain peoples under alien rule—should burn with such intensity, especially where violence has been such a commonplace for centuries. Small wonder too, that exchanges of population, Slovaks for Hungarians, for example, seemed the only way of settling border problems in some of the more sensitive areas.

[2] See Martin Gilbert, *Recent History Atlas*, for maps clearly presenting some complicated changes of frontier.

Important though nationalism is, perhaps overridingly important, it has not been the whole story. Sometimes it has been cut across by shared antipathies, as when Hungarians and Rumanians co-operated in Jew-baiting during the war, or when quarrelling nations sank their differences briefly to fight the Turks at various points of time. Sometimes class interest has proved stronger. Many of the landed interests collaborated with the Turks, later with the Germans, in what is now Yugoslavia. During the war, some of the most extreme Hungarian and Rumanian nationalists, while whipping up race hatred at home, continued to co-operate with their opposite numbers across the border.[3] Before the war, the Rumanians used to laugh at Hungary's Admiral Horthy as "an Admiral without a Navy" ruling a "kingdom without a king",[4] but were well aware that it was Rumanian troops that had put him in power in the first place, when they intervened to overthrow Béla Kún's Hungarian Soviet Republic in 1919. At times, too, working-class solidarity has managed to cancel out nationalism; for a while in Rumania, for instance, relations between Rumanians, Germans, Magyars and Serbs in the mixed areas were reasonably good. But there, as we have seen, they have proved rather fragile. In spite of temporary realignments, national feeling has always been quick to rear its head again, a legacy of history that communist governments have had to recognize.

One side-effect of East European nationalism in education has been the increasing stress on national traditions. To be realistic, it has been necessary to recognize the backwardness of most of these countries in the educational field; to make the most of achievements since the war, it has been felt necessary to point out this backwardness—and the further difficulties raised by war devastation—by way of contrast. As Communists, too, the authorities have been inclined to stress the positive contribution of post-

[3] Jack Lindsay and Maurice Cornforth, *loc. cit.*
[4] Hungary, then as now, had no coastline. Hungary remained nominally a kingdom with the Emperor of Austria as king (and Horthy as regent) until after the Second World War. But since there had been no Austrian Emperor since the end of the First World War, few could take seriously Hungary's official subjection to the Crown of St. Stephen.

war effort in the building-up of new educational systems, with or without acknowledgements to the U.S.S.R. But national pride will not be gainsaid, and it is remarkable how far Eastern European writers will go to emphasize the "positive" aspects of their traditional educational systems. Thus we hear a good deal about the ancient universities in Poland and Czechoslovakia, the Jagiellonian University of Kraków and the Charles University of Prague; one Rumanian author[5] not only praises the work of eighteenth- and nineteenth-century pioneers and of the traditional *lycées*, but emphasizes the "concern for education" evident from archaeological research as far back as the Roman colonies in Dacia; a Bulgarian writer not only insists that during the nineteenth century, "before thinking of building churches in their villages, the Bulgarians built schools", but goes on: "But the picture of the old Bulgarian school would be incomplete without stressing its profoundly democratic character. It was so strong that neither the Ottoman oppressors nor the reactionary and fascist Bulgarian bourgeoisie were able to crush this democratic spirit."[6]

Later, he concedes that the system as a whole was deficient, and that "despite this extensive system, Bulgarian schools in that form were not able to cope with the demands which the new life and socialist construction put to them"[7] and goes on to list the improvements carried out since. This last is what one would expect, but it is interesting to see how condemnation of many aspects of the old education is so often tempered by pride in a nation's achievements, even under politically unacceptable régimes.

Another legacy of Turkish rule in the south was to add cultural and religious differences to the national ones. This affected the northern countries less in recent times, and in the southern countries where Turkish rule was replaced by Austrian (as in Hungary, Transylvania, Croatia) its long-term effects were slight. Conse-

---

[5] A. Manolache, *General Education in Rumania*, pp. 7–13. (Meridiane, Bucharest, 1965.)

[6] Nevena Geliazkova (ed.), *Prosperity and Culture in Bulgaria*, p. 100. (Foreign Languages Press, Sofia, 1964.)

[7] *Ibid.*

quently the northern countries, together with Hungary and Croatia, tended to look to the West, to Vienna and Berlin rather than Moscow or Belgrade. North and west of the line, the Roman Catholic Church was dominant; south and east of it, the Orthodox Churches. There was also, not surprisingly, strong Islamic influence in some places, such as Albania, Bosnia and Bulgaria. The Poles, Czechs, Slovenes, Croats and Hungarians chafed often enough under the rule of the Habsburg Empire, and contributed their own quota to the nationalist upheavals of the mid-nineteenth century; but even after the break-up of Austria-Hungary, they felt themselves part of a Catholic European tradition and rather superior to their backward "Asiatic" neighbours. This division not only cut across the area as a whole but across individual countries, notably Yugoslavia, where religious, cultural and national differences provided fruitful soil for Axis policies of divide and rule during the Second World War.

Religion was more than a matter of theological conviction in most of these countries; it became a symbol of national identity. Catholic Poland could assert its Catholicism against the Russians and its Polishness against the Austrians, thus keeping a sense of national unity under partition. Catholic Hungary, likewise, could find in its religion a spur to greater struggles against the Muslim Turks, and in its Magyar consciousness a force of resistance to undue Austrian domination—though, by the same token, denying similar rights to Slovaks, Slovenes, Croats and Rumanians, to say nothing of Jews and Gypsies. In the southern Balkans, the Orthodox Churches of Serbia, Rumania and Bulgaria became the chief repositories of national cultures in the Christian idiom while these countries were under Muslim rule. The Orthodox Churches were a last tenuous link with the culture of Byzantium, a link with Russia—that country was Christianized by Orthodox Bulgars Cyril and Methodius, and used Old Bulgarian still as a liturgical language—and, eventually, a focal-point for national revolt. Thus developed a close link between the Orthodox Churches and national politics, a tradition that has stayed alive to this day, as witness the part played by the Orthodox Ethnarchy under Archbishop Makarios—a part that seems quite normal to any of the Orthodox, Greek or not—in the struggle for Cypriot independence.

The *national* character of the Orthodox Churches has had other important consequences. Unlike the Catholic Church, they are not effectively under any supranational control—there is no Orthodox equivalent of the Vatican—and have long been accustomed to working closely with the state, national and religious life being so closely intertwined. For this reason the churches have given the communist governments very little trouble in predominantly Orthodox countries; even with officially atheist régimes, they have been able to coexist, with some loss of power and prestige, not too uncomfortably. The "turbulent priests" of Eastern Europe, men such as Mindszenty, Stepinac, Wyszyński, are Catholics. Thus we have the paradoxical situation of comparatively docile co-operation from the national Orthodox Churches, while the international Roman Catholic Church frequently acts as a focus for national self-assertion, and provides a major obstacle to plans to secularize national life—including education—in accordance with the precepts of Marxism.

This has proved to be something of a mixed blessing. It is true that in Hungary, Czechoslovakia, and above all in Poland, the Church has sometimes played an important part in modifying some aspects of communist rule. When Władysław Gomułka came to power in Poland in 1956 and began to liberalize the régime, he did so in the face of some considerable Soviet opposition. To resist this, he needed considerable popular support, and it is quite likely that he owed a good deal of it to his temporary *rapprochement* with Cardinal Wyszyński. The teaching of religion was, for a while, allowed in the schools. Less ephemerally, much of the coercive apparatus of the state was trimmed, the unduly pro-Soviet old guard was removed from the government, agriculture was rationalized, the communist government became much more of a *national* Polish government. In Hungary, although the revolt of 1956 was crushed by Soviet forces, it had some lasting effect in that the régime of János Kádár was much more liberal than that of Stalinist Mátyás Rákosi; and although Cardinal Mindszenty still has to shelter in the American Embassy, it is arguable that the Church played some part, even if indirect, in this process.

But it is also true that the Catholic Church has in the past been associated with the *ancien régime*, to an extent that makes it present not only an anti-communist but often reactionary face. In Poland, the squabbles between Church and State are raging once again (though Wyszyński is still at liberty), culminating in the recent government restrictions on foreign pilgrims (including the Pope) who wished to visit the celebrations of 1000 years of Christianity in Poland in 1966 at the shrine of the Black Madonna of Częstochowa. Catholicism, no less than Communism, has its traditionalist and progressive wings, and Wyszyński is regarded as standing firmly on the right. Not surprisingly, there are many areas of social as well as religious policy where clashes between Church and State are likely to occur. Whatever the failings of the Gomułka government, Wyszyński is not renowned for his tact; he once wrote to the Spanish bishops comparing the struggle of the Church in Poland with that of the (Fascist) defenders of the Alcázar during the Spanish Civil War. Thus the quarrel continues with loss to both sides. In the Hungarian border zones, the Church has been tarred with the brush of forcible Magyarization; in Czechoslovakia, it is suspected of giving support to Slovak separatism. In Yugoslavia,[8] the Catholic Church has to live down a record of collaboration with the Axis. Under the puppet Republic of Croatia, the Ustaše—Croat Catholic terrorist bands—forcibly converted and then massacred thousands of Croat and Serbian Orthodox; they boasted of their exploits so loudly, even making films of them, that even the Nazis, whose own behaviour was bad enough in all conscience, were shocked. How far Archbishop (later Cardinal) Stepinac really was implicated in this is a matter of some controversy, but he was jailed by Tito after the war, and the association of the Church in general with the doings of the Ustaše has done the Church little good in Yugoslavia. It was never

[8] See Dedijer, *op. cit.*, and Domenach and Pontault, *op. cit.* Also: Fitzroy Maclean, *Eastern Approaches*, Part III. (Jonathan Cape, London, 1951.)

actually suppressed, but there has been considerable tension with the authorities since the war, though Tito's resumption of relations with the Vatican in 1966 may have done something to alleviate the situation. The handling of relations between Church and party in any Eastern European country is a matter for considerable tact, in view of the ideological gulf alone; but, particularly in areas where the issues are confounded by the national question as well, tact is a rare commodity. The stand of the Church has, in some areas, modified the régime, but there is never any guarantee of this. Association with right-wing forces is just as likely to lead to a hardening in the Party line.

Unlike Catholicism, but like Orthodoxy, Islam has given the communist governments little direct trouble in Eastern Europe. There are virtually no Muslims in the northern countries, but in the south they are by no means numerically insignificant. There are three-quarters of a million in Bulgaria, even a few in Rumania; most Albanians are Muslims, as are 11 per cent of the population in Yugoslavia. This last figure is misleading, in a way; Muslims form a majority in Bosnia and in the Kosmet, and a substantial proportion in Macedonia and even in Serbia. Their problem is social rather than political. They are likely to be more backward than their compatriots, and by their conservatism, tend to resist change, whether in farming, medicine or education. It is often not all that easy to get them to send their sons to school, but much more difficult to get them to send their daughters, or let their wives take adult courses. This, of course, can get in the way of national educational policy, which takes a stand on sexual as well as religious equality. One example will serve: in Belgrade there are large numbers of Muslim Shyptars (Albanians). Some of them have drifted into the city from the Kosmet, some from across the Albanian border which, although officially closed, is difficult to police. Many of them work as woodcutters, live on very little (even the low living standards of Serbia seem high to them), then return home with their savings to buy a wife. But a few settle permanently, and assimilate to some extent. The wife of one of these woodcutters—young and strikingly attractive—was persuaded by her neighbours to take an elementary school course at one of the adult institutions. At first her husband refused his consent, but eventually gave way, and took her along to enrol at the adult school, on condition that he could wait outside the classroom for her every evening. The principal agreed, being accustomed to dealing with the more delicate areas of national sensitivity. The experiment lasted a month. It was bad enough for the woman to see her husband waiting with his axe on his shoulder whenever she came out of classes. But when he swung it in his hand or began to hone it thoughtfully whenever he saw a man speak to her, some of the other students objected, and she thought it best to leave school before damage was done.[9]

This isolated (but not unique) anecdote casts light on some statistics. According to the 1961 census,[10] nearly 20 per cent of the Yugoslav population were illiterate; 10 per cent of the men, 29 per cent of the women. The lowest rate was in Slovenia, with 1·8 per cent, the highest in Bosnia, with nearly a third of the population illiterate. More instructive, though, is the difference between the sexes; in Slovenia, it was 1·7 per cent men, 1·9 per cent women, but in Muslim Bosnia, whereas "only" 16 per cent of the men were illiterate, over 47 per cent of the women were. Polygamy and wife-buying have proved difficult to abolish completely, and although the veil is no longer worn, the attitudes that it symbolized are clearly defined in figures such as these.

The social structure of the Eastern European countries also contributed to the general backwardness. The word "feudal" has been loosely used, and has become as much a term of abuse as description, especially in communist vocabulary. But if allowance is made for the fact that actual serfdom was largely abolished during the nineteenth century,[11] it is not too bad a description. In Eastern Germany, especially Prussia, the Junker landlords were still powerful by the time of the Second World War; so were the

[9] Oral communication, Belgrade, 1965.
[10] *Statistički Kalendar Jugoslavije 1965*. (Savezni Zavod za Statistiku, Belgrade, 1965.)
[11] Not always in fact, however; see Dedijer's description (*op. cit.*) of his grandfather, Jovan Babić, and his household.

landed aristocracy in Poland, Hungary, Rumania, Bulgaria. More than anywhere in Europe, the Eastern European countries still exhibited the classic division into landlords and peasantry, with a group of more substantial farmers (whom the Communists called by the Russian term *kulak*)[12] in between. Outside the major urban centres, both the industrial working classes and the professional middle classes were, compared with Western Europe, weakly developed, and society was relatively stagnant. Economically, this was reflected in a low level of industrial development, in the southern zone at any rate; politically (apart from liberal-democratic Czechoslovakia) in various types of right-wing and often dictatorial régimes, such as those of Piłsudski in Poland, Horthy in Hungary, Antonescu in Rumania. This situation was, of course, a fruitful source of political tension before, during and after the war; frightened by the "red menace" the landowning and often the middle classes were in many countries inclined to side with the Axis, which they saw as a protection against Communism, and were thus after the war widely discredited as political forces by the taint of collaboration. This made the communist take-over rather easier in many of these countries, especially when combined with the presence of Soviet troops. On the other hand, the relative weakness of the industrial working classes in most countries provided an unsteady basis for social revolution. As we shall see, there were attempts in many places on the part of the local communist leaders to establish socialist régimes of an independent type, but these quickly gave way to a "revolution from above", communist régimes largely imported from the Soviet Union. This was a complex development, but it is quite likely that one factor in this was the comparative weakness of the political forces in the countries concerned; and this, in turn, can be connected with the weakness (outside Czechoslovakia) of the industrial working class.

More to the point for present purposes, stagnant society meant,

[12] *Kulak*—a fist (Russian). The term was used as an official classification during the drive to collectivize agriculture in the U.S.S.R. in the 1930's, especially in the Ukraine.

all too often, stagnant education. We have seen something of the illiteracy that was widespread through much of the area, the neglect of the technical sector, the general unevenness of educational provision, especially in the countryside. Highly selective systems of secondary and higher education provided little scope for social mobility through education. In pre-war Rumania,[13] for instance, seven years of elementary schooling were nominally compulsory, but only 5·4 per cent of children pursued it beyond the fourth year; further, although the peasantry accounted for about four-fifths of the population, less than 1 per cent of their children completed more than four years of school. In Bulgaria,[14] although primary education was compulsory, 100,000 children (principally the children of peasants) did not attend school at all, and there were still in 1944 1780 villages with no schools. In Poland,[15] at least 10 per cent did not go to school and only a little over a quarter of any age group completed seven years of elementary schooling—hardly any of them the children of peasants. Further, the less social and economic change, the less was the stimulus to educational expansion; school-enrolment figures from before the war are of doubtful accuracy, but they seem in effect to have stood nearly still for decades. Either economic or social change was needed to shake up the educational system; both were provided by the war and its aftermath.

Social backwardness, a history of constant upheaval—these reinforced each other and made for educational impoverishment. The war, while setting in motion a good deal of change, also increased existing difficulties with its widespread devastation. This varied considerably from place to place. Rumania and Bulgaria, being first allied to the Axis powers, then occupied by them, then overrun by the Red Army relatively quickly, suffered comparatively little. But the story was very different elsewhere. In Poland, quite apart from the damage and casualties of the

[13] Herta Hasse and Seymour Rosen, *Education in Rumania*, p. 2. (U.S. Office of Education, Washington D.C., 1960.)
[14] Nevena Geliazkova, *op. cit.*, p. 100.
[15] *Poland 1944–1964*, p. 153. (Polonia, Warsaw, 1964.)

fighting, the Germans pursued what became virtually a policy of genocide; by the end of the war, Warsaw and most other cities were almost totally in ruins, nearly 40 per cent of the national wealth had been destroyed, and between deaths on the battlefield and the extermination camps, 22 per cent of the population had lost their lives. As a measure of the educational loss, 33,000 classrooms had been destroyed.[16] In Czechoslovakia the fate of Lidice is well known, but it was not the only instance of a policy of reprisals; teachers in particular, as active members of resistance movements, were shot or imprisoned in large numbers. In Albania, continuous partisan warfare took its toll. In Yugoslavia, armed resistance to the Axis coincided with social revolution and civil war. One Yugoslav in every nine was killed, usually by other Yugoslavs—Ustaše and Četniki (Serbian royalists) killed partisans, partisans killed them and the Germans, and there were other active groups—Slovene White Guards, Bosnian Muslim Nationalists—who fought and massacred each other, but concentrated on Tito's partisans. The Germans played their part too, both in the actual fighting and in reprisals against the civilian population; Kragujevac, where they shot the entire male population over the age of 15 in 1941, was the Yugoslav Lidice, but there were others. In East Germany Dresden was flattened by Allied air-raids, and much else by the Soviet Army. Even reckoning in strictly practical terms, the great loss of life and property—including of course teachers and schools—rendered an area already backward even more so. While dramatically underlining the need for reconstruction, the devastation of war severely limited the means of carrying it out.

History has been cruel to Eastern Europe. The wars and feuds began before written records, and have made up much of their substance ever since. As for the great powers on the fringe, they have regarded the peoples of the area as fit subjects for exploita-

---

[16] *Poland 1944–1964*, p. 32. Among the dead were some 27,000 teachers. (Mieczyslaw Pęcherski, *Das Schulwesen in Volkspolen.* p. 291. In: Deutsches Pädagogisches Zentralinstitut, *Das Schulwesen sozialistischer Länder in Europa.* (Volk und Wissen Volkeigener Verlag, Berlin, 1962.))

tion; the Venetian diplomat Paolo Sarpi once said, "If you want the Dalmatians to be your faithful servants, keep them in ignorance and hunger",[17] a maxim which was applied by other powers to other peoples as well. Alternatively, the powers have treated them with indifference; Chamberlain's casual dismissal of Czechoslovakia as a "far away country of whose people we know nothing" was also in the classic tradition. The legacy of the past in material backwardness has been obvious enough, though this can be overcome. A legacy less easy to adapt is the cast of mind that a turbulent past has put on these peoples. To survive, they have clung in troubled times to pride of nationality or religion; but while patriotism and faith have often proved a spur to effort, they can all too easily turn into chauvinism and bigotry, which have often added to the already great obstacles in the way of betterment. In education, as in other things, the past has bequeathed the peoples of this region obstacles that any kind of régime—left, right of centre—would have found daunting. As it turned out, the régimes landed with these tasks were communist. This, as we shall see, made it possible to overcome some of the problems, while raising others at the same time.

[17] Quoted by Domenach and Pontault, *op. cit.*, p. 114.

CHAPTER 4

The Making of Eastern Europe (II)—The Political Background

MYTH-MAKING is not confined to the ancient world. It is a process parallel to the making of history; and around the political developments in Eastern Europe after the war, whereby communist governments were established between 1945 and 1948, we can see the emergence of two myths, one on each side, that have served to explain events and justify attitudes to them.

One myth goes thus: before the war the countries of Eastern Europe were ruled by pro-fascist cliques, supported by the landowning and bourgeois classes. During the war, they were occupied by the Nazis, with whom the anti-democratic forces collaborated. As the tide of war turned, the mass of the people, forming democratic alliances between the workers and peasants, and helped by the liberation of their countries by the Soviet armies, established people's democratic governments under the leadership of the parties of the working class. Since then, with the help and support of the U.S.S.R., they have been overcoming great difficulties and building their own socialist societies.

The alternative myth goes like this: before the war, the countries of Eastern Europe were in some cases free, in others under dictatorships. During the war they were occupied by the Nazis, but when they were driven out democratic forces began to emerge. These, however, were soon suppressed by the U.S.S.R. which, having its armies on their soil, was able to impose communist régimes totally subservient to Soviet interests. Since then these countries have formed a Soviet colonial empire in Europe, holding down their people by force.

These, of course, are crude statements, of which many variations and refinements are possible. To say that they are myths does not necessarily mean that they are untrue, merely that they are designed to convince rather than describe. As usual, both myths contain elements of truth and of fiction. Disentangling the two is both controversial and complex, but has to be attempted; neither myth, as it stands, satisfactorily explains the political developments of the last few years, the present structure of society, or the current state of thinking on social problems, including education.

Both myths overlap to some extent. Communist governments did take over, the Red Army was a major factor, and they did look to the Soviet Union for guidance. But from any point of view it was not a simple process; there were many important differences in the way in which the Communists came to power—differences that were to prove crucial in the years to come. For the sake of convenience, they can be grouped under three main heads:

1. Importation of communist régimes with the help of the Soviet Army. This happened in Poland, Hungary, Rumania, Bulgaria and, most obviously of all, in East Germany, where the territory of the "German Democratic Republic" coincides exactly with the zone of Soviet military occupation.
2. Home-made revolutions based on wars of resistance to the Axis occupying forces. Yugoslavia and her one-time protégé, Albania, are examples.
3. Internal revolution or *coup d'état*. Czechoslovakia is the only example.

The division, of course, is not absolute; there was a good deal of overlapping. In Poland, there were communist as well as non-communist resistance forces, and there were Polish units in the Red Army that finally pushed the Germans out. In their wake came a provisional government consisting (mainly) of Polish communists which was established at Lublin while the fighting was still going on; it was later moved to Warsaw as a recognized government, thus presenting the Western powers with a *fait accompli*. Armed brigades of workers did fight against the Germans in Rumania, and in Bulgaria armed uprising did play a part in the overthrow of the Axis and their sponsored régime. In Yugoslavia there had been hardly any help from Russia during the partisan war, but the Soviet forces did play some part in liberating the country; they took Belgrade, for instance, which the partisans had been unable to do. Generally, though, the presence of Soviet troops proved to be a decisive factor. But it was not the only one; their importance in Yugoslavia was marginal, and in the case of Czechoslovakia there were no Soviet troops at all in the country when the *coup* took place in 1948. Nor did the presence of Soviet troops necessarily mean political take-over; Finland was occupied by the U.S.S.R. after the war, but no communist régime appeared there, either then or later.

Stalin has often been accused of exporting and imposing "revolution from above" in Eastern Europe, but, ironically enough, there is considerable doubt that he was particularly interested in revolution of any kind, at least to begin with. During the war he acted much of the time like a traditional Russian ruler; he appealed to national rather than political solidarity; he came to terms with the Orthodox Church and even in relatively small things, like changing the national anthem or service uniforms or the titles of governments posts, he consistently soft-pedalled the revolutionary aspects of the Soviet régime. Foreign policy was more Russian than communist; for example, much of his justification for joining the war against Japan was that this would be a revenge for the humiliating defeat of Russia by Japan in 1905—which would have come as something of a shock to revolutionaries of the old school, who had hailed that defeat as a blow to Tsarism.[1]

This approach was to be seen in all Stalin's dealings with Europe after the war. He played up pan-Slavic sentiment,[2] he joined with Churchill in carving up Eastern Europe into "spheres of influ-

[1] Isaac Deutscher, *Stalin: A Political Biography*. (Penguin, 1966.)
[2] Milovan Djilas, *Conversations with Stalin*, pp. 24–26, 48. (Penguin, 1963.)

ence" on the traditional pattern,³ and, as Isaac Deutscher has pointed out,⁴ pursued a policy that might have been designed to cripple the chances of genuine communist revolution by exacting heavy reparations from Hungary, Bulgaria, Rumania, Finland and Eastern Germany. In many places, too, he allowed his forces to behave like conquerors rather than liberators, thus putting the local Communists in a most awkward position.⁵ In Western Europe Stalin put heavy pressure on the communist parties to play subservient roles in the post-war governments, from which they were soon ousted. He did nothing to help the communist-led ELAS in the Greek civil war, even with moral support, although the British Government intervened on the other side. He had given practically no aid to the Yugoslav partisans; what outside help they did get came mainly from Britain, once Churchill had decided that they were a more effective anti-German force than the Četnik units of Draža Mihajlović.⁶ There was no attempt to encourage a communist government in Finland; for one thing, control of Poland and East Germany removed anxieties about security in the Baltic, and for another, the reparation agreements made it possible to dominate Finland economically without the troubles of political control as well.⁷

³ Churchill describes his deal with Stalin in 1944 in his *Second World War*:
"I wrote on a half-sheet of paper:
Rumania: Russia 90 per cent, others 10 per cent
Greece: Great Britian (in accord with U.S.A.) 90 per cent, Russia 10 per cent
Yugoslavia: 50–50 per cent
Hungary: 50–50 per cent
Bulgaria: Russia 75 per cent, the other 25 per cent.
I pushed this across to Stalin, who had by then heard the translation. There was a slight pause. Then he took his blue pencil and made a large tick upon it and passed it back to us. It was all settled in no more time than it takes to set it down."
⁴ Isaac Deutscher, *Russia After Stalin*, p. 79. (London, 1953.)
⁵ Milovan Djilas, *op. cit.*, pp. 70 ff.
⁶ Fitzroy Maclean, *op. cit.*, Part III.
⁷ Under the agreements, Finland had to deliver part of the reparations to the U.S.S.R. in machinery. As Finland had no machine industry to speak of, she had to create one. While this was of benefit to Finland in the long run, the industry had to depend on Soviet markets after the reparations were complete.

In fact, there is strong evidence to suggest that at the end of the war Stalin's interests in Eastern Europe were mainly strategic and economic; strategic, because the Soviet Union, with good reason, was nervous about her western frontier. What Stalin wanted was a *cordon sanitaire* to protect it, and any ideological considerations were relatively unimportant. Finland was no longer a threat, and therefore was left alone politically; Greece was no threat, and therefore the Greek Communists were left to their own devices. But Poland, Hungary, Rumania and Bulgaria were on the frontier, and Stalin's first concern was to keep them under control with a Soviet-sponsored network in economic, police and military affairs. Actual communist governments came later, usually sharing power at least nominally with a coalition of parties, and strengthening their position by arranging unions of communist and social democratic parties; the Worker's Parties of Poland, Hungary, Rumania, Bulgaria and the East German SED (*Sozialistische Einheitspartei Deutschlands*—Socialist Unity Party of Germany) were the outcome of mergers of this kind. Significantly, in these countries the Communist Parties had been weak after decades of suppression, and were thus heavily dependent on Soviet support. Apart from those who had spent the war years in jail or hiding, most of the leaders had quite literally been brought back into their own countries by the Soviet Army. Stalin's interest in them was as instruments of domination rather than of social revolution. In economic matters—bilateral trade and industrial schemes were arranged which worked to the Soviet Union's advantage—as well as in political, military and security matters, these countries were under Stalin's effective control in all but name.

Yugoslovia was a very different matter. Tito's coming to power owed nothing to the Soviet Union, but was based on the efforts of the Partisan Army and the Yugoslav Communist Party; furthermore, of all the groups that engaged in the fighting during the war, the Communists were the only one that could claim to be *Yugoslav* rather than Slovene, Croat, Serbian or Bosnian. Tito worked to carry through social and political revolution at the same time as national resistance, and, significantly, encountered discouragement from Stalin—genuine home-made revolution was not part of his strategic plan, or of his deal with Churchill. Soviet–Yugoslav tensions began long before the final break in 1948. The Yugoslav Communists had achieved power by their own efforts, and it is not surprising that they continued to insist on their right to go their own way. It soon became apparent that Yugoslavia, and the kind of political thinking that went on there, was going to cause trouble. Many of the Communist Parties contained what have been termed "nativists" (as opposed to "Muscovites") for whom the idea of an independent kind of Communism had a strong appeal.[8] By 1947 the Polish Communists, led by Gomułka, were insisting on going their own way in matters like the organization of agriculture. Dimitrov in Bulgaria was declaring that the country would not "be a Soviet Republic, but . . . a people's republic . . . a free and independent state with its national and State sovereignty",[9] and spelled out some of the differences, in attitudes to the ownership of property, for example. The Yugoslavs, Albanians and Bulgarians began talking openly of plans for federation, and by the beginning of 1948 the idea (or a modified version of it) was being sympathetically looked at by the Rumanians, Poles and Hungarians as well. The stage of firm proposals had not been reached, but the idea of some kind of federal union of communist states, independent of the U.S.S.R., was clearly in the air. Equally clearly, Yugoslavia was the main focus for this kind of thinking. On Marxist grounds this sort of development should have been welcomed rather than discouraged; but Stalin's interests were national —communist régimes were a good thing in so far as they served the interests of his own country, no more and no less.

The clamp-down came in 1948. This was the year of the *coup* in Czechoslovakia, which, although presumably timed by the Czechoslovak Communist Party to suit Soviet purposes, was an internal affair; the broad coalition government broke up, and it was Czech workers demonstrating in the streets of Prague, not

[8] Ghiţa Ionescu, *op cit*.
[9] *Ibid*., p. 26. See also Djilas, *op. cit.*, pp. 99 ff.

Russian soldiers, who put the pressure on President Beneš to accept a communist-dominated government. But whatever the method, the result in international terms was to bring Czechoslovakia into the Soviet *bloc*. The *coup* took place in February, and was finally consolidated by the beginning of June. On 28 June the Yugoslav–Soviet quarrel came to a head with the expulsion of the Yugoslav Communist Party from the Cominform. The expectation was that Tito would crumble: "I have only to lift my little finger", Stalin is reported to have said, "and there will be no more Tito." But Tito, enjoying as he did considerable support at home, and being used to striking out on his own, remained. It was probably the greatest single defeat of Stalin's career.

"Titoism" then became the chief deadly sin in the communist world. It was represented as the inheritor of the heresy of Trotsky, and the tool of American imperialism, and was used as a stick with which to beat (usually fatally) the "national" communist leaders in a series of purges in the style of the 1930's. Pătrăşcanu was expelled from the Rumanian Workers' Party in 1948, and shot some years later; Gomułka in Poland was expelled from office, then from the Party, and was put in prison, but not shot—he was to re-emerge later with interesting consequences. In 1949 it was the turn of Xoçe in Albania, Kostov in Bulgaria, Lászlo Rájk in Hungary—all were executed. So, in 1950 and 1951, were Clementis and Slanský in Czechoslovakia. By 1951 all the East European countries, apart from Yugoslavia, were under completely Stalinist régimes, closely tied to the Soviet Union and casting themselves more and more in the Soviet mould.

It was not to last for long. Stalin's death left the way clear for considerable political changes in the U.S.S.R. itself. In due course, the "collective leadership" of the early days gave way to the predominance of Nikita Khrushchov who, though himself as involved as any in Stalin's policies, seems to have been aware of the need for some change of direction, though it is unlikely that he intended the process to go as far as it did. There is little evidence that he or his associates had any long-term grand design or master plan; he played it by ear—this, at least, is an explanation that fits both the course of events and what is known of his character. His energies were for the most part concerned with internal Soviet affairs. These need not detain us here, except in so far as they had repercussions outside, particularly in the area of Eastern Europe.

The repudiation of the "cult of personality" and many of the policies that went with it began even before the famous speech to the Twentieth Congress of the Communist Party of the Soviet Union. This speech, "secret" though it was, announced in the most dramatic fashion possible that a different way would now be pursued, and it was soon noticed that some loosening up of Soviet society—the "Thaw"[10]—had begun. This, of course, was bound to have some effect in Eastern Europe, where restlessness had been sporadically evident even after the Stalinist purges. There had been riots in Czechoslovakia and East Germany, which were later to assume much more serious dimensions in Poland and Hungary. Even before the "secret speech" Krushchov had visited Tito in 1955 and practically admitted that Soviet policy towards Yugoslavia had been mistaken (though he blamed it on Beria at the time);[11] later in 1956 (after the speech) the Cominform—Stalin's agency for the control of the other parties—was dissolved, and the Soviet and Yugoslav parties resumed relations. This was not to be taken as the sign for a break-up of the *bloc*, however; Khrushchov, while repairing relations with Tito, had been consolidating the other countries. This he did militarily by setting up the Warsaw Treaty (a counterpoise to NATO), and economically by establishing COMECON, the Communist Common Market. Yugoslavia, though in a sense back in the fold (on her own terms), remained outside both organizations.

---

[10] So called after a novel of that title by Ilya Ehrenburg, an early example of a move away from the period of "Zhdanovshchina"—Andrei Zhdanov's subjection of the arts to strict party control and a dogmatic interpretation of "socialist realism".

[11] Lavrenty Beria was Deputy Premier for State Security under Stalin, and as head of the MVD (Security Police) one of the most hated men in the Soviet Union. He was "purged" and shot in 1953 after Stalin's death.

The year 1956 was one of crisis for the communist world. From the Twentieth Congress of the CPSU in February to the end of the year, complex events moved with breakneck speed. Poland achieved a greater degree of independence when unrest, especially among the industrial workers and students, brought Gomułka out of disgrace and back into power; as has already been noted, the new régime made many important modifications in the running of society, asserting a greater degree both of liberalization and national independence. Tito's revisionism (and Khruschov's) had spread. After some vacillation, Khrushchov accepted the compromise. Anxiety about Germany, if nothing else, would keep Poland from breaking away completely. In Hungary events took a more violent turn. Rákosi was removed from office, and popular upheaval brought Imre Nagy to power at the head of a coalition government of Communists and non-Communists, which attempted to take Hungary out of the Warsaw Treaty and seek neutral status. In the fluid situation János Kádár (himself, like Nagy, a "national" communist) set up a rival government and condemned the rising as a counter-revolution; there were indeed some counter-revolutionary groups at work, but they were hardly the main force of the rising. The Kádár government, having lost control over the Hungarian army, appealed for Soviet military help to restore its authority. This (again after some vacillation) was forthcoming, and Soviet troops crushed the rising. Hungary had been brought back into camp and, whatever points can be made about the legailty of the Nagy or Kádár governments, clearly by force. Apparently Yugoslavia's road was not to be followed by anyone else, at least not all the way. Gomułka and Tito, both worried by some aspects of the rising, and possibly by some elements that emerged, accepted the Soviet action, though without enthusiasm. The other Eastern European governments supported it much more readily; one of the political quips of the time was "The Hungarians are behaving like Poles, the Poles like Czechs and the Czechs like pigs". This last referred not to their hygiene but their docility, and could have been applied widely throughout the area after the end of the Hungarian episode.

But things could never be the same again. To begin with, the U.S.S.R. had publicly renounced the Stalinist claim to infallibility; Tito's presence on the fringes of the *bloc* as a tolerated heretic further weakened the monolith by providing an alternative pattern; and although there was some back-tracking, most of Poland's gains were kept. The suppression of the rising in Hungary in 1956 did not bring back a régime of the Rákosi type; Kádár turned out to be considerably more liberal than many of his neighbours. The deviations have continued. Albania has been at loggerheads with the U.S.S.R. since the *rapprochement* with Tito. Rumania has been asserting an independent line since the beginning of this decade, and by 1966 had come to be regarded as Eastern Europe's equivalent of Gaullist France. In spite of the Soviet action in Hungary, the logic of revisionism has continued to work; the governments of Eastern Europe, while still communist, are more and more going their own way.

The course of events has been so uneven that it is difficult to reduce it to a single pattern. The "Thaw" has certainly not been steady, though events do seem to move generally in that direction. There has been none in Albania, relatively little in Bulgaria, and for a long time there was less in Rumania and Czechoslovakia than in other places. There have been partial refreezes, as in Poland and more so in East Germany; generally, movements are so uncertain that the currently popular exercise of arranging these countries in a "dogmatist-revisionist" league-table is at best difficult, at worst speculative. On the whole, though, one can still put Albania at one end of the scale and Yugoslavia at the other with reasonable certainty; and over the area as a whole one can discern a spread, albeit patchy, of more liberal interpretations of communist policy in economic and social affairs.

One consistent trend, as we have seen, is towards greater diversity, but this works in various ways. In asserting their independence of the U.S.S.R., East European countries tend to liberalize their régimes or play on national sentiment. Usually there is some of both but not always. Nationalism is more apparent than liberalism in Rumania; Hungary and Czechoslovakia are more liberal than they were; so is Poland, though less dramatically so than in 1956, and national consciousness is as prominent as ever. Yugoslavia has done both for a long time, and now, with the dismissal of the head of the Security Police and the shifting of the emphasis of power from the League of Communists to the Socialist Alliance, is going much further than any other country in the area in effectively dismantling the apparatus of party control. Bulgaria is slower than most in pressing on with liberalization, though there have been some moves in that direction, and still makes more gestures of solidarity with the U.S.S.R. than is now customary. East Germany is one of the most "dogmatist" of all; for reasons we have seen the authorities there hesitate to try any particular appeal to German national sentiment, and there have been signs in the last year or two, illustrated by the expulsion of Professor Havemann—a prominent advocate of democratisation of the Party—from the SED and the Academy of Sciences. Albania is the most "Stalinist" of all, and seems likely to remain so in present circumstances. It is clear, then, that even when assurances of unity are loudly proclaimed (Nicolae Ceauşescu recently referred to the Warsaw Pact as a "band of brothers", even when casting doubt on the need for any military pacts at all), the one-time monolithic unity of the Communist world has broken down—as it was bound to do once the Soviet Union had countenanced Yugoslavia's position. This can be seen in greater variations in economic policy, where Czechoslovakia, Hungary and Poland have taken "Liebermanism"—a more flexible attitude to economic planning—much further than the Soviet Union has; or in agriculture, where some countries such as Yugoslavia and Poland have abandoned the classical Soviet model of collectivisation, and others prefer to work with more loosely organized cooperatives. Party control of the arts has practically gone in Yugoslavia,[12] and although still present (and occasionally reasserted) in Poland and Czechoslovakia, it is nowhere near as tight as it was during the Stalin era. In education, too, there has been a move

---

[12] But not quite, as Djilas and Mihajlov—both political dissidents now in jail—know to their cost.

away from a strict adherence to Soviet models; Yugoslavia began this process a long time ago, and Rumania has been the latest to follow, de-Russianizing the curriculum (Russian is no longer a compulsory language in the schools, for example), making more contacts with Western countries, especially France, and relying more on experiment and pragmatic solutions to problems than on the use of Soviet precedent. We have noted already the tendency in many of these countries to emphasize the "positive" aspects of the traditional systems; to this is being added a more local approach to the solution of local problems, and a corresponding reluctance to use the Soviet schools as a master-model for their own.

The story of Eastern Europe since the war may be seen as the story of three men; Stalin who built up Soviet control, Tito who challenged it, and Khrushchov who (to some degree unwittingly) presided over its disintegration. The various countries of Eastern Europe thus share three characteristics: they all have communist governments that grew out of the dislocation of war; all have at some time been in a "special relationship" with the Soviet Union; and in recent times they have been reinterpreting communist policy in ways that seem more suited to their own circumstances. Post-war Communism, Sovietization, national deviation—all these have made their mark on education as on other aspects of life. The communist character of the régimes has led them to reconstruct education in accordance with the principles of Marxism, to change the social role of education, to reinterpret its aims and functions, to change the content and administration and structure of education with a thoroughness that other kinds of régimes are seldom able to muster, because of lack of power or motive, or single-mindedness. In short, communist régimes have felt obliged to make radical changes in society and have always seen education as one of the ways of achieving this. Further, the fact of Soviet tutelage led them to rely heavily on Russian models, even if these had little to do with communist theory as such. Finally, the irregular move towards "national communism" has led them to ring further changes on their systems in accordance with their own national individuality; this, while not necessarily creating liberalization, is likely at least to create an atmosphere of greater flexibility. In no case has there been a sharp break; each stage has had some influence on the schools systems as they have developed. While present trends towards differentiation are important, therefore, what the different systems share is important too, and should not be obscured. To appreciate this, it is necessary to examine both the common ground of communist theory, and the "working model" of Soviet practice in education.

CHAPTER 5

Communist Education—Marxist Theory and Soviet Practice

"PHILOSOPHERS have only interpreted the world in various ways; but the real task is to change it."[1] This, perhaps one of the best-known quotations from Marx, is inscribed over the entrance to the Humboldt University in East Berlin, and sums up the basic objectives of communist education. According to various official sources,[2] Marxism is recognized as the ideological basis of education in the countries of Eastern Europe; and this means, among other things, that education is regarded not only as a means of instruction and information, but is to be used quite deliberately as a means of pursuing the "real task" of altering man's environment.

Fundamental though this idea is, it does not go the whole way in explaining how communist education takes the forms that it does in practice. Marx himself never worked out any detailed blueprint for educational policy, but provided a framework of ideas—what might be regarded as a set of guiding principles against which action could be assessed.[3] He had a good deal to say about the essential position of productive work in the shaping of man's nature, and the desirability of combining it closely with learning; he insisted on the need for the unity of theory and practice, so that theory would not only explain why things are as they are, but would go on from there to inform practice and find solutions—which is, of course, the whole point of the quotation referred to. But as it stands Marxist thinking in education leaves plenty of

[1] Karl Marx, *Eleven Theses on Feuerbach* (1845).
[2] See Chapter 7, § 1.
[3] P. N. Grusdew (ed.) *Marx/Engels: Über Erziehung und Bildung.* (Volk und Wissen Volkeigener Verlag, Berlin, 1962.)

room for interpretation when it comes to the practical issues of organizing school systems; yet, apart from Yugoslavia to some extent, communist governments in Eastern Europe have not set themselves to rework their educational systems from the ground up, adapting Marxist principles to their own particular conditions. They have, rather, looked to a system where the theory had been worked out in practice some time before, namely that of the U.S.S.R. Thus, when the communist régimes of these countries began to reform their educational systems, what they brought to the task was not just a set of principles, but a ready-made "working model". Most of the interpretation had in effect been done already; and when any further reinterpretation was thought necessary, they were for the most part content to follow the lead of the U.S.S.R. once again. Often a virtue has been made of this. The Czechoslovak Minister of Education and Culture, writing of the school reforms of 1960, described the Soviet Union as "a model to us in all respects".[4] Not many are quite as fulsome as this nowadays, but it is not long since acknowledgement of Soviet tutelage was well-nigh universal in Eastern Europe. Initially at least they turned not only to Marxism, but to the U.S.S.R. as its chief interpreter. In view of the relationship between the Soviet Union and the other countries this is hardly surprising; but it does underline the fact that we cannot examine the mainsprings of communist education in Eastern Europe in terms of Marxist theory alone. What these countries adopted (and adapted) was certainly communist, but it was a specifically Soviet version of it, and this owes much of its form to its Russian past, as well as to its Marxist–Leninist rationale.[5]

Soviet education falls outside the scope of this book, and has in any case been fully dealt with elsewhere. But it is impossible to ignore it for that reason—its influence on Eastern European

[4] František Kahuda, *Učitelske Noviny*, **10**, 51/52, pp. 1–2, 21 December 1960. Quoted in: Nellie Apanasewicz and Seymour Rosen, *Education in Czechoslovakia*, p. 22. (U.S. Office of Education, Washington D.C., 1963.)

[5] For a full treatment of the historical antecendents of the Soviet system, see Nicholas Hans, *The Russian Tradition in Education*. (Routledge & Kegan Paul, London, 1963.)

education has been too profound. Although it is not possible, therefore, to attempt anything like a full treatment even in bare outline, it is necessary to take note of some of its most important features in so far as they have influenced post-war developments in the other communist countries.

Communist education has undergone many changes and re-interpretations since the Revolution of 1917.[6] In the early days, it was characterized by a virtually complete rejection of all that had gone before. In these heady times of innovation in everything from family relationships to literature and art, the philosophy of the "clean sweep" was applied to education as well. Special decrees threw open the doors of all universities and colleges, strictly forbidding the use of any kind of entrance examination or other selective procedure. There were massive campaigns for the "liquidation of illiteracy" and the popularization of education at all levels. Attempts were made to break completely with the past in curriculum, teaching methods, school organization and practically everything else, as the new Soviet Republic embarked on a period of experiment that went on until Stalin tightened up the system in the 1930's. During that time, communist education presented a very different picture from the one that confronted the East European countries after the Second World War. As well as turning to Marx, the Soviet schools shopped around the world for ideas. Various kinds of "Progressivism" were espoused; the ideas of John Dewey, the educational exponent of American Pragmatism, were favourably received; all sorts of new techniques—projects and activity methods, the Dalton Plan of teaching through individual work assignments, methods of teaching through play—were pressed into service for the creation of a totally new kind of education. Lenin and his wife, Nadezhda Krupskaya, advocated polytechnical education—education based on the mastery of the tools, skills and materials of production—rather

---

[6] For an historical treatment of the early period of Soviet education: Oskar Annweiler, *Geschichte der Schule und Pädagogik in Russland vom Ende des Zarenreiches bis zum Beginn der Stalin-Ära.* (Erziehungswissenschaftliche Veröffentlichung des Osteuropa-Instituts an der Freien Universität Berlin, 1964.)

along the lines suggested by Marx (borrowing from Robert Owen) in *Capital*; this policy was rather spoiled from being carried to often extreme lengths. Anton Makarenko worked with the *bezprizornie*—waifs made homeless by the Civil War, who roamed the countryside in bands—and developed his theories, which were to find a permanent and important place in Soviet educational thought, of socially based moral education centring on the "collective" (the group of which the pupil was a member) as the mainstay of moral responsibility and awareness. Soviet education during this period often lacked cohesiveness, and even looked chaotic at times; doubtless, too, there were many failures arising from the hasty implementation of plans ill thought out, or the carrying of sensible ideas to absurb lengths, such as the attempts in the name of polytechnical education to base *all* instruction on some kind of productive work. But it did have a vigour, flexibility and open-mindedness that has never been recaptured. Given favourable circumstances, it might have developed into something really unique.

But circumstances were not favourable. The Soviet Government had inherited from the Tsarist régime a legacy of backwardness in education as in much else. Literacy (usually quite a good rough guide to educational development) has been variously estimated, but probably was not much over 30 per cent for the country as a whole; it was, of course, rather higher in European Russia—perhaps 40 per cent or more—and much less in the Arctic, the Far East and Central Asia, approaching vanishing-point in some places. The First World War and the Revolution had thrown the country into chaos, and the Civil War and Intervention that followed had devastated it. If the country was to be put back on its feet and developed into an advanced industrial state, three pressing needs stood out amongst a host of others: they needed more engineers, agronomists, doctors, scientists, teachers, highly trained specialists of all kinds, as many had perished or emigrated during the Civil War, and there had never been enough in any case; industrialization programmes needed a greatly increased force of skilled workers; and among the population at large there had to be a much higher level of literacy, for without this the first two aims, to say nothing of longer-term political and social objectives, would have little chance of success.

Output and efficiency thus became the chief criteria; in such a situation, all this experimentation seemed something of a luxury. By the 1930's "irresponsible experiments" had been outlawed, the administration of the system had been tightened up and almost complete uniformity imposed in content and method. Back came formal lessons, examinations, the five-point marking-scale for homework and classwork, strict classroom discipline, school uniforms, and many other features of the schools of Tsarist times. The Soviet school was no longer something totally new in the educational world; it was the traditional school of old Russia, planted firmly in the familiar European tradition. There remained some important differences, however. It was a planned system, geared to social needs. It was a system open to the masses, not one intended for an élite. Something of the scientific and technical bias of the 1920's remained; and the political orientation had, of course, changed. But in external at least it would have seemed familiar enough to a pupil from pre-Revolutionary days. It was this kind of school, not the "educational workshop" of the 1920's, that served the Eastern European countries after the Second World War as the model for communist education.[7]

One feature that has remained constant throughout all other changes has been the system's ideological bent. To some extent, of course, all societies put across their fundamental assumptions to their future citizens, whether through the schools or by other means. Few, however, do it as consciously as the Soviet educators, and few are as thorough and all-embracing in the view of the extent to which they think it proper to mould young minds in an approved pattern. Education, they argue, must serve the need of society; Soviet society is engaged in the building of Communism; accordingly, the schools must play their part by teaching the

[7] For a fuller treatment of the Soviet Educational system: Bereday, Brickman and Read, *The Changing Soviet School*. (Constable, London, 1960.) Nigel Grant, *Soviet Education*. (Pelican, 1968; University of London Press, 1965.)

younger generation the knowledge and skills—and the attitudes and values—that will make them able and willing to work to this end. The teaching of political attitudes is seen as an essential part of the essential task of communist education, the creation of a new kind of person—the "New Man"—to build a new kind of society. The use of words like "indoctrination" and "propaganda" trouble them not in the least, and usually are countered by Lenin's declaration that non-political education is "a hypocrisy and a lie". Social, moral and political education are therefore treated as essentially one process, and a great deal of attention is given to it in the schools.

The teaching of actual political theory does not take place until the later stages, when "Social Study" (*Obshchestvovedenie*) figures in the curriculum of final-year classes in the secondary school, and extensive courses in Party history and Marxist–Leninist doctrine form part of all higher-educational programmes. But just as no Catholic would be prepared to postpone moral education until the pupil could grasp the finer points of, say, the doctrine of the Trinity, no communist would put off his kind of moral education until the dawn of understanding of the theory of surplus value or basis and superstructure. Accordingly, the child is presented at an early stage with the basic ideas in lessons on other subjects—history, geography and literature in particular—where material can be selected from the approved point of view. It is done also by direct teaching, in lessons on moral education and the like, by the intensive use of posters, slogans and the omnipresence of Lenin as father-figure, and through the youth organizations whose activities, if rarely directly political at the younger levels, are strongly flavoured with political attitudes and symbols none the less. The message is reminiscent sometimes of religious teaching, with red flags and portraits of leaders interspersed with exhortations to good works, and sometimes looks more like advertising, where simple slogans ("Peace to the World", "Onward to the Building of Communism", etc.) build up a favourable "brand image". The use of all these agencies for putting across the approved socio-political attitudes has long been developed into a fairly elaborate procedure in Soviet schools. We shall see later how closely most of the East European systems have followed Soviet practice, often in rather different circumstances, and how far they have rung their own changes on it.

The pre-eminence of political objectives implies careful political control. Here too the Soviet Union has set the pattern. This has been achieved from the beginning by virtually complete governmental control, highly centralized, with a marked degree of uniformity throughout the educational system; by Stalin's time this had been extended to details of curricula, schemes of work, teaching methods, and even such matters as the running of parent's committees. The actual agencies of government have varied from time to time; the *Narkompros* (People's Commisariat for Education) giving way eventually to a more complex system whereby higher and specialized secondary education is attended to by a U.S.S.R. Ministry, with Ministries for the constituent republics, school education by the republic Ministries of Education (with on centralized Ministry for the entire country until recently), and vocational–technical education by a special committee of the Council of Ministers. But the real control, from the high-level formulation of basic policy down to the individual schools, is in the hands of the Communist Party. It therefore matters little whether the governmental agencies are centralized or not; the Party is. This pattern too has been taken over in essentials by the East European countries. As we shall see, the arrangements for government control vary; Rumania, for instance, has one Ministry of Education responsible for everything from kindergartens to universities throughout the country, while Yugoslavia, as usual, diverges most, with a comparatively decentralized system. But whatever the details of the organization of Ministries, the principle of Party control, even in countries with nominally multi-party systems of government, obtains generally. Again, only in Yugoslavia is there any great departure from it, and that only recently.

In the structure of the educational system, too, the U.S.S.R. has provided the template. From the Marxist–Leninist point of view, any school system would have to be organized on a mass basis, and as we have seen practical considerations in any case tended to reinforce the principle—selective systems are liable to be wasteful, and, particularly in the first decades after the Revolution, the Soviet Union could not afford to overlook any possible source of talent. This has meant, in spite of difficulties, pursuing a policy of comprehensive schooling of a thoroughness quite startling to most Western observers. "Streaming" of children into different classes according to ability, whether by the use of intelligence tests or other means, has long been forbidden in Soviet schools. Each class is supposed to contain a complete cross-section and follow the same programme. Apart from those who fail to make the grade and have to repeat the year's work (a figure hard to estimate exactly, but possibly between 10 and 20 per cent on average), all children in any given year move on to the next grade with the whole class. There is no "eleven-plus", and the divisions, familiar in Britain, into Grammar School and Secondary Modern, or Senior and Junior Secondary, do not exist. There are shortcomings, of course; 20 per cent repeating does seem rather high, even if all the rest have passed a standard that we normally think of as within the limits of the top 30 per cent only; there is evidence of "concealed streaming" in some places, and it has been suggested that many teachers use the examinations—mainly oral—rather more leniently than they should. The retention from Tsarist times of a small number of special schools for the artistically gifted, and the opening of new ones for the scientifically gifted as well, provide another break in the picture of universal comprehensive education. But the principle is well established. In spite of the statements of some Western observers (and, be it said, some incautious Soviet educators too), neither Marxist theory nor Soviet teachers deny the existence of differences of individual ability. But they do argue that far too deterministic a view is taken in the traditional selective systems; they point out that while the less able benefit from the stimulus of their abler fellows, the bright ones are not held back; and it is also held that encouraging the quicker ones to help those who are having difficulty with their work is a valuable form of social training for both. No class places are given; pupils are encouraged to feel that it is their job to help the whole class to pass. All take credit for the success of others, and feel responsible for their failures; this, at least, is the aim. It is not, of course, always realized, but it does seem to work more often than outside observers, used to a quite different set of assumptions, might expect. By the end of the Second World War comprehensive education, in this form of undifferentiated groups working to the same programme at each stage, was so thoroughly established that it had come to be regarded as a *sine qua non* of communist educational practice, and was treated as such, with some modifications, by the communist régimes of Eastern Europe.

The details of school organization were less important. They have changed frequently in the U.S.S.R., and could not in any case have been imported as they stood into the other countries. In the post-war years there was a unified ten-year school, taking pupils from the age of 7 to 17; it was hoped to make this eventually compulsory for all. Most pupils completed only the shorter version, the seven-year school (7–14), though many followed general or vocational part-time courses afterwards; and in some remote areas there were still only four-year schools (7–11). In 1958, under what became known as the Khrushchov reforms, this system was replaced by a basic compulsory eight-year school (7–15), comprehensive and unified throughout. Thereafter, pupils could follow a mainly general course at a *Secondary Polytechnical School* (three years), a professional course at a *Tekhnikum* or *Specialized Secondary School* (four years), or a trade course at a *Vocational Technical School* (from six months to three years, depending on the trade). More part-time schools, especially of the first type, were also set up. There have been further changes[8] since Khrushchov's fall from power, though some of them were under way when he was still in control: the length of the complete school course is now once again ten years, and there have been alterations in Tekhnikum and higher educational courses. The eight-year school, however, remains the basic unit.

[8] Nigel Grant, "Recent Changes in Soviet Secondary Schools" (*International Review of Education*, XI 1965 **2**, pp. 129–43.)

The "Khrushchov reforms" also introduced an increased element of polytechnical education into the ordinary schools. This, as we have seen, was nothing new, though it had been eclipsed somewhat during the Stalin era. Under the 1958 system it was increased at most levels, and pupils in secondary classes (age 15 and over) were required to undergo industrial training in factories or farms for a third of their curricular time. This was cut to a quarter in 1964, and since then the whole question of polytechnical education has been under re-examination, with calls for rationalization and reduction of time spent on it—there have been many complaints in the press that the time was too often spent in repetitive activities which yielded neither educational or industrial advantage. The relationship between polytechnical and general education has been a vexed question in communist schooling, and this has not been confined to the U.S.S.R., but has been echoed in the Eastern European countries. Most of them produced reforms of their own[9] in the years following the Soviet changes—Bulgaria, East Germany and Czechoslovakia in 1959, Poland and Hungary in 1961, Rumania in 1962—and although they did not copy them exactly (they hardly could) the twin factors of expansion and increased emphasis on polytechnical education figured prominently. Much was made of the necessity, in communist education, of securing the unity of theory and practice, linking learning with productive work and, in a phrase taken straight from the title of the 1958 Soviet law, "strengthening the ties of the school with life". Marxist–Leninist theory was, of course, invoked at length; more specifically, the Soviet example in the phrasing of the reforms and the actual enactments was clear enough and was, usually, acknowledged. One writer[10] even mentions Czech officials consulting a *Russian* source to settle some point on polytechnical education policy, which suggests that they owed more than the broad outlines to the U.S.S.R. But not every

---

[9] Rudolf Weissner, Helmut Brauer and Willy Mann, "Das Bildungswesen der zweiten Stufe in einigen sozialistischen Ländern (Eine vergleichende Studie)" (*Vergleichende Pädagogik*, **10**, 1964, p. 10).

[10] Edmund King, *Communist Education*, p. 13. (Methuen, London, 1963.)

shift of Soviet practice has been followed everywhere, particularly in the last year of two; while the Soviet authorities were retrenching by cutting the extra year off the eleven-year school, for example, the trend in the other countries remained one of increasing the length of schooling. Even in countries where the importance of Soviet example is still declared, what happens in practice tends to diverge more and more.

Among many other features of communist education as interpreted in the U.S.S.R. which have proved important for Eastern Europe, one may single out the role of adult and higher education, the emphasis on science and technology, and the great importance accorded to extra-curricular agencies, notably the youth organizations. Adult education in various forms, from literacy classes to workers' faculties, has played a vital part in the Soviet system from the Revolution onwards. This is what one might expect of an initially backward country bent on expansion in a hurry, conditions which also obtained in many parts of Eastern Europe after the war. Encouragement to pursue part-time studies, and the provision of elaborate facilities for this has become one of the hallmarks of the system. The same "expansionist" philosophy has been applied to higher education, so that the Soviet Union, with over 4 million students, has now one of the highest proportions in the world of population engaged in higher studies. This has been accomplished partly by making more places available, partly as a corollary to the expansion of secondary schooling. As has happened in other countries, the potential number of entrants has increased more than might have been expected and, as the demand became overwhelming, the authorities have resorted once more to some degree of restriction, noticeably greater since 1958. This has been modified by taking up some of the increase in various types of part-time course—evening and shift classes, correspondence schools, and the like—so shifting the emphasis that such students now make up about half the total number. Since they remain in contact with the workaday world, this is approved of on social as well as economic grounds. Some of the East European countries, notably Poland and Czechoslovakia, had much longer established higher educational systems than the U.S.S.R., but followed the general trend of accepting Soviet practice in some detail. The adoption of expansionist policies, and the use of such devices as part-time courses to make them feasible, was only to be expected, given the basic acceptance of the basic policies of mass education and the maintaining of links with the economy. But assimilation has gone further, sometimes to the extent (as in Czechoslovakia)[11] of renaming degrees in accordance with Soviet usage, which surely has much less relevance either to political philosophy or policy decisions on the admission of students.

Not even a rough outline of communist education could be complete if only the schools and higher institutions were considered. The youth organizations—in the U.S.S.R., the Octobrists for the very young, the Pioneers for the 10 to 15-year-olds, and the Komsomol from 15 to 27—are much more than bodies for social mixing and the organization of sports and hobbies and other leisure activities, though of course they attend to these things as well. They are so closely bound up with the work of the schools as to be virtually part of the educational system. It has already been noted that they are one medium for the transmission of social and political ideas. They are also one of the mainstays of class discipline, voicing the disapproval of the "collective" towards shirkers and delinquents and its encouragement to greater efforts. They run many school activities, from weeding the school yard to putting on plays or arranging excursions. They hold meetings to discuss each other's work, and arrange for some of their own number to coach those in difficulty. They act as a liaison body between pupils and staff. In short, whether in the school or in the Pioneer houses, they impinge on practically every aspect of the pupil's life.

This feature of Soviet education has been taken over throughout Eastern Europe. The Yugoslav Youth League, the East German FDJ (Free German Youth), the Bulgarian Dimitrov Youth League

[11] Stanislav Vodinský, *Czechoslovakia: Education*, pp. 58–59. (Orbis, Prague, 1963.)

and others play the same role as the Soviet Komsomol, while all the countries in question have the equivalent of the Pioneers for younger children. There are differences in age-levels and organization, especially in Poland, where the Komsomol-type ZMP (Union of Polish Youth) has been divided into two senior organizations, and where the junior organization, the League of Polish Scouts (ZHP), still owes more, at least in externals, to the Baden-Powell model than to the Soviet one. But generally the resemblances between these bodies and their Soviet counterparts is close, not only in function but in externals; even in Rumania, the "solemn promise" is practically a word-for-word translation of the Promise of the Soviet Pioneers. Whatever the difficulties or undesirability of importing school systems wholesale, this immensely useful means of reinforcing the work of the school in social, moral, political and leisure education was not be to missed. Perhaps more than any other feature of Soviet education, this has been taken over by the other countries with the minimum of change.

These, then, are the chief aspects of the Soviet system which influenced the communist régimes of Eastern Europe when they set themselves to overhaul their educational systems in accordance with communist principles. There were many others, often extending to details like the style of uniforms and the titles of diplomas, but they were less universal and less essential to the nature of the system. The dominance of the Soviet Union led to the adoption of many specifically Russian features too, hence the prominence of the study of Soviet political institutions in Czechoslovakia and elsewhere, of Russian revolutionary history in, for example, East Germany, or Russian language and literature in the school curricula practically everywhere, and so on. These Russian features have tended to be the first casualties in countries like Yugoslavia and Rumania when they have started to assert national individuality; in both countries the compulsory study of Russian, for instance, has been dropped in the schools.

The dual nature of the Soviet system—at once communist and very Russian—has in itself made the borrowing process an extremely complex one, considering the tangle of cultural traditions and areas of national sensitivity that characterize every aspect of life in Eastern Europe. It was, of course, further complicated by the particular problems and the pre-existing school systems of the various countries. We shall see later the different ways in which the Soviet "working model" was adopted for use in these countries; but it was never a case of simple importation. Even the most backward states already had school systems of some kind, however rudimentary, and in many cases they had well-developed educational traditions of their own. The influx of Soviet ideas and practices could never take place in a vacuum; even when determinedly turning their backs on the past, communist régimes had to use the teachers and the schools that they had already, at least to begin with, and inevitably found that their freedom to innovate was circumscribed by the existing systems. Even before the resurgence of national feeling led them to stress the "positive aspects" of their inheritance from the past, the patterns and assumptions of the traditional systems had left their mark on the development of education in these countries. We shall, therefore, examine briefly the kind of schools that existed before the major changes were made, then consider the blend of the old and new that characterizes Eastern European education at the present time.

CHAPTER 6

Educational Patterns—The Old and the New

WHATEVER kind of régime had taken over in the East European countries after the war, they would have been faced with obvious and pressing need for reform of some kind. The pre-war picture in education, as in much else, was uneven, but in most areas was extremely backward. This, as we have seen, was true not only in the more predictable case of the "Southern Tier", where Yugoslavia had an illiteracy rate of over 40 per cent,[1] Bulgaria 31,[2] Rumania 25,[3] and Albania 80,[4] but in some of the northern countries as well. Over 25 per cent of all Poles were illiterate;[5] Hungary had a more modest level, but still reached 8 per cent.[6] Even Czechoslovakia, advanced by East European standards, had an illiteracy rate of over 4 per cent in 1931.[7]

This backwardness was, of course, partly due to the low level of economic development throughout most of the area, especially in the countryside. But it was often exaggerated by the structure of the systems themselves. The standard of instruction was by no

[1] Stana Tomašević and Mustafa Begtić, *Vocational Training in Yugoslavia*, p. 37. (Belgrade, 1961.)
[2] Naiden Čakarov et al., *Das Schulwesen in der Volksrepublik Bulgarien*, p. 139. In: Deutsches Pädagogisches Zentralinstitut, *Das Schulwesen sozialistischer Länder in Europa*. (Volk und Wissen Volkseigener Verlag, Berlin, 1962.)
[3] Herta Haase and Seymour Rosen, *Education in Rumania*, p. 2. (U.S. Office of Education, Washington D.C., 1960.)
[4] *World Survey of Education*, III, p. 169. (UNESCO, Paris, 1961.)
[5] Zygmunt Parnowski, *Education in Poland*, p. 7. (Polonia, Warsaw, 1958.)
[6] Márton Horváth, *Public and Higher Education*, p. 81. In: János Veres (ed.), *The Experiences of Building a New Society*. (Pannonia, Budapest, 1964.)
[7] Jemnović, *op. cit.*, p. 4.

means universally low. In higher education, for example, the Polish and Czechoslovak universities could look back on a long tradition and a level of excellence equal to most other countries. The high scholastic standards of the German *Gymnasien* (academic secondary schools with an intensive ten-year course) were justly famous, but had also been attained elsewhere; the best of the Polish and Rumanian *lycées* and of the Czech, Hungarian and Yugoslav *gymnasia* were as good as anything in the West. Some of these schools boasted ancient lineage as well as high attainment; even now, Bulgarians and Rumanians are inclined to take almost as much pride in the Gubrovo High School and the Bălcescu *lycée* as do Poles and Czechs in the Jagięllonian and Charles Universities.

Nor were these isolated examples. The pre-war systems offered a wide range of high-quality courses at secondary level at least. Drawing their inspiration mainly from France and Germany, they paid particular attention to the chief pride of these countries, the *lycée* and the *gymnasium*. In detail, the school systems naturally differed a good deal, but a couple of examples will serve to illustrate the general pattern.

The Rumanian[8] elementary school admitted children at the age of 7, and offered two types of course: four years for those going on to secondary schools, and seven years (7–14) for the rest, a complete self-contained course designed to cover the entire period of compulsory schooling. This was the theoretical situation; in practice, this seven-year "terminal" elementary course did not amount to much. It was true that schooling was compulsory in principle until the age of 14; but since, according to official figures, less than 6 per cent continued elementary schooling beyond the fourth year (age 11), enforcement cannot have been very effective. The choice for the 11-year-olds was in practice much starker than the official position made out—either they

---

[8] *Sistemul de învăţămînt în Romînia burghezo-moşierească.* In: A. Dancsuly A. Chircev and A. Manolache, *Pedagogia*, pp. 74–77. (Editura Didactică şi Pedagogică, Bucharest, 1964.) Herta Haase and Seymour Rosen, *op. cit.*, pp. 2, 7.

went on to secondary schools, or they left. The great majority left, especially in the countryside.

For those who did go on to secondary schooling, there was considerable variety. There were some vocational schools, though these had a lowly place in the system. There were pedagogical or "normal" schools with a seven-year course for the training of primary school teachers. There were theological schools (six to eight years); and there were the *lycées* (seven years). *Lycées* were of three types—academic, commercial, military; the curriculum was much the same for all for the first three years, but was differentiated thereafter. At the end of the course, students could take the final examination (*bacalaureat*) and go on to higher education or jobs in industry and government. For those who hoped to enter university, the narrow path of an academic *lycée* was the obvious one to follow; entering the other types of secondary school meant a rather firmer vocational commitment.

The pre-war system in Czechoslovakia[9] was more complex and also more effective. It differed first of all in being organized in three tiers, not two. The stages were: (1) the elementary school, from 6 to 11 years of age; (2) the "Civic" school (*měst'anská škola*), an advanced primary or lower secondary school, from 11 to 15 years; and (3) the secondary schools (*střední školy*). These stages were not usually taken in sequence, however; the first parting of the ways came at the end of the elementary school. The 11-year-old who qualified for admission (and paid the fees or got a scholarship) could go directly to a secondary school. There were five types: (1) the *gymnasium*, with the emphasis on Latin and Greek; (2) *reálné gymnasium* ("Modern" gymnasium), with Latin, but substituting English or French for Greek; (3) the reformed *reálné gymnasium*—much the same, but with more stress on modern languages and less on Latin; (4) the *reálka* ("modern school"), which concentrated on mathematics, natural sciences and modern languages, to the exclusion of the classics; and (5) the "higher modern gymnasium" (*vyšší reálné gymnasium*), which offered

[9] Nellie Apanasewicz and Seymour Rosen, *Education in Czechoslovakia*, pp. 3–5. (U.S. Office of Education, Washington D.C., 1963.)

classical, scientific or modern language options half-way through the course. All of them had the same basic course in other subjects—Czech, Slovak, history, and so on. The courses all lasted for eight years (seven years in the *reálka*); the first four years were virtually the same in all the schools, differentiation taking place from the fifth year. Passing the final examinations (*maturita*) qualified students for entry to higher educational establishments. In general and humane studies, this was the normal route to university or college.

Pupils who did not go on to secondary education at 11 entered the civic school, where the four-year course was less exacting than secondary but advanced beyond primary—it included geometry, physics and a foreign language, for instance, and subjects with a vocational bent like book-keeping and manual skills. This could be regarded as a "terminal" course; indeed, it went one year beyond the age of compulsory schooling (14). It could also be regarded as preparatory, for pupils completing it successfully could apply to professionally inclined secondary schools. These were vocational–technical schools (engineering, electrotechnics, etc.), agricultural and forestry schools, and commercial academies. The length of course was four years. On completion, students could take up employment, or enter the appropriate higher institutions—technical, agricultural or commercial colleges.

The influence of German models is clear throughout, especially in the academic secondary schools. Enforcement of attendance was much more effective than in Rumania (and most other countries), and opportunities were less limited, notably by virtue of the provision of a viable "second road" to higher studies. A glance at the literacy levels of the two countries is enough to point the greater efficiency of the Czechoslovak system. But it did have its black spots. As the name hints, the civic schools were essentially urban; many country districts lacked them altogether, and it was in the country that the system fell furthest short of its aims. Although the 1922 Law had made schooling compulsory till the age of 14, this did not always hold in practice. There was a good deal of "leakage", and in predominantly rural Slovakia only 38 per cent went on to *any* kind of post-primary education, whether secondary or civic; the rest left with only five years of elementary schooling.[10] Czechoslovakia was more fortunate than most in being able to provide alternatives for the majority who could not proceed to secondary school, but even there there were shortcomings, sometimes glaring.

Over Eastern Europe generally similar patterns were to be found: basic elementary schooling for the majority (and nothing else, except when there were junior secondary schools after the Czech pattern), and a selected minority going on after four or five years to secondary schools, often of high quality, to prepare for white-collar jobs or higher studies. The trouble with these traditional systems was not the quality of instruction, which was often excellent, but that they were too limited in scope. Geared to preparation for higher education and centred in the towns, they were largely urban middle-class institutions. They charged fees; and although it was often possible to win scholarships or at least earn remission of fees, this drastically limited the social range of the pupils that were admitted. A Hungarian writer, Ernő Bajor Nagy, describes his own dismay when, armed with excellent reports from his village school, but totally lacking funds, he tried to persuade the headmaster of a *gymnasium* to let him in:

> The headmaster asked with concern: "And how will you pay your fees?"
> "I intend to be an eminent scholar and earn exemption from paying," I promised.
> "And how will you be able to buy your books?"
> "We have already saved up for them."
> With mild patience he explained things to me: "And next year? The year after? And your gymnastics gear? Your drawing equipment? The excursions? And what if your mother should fall ill?..."
> I could not find arguments to oppose his. Finally all I could stammer was:
> "I want to be a gymnasium student."
> And this is what he replied:
> "Why do you want to be?.... What would happen to the world if everybody wanted to be a gymnasium student? You will be a very fine man

---

[10] Stanislav Vodinský, *Czechoslovakia: Education*, p. 25. (Orbis, Prague, 1963.)

even without that.... The Latin proverb says—like prefers like. You are different from the gymnasium students."[11]

Such experiences were repeated all over Eastern Europe; and for every Nagy there must have been countless others who never felt it worth while trying to crash the barriers. For the barriers were formidable. Even in advanced countries, selection procedures, even when made as "objective" and "culture-free" as possible, tend to discriminate heavily against the children of non-professional families. Add to that the financial barriers, and very few children of working-class or peasant families had much chance of entering secondary education, even if they did succeed in finishing primary school. In Poland, only 14 per cent of the entrants to secondary schools came from peasant or working-class families; in Hungary it was only 4 per cent. Even where universal elementary schooling was effectively enforced (as in Germany and, to some extent, in Czechoslovakia) it was hard to avoid class bias in secondary schooling.

But it was not fully effective. The provision of elementary education, and its enforcement, was uneven. Bulgaria had seven-year basic schools (four years elementary plus three years pre-secondary); Hungary had six years (6–12), Poland seven, Germany eight (*Volksschulen* from 6 to 14), and Yugoslavia, less ambitiously, only four years (7–11). All of these were, in theory, compulsory; but apart from Germany, this was not completely enforced. We have seen something of the different degrees by which Czechoslovakia and Rumania fell short of the official position. In Bulgaria, as late as 1944, there were nearly 2000 villages with no schools at all, and 100,000 children with no schooling.[12] In Hungary, in the 1930's, less than half the age-group were completing even the six-year elementary course.[13] In pre-war Poland over a million school-age children were not at school, and in any case many rural elementary schools were taking

---

[11] Ernő Bajor Nagy, *A Country at School*, pp. 8–9. (Pannonia, Budapest, 1962.)
[12] Nevena Geliazkova (ed.), *Prosperity and Culture in Bulgaria*, p. 100. (Foreign Languages Press, Sofia, 1964.)
[13] Márton Horváth, *op. cit.*, p. 83.

seven years to cover four years of the course, so that few country children had any chance of qualifying to apply to secondary schools, even if they did manage to stay on for the statutory seven years.[14] In most of Eastern Europe, then, the secondary schools rarely had a nation-wide network of elementary schooling to draw on, but were limited to the fraction who could overcome the obstacles of residence, sub-standard schooling, absence of enforcement, absence of money, and the severely limiting entrance requirements of the secondary schools.

These limitations were further aggravated by another characteristic, namely the "academic" bias of the secondary schools—at once their greatest pride and their greatest weakness. As we have seen the technical and vocational sectors had been widely neglected. The extent of this neglect varied from place to place—less in Germany and Czechoslovakia, more elsewhere. Most countries had some kind of non-academic provision beyond the primary stage, but such schools were usually few in number and often (a corollary of the prestige of the *gymnasia* and *lycées*) types as "poor relations" of the academic schools. In Hungary, to cite one example, 70 per cent of post-primary schools were of the "grammar" type.[15] This bias, of course, made itself felt at the level of higher education as well. Once again, Germany and Czechoslovakia were better off in this than most, in providing ways whereby the more technical-minded, by means of the vocational secondary schools, had some chance of reaching the higher levels. But they were exceptional; generally any way to higher education other than through the academic secondary schools was virtually non-existent (as in Bulgaria and Yugoslavia) or severely limited. Thus, the selective nature of the *gymnasia* and *lycées* ensured that the doors to the higher institutions shut early; and the academic bias of the secondary system, with its scarcity of alternative types of secondary school, preserved this exclusiveness. For all but a tiny minority, the doors stayed shut.

[14] Maria Paschalska, *Education in Poland*, p. 9. (Polonia, Warsaw, 1962.) Zygmunt Parnowski, *op. cit.*, p. 7.
[15] Márton Horváth, *op. cit.*, p. 83.

When the communist régimes came to power after the war, they inherited such traditionally minded systems and an obligation to alter them to meet new needs. In some cases they took over developed systems, as in Germany and Czechoslovakia; in others, backward systems, as in Rumania and Bulgaria; and again in others, backward systems where the situation was made much worse by the devastations of war, as in Poland and Yugoslavia. Yugoslavia, badly off enough for school provision in pre-war-days, emerged from the horrors of occupation and civil war with a major task of reconstruction in hand; 14 per cent of the schools had been totally destroyed and 36 per cent badly damaged. Some areas had been worse hit than others. Backward Bosnia had lost 39 per cent of the schools, while a further 21 per cent had been severely damaged, 27 per cent slightly damaged; only 13 per cent were fit for immediate use. Over the country as a whole, perhaps 50 per cent of the schools could be used after the war, if staff could be found for them—no easy matter, since an already inadequate teaching force had been depeleted by the killing of some 10,000 teachers during the fighting.[16] Poland, where the Nazis had closed and destroyed schools and shot large numbers of teachers as a deliberate policy (one estimate is over 27,000 altogether), was an even worse case.[17] It might be thought that the traditional systems were so shattered as to have little influence on the pattern of reconstruction after the war; but, by the same token, this made the building up of any other system extremely difficult. The authorities, communist or not, had to make use of whatever schools and teachers they could get.

The coming to power of the communist governments saw a rash of legislation throughout Eastern Europe. In the constitutions of the new states, basic principles for the running of the educational systems were laid down:

> Citizens have the right to education. Education is secular, and is imbued with the democratic and progressive spirit. National minorities are guaranteed the right to have instruction in the mother tongue and to develop

---

[16] Tomašević and Begtić, *op. cit.*, p. 43.
[17] Mieczysław Pęcherski, *Das Schulwesen in Volkspolen,* p. 291. In: DPZI, *op. cit.*

their national cultures.... Basic education is compulsory and free. The schools are state schools.... The right to education is guaranteed by means of schools and other educational establishments, universities and the provision of scholarships, hostels.[18]

This is from the Bulgarian Constitution of 1947 (Article 79), and in its main points is typical of the many declarations of this sort that were made in Eastern Europe. They were normally reinforced by clauses on the equality of the sexes, classes, religions, etc., in the right to education as to other things. Constitutions, of course, need not be effective guarantees in practice; but they do give some clue to official attitudes, and can be taken as a statement of the declared ideals of the régime. The stated principles formed the guiding lines for the educational reforms of the post-war period.

Obviously there could be no clean sweep of the old and the introduction of new systems in detail, whether copied from the U.S.S.R. or not. What did emerge was a series of modifications to bring existing systems into line with the Soviet model—or at least its basic features—in so far as objective circumstances allowed. These often imposed severe limitations. Rumania, for instance, carried through some sweeping changes in the 1948 Law for the Reform of the Educational System. The major objectives were:

> To eliminate illiteracy; to broaden and democratise the basic educational system so as to include all children of school age, as well as adult illiterates; to educate the youth in the spirit of popular democracy, and to instill in them the spirit of socialist patriotism and proletarian internationalism.[19]

Steps were also taken to ensure more stress on science and technology, and link the work of the school more closely with the needs of the national economy. But the expansion needed for such a programme was held up by the hard facts of life; schools had to be built, teachers trained, and money found for this—they could not simply be legislated into existence. To begin with, therefore, only four years of elementary schooling could be made compulsory; it was not until 1964 that, after a hard struggle, eight-year basic

---

[18] Naiden Čakarov et al., *Das Schulwesen in der Volksrepublik Bulgarien*, p. 137. In: DPZI, *op. cit.*

[19] Herta Haase and Seymour Rosen, *op. cit.*, p. 1.

schooling became compulsory for all.[20] The policy of "democratizing" education by making it universally available thus had to wait on circumstances, and this can be observed in other countries as well. But the policy, at least, was decided on and kept in mind from the very beginning. Educational expansion was regarded as absolutely fundamental to all their economic, social and political objectives; since most countries had to make up a backlog of centuries, there can be no denying the impressiveness of the expansion that has taken place.

Expansion, unification, the "open-door" policy—these, together with increased stress on technology and the needs of the economy (and, of course, the expected political orientation), characterized the post-war educational reforms. Bulgaria was early in the field with an education law in September 1944 which "comprehensivized" the basic schools, set up special schools, and founded a network of external schools, evening and correspondence classes, etc.[21] In Poland the Minister of Education called a conference on public education at Łódź in 1945, and brought away recommendations that education should be thenceforth unified, free, compulsory, and open at all levels. More specifically, the conference suggested a basic comprehensive eight-year school, to be followed by three-year secondary schools and trade schools —rather on the model of the Soviet system, with additions. It was also suggested that all pupils not pursuing full-time secondary schooling should be required to attend a part-time trade school till the age of 18—an idea presumably derived from the German *Berufsschulen*. Not all of this proved possible, in view of the country's economic situation; the Decree on the Organization of the School System of November 1949 was more modest in its aims. There was to be a compulsory seven-year basic school; the existing secondary schools (the four-year *gimnazjum* topped by the more specialized two-year *liceum*) was replaced by a single four-year *liceum*, much more broadly based than before, and entry to it was

[20] Ministry of Education of the Rumanian People's Republic, *The Educational Movement in 1964–1965*, p. 21. (Meridiane, Bucharest, 1965.)
[21] Naiden Čakarov, *op. cit.*, pp. 137 ff.

to be postponed until the completion of basic schooling. This step reduced the total length of course from twelve or thirteen to eleven years (with regrets), but it has since been raised to twelve again. At the same time, the technical network was greatly expanded, as were part-time schools of all kinds. To remove one of the worst blots on the system, an anti-illiteracy campaign was mounted on a national scale in April 1949.[22]

In Hungary[23] the dual nature of the elementary school was abolished in 1945, and replaced by a single basic eight-year school (age 6–14), leading on to three types of secondary school: *gymnasia*; technical, agricultural and economic schools; and teacher-training schools, all with a four-year course. The new *gymnasium* differed from the old in the absence of early selection—all had to complete the basic comprehensive school first. Again, there were moves to expand technical and vocational courses, and evening and correspondence classes, apprentice training centres, adult education courses—all these were expanded to an unheard-of extent. In Czechoslovakia,[24] the 1948 School Law was passed "to make culture, training and education democratic". All schools were brought under state control. As before, the system was organized in three tiers: (1) the basic school (*národní škola*—national or people's school) from age 6 to 11; (2) middle schools (11–15); and (3) four-year *gymnasia* and vocational secondary schools (15–19). Once again, early entry to the selective schools was stopped; each stage had to be gone through in turn, thus postponing decision on selection and keeping open the doors to the upper levels for a longer period. This system was later to develop into a basic eight-year (subsequently nine-year) comprehensive school, followed by different types of secondary school on the familiar pattern. Other moves noted elsewhere, particularly the expansion of technical and adult education, were also made, and special schools—there had been only a few private schools for the handicapped before the war—were set up. Yugoslavia also

---

[22] Mieczysław Pęcherski, *op. cit.*, pp. 291 ff.
[23] Márton Horváth, *op. cit.*, pp. 81–82.
[24] Apanasewicz and Rosen, *op. cit.*, p. 11.

pressed forward with the pattern of the basic school followed by various secondary schools, but this took time; it was the early 1950's when the major legislation was worked out, and there were more variations from place to place. But there too, as far as possible, the innovations were on the same general lines.

East Germany is something of a special case.[25] There the position was complicated by the role of the occupying powers and their relations with each other, by the division of Germany, and by the special position of Berlin. It will, therefore, be considered separately in a later section.

There were, of course, further changes in the East European countries in the years that followed, but it can be seen that the pattern was established right from the start. In the structure of education, the traditional systems were adapted to move them closer to the Soviet model. With all the variations, the new systems were alike in bringing in unification, comprehensive education, expansion at all levels, greater emphasis on technical schools and on part-time and adult courses. In short, selective systems were converted into mass systems, and brought under complete state control to make overall planning for this possible.

The same process was applied to the content of education, though here again there were variations. The most significant moves in this field were the shifts of emphasis towards the natural sciences, with correspondingly less attention to the classics. Technical and polytechnical education too acquired a place in the general schools, though they did not fully come into their own until the "second wave" of school reforms in the early 1960's. Such subjects as "civics" or "citizenship" were either reinterpreted along Marxist lines, or replaced by more directly political teaching, such as the subject of "scientific socialism" in the Rumanian *lycées*. Russian became the first foreign language in the schools, and was taken by all pupils. Unlike the Soviet schools, however, most of the East European systems did not limit themselves to one foreign language, but offered two or even three, so that the study

---

[25] Weissner, Brauer and Mann, *Vergleichende Pädagogik*, **10** (June 1964), pp. 33–38.

of English, French and German was still available—more so than under the old systems, frequently, in view of the expansion of secondary schooling. Rumania even continued to keep Latin as a standard part of the *lycée* curriculum, Rumanian being a Romance language. Religious education was generally removed from the school curriculum, though it made a temporary reappearance in Czechoslovakia and Poland.

Close though the curriculum came to that of the Soviet schools, there remained some important differences. The range of languages taught was greater, as was the time available for their study. Classical studies, though diminished in importance compared with their place under the old systems, survived to a far greater extent than in the U.S.S.R. Latin, for example, is not found in the Soviet schools; it is taken at university, if anywhere; but it is commonly taught in the schools of Poland, Czechoslovakia, Hungary and East Germany, as well as Rumania. More fundamentally, the prominence of *Russian* language, *Soviet* institutions, *Soviet* history and geography—alongside those of the countries concerned—meant that while the content of the Soviet curriculum was, as it were, self-sufficient, that of the Eastern European schools was outward-looking—towards the U.S.S.R. Finally, the Soviet practice of having a uniform curriculum throughout was not fully adopted. Though uniformity became normal throughout the basic schools (expanded to cover the first years of the secondary stage), some choice was generally retained in the later stages, either by the offering of distinct courses (such as the science or humanities "sides" in Rumania and Yugoslavia), or by leaving room in a common curriculum for optional subjects, as in Poland and Bulgaria. In the U.S.S.R., the 1958 reforms allotted a small proportion of curricular time to optional subjects, and there is now talk of expanding the principle of variety in the senior classes. There may, of course, be no connection, but some teachers in Eastern European countries have suggested that this is one instance of ideas and practices going the other way, and that they are now having some influence on the Soviet Union, rather than the other way round.

Another apparent irony, incidentally, is that most countries have managed to extend their length of schooling beyond that of the Soviet Union. This took time, but by the early 1960's East Germany (taking basic and secondary schooling together) had a twelve-year course of general education; by the middle of the decade, so had Rumania, Hungary, Yugoslavia, Czechoslovakia and Poland, and Bulgaria had eleven years. The U.S.S.R., on the other hand, had to cut back from eleven to ten years in 1964. East European technical courses, too, tend to be longer (and broader) than their Soviet counterparts. Much the same holds good for the proportion of pupils going on with some kind of education (general or trade) after the basic school. By the early 1960's East Germany was in the lead with 97 per cent, followed by Bulgaria (surprisingly enough) with 95 per cent. Czechoslovakia had reached 90 per cent, Poland 80 per cent. At the other end of the scale, the U.S.S.R. had 55 per cent, Rumania just 50. These figures,[26] of course, include *Berufsschulen* and part-time and day-release schemes of all kinds, which greatly inflates some of the figures, especially those for East Germany and Czechoslovakia. If only the general schools or, alternatively, full-time courses were counted, the total picture (and the order in the "league table") would be rather different. But such figures do serve as a timely reminder that although it served as a model for other countries the Soviet Union, with its vast Asian areas and underdeveloped regions, is poorer than Eastern Europe; the resources are there, but they are sorely stretched. They also seem to indicate that the expansion of the educational systems since the war has been a continuous process; while the Soviet Union has been forced to draw its horns in from time to time, the East European impetus is still there. Regardless of the relative positions of the various countries, it is worth noting that in all of them a majority—often overwhelming—of pupils go on to some kind of schooling, full or part-time, beyond the leaving-age (15 or 16). This again, especially when compared with the pre-war position, is eloquent testimony to the serious with which the idea of "mass education" is regarded.

[26] Weissner, Brauer and Mann, *op. cit.*, pp. 20–21.

Since the first wave of legislation brought the traditional systems more into line with the U.S.S.R., a great deal has changed. Both in the Soviet Union and the other countries development has continued, sometimes with baffling speed; and although many of these countries have to some extent kept in step with Soviet developments—notably in echoing the increased stress on polytechnical education after 1958—there have been more and more exceptions as time goes on. Some of these developments, such as the changing attitude towards things Russian, for example, have been noted already, stemming as they do from wider political developments like the reassertion of nationalism in Rumania. Others are more directly educational, such as the toying with the idea of "streaming" (at least to the extent of setting up "special experimental classes") in certain Rumanian *lycées*,[27] or the use of specialist teachers in primary classes (Rumania again),[28] or the use of mental tests in Yugoslavia, the nondogmatic approach to education for citizenship in Poland, and so on. The point is increasingly made that even if they are working within the same framework of ideas, communist countries have to solve their own problems in the light of their own conditions; more attention is being paid to experiment on the spot and less— even if gestures are felt necessary—to following Soviet example. Rumanian journals are full of accounts of experimental teaching schemes;[28] new techniques of all kinds, particularly the use of audio-visual aids, are examined with lively interest by teachers in Yugoslavia, Hungary and Poland. East Germany and Czechoslovakia, for all their constant declarations of indebtedness to the U.S.S.R., do a great of work on their own. Until very recently, the Soviet schools were relatively behind in the use of aids of any kind, and their textbooks were famous for dullness of content and layout; these, however, are two fields where the advances made by the Czechoslovaks have often been remarked on. The East

[27] Oral communications, Bucharest. 1965.
[28] Stanciu Stoian: "Cercetări privind experimentarea noului sistem de predare la clasele I-IV", *Revista de Pedagogie*, **5**, pp. 24–42 (1965). P. Popescu-Neveanu, "Particularitățile pedagogice ale sistemului profesor-obiect la clasele mici", *ibid.* **8**, pp. 21–30.

Germans have made considerable study of programmed learning (so-called "teaching machines") and other mechanized techniques, and have built special experimental schools where these can be studied. These are often dingy in appearance, but are elaborately equipped; some even have *cabinets de voyeur* with one-way glass screens for the observation of experimental lessons, which some observers find faintly sinister.[29] There is also a keen interest in ideas and techniques from the West; be they dogmatist or revisionist, the East European countries are "shopping around" in a way reminiscent of the Soviet Union during the 1920's.

Rather more vaguely, the general atmosphere differs from place to place more than it did. Here one is on dangerous ground —"atmosphere" is notoriously difficult to pin down, and personal impressions are liable to be unreliable or unrepresentative— but one does sense a difference between the classrooms of East Germany and Poland, Czechoslovakia and Hungary, Rumania and Yugoslavia, with more formality as a rule in the former cases, and more flexibility, even relaxation, in the latter.[30] This is a change from the 1950's, when most observers reported that the same aura of formality reigned throughout. It is still changing, and as such changes take place the unevenness of the whole area is emphasized. This, again, is partly tied up with broader developments in society at large; but it may lie partly within the school themselves. The perceptible move in some countries away from one prescribed teaching method or lesson structure, the greater part being played by teachers' study-groups in assessing their methods of teaching, and other developments of this kind may arise from the growing suspicion that there is not always one "correct" solution to be applied to a problem in any set of circumstances. One expects controversy over educational policy—specialization, say, or the place of examinations—in Yugoslav staffrooms, but when one hears it in Rumanian or East German schools as well, it shows the general drift; flexibility appears to be

[29] Personal observations, Berlin, June 1965.
[30] Personal impressions, 1965 and 1966.

in the air, not only in the East European area as a whole, but within the individual component systems.

We have seen how diverse educational systems, in their own ways, were adapted under communist régimes to the Soviet pattern after the war. We have further seen how some differences, inevitably, persisted, and how in the last years diversity has grown further, whether from pedagogic or political causes. But it would not do to stress the differences unduly, real and growing though they are; fundamental features underline the details, and these are still generally shared. It is still possible to generalize about the patterns of communist education in Eastern Europe at the present time, before going on to examine the national systems individually.

CHAPTER 7

Eastern European Education Today: Some General Features

1. EDUCATION AND IDEOLOGY

The aim of education in Eastern Europe is primarily ideological; this has been made abundantly clear from the first reforms onwards. For example, when the new school curricula were drawn up in Czechoslovakia in 1948, the basic aims of the system were spelled out thus:

> The guiding principle... is to make culture, training and education democratic. Emphasis is given to the idea of the "policital" school: the school should train young people to take an active part in the building of a people's democracy.... Children are brought up in the spirit of the country's progressive traditions and that of socialist morality.[1]

Again, in East Germany:

> (The School) has the task of developing the socialist national awareness of youth, of teaching youth love for the German Democratic Republic, and to be conscious builders of socialism in the spirit of socialist morality, proletarian internationalism and firm friendship with the Soviet Union.[2]

Or again, picking at random, in Yugoslavia:

> The general aim of education in our country... is... to enable the younger generations to contribute by their work... to the continuous development of productive forces, to the strengthening of socialist social relations... to provide the foundations of a scientific conception of the world... to make youth familar with the history and achievements of the

---

[1] *International Yearbook of Education*, 1949, pp. 106–7.
[2] *Programm der Sozialistischen Einheitspartei Deutschlands*, V/1. *Die weitere Entwicklung des sozialistischen Bildungswesens.* In: *Sozialistische Schule*, p. 22. (Staatsverlag der DDR, Berlin, 1964.)

Yugoslav peoples and the entire human race ... to raise young people ... so that they may come to be loyal to their socialist homeland ... and to value the international solidarity of the working people ... , etc.[3]

Official statements such as these could be multiplied indefinitely. Apart from obvious similarities in vocabulary (though the Yugoslav phrasing runs less to pattern), the same basic assumptions can be seen throughout Eastern Europe—namely, that the chief purpose of education is to serve the needs of society. That is, the schools must help in the building of communist society by producing people imbued not only with the necessary knowledge and skills but with communist values as well. As in the U.S.S.R., this is done by various means: by direct teaching of political theory; through other subjects in the curriculum; by the use of posters, slogans and the like; and through extra-curricular agencies such as the youth organizations. Whether the interpretation is "revisionist" or "dogmatist", whether its presentation is subtle or crude, it is always there in some form and to some extent.

The direct teaching of political theory appears, as in the U.S.S.R., comparatively late. In Czechoslovakia, "civics" is taught for one hour a week from the sixth year of the basic school onwards.[4] This, for the most part, is straightforward education for citizenship of the kind familiar in most countries, but the theoretical content increases as time goes on. Not only is the organization of the Czechoslovak Socialist Republic dealt with, but also the constitution and state system of the U.S.S.R. "and its advantages as compared with the exploiting organization of the capitalist states". Citizenship (*Staatsbürgerkunde*) comes into the East German curriculum only in the ninth form. At first, its object (along with history and geography) is declared to be "to give the children historical and political knowledge, to perceive the laws of social development. The questions arising from ... current political events are to be dealt with in all subjects ... and answered comprehensively and convincingly, in accordance

---

[3] *General Law of Education in Yugoslavia*, I, Article 3, pp. 51–52. (Edition Jugoslavija, Belgrade, 1959.)
[4] Stanislav Vodinský, *Czechoslovakia: Education*, p. 21. (Orbis, Prague, 1963.)

with the age of the pupils."[5] Later, at secondary level, the emphasis of citizenship and the social sciences moves much closer to straight political teaching:

> The pupils ... learn the laws of social development and are enabled to apply historical and political knowledge independently to present-day problems. Instruction in citizenship imparts economic, philosophical and political basic knowledge in close connection with life and thus introduces the pupils to Marxism–Leninism.
> The pupils are to be led to recognize the historic role and national task of the German Democratic Republic. They are to gain the conviction that the future belongs to socialism in the whole of Germany.[6]

In Rumania "education for citizenship" (*educaţia cetăţenească*) appears in the eighth year of the basic school (age 14) with the object of "forming the morals of young people, to prepare them in the future to participate consciously in the life of our socialist society".[7] It is certainly political in bent, but not yet greatly concerned with theory. That comes later; half-way through the *lycée* course, Political Economy (Marxist) appears on the timetable, and is succeeded in the following year by "Scientific Socialism", a basic course in Marxist–Leninist political philosophy, historical and dialectical materialism, etc. To give some idea of the weighting, this means that over the four-year secondary course the student spends 128 hours on *directly* political subjects. This is roughly 3 per cent of the total curricular time, and takes up about the same number of hours as industrial practice, nearly as many as geography, half as many as history and chemistry, and twice as many as drawing.[8]

Social study in the Yugoslav schools[9] also presents political points. Much of the content concerns the country's constitution

---

[5] *Law on the Integrated Socialist Educational System*, 1965, IV, I, par. 15(2), p. 87. In: *Education and Training in the German Democratic Republic*. (Staatsverlag der DDR, Berlin, 1966.)

[6] *Ibid*. IV, I, par. 16(2), p. 89.

[7] *Conţinutul procesului de învăţămînt*, p. 133. In: A. Dancsuly, A. Chircev and A. Manolache (eds.), *Pedagogia*. (Editura Didactică şi Pedagogică, Bucharest, 1964.)

[8] A. Manolache, *General Education in Rumania*, pp. 36–39.

[9] Ljubomir Krneta (ed.), *The Elementary School in Yugoslavia*, pp. 141–52. (Edition Jugoslavija, Belgrade.)

and system of government, workers' control of industry, cultural life and so forth. The aim of the course is to introduce children to social living in general, and Yugoslav socialist society in particular. In classes IV and V (age 10–11 years) the main topics covered by the social study scheme are: the peoples of Yugoslavia; life on the littoral; the Pannonian plain; the mountainous regions; life and work in mining districts; modern agriculture; modern industry—factories to the workers (with accounts of Marx, Engels, Lenin and "brief talks on the workers' struggle for a socialist society", as well as an explanation of technological developments); life of modern man (town and country, hygiene, medical services, etc.); exchange of commodities; transport and communications in the service of man; cultural wealth; and finally, "Yugoslavia—a free country of socialism". This last section examines the history of the struggles of the Yugoslav peoples for independence from the Turks and Austrians, the People's Revolution and its heroes, the Partisan War, the proclamation of the Republic, Tito, and ends with the structure of the Federal Republic, the People's Assemblies, People's Committees, and so forth. In class VI Social Study is replaced by history and geography as separate subjects, but moral education—intended, among other things, "to familiarize pupils with the fundamental standards, requirements and norms of socialist morals"—continues in the educational scheme.[10] In the secondary schools philosophy is taught, but is more broadly interpreted than is usual in most Eastern European countries.

Political studies appear in the final year of the Bulgarian schools for two hours a week under the title of "Basic Principles of Communism";[11] so does "Study of the Constitution" in Albania.[12] In Poland, there is a final-year course (two hours a week) on "Poland and the Modern World". This is designed to "give pupils knowledge of the problems of People's Poland and the world, and to prepare them to take an active part in social and

[10] *Ibid.*, p. 179.
[11] Mihajlo Juhas, "Općeobrazovna škola i produženi boravak u SR Bugarskoj" (*Revija Školstva i Prosvetna Dokumentacija*, **1**, 1965, pp. 23–29).
[12] *World Survey of Education*, III, p. 174. (UNESCO, Paris, 1961.)

political life".[13] There is also a course in philosophy which deals more directly with Marxist–Leninist theory.[14] These subjects are now to be replaced by a more integrated course of "Social Study".[15] In Hungary, where until recently political subjects as such did not appear on the time-table at all, a new course, "The Basis of our World View", is being introduced. The plan leaves room for some improvisation by the teacher and discussion with pupils, but the main topics are prescribed:

I. Basis of the Marxist–Leninist world view.
  1. The general laws of natural change and development.
  2. The fundamental laws of change and development of society. (Under this heading come such themes as the development of modes of production and class struggle, basis and superstructure in society, and the role of social revolution in the development of society.)
  3. Semblance and reality in human consciousness.
  4. The Marxist–Leninist world view is the most progressive world view of our age.
II. The position of socialist Hungary in the world. Some leading problems of our time.
  1. The social, economic and state system of our homeland.
    (a) The structure of our society.
    (b) The economic life of our society.
    (c) Political and state organization of our society.
  2. The two world systems.
  3. The collapse of the imperialist colonial system. Situation and problems of underdeveloped countries.
  4. The ways to world-wide victory of socialism.
  5. The chief problem of our age: the question of war and peace.

[13] Mieczysław Pęcherski, *Das Schulwesen in Volkspolen*, p. 319. In: Deutsches Pädagogisches Zentralinstitut, *Das Schulwesen sozialistischer Länder in Europa*. (Volk und Wissen Volkseigener Verlag, Berlin, 1962.)
[14] *Ibid.*, pp. 319–20.
[15] Zbigniew Sabiłło (ed.), *Program Nauczania Liceum Ogólnokształcącego*, pp. 158–67. (Państwowe Zakłady Wydawnictw szkolnych, Warsaw, 1965.)

6. Communism, the future of mankind.[16]

In most Eastern European countries, Marxist–Leninist studies are also a prominent part of all courses in higher educational institutions, in order to "deepen and strengthen the social consciousness of the students and to enable them to apply the general laws of the development of nature, society and human thinking in life".[17] The role of political theory throughout the system is thus not just to secure conformity, though this is obviously expected; what the authorities are trying to achieve is understanding of the theoretical basis of society, informed conviction rather than mere acceptance. In view of the importance attached to this aim, it may seem surprising at first glance that studies of this kind appear on the curriculum comparatively late, and reach their maximum intensity after the majority of students have ceased to be involved in formal education.

But the presentation of political attitudes does not wait for the introduction of "Political Economy", "Basic Principles of Communism", "Study of the Constitution" and the rest; it permeates other subjects, often to saturation point.[18] The extent to which the ordinary school subjects are suitable vehicles naturally varies; in contrast with the Stalin era, mathematics, the sciences and to a large extent, the fine arts, are left alone for the most part. Foreign languages can be used more extensively, however, by judicious selection of texts. This is often a declared purpose; one East German document puts it thus:

> In our school system, Russian is taught as the first foreign language because in politics, economics, technology and culture, the Soviet Union is the primary example of a socialist state, and also holds the leading position in the peace camp. For these two reasons, instruction in Russian shall.

---

[16] József Farkas, "Gymnasiallehrplan 'Grundlagen unserer Weltanschauung'" (*Informationsdienst zum Bildungswesen in Osteuropa*, 10/11, pp. 50–52. Osteuropa-Institut an der Freien Universität Berlin, 1965.)

[17] *Education and Training in the German Democratic Republic*, p. 108. (Staatsverlag der DDR, Berlin, 1966.)

[18] *Das Schulwesen sozialistischer Länder in Europa, passim.*

deepen the friendship between the German people and the peoples of the Soviet Union.[19]

Similar reasons are given in Polish statements, though they also make the point that Russian is a kindred Slav language.[20] By a reverse process, textbooks in Western European languages can be used to give an unfavourable picture of life in Britain, America, France, etc. Sometimes they resort to complete falsification; Edmund King describes a Czechoslovak textbook, *Anglický od A do Z* (English from A to Z), which represents the typical British worker as trying to live on £4 10s. a week.[21] In fairness, this kind of thing makes most communist intellectuals wince, and there is much less of it than there used to be; but more subtly, and less maliciously, points continue to be put across, if only by a bias towards left-wing authors in the choice of novels for senior classes.[22] In readers in the native tongue, too, the opportunities are many; and if first-year readers no longer portray Stalin as a Dutch uncle patting children on the head (as did one Hungarian book produced in 1953), the opportunities are often taken, particularly if a nationalist as well as communist message is required.

History and geography offer considerable scope for political interpretation. This is usually stated quite specifically as one of the chief purposes of these studies. In the Czech schools, geography concentrates on "Czechoslovakia, Europe, and above all the Soviet Union and the socialist countries",[23] and sets out to evaluate

---

[19] *Deutsche Lehrerzeitung*, 12 September 1958, p. 2. Quoted in Paul S. Bodenmen, *Education in the Soviet Zone of Germany*, p. 21. (U.S. Office of Education, Washington D.C., 1959.)

[20] Mieczyslaw Pęcherski, *op. cit.*, p. 315.

[21] Edmund King, *Communist Education*, p. 25. (Methuen, London, 1963.)

[22] See also M. J. Moore-Rinvolucri, "Foreign Languages in the German Democratic Republic". (*Modern Languages*, **47**, 2 (June 1966), pp. 67–68.) The author describes English schemes which concentrate on housing problems, the life of Welsh miners, the London bus strike and the Aldermaston marches, with passages from *World Youth* and the *Morning Star* to the exclusion of other newspapers. She also stresses the constant theme of international friendship running through the textbooks.

[23] Mojmír Dýma and Jaroslav Kojzar, *Das Schulwesen in der Tschechoslowakischen Sozialistischen Republik*, p. 481. In: DPZI, *Das Schulwesen sozialistischer Länder in Europa*.

Education Today: Some General Features 97

as well as describe. Textbooks there, as in Rumania and elsewhere, still tend to use "socialist countries" and "capitalist countries" as a geographical as well as political classification, and present them to the advantage of the former. In the Yugoslav schools the programme[24] concentrates on physical and economic geography, and the classification is regional, not political. But political issues are raised frequently. In class VII, for example, the treatment of the U.S.S.R. includes "the October Revolution, the socialist social system, the solution of the nationalities problem". The sections on Africa comprises: "Configuration of land; climatic and vegetation zones (desert oases, steppes, savannas, forests) and fauna ... struggle of Africans for liberation", etc. Under North America, after treatment of physical geography, we find: "Colonization of North America; penetration from East to West, extermination of American Indians, importation of Negro slaves", etc., followed by a straightforward account of the economic geography of the U.S.A. In an area where disputed territories have always been a sore point, even maps and place-names have political significance; even in East German atlases,[25] Stettin now appears as Szczecin, Breslau as Wrocław, and Königsberg as as Kaliningrad, studiously accepting the post-war frontier settlement. (The West Germans, of course, do the opposite just as studiously, and cling stubbornly in their maps to the 1937 frontiers.[26] In these circumstances, no interpretation can be neutral.)

History can be similarly used in a number of ways. Modern history, obviously, can be presented so as to reinforce the approved interpretation of world affairs. Sometimes this emphasis is overwhelming; an East German ninth-form history textbook,[27] for instance, sets the tone on the cover with a picture of the storming

---

[24] Ljubomir Krneta, *op. cit.*, pp. 153–67.
[25] See *Weltatlas: Die Staaten der Erde und ihre Wirtschaft.* (Verlag Enzyklopädie Leipzig 1960.)
[26] See any West German map of Germany. The Eastern Territories are usually shown as "under Polish occupation" and "under Soviet Occupation", and East Germany as "The Soviet-occupied Zone of Germany".
[27] Wolfgang Heidler and Gerhard Ziegler (eds.), *Lehrbuch für Geschichte der 9. Klasse der Oberschule.* (Volk und Wissen Volkseigener Verlag, Berlin, 1963.)

of the Winter Palace in Petrograd in 1917, and throughout its 298 pages gives a detailed and partisan account of the period from 1917 to 1939. It main headings give a good idea of its content and approach:

1. The Great October Socialist Revolution.

   The bourgeois-democratic February Revolution; the transition to Socialist Revolution; the victory of the Great October Socialist Revolution; the struggle for the consolidation of Soviet power; the world significance of the Great October Socialist Revolution.

2. The November Revolution in Germany. The Founding of the Communist Party of Germany.

   The origins and tasks of the Revolution in Germany; the victory of the revolutionary masses over the monarchy; Soviet power or national solidarity; the founding of the KPD—the most significant outcome of the November Revolution; counter-revolutionary terror on the suppressing of the revolution; the outcome and lessons of the Revolution.

3. International Developments from 1919 to 1923.

   The founding of the Third International; the victory of the Soviet workers in the Intervention and Civil War; the revolutionary and liberation movement of exploited and suppressed peoples from 1919 to 1923.

4. The Weimar Republic during the Revolutionary World Crisis.
5. The Building and Victory of Socialism in the U.S.S.R.
6. The Weimar Republic from 1924 to 1929.
7. The World Economic Crisis 1929–39. The Last Years of the Weimar Republic.
8. Germany during the Fascist Dictatorship 1933 to 1939. The First Fascist Aggressions and Preparation for the Second World War.

   The establishment of fascist dictatorship in Germany and the heroic struggle of the anti-fascist forces under the leadership of the KPD; the economic ideological and military war preparations of German imperialism and militarism; the struggle of the KPD for the formation of a united working-class and popular front against fascism and the threat of war; the first fascist aggressions; the heroic struggle of the Spanish people against fascist enslavement; the next aggressions of the German fascists and resistance of the peoples; the U.S.S.R.'s struggle for collective security against fascist aggression: the Bern Conference of the KPD and its significance in the struggle for a democratic, peaceloving Germany.

9. The Struggle of the Chinese People for National Independence.

As can be seen even from this summary, the role of the German Communist Party is emphasized throughout, with obvious implications of approval for the post-war policies of the SED.

In the rather different political atmosphere of Yugoslavia, to take another example, the treatment of history is less determinedly sectarian. Nevertheless, the same general approach, in essentials, can be seen here too.[28] In class VII of the basic school the modern history programme covers the period from the French Revolution to the Russian Revolution and the foundation of Yugoslavia, and includes the struggles of the Communist Party against the royal dictatorship. In class VIII (the final year of compulsory schooling) World War II is dealt with. Then, under the heading "People's Liberation Struggle", the following topics are covered: "Yugoslavia joins the Axis Tripartite Pact. The 27th March 1941. Attack on Yugoslavia. Occupation and division of the country. Preparations for armed insurrection and the beginning of the insurrection. Development of the People's Liberation Army. Terror of invaders, and anti-national activities of domestic bourgeoisie. Development of people's government. Foundation of people's state. Second session of AVNOJ (Anti-fascist Council for the National Liberation of Yugoslavia). International significance of this session. Final military operations and liberation of Yugoslavia. Proclamation of the Republic." Two further sections, "The Development of Socialist Yugoslavia" and "Treatment of Current Topics"—a summary of international events—wind up the course.

In the other countries similar use is made of modern history. Between that, and the teaching of the history of the homeland, efforts are made (to cite the Polish statement)[29] "to develop

[28] Ljubomir Krneta, *op. cit.*, pp. 168–77.
[29] Mieczysław Pęcherski, *op. cit.*, p. 315.

patriotism and internationalism" as interpreted by the authorities. In a less obvious way ancient and medieval history play their part too, by looking at history as a process of social change based on changes of the modes of production and brought about by class struggles, to "train the pupils to a historical-materialist view of social phenomena".[30] Ancient history is not, therefore, just the glory that was Greece and the grandeur that was Rome, but is examined as slave-society as well. Medieval Europe, likewise, is examined in the light of feudal socio-economic relations. World history, in fact, is shown as a process evolving in the Marxist pattern. The idea is not just to secure conviction on abstruse theoretical points, but to convince pupils that the kind of society they are being called upon to build is not simply a rejection of the past, but the culmination of the whole march of history. As one Rumanian authority puts it: "By basic understanding of the causes and facts of history . . . pupils will reach the conclusion that *mankind moves inevitably towards socialism and communism.*"[31]

Thus, throughout the curriculum, by direct and indirect means, political doctrines are put across to the pupils. But this goes beyond formal teaching in the classroom. Communism is advertised as well as taught, and here the differences between the countries are rather greater—and rather more obvious, perhaps they strike the eye. In Poland, for instance, posters and slogans are normally absent, in marked contrast with the early 1950's. On the other hand, they are common enough in Bulgaria, and East Germany, where pupils are constantly being exhorted to "Live and work like communists", "Study for the building of socialism", "Struggle for the peace of the world", and so on. The use of portraits of leaders as political symbols varies, depending on current attitudes towards the "cult of personality". In former days, Stalin looked down on the children from every other wall, but has now vanished, except presumably in Albania, where he is still a major

---

[30] Ferenc Ábent *et al.*, *Das Schulwesen in der Ungarischen Volksrepublik*, p. 555. In: DPZI, *Das Schulwesen sozialistischer Länder in Europa*.

[31] A. Dancsuly, A. Chircev and A. Manolache, *Pedagogia*, p. 133. (Italics in original.)

cult-figure.³² In Poland, nobody has taken his place. Nor in Rumania; there, although slogans and republican banners are common enough, portraits of Party leaders such as Maurer and Ceauşescu are not part of the scene; they do hang Darwin and Michurin, Shakespeare and Pushkin and Caragiale in the classrooms and corridors of *lycées*, but that is rather different. In East Germany Walter Ulbricht gazes from the walls; so did Khrushchov until recently, so does Lenin still. So does Novotný in Czechoslovakia. In Yugoslavia, where slogans are rarely to be seen, Tito is everywhere; there is not a classroom, school hall or staffroom (or, for that matter, shop or office) where his picture does not hang.

It is hard to judge what effect, if any, such visual aids to political education have. Many of the slogans in the schools are only marginally political, encouragements to greater effort such as "We are studying for tomorrow" or "Let us follow their example" (on the honours board in a Rumanian school). Nobody has discovered whether such exhortations ever actually make anyone *do* anything, but it is possible that they may become part of the pupils' mental scenery if absorbed for long enough. Like the portraits, they may act as visual focal points for ideas that take a long time to put into words; by themselves, they may not accomplish much, but they are never by themselves. As part of a total effect they may have some influence in serving as a reminder of the expected attitudes.

Little of this propagandizing, direct of indirect, is peculiar to communist schools. The treatment of history and geography, for example, need not involve distortion and falsification, merely an appropriate selection and emphasis; and in the West as well as the East school curricula are used to encourage patriotism and present the accepted ideologies of Christianity, the American Way of Life, etc. Party control of education is paralleled, in principle at

³² Whereas most of the East European countries had cities named after Stalin at one time, they have all been renamed; Albania alone retains its symbolic allegiance with Qyteti Stalin unrenamed, and references to Stalin figuring in public pronouncement in a way once familiar throughout Eastern Europe but now unknown outside Albania.

least, by the dual-purpose ministries for church and education in Greece and the Scandinavian countries; the teaching of communist doctrine is justified on the same basis as the teaching of religion in many Western countries, whether denominational as in Spain and Portugal or rather broader as in the United Kingdom. Even the posters and portraits have their counterparts in the royal pictures, national flags, crucifixes and other devotional objects of other cultures. The use of schools as vehicles of ideological persuasion is wellnigh universal, and to argue that communist schools indoctrinate while Western ones do not is to miss the whole point. The main difference is that the communist systems give this part of the schools' work a higher priority than some Western systems, and present political viewpoints more consciously, deliberately and thoroughly than is usual elsewhere. In many Western school systems the dominant values are taken for granted—so much so that teachers are often unaware of putting over ideological points at all. In the communist systems, as the official statements and official schemes show, they are carefully worked out and prescribed in some detail by the authorities.

2. DISCIPLINE AND MORAL EDUCATION

Teachers in Eastern Europe are fond of quoting Comenius' saying: "A school without discipline is like a mill without water."[33] Most teachers elsewhere would agree; while there are some who feel that they can work in an environment of continuous uproar, the great majority would regard some degree of control as essential if anything is to be accomplished at all. This is certainly the view in Eastern Europe. For one thing, there is a long-established tradition of formal classroom discipline; for another, the great things that are expected of the schools would have scant prospect of success without at least enough discipline to oil the wheels. The teacher, therefore, appears as a figure backed with all the authority of adult society. He is expected to be in control

[33] Jan Amos Komenský, *The Great Didactic*.

in the class, and in most countries is supported by an official set of "Rules for Pupils' Conduct" which all children are expected to know and observe. These rules deal with the whole range of school conduct—how to behave towards the teacher, procedure for homework, etc.—so that the teacher is not faced with the situation of having to work out the boundaries of the permissible afresh with every class, but can start off from a background of common expectations. But regulations of this kind do more than lay down norms of classroom conduct; dealing as they do with behaviour in the home and the street, with helpfulness towards parents, the very young, the sick and the old, responsible attitudes towards work, etc., they also indicate the *attitudes* expected of pupils in the school and out of it.

As always, details vary, but in one respect there is unanimity: there is far more to discipline than keeping order in class. This, while obviously necessary, is regarded as wholly inadequate. Discipline, to be worth anything, must not only affect what a person *does*, but what he *is*. In short, it is part of the wider field of moral education. Pupils are therefore not only expected to know and observe the rules, but to understand why they are made. Enforcement there must be, if necessary; but since discipline based on sanctions is only effective while the sanctions are there, teachers are strongly discouraged from relying too much on punishments. The aim is to get pupils to understand the need for certain standards of behaviour, in the hope that they will absorb them as part of their own natures. Looked at in this way, class discipline is only to a minor extent a device for making orderly teaching possible; it is principally a support for moral education, shaping the attitudes and behaviour of the future adult as well as the present school-child.

Communist educators take moral education very seriously indeed, quite as seriously as education for technology or science or language or anything else. Apart from Yugoslavia,[34] it does not normally figure as a distinct subject on the time-table, but

---

[34] Ljubomir Krneta (ed.), *The Elementary School in Yugoslavia* (Edition Jugoslavija, Beograd, 1960), p. 32.

most systems[35] have a "class-teacher's period" which comes to much the same thing. In any case, it is expected that the whole curriculum, and the extra-curricular activities, will be put to appropriate use in creating "a new type of person".

The morality taught in the communist schools is, of course, secular. Marxism regards supernatural religion as a delusion, and a diversion of man's attention from real problems—the "opium of the people"—and argues that the real task is not to seek grace or save one's soul, but to change the nature of reality for the better. There can, therefore, be no appeal to a divine will as the justification for one's actions. Although there has been some antireligious teaching from time to time in most communist countries, the emphasis is generally more positive, an attempt to present an alternative standard of judgement. Basically, this is a social standard; what is good is what benefits social man.

This needs further elaboration. Marxists recognize many problems here, of which space does not permit anything like a full account. But some of the difficulties are obvious; it is not easy to relate *every* human action to the good of mankind at large, nor will it do to dismiss any that are not as devoid of moral content. At the personal level, one can argue that the individual virtues—kindness, consideration, honesty, etc.—are a necessary social lubricant; people live and work together better as groups, and are happier as individuals, if they are pleasant and helpful to each other in their relationships, refrain from robbing and killing each other, and so forth. Even in moral problems where other individuals are not involved (and these must be few indeed) similar social standards can be applied; if someone becomes alcoholic, say, or stupefies himself with heroin, or even fails to make the best of his potential at school work, he is depriving society of his contribution. But moral responsibility is not left at the personal level; no clear-cut distinction between public and private morality is recognized, and the view that there is some qualitative difference between robbing a neighbour and robbing the community (by

[35] Deutsches Pädagogisches Zentralinstitut, *Das Schulwesen sozialistischer Länder in Europa* (Volk und Wissen Volskeigener Verlag, Berlin, 1962), *loc. var.*

tax-dodging, for example) is held to be totally pernicious. From the way a child treats his parents to the way he reacts to the war in Vietnam, the same ultimate standards are applied. A prominent Polish educationist, Bogdan Suchodolski, puts it thus:

> Questions of "small-scale moral practice"—everyday good deeds towards people in our immediate environment—have an unbreakable link with those great moral problems of the epoch in which human aspirations, fears, hopes and efforts find their deepest reflexion. . . . Therefore all actions are subject today to an assessment from the moral point of view—not only the individual's actions concerning some other person, but also the individual's actions which promote or retard definite social processes . . . Moral education . . . is now focusing its attention upon the problems of man's responsibility for the environment he creates.[36]

Moral education thus blends completely with ideological education. Personal actions are good not "just because they are good", or because they are in accordance with the will of God, but because they benefit other people, one's friends, school, family, country at one level, mankind at the other. There is a further refinement: it is held that capitalist society is based on the exploitation of man by man. Since this is a violation of the principle of human dignity, and since socialist society is a stage in the removal of this state of affairs, socialist society is morally preferable. Further, Marxist theory holds that some moral values take their form from the kind of society in which they arise; that is, bourgeois morality is a code of values designed to justify the actions of the ruling classes, while socialist morality is designed to serve the interests of the working classes. Each stage of the argument, of course, is much more complicated than in this potted account, but the upshot is that socialist morality, where it differs from bourgeois morality, is of a superior type, conforming more closely with the needs of mankind. In the Marxist view, then, morality and politics are inseparable. The "good man" and the "good communist" are practically interchangeable terms; loyalty to the teachings of Lenin, one's socialist motherland, the international

[36] Bogdan Suchodolski, *Poland—A Statement of Aims and Achievements*. In: E. J. King (ed), *Communist Education*, pp. 243–4. (Methuen, London, 1963.)

working-class movement, and the like, are no less moral obligations than the right kind of behaviour in school, home, playground or street. In the East European countries, they are part of the total picture. "Moral education", says Suchodolski, "is concerned with the individual in the context of his social duties."[37]

This does not mean that the requirements of communist moral education are totally alien from the Western point of view. *Mutatis mutandis*, the whole approach has a surprisingly close similarity to many religious formulations, and when it comes to the actual qualities desired, there is a large area of overlap. A Yugoslav programme[38] mentions, among others, comradeship, loyalty to one's friends, truthfulness, courage, assiduity, courtesy, civilized behaviour, unselfishness, etc. A Rumanian textbook mentions determination, perseverence, the spirit of initiative and independence, conscientiousness, self-control, respect for others, and many more.[39] Although presented in the context of Marxist morality, there is nothing at this level that would not be heartily endorsed by the YMCA, the Headmasters' Conference or the late Lord Baden-Powell. The main difference arises when the communist schools particularize further, and seek to inculcate "respect and love for working people", "positive attitudes towards labour", "feelings of solidarity with colonial peoples in their struggle for freedom", "loyalty to the socialist homeland", and so on. In the Marxist view of morality, "socialist patriotism" and "proletarian internationalism" are moral as well as political virtues, and are emphasized as such in the work of the school in moral education.

Every opportunity of putting moral lessons across is seized upon. As the Yugoslav programme puts it:

> The joint life of the children in school, in their societies and various corporate activities offers, from day to day, numerous examples which may

---

[37] Bogdan Suchodolski, *op. cit.*, p. 243.
[38] Ljubomir Krneta, *op. cit.*, p. 181.
[39] A. Chircev et al., *Educarea elevilor în spiritul moralei comuniste*, pp. 222–331. In: A. Dancsuly, A. Chircev and A. Manolache (eds.) *Pedagogia*. (Editura Didactică și Pedagogică, Bucharest, 1964.)

be used to analyse the acts of individuals and of groups, of smaller or larger bodies. . . . The teacher's standards of conduct should be high, since they are invariably passed on to his pupils. Success in the moral training of pupils will best be secured through preparation. At all events, improvisation and "preaching" should be avoided.[40]

It does not always work out like this in practice; whatever official programmes say, preaching, even finger-wagging hectoring, is by no means unknown. But on the whole a more positive approach is encouraged. A great deal is made of the importance of the example of adults, especially of teachers and parents, in providing children with a model of "civilized behaviour"; and to minimize conflicts of standards between teachers and parents, home–school contacts of all kinds are encouraged—parents' meetings in the schools, "open days", home visiting by the teachers, and the like. Discussions are held in class, often in connection with the "Rules for Pupils' Conduct". First-year children in Rumania, for example, are asked to consider "How should you behave towards teachers?", "How should you behave towards old people?" and, as far as possible at their age, to consider why. In the second year: "How should you behave in school?", "How can you show your love for your parents?", "What does 'comradely help' mean?". In the third year there are themes like "Cleanliness and tidiness", "The Pioneer is an example to all"; in the fourth, "How can we help the very young, the sick, the old?". By the time they reach the fifth and sixth years, they are presented with topics like "What does it mean to be a good patriot?", "How should we organize our free time?", "The contribution of our class to the work of the school"; and in the last two years of the basic school the discussion becomes more general and abstract—"My work at home and at school", "The value of intellectual and physical work", "What is a firm character?", "Courage and modesty", etc.[41] Set themes of this type are only one factor, however. The same programme suggests that examples should be taken as they arise in lessons, or from school activities and events outside the school, and

[40] Ljubomir Krneta, *op. cit.*, p. 179.
[41] *Pedagogia*, p. 253.

"explained, analysed and presented in a form that they can understand".[42] Further, assuming that knowing right is of little use unless one also does it, theory is put into practice in the children's groups activities—pioneer organizations, class groups, anything where they join together for a common purpose, even sports and games.[43] This, of course, is Makarenko's "collective" in action, and in many ways not unlike Dewey's "shared experience", except that it admits of rather more direction by the teacher. Approval and disapproval, praise and blame, applied by classmates, teacher or school director—all of these are to be used not just to keep order but to reinforce the development of right sentiments. This is one reason why sanctions and punishments are sparingly used; they will not always be there, but it is hoped that the teacher can lay the foundations of *internalized* discipline through precept, example and the organization of school life.

The seriousness with which moral education is taken is apparent from its place in the training of teachers. That it is constantly emphasized in the course goes without saying; more striking is the detailed treatment it receives in the textbooks. Useful though they may be, some hints on "Class control", pious hopes about good example rubbing off on the pupils, and impeccable precepts for good behaviour will not do. Teachers must not "play it by ear"—they must know exactly what they are doing. In the Yugoslav pedagogy course,[44] for example, student teachers are first of all given a detailed analysis of the "Concept of morality", which includes such issues as "The social and class nature of morality", "Moral norms and moral awareness", "Moral sanctions and moral consciousness", etc. From there, they go on to consider "The concept, tasks and content of moral education", with exhaustive treatment of the principles involved, the characteristics to be aimed at, the methods that can be used.[45] Ultimately,

[42] *Pedagogia*, p. 257.
[43] *Ibid.*, pp. 258–64.
[44] Nikola Potkonjak, *Moralno Vaspitanje*. In: Ljubomir Krneta, Milena Potkonjak and Nikola Potkonjak, *Pedagogija*, pp. 176–203. (Zavod za Izdavanje Udžbenika SR Srbije, Beograd, 1965.)
[45] *Ibid.*, pp. 182–7.

Education Today: Some General Features

this is linked with the development of "Yugoslav socialist patriotism and proletarian internationalism"—carefully distinguished from "bourgeois nationalism, chauvinism and cosmopolitanism" —which in turn is linked with "Work discipline; discipline of behaviour; respect for social property; education in humanism, comradeship, friendship, and true respect between the sexes".[46] Once again, the wheel has turned full circle; the personal virtues and the civic and political virtues are all of a piece in the upbringing of moral man. Nor are the students expected to absorb these principles in a doctrinaire way; they have to examine and apply them practically. They are asked to consider, for instance, ways of using geography lessons to encourage brotherhood and unity among the Yugoslav peoples, ways of using literature to foster international understanding, or how to use films to encourage mutual respect between men and women, etc.[47] They are also reminded of the difference between moral education and the teaching of morals—that is, that their task is not only to put over the approved norms, but to help pupils develop the ability to make moral judgements.[48] This theme runs through many writings on moral education; and if it seems contradictory to encourage individual judgement assiduously while presupposing the result in such detail, it is worth remembering that all systems of moral education do this in principle. The difference is one of degree.

It is also significant that moral education is regarded throughout Eastern Europe as a suitable subject for research, experiment and publication, no less than teaching methods, curriculum design or any other of the more familiar areas. Much attention is paid to this aspect in the running of boarding establishments or remedial centres, like the Fót Children's Village in Hungary.[49] One Polish controlled experiment has applied the technique of putting children under two types of leadership ("authoritarian"

---

[46] *Ibid.*, pp. 188–202.
[47] *Praktična vežbanja; ibid.*, p. 203.
[48] *Moralno vaspitanje i nastava morala; ibid.*, p. 187.
[49] "Fót Children's Town: The Makarenko Approach", *Times Educational Supplement*, 27 November 1964.

and "democratic") to study the development of social and moral attitudes.[50] Whether for specialists or laymen, teachers or parents, books and pamphlets dealing with various problems or moral education are continually coming off the presses. To cite Suchodolski again:

> Moral education has ... become a far-reaching and many-sided endeavour in the upbringing of youth, so as to prepare them for creative participation in the work of building a social order that will be the expression of people emancipated from the demands of nature and from man's wrong ideas.[51]

Naturally, problems remain. There are times when the more immediate tasks of keeping order in class loom rather larger than long-term objectives. Though reliance on punishment is discouraged, therefore, teachers do have a battery of penalties at their command for dealing with the lazy or badly behaved child. These are carefully graded from mild reproofs by the teacher to severe reprimands by the director of the school, which are reported to be highly effective.[52] If these fail, the conduct mark can be reduced. The requirements for conduct are always higher than for academic subjects, and if the pupil does not make the grade he may have to repeat the year—clearly a useful spur for the ambitious.[53] As a last resort, a pupil can be expelled, but this is said to be very rare. There was a case in Yugoslavia in 1965 when about a quarter of the pupils were expelled from a *gimnazija* in Banja Luka; this caused a national uproar, and it does seem that there was something far wrong with the running of the school.[54]

---

[50] Heliodor Muszyński, "Stosunek zespołu do wychowawcy i jego znaczenie w procesie wychowania moralnego" (*Ruch Pedagogiczny*, **3** (XXXV), 1961, 4, pp. 30–43).

[51] Bogdan Suchodolski, *op. cit.*, p. 243.

[52] Oral communications.

[53] In Rumania, for example, pupils are graded for all subjects from 1 up to 10. If they have an average mark of 5 or less at the end of the year, they have to repeat; but for conduct nothing less than 6 will do.

[54] M. Grubor, Il "Momento della Verità" (Centro Studi e Ricerche sui Problemi Economico-Sociali, *Documentazione sui Paesi dell'Est*, Bolletino settimanale no. 1, 6 March 1965.) Trans. from article in *Vjesnik*, 18 February 1965.

Expulsions on this scale are unheard of—hence the outcry—and it is said that even individual ones are uncommon. The existing punishments usually seem more than adequate, and the visitor at least gets the impression that they are rarely needed. Corporal punishment, incidentally, is not one of them; not only is it condemned by public opinion and educational theory, it is also forbidden by law.

One reason for what one observer[55] calls the "serenity" of the pupils may be that the thorough programme of moral education does work in practice; certainly, it does frequently happen that long before a teacher exhausts his supply of reproofs and reprimands with some troublesome child pressure from the "collective", in the form of the Pioneer organization, takes over. Even without being told that he is letting down the class, the school, the city, the country, the future of socialism, etc., any child must find it hard to resist the group pressure of his classmates. Self-interest may play some part too; for the ambitious, education is practically the only road to advancement. Thus, conveniently enough, a child working diligently at his studies can serve his own career interests, gratify his parents, yield to the expectations of teacher and classmates *and* fulfil his moral and political duty, all at the same time. Whatever the reasons, it is impossible for the visitor not to be impressed by the keenness, even Boy Scout eagerness, shown by the average pupil in the schools.[56] Nor does it seem strained or artificial; the classroom atmosphere is certainly formal, but it is a formality tempered by friendliness and genuine concern for children on the teachers' part. The children do not give the impression of being continually under restraint; when the situation is appropriate—between lessons, say, or when crowding round a visitor to ask questions—they can become relaxed and informal without running wild, and when lessons begin again they usually step straight back into the formal classroom routine without

---

[55] E. J. King, *Comparative Education*, **1**, 2 (1965), p. 134.
[56] Personal impressions, various. See also W. Kenneth Richmond, "No Trouble for the Teachers" (*Scotsman*, 27 October 1964); "Budapest's Puritan Aspect: Lively Conformity" (*Times Educational Supplement*, 16 October 1964).

fuss or harassment.[57] There are delinquent children, of course, and doubtless there are whole classes, let alone individuals, with whom control is something of a problem; these are the failures of the moral education and disciplinary system. There may also be children who behave reasonably well and work hard enough, but *only* because they are kept in order by the teacher and the sanctions at his command; these, too, are regarded no less as failures in the long run. How far the moral education programme has succeeded in making its political points has been called in question.[58] But the general standards of behaviour, from kindergarten onwards, do seem high; good manners are commonplace; and most teachers assume, as a matter of course, that the class is on their side from the start—which is as good a basis for real discipline as any teacher, East or West, could ask for.

3. SCIENCE AND TECHNOLOGY

There is not much talk in Eastern Europe about the "two cultures" as an educational problem. The Western observer, familiar with tensions and lack of communication between the sciences and the arts and accustomed to controversies about their relative importance in the educational scheme of things, finds it taken for granted in the communist schools that science should occupy a central place. Indeed, the idea that there can be a single subject called "science" (as one still finds in some British schools) strikes their teachers as rather odd, since it artificially squeezes a whole range of thought into one pigeon-hole, and usually a constricted one at that. They do not teach "science", but sciences—

[57] Personal impressions are always open to the objection that visitors may be shown specially selected schools, or that everyone may put on their best behaviour for their benefit. There is doubtless some truth in this, and allowances have to be made; but on various occasions I visited schools at extremely short notice and sometimes (by going to the wrong place) without any notice. Also, to dismiss the children's behaviour as totally assumed for the occasion is to strain belief in their acting capacity.

[58] George Z. F. Bereday, "Education and Youth" (*Annals of the American Academy of Political and Social Science*, **317** (May 1958): pp. 63–70. The author writes of the "ebbing fortunes" of political education in Poland, Hungary, Czechoslovakia and Rumania.

mathematics, physics, chemistry and biology—to *all* pupils in the basic schools. The actual proportion of time devoted to them varies from country to country, from 25 per cent over the whole course in Rumania to over 32 per cent in East Germany, but it works out at about 30 per cent for Eastern Europe generally.[59] Considering that only mathematics is taught from the beginning, with biology, chemistry and physics usually appearing about the fifth year or later, this means a heavy concentration on the sciences for the older pupil in the compulsory school, as a look at the curricula of the individual countries will show.[60] In the secondary general schools, some degree of specialization is possible in most countries, but nothing approaching the degree familiar in English grammar schools—the idea of letting pupils drop one side or the other at the age of about 16 is unthinkable. Even pupils specializing in the "humanities" carry all the science subjects right through to the end of the course, usually adding astronomy for good measure, and sometimes psychology as well.[61]

If one adds work study and technical training—the practical side of the sciences and an integral part of the curriculum in terms of the "polytechnical" principle—the time devoted to all kinds of scientific and technological studies, in the widest sense, rises considerably. In the early 1960's, when most of the systems were reformed to increase the practical content of the courses, the total proportion rose to between 34 per cent in Hungary and 42 per cent in East Germany—an average of about 37 per cent for scientific, technical and practical subjects over the whole basic course.[62] There has since then been some reduction in the time set aside for polytechnical studies, but the emphasis on this side of general education remains strong.

It is in this bias to the practical and applied that the trend is most noticeable in higher education. Generally, the "pure"

[59] Rudolf Weissner, Helmut Brauer, Willy Mann, "Das Bildungswesen der zweiten Stufe in einigen sozialistischen Ländern—Eine vergleichende Studie" (*Vergleichende Pädagogik*, **10** (1964), pp. 12–14).
[60] See pp. 188 ff.
[61] See pp. 194 ff.
[62] Weissner, Brauer and Mann, *op. cit.*, table 2, p. 13 (adapted).

sciences claim fewer students than the "humanities", especially if this includes economics, law and the like—there are about three-quarters as many science as arts students in Albania,[63] for example, half as many in East Germany,[64] and well below that in Yugoslavia.[65] But the bias towards practical courses—engineering, technology, agriculture—is strong indeed; in East Germany, there are three times as many students of technology as there are of pure science.[66] Again, there are many variations, but there is a general pattern of preference for the science-technology side; in Yugoslavia[67] it accounts for over 30 per cent of all students,[68] about 35 per cent in East Germany,[69] over 40 per cent in Albania,[70] over 50 per cent in Bulgaria,[71] and so on. This tendency appears in different ways at all points in the educational system, from kindergarten handwork to post-graduate agronomy—witness the expansion of all kinds of secondary vocational and technical schools since the war, the proliferation of apprentice and adult training schemes, the emphasis on part-time courses in higher education to keep students in touch with practical work. In these and other ways, one has the impression of educational systems fully committed to science and technology in general and special courses alike.

There are a number of reasons for this, practical as well as theoretical. In both industry and agriculture, the need for trained personnel at all levels, from the skilled worker to the post-grad-

[63] *Vjetari Statistikor i R.P.Sh.* 1964, p. 373. (R.P.Sh. Drejtoria e Statistikës, Tirana, 1964.)
[64] *Statistisches Jahrbuch der DDR 1964.* (Staatsverlag der DDR, Berlin, 1964.)
[65] *Statistički Kalendar Jugoslavije 1965.* (Savezni Zavod za Statistiku, Belgrade, 1965.)
[66] *Statistisches Jahrbuch der DDR 1964.*
[67] *Statistički Kalendar Jugoslavije 1965.*
[68] "Other students" includes all those in universities and other higher educational institutions, including teacher training colleges; students of medicine, dentistry, veterinary medicine, planning and economics are not counted in the figures for "technology and science".
[69] *Statistisches Jahrbuch der DDR 1964.*
[70] *Vjetari Statistikor i R.P.Sh. 1964.*
[71] *Statističeski Godišnik na N.R. Bŭlgarija 1963*, p. 347. (NRB Centralno Statističesko Upravlenie pri Ministerskija Sŭvet, Sofia, 1963.)

uate specialist, is obvious enough; in countries where programmes of industrialization have been adopted to lift economy and living standards into modern times, the need is even more pressing. As Albania's Enver Hoxha has put it, "Out country has become not only a big construction-site, but a great school where one out of every five persons studies".[72] Rhetorical flourish though this was, the connection between the state of the economy and the state of the educational system was seriously meant. In this respect Albania is unique only in having had a later start than any; and the intimate connection between education and living standards has been underlined in similar terms by other East European leaders who would probably agree with Hoxha in little else. The needs of the economy alone would explain the emphasis on technical schools and technological courses at college level. But there is a practical sociological aspect too. As in the U.S.S.R., the expansion of secondary schooling produced more potential students than higher institutions of any kind could take. It was generally recognized that this was not a healthy situation; a statement by the Bulgarian Ministry of Education and Culture in 1959 is typical of the general official view:

> The main defect of the general secondary school has lain in its orientation, in the lack of realism which has seen its essential task as preparing candidates for higher education and government posts, with no attempt to train for productive work. This shortcoming was less apparent when secondary education was reserved for the few and the number of pupils completing the secondary course coincided with the number entering higher educational institutions. But it can no longer be tolerated now that the secondary school has been democratized and the normal outlet for its graduates is into employment in production.[73]

The general schools, therefore, as well as the vocational schools, had to take account of the possibility that their pupils would work in industry or agriculture, and an unduly bookish curriculum would not meet their needs. There were, of course, other reasons

---

[72] Enver Hoxha: "Speech delivered at the festive meeting devoted to the 20th anniversary of the founding of the Party of Labour of Albania and the 44th anniversary of the Great October Socialist Revolution", p. 21. *Bulletin of the State University of Tirana*, Supplement, 1961.

[73] *World Survey of Education*, III, p. 289. (UNESCO, Paris, 1961.)

for introducing polytechnical education in the schools, but this was probably the most clearly practical of them. When it came to practice, the details varied, but not radically; the scheme introduced in Bulgaria in 1958 gives some idea of the content of polytechnical education in the general school.[74] The main emphasis was on "Experience of productive work", starting in the first year with simple handwork—paper-modelling and the like—rising to three hours a week in the fifth, sixth and seventh years of workshop practice, excursions to public utilities, work on experimental plots, and a general coverage of the basic processes of industrial and agricultural work. Crop and stock management came on to the time-table for two hours a week in the eighth year, and in the ninth there were two hours a week of technical drawing, one of rural mechanization, and three of the "Elements of machine operation". Cars and tractors were studied in the tenth form (two hours), and practical electronics in the eleventh. This course was designed for all pupils, regardless of their future occupations; but there was industrial training in the last three years as well, rising from five to twelve hours a week, and this could give vocational qualifications as well.

Apart from practical pressures, economic and sociological, the stress on science, technology and polytechnical education is closely tied up with the objectives of communist political and moral education. Article 1, part 3, of the Czechoslovak Education Law of 1960 states the aims thus:

> Training and education are based on a scientific concept of the world, on Marxism–Leninism; they are closely tied in with the life of the people, and are based on the latest knowledge of the sciences and progressive cultural traditions. The entire training and educational work of the schools is linked with the study of the fundamentals of science, polytechnical instruction and labour training in socially useful, especially productive, work.[75]

Emphasis on the sciences, therefore, is made partly for ideological

---

[74] *World Survey of Education*, III, p. 283.
[75] *Zbierka zakonov*, No. 82, p. 645. (Bratislava, 1960.) Quoted in: Nellie Apanasewicz and Seymour Rosen, *Education in Czechoslovakia*, p. 21. (U.S. Office of Education, Washington D.C., 1963.)

reasons. Instruction in physics, biology and astronomy does not in itself, of course, create Marxists; but in so far as it encourages a "scientific concept of the world", as opposed to a religious or mystical one, it is regarded as a necessary first step. As for polytechnical subjects, they are intended to do more than prepare pupils for actual employment; by familiarizing them with tasks they may well *not* perform in later life, it is intended to make for greater social understanding and social cohesion. Work practice is also intended to have salutory effects on the development of the pupils' attitudes and personal conduct. As another Czechoslovak statement says: "Education for work ... is intended to give the children a positive attitude to manual labour. They will acquire basic working skills and habits, learn to be accurate and tidy in their work, and to work for the common good."[76] The connections here with some aspects of political and moral education are clear enough. Many of the moral education programmes make much of teaching "respect for manual work" and "feelings of solidarity with working people" as part of the development of socialist morality, and neither can make much headway if pupils grow up disdaining to do any manual work themselves and despising those who do as failures. Polytechnical education, from this point of view, is intended as a means of strengthening the pupils' social awareness, and thus strengthen his acceptance of the socially based moral code. According to a Hungarian headmaster:

> In Hungary, education is in the first place a question of community education. No one can be good or bad in himself. This or that kind of attitude reacting on others evokes a positive or negative response. We therefore educate the child, the young person, to realise that he is a social being, who through his actions moulds the life of society.[77]

Much has been written about the reasons behind the policy of "bringing the schools closer to life", and about some of the difficulties that it has run into, especially the side concerned with practical industrial training in actual factories or farms for senior

---

[76] Státní pedagogické nakladatelsví (eds.), *Development of the Czechoslovak School System in the School Year 1960–61*. Quoted in *ibid.*, p. 23.

[77] Ernő Bajor Nagy, *A Country at School*, p. 43. (Pannonia, Budapest, 1962.)

pupils. There seems little doubt that liason between school and factory has often been at fault, that the programme was often interpreted without imagination, and that many managers regarded the pupils as more of a nuisance than anything else. There were numerous complaints about the disruption of school work for the sake of putting in time in the factories at repetitive tasks that benefited neither the pupils' education nor the factories' output. The rather naïve assumption that four hours at a lathe or in a field is necessarily more valuable *educationally* that two or three came under scrutiny too. All this—and probably the lack of adequate facilities in some areas—led to some reorganization of polytechnical education, and particularly of industrial training. This generally meant a reduction. Czechoslovakia, for instance, cut "Principles in Production" in the secondary school from eight to six hours a week in 1964, and made other minor reductions, with the promise of more to follow.[78] Bulgaria cut industrial practice drastically (from twelve to six hours a week) in the final year, trimmed other subjects less drastically, and moved technical drawing and "Car and tractor" into the category of optional subjects.[79] But while it remains, even in attenuated form, it underlines the desire of the authorities to link theory and practice, and to try to break down the division between mental and physical work, a division stigmatized as a legacy of the class divisions of capitalist society.

This attitude to the relationship between mental and physical work is important, for it lies behind the approach to many problems. The assumption that there can or should be a clear-cut division between general education and vocational training (roughly associated with intellectual study and manual operation respectively) is all too easily made. Almost everywhere, in recent years at any rate, the clarity of the division has been called in question, and many teachers have become uncomfortably aware

[78] Johannes Faensen, Tschekoslowakei: Verkürzung des Produktionsunterrichts. (*Informationsdienst zum Bildungswesen in Osteuropa*, **8/9**, pp. 44–45. Osteuropa Institut an der Freien Universität Berlin, 1964.)

[79] Mihajlo Juhas, Općeobrazovna škola i produženi boravak učenika u SR Bugarskoj (*Revija Školstva i Prosvetna Dokumentacija*, **1** (1965), pp. 24–25).

that the grammar-school pupil studying Latin or English literature is just as likely to be vocationally motivated as his counterpart studying building trades at a further education centre. Communist theory seeks to minimize the distinction. As one Rumanian writer has said:

> At the risk of appearing paradoxical, we venture to affirm this: there exists in any general education a vocational aspect or intention, just as in any serious vocational training there exists an element of general education. The classical *lycée* of the past half-century was vocational by nature; it trained functionaries for the bourgeois-landlord state. The "modern" or "real" *lycées* were also vocational in this sense; they trained future lawyers, businessmen, engineers. ... [80]

The author here is dealing with the proposal to set up industrial and agricultural *lycées* combining general and vocational education, and is concerned with reconciling the two elements. This approach, as we have seen, lies behind much of the "polytechnizing" of the humanities and general education. But there is another side to the coin; no less striking, though less commonly reported, is the converse of this policy, stemming equally logically from the same premises—the "humanization" of technology and vocational training.

Most East European countries have two main types of technical schools: *trade schools* (or apprenticeship centres, etc.) for the training of skilled workers, and *secondary technical schools* (often called *Technicums* on the Soviet model) which train pupils who have completed the basic school course for "intermediate" professions —engineering, agriculture, communications, computer programming, animal husbandry, or for such occupations as librarianship, nursing, veterinary work, clerical work, and so on. The main emphasis is, of course, vocational, but a considerable amount of time is spent on "general culture"—mother tongue, literature, social studies, foreign languages and the like. In Albania, for example, the time in industrial technicums is divided thus on average: 23 per cent for practical work in school and in production,

---

[80] Stanciu Stoian, "Un obiectiv important al politicii noastre" (*Revista de Pedagogie*, **8**, 1965, pp. 9–10).

42 per cent for technical subjects, and 35 per cent for general educational subjects. In agricultural technicums the pattern is: 29 per cent for practical work in school, farm and plot, 38 per cent for theoretical studies in agriculture, 32 per cent general subjects. The general educational content is even greater in the economic technicums: 37 per cent general, 55 per cent vocational subjects, and barely 8 per cent for practical work.[81] Likewise in the Czechoslovak technical schools: in those specializing in mechanical engineering, for instance, the four-year course is divided 60 per cent for vocational subjects (electro-technology, mechanics, technical drawing, machine parts, workshop training, etc.) and 40 per cent for general subjects (including the sciences, Czech or Slovak language and literature, history, civics, Russian and physical education). In addition there are three-week periods of work practice in the first three years on the one hand, and time for optional subjects—a second foreign language, for example, or more sport—on the other. In agricultural secondary schools (e.g. those specializing in plant cultivation and animal husbandry), the proportion is about 54 per cent for vocational studies, 46 per cent general, and also time for optional subjects and rather more extensive periods of work practice—six weeks in the first year, nine in the second, eight in the third.[82] This kind of pattern is characteristic of secondary technical schooling generally. Apart from the "humanizing" influence of the general studies, they make it possible for students to take their secondary school certificate as well as qualifying for a job. The technical schools thus become one route to higher education as an alternative to the academic *gymnasia* and *lycées*.

The trade schools which train workers for industry are, as one might expect, more immediately concerned with the mastery of particular skills. But here too a not insubstantial proportion of the curriculum is devoted to general subjects. In the Czechoslovak

---

[81] *World Survey of Education*, III, p. 175. (UNESCO, Paris, 1961.) Figures adapted and rounded off.

[82] Stanislav Vodinský, *Czechoslovakia: Education*, pp. 46, 47. (Orbis, Prague, 1963.) Figures adapted and rounded off.

apprentice training schools (which admit about two-thirds of all pupils leaving the basic school), they study Czech or Slovak language and literature, Russian, Civics, mathematics, physics and physical education as a normal part of the course, and a second foreign language is available as an option. The emphasis on the vocational side is much stronger than in the technical secondary schools, but even so it amounts to about 20 per cent of the time on a three-year course.[83] This proportion is about 16 per cent in the East German two-year apprenticeship schools,[84] 32 per cent in the Polish trade schools,[85] and so on. There are variations from place to place, but whether the proportion of time for general studies is greater, as in the *Technicum*, or less as in the trade schools, it amounts to rather more than a token gesture in the direction of "liberal studies".

Occasionally one hears suggestions that the principle of "unity of theory and practice" should be carried to the point where the general content of technical and vocational courses would be directly relevant, in detail, to the technical bias of the main courses, something after the idea of "centres of interest" or the Horological School in Paris where everything is studied from a horological angle.[86] The practical difficulties would be immense, and in any case it has never been suggested that any schools should train people *only* for a job. If there have been temptations to slant literature towards mechanics or foreign languages towards animal husbandry, they have been resisted. General subjects are treated much as in the general schools, and the fact that someone is going to be a mechanic or weaver is not accepted as a reason for supposing that he should not read Goethe or Gorki. One example will

---

[83] *Ibid.*, pp. 36–37.

[84] *Vocational Training in the German Democratic Republic*, p. 56. (German Institute for Vocational Training, no date.)

[85] Mieczysław Pęcherski, *Das Schulwesen in Volkspolen*, pp. 344–5. In: DPZI, *Das Schulwesen sozialistischer Länder in Europa*. (Volk und Wissen Volkseigener Verlag, Berlin, 1962.)

[86] Kenneth Smart, "The Polytechnical Principle", p. 161. In: E. J. King (ed.), *Communist Education*. (Methuen, London, 1963.) This chapter can be recommended for a thorough treatment of the theory and practice of polytechnical education.

serve: in the Electro-Technical School[87] in Belgrade (a school of the *Technicum* type) the four-year course concentrates on basic technical studies—mechanics, technical drawing, basic electricity, and so on; and special technical studies—in this case, various branches of electrotechnology; but nearly 40 per cent of the time is allotted to general mathematics and siences, Serbo-Croat literature and language, history and social studies, a foreign language, and so forth. The literature course deals with Slovene and Macedonian as well as Serbo-Croat literature, and as each form is treated—epic poetry, lyric poetry, drama, short stories, the novel—examples for other literatures are included. The budding electrotechnologist is therefore expected to know something of Gorki, Turgenev, Pushkin, Balzac, Shakespeare, Hemingway, and to read a selected list in translation along with a sizeable list of Yugoslav works. This breadth can be seen throughout the general education programme, and holds good for the rest of Eastern Europe. Not only does the structure and content of technical and vocational education reflect a desire to humanize the whole process, but shows the determination of the authorities to raise this sector of the system in general esteem, and end the state of affairs whereby technical schools were poor relations of the academic schools.

Many problems remain. The difficulties of putting the polytechnical principle into practice in the general schools have already been mentioned, and doubtless similar difficultier saise in integrating general education with the technical and vocational courses—one does meet disgruntled youths who want to spend all their time on the machines instead of bothering with foreign languages and civics. There have been failures, and there will doubtless be more, in the practical organization of such new courses. More fundamentally, there are doubts about how far a simple additive of arts subjects can humanize a technical course or student, or vice versa. Further, there is some uncertainty on the part of the authorities how far "bringing the schools closer to life" should involve a precisely vocational bent. What does seem

[87] *Tehnička Škola: Nastavni Plan.* (Belgrade, 1965, unpublished.)

clear is that they are trying to bring the disparate elements of education and training—general and special, academic and practical—into some kind of unity, to find a way of educating at the same time the worker, the citizen and the person. This kind or problem touches us closely too; whatever reservations we may have about the way the East Europeans go about solving it, therefore, and whatever difficulties they have, the attempt to realign the different sides of the educational programmes merits close attention.

4. THE YOUTH ORGANIZATIONS

"School life today", says a Czechoslovak writer, "would be unthinkable without the organizations of children and youth." This could be said for the whole of Eastern Europe, where the various youth organizations play a much more important part than they do in Western countries. For one thing, their membership is wider; while the Scouts, Guides, Boys' Brigade and the rest attract only a minority, the youth organizations in communist countries have a virtually complete membership among school-age children at least. For another, their activities are so closely tied in with the work of the school that they can be considered part of the educational system. From one point of view they are junior political organizations, as some of their names indicate—the Communist Youth League or KISZ (*Kommunista Ifjúsági Szövetszége*) in Hungary, the Dimitrov Communist Youth League or DKMS (*Dimitrovski Komunističeski Mladežki Sŭjuz*) in Bulgaria, etc. Their political role is proclaimed in their constitutions and their mottoes (e.g. "Young masses, forward to a socialist Hungary!"), and their relationship with the Communist or Workers' Parties is usually formally spelled out, whether they are technically junior branches of the Party or not. But the political side is not the whole story; they also organize all sorts of spare-time activities, cultural circles, sports clubs, holiday camps and so forth, so that they are not only the East European equivalents of the Young Communist League (or, *mutatis mutandis*, the Young Socialists or the Young Conservatives), but of the Cubs, Scouts, Brownies,

Guides, Girls' Guildry, Sea Cadets *and* the Youth Service, youth clubs and school societies as well, drawn together under the umbrella of single unitary organizations. In most cases they are quite specifically formed on the Soviet model,[88] whose pattern they follow fairly closely—Pioneers for children and young adolescents, and the Komsomol for older adolescents and young adults. There are, of course, differences from country to country, but generally they correspond closely both in organization and function. For boys and girls of basic school age—generally up to 15 or thereabouts—the most important are the junior organizations, normally called the Pioneers.

Pioneers—the Junior Organizations

Even before he joins, the child is aware of the Pioneers as soon as he comes to school. In most cases, he cannot join immediately, but must wait for two or three years. In Hungary, for instance, the minimum age for entering the Hungarian Pioneer League or MUSZ (*Magyar Uttörők Szövetszég*) is 8, and pupils can stay on till the age of 16. In Bulgaria, the Septembrist DPO or Dimitrov Pioneer Organization (*Dimitrovska Pionerska Organisacia "Septemvrijče"*) takes pupils from the age of 10 to 15. In Rumania they have the Pioneer Organization (*Organizaţia de pionieri*) for children of 10 to 15. The League of Polish Scouts or ZHP (*Związek Harcerstwa Polskiego*) is open to young people up to the age of 18, thus providing an overlap with the senior organizations (entry age 16), but pupils cannot join till they are 8 or 9.

But ways are found of introducing children to the Pioneers from the moment they enter the school. Pioneer flags and large-scale emblems decorate the schools, occupying prominent positions in entrance halls and assembly-halls, Pioneer posters are in classrooms and corridors. In countries where the entry age is 8 or over,

[88] e.g. Mojmír Dýma and Jaroslav Kojzar, *Das Schulwesen in der Tschekoslowakischen Sozialistischen Republik*, p. 495. In: DPZI, *Das Schulwesen sozialistischer Länder in Europa*. (Volk und Wissen Volkseigener Verlag, Berlin, 1962.) The influence of pre-war communist youth movements is, however, also stressed in most countries.

the teachers of the younger classes, helped by older pupils, prepare the children by telling them about Pioneer activities, familiarizing them with the Rules and Promise, the mottoes, badges, banners, and their meanings, and brief them in all the admission ceremonial as well as the standards of behaviour expected of Pioneers. This does not necessarily mean forming a definite (if comparatively informal) preparatory stage like the Soviet "Octobrists".[89] Some countries do feel that the young children are better off in an organization of some kind—hence, in Czechoslovakia, the founding in 1959 of the *Jiskry* (Sparks) for the 6- to 9-year-olds. The Yugoslav Pioneer League or SPJ (*Savez Pionira Jugoslavije*) simply admits children right from the start, at 7 in this case. Similarly, the East German "Ernst Thälmann" Pioneer Organization (named after the pre-war German communist leader) admits children when they enter school at the age of 6. But there the organization is on two levels: younger children are *Jungpionieren* (Young Pioneers). Not until they reach the fifth year (age 10–11) do they become fully fledged *Thälmannpionieren.*

The Poles have taken this policy of organization by stages a step further. The ZHP has a three-tier structure, with "Little Scouts" (*zuchy*) from 8 or 9 to 10 or 11, Junior Scouts (*młodsi harcerze*) up to 15 or 16, and Senior Scouts (*starsi harcerze*) up to 18.

Membership of the Pioneer and other organizations is officially voluntary; indeed, it is represented to the young children as a privilege and an honour for which they must show themselves worthy by good behaviour and hard work. Much is made of the voluntary principle, though it is expected that all should voluntarily join. As one Hungarian writer puts it: "The voluntary principle and the character of the Pioneers as a mass organization are not contradictory."[90] It certainly is a mass organization: practically all do join. This is what is expected by officials and teachers, and one finds in lesson-plans and the like a built-in

---

[89] Expulsion or suspension from the "Octobrists" cannot, for example, be used as a disciplinary measure.

[90] Ferenc Ábent *et al., Das Schulwesen in der Ungarischen Volksrepublik,* p. 570. In: DPZI, *op. cit.*

assumption that all the class will be Pioneers as a matter of course.[91] One does occasionally see a pupil or two not wearing the characteristic red scarf (or blue in East Germany). They may be individualists who do not want to join, but it usually turns out that they have been suspended from membership by their comrades for letting the class down by persistent laziness or bad behaviour—a keenly felt disgrace and, accordingly, an effective disciplinary measure. There is no need to put this practically total membership down to coercion; it is more likely due to the desire of children to "belong". Further, it is generally expected, and most people—especially children—do what is expected unless they have stronger reasons for doing otherwise. On the positive side, there are all the activities, from art clubs to holiday camps, from football teams to orchestras, that membership offers.

Strictly speaking, a pupil does not have to be a member of the Pioneers to join in their activities. The adult Communist or Workers' Parties are as a rule fairly exclusive; one cannot just join, but must be deemed acceptable—"the most advanced individuals, politically and morally", are accepted, according to one source, into the Czechoslovak Party.[92] But linked with the Parties though they are, the Pioneer organizations are not exclusive; they are "mass organizations" whose task it is to draw children into social, political, cultural and other activities. The non-joiner will not, therefore, find himself excluded from the basketball club or the canoe excursion just because he will not wear the red scarf. He will, on the contrary, be encouraged to take part, on the assumption that he will soon want to belong completely, red scarf and all. Not surprisingly, this is the way it usually works out.

Joining the Pioneers is something of an occasion. Typically, there is an induction ceremony in the school, the Pioneer House or Palace, or sometimes on the premises of the "patron" organiza-

[91] e.g. A. Felea and C. Fogarasi, "Contribuții metodice la problema dezvoltării exprimării elevilor într-o limbă străină (limba rusă)" (*Revista de Pedagogie*, **5** (1965), p. 89).

[92] Stanislav Vodinský, *Schools in Czechoslovakia*, p. 116. (State Pedagogical Publishing House, Prague, 1965.)

tion, a factory or collective farm that has taken the detachment under its wing. The new Pioneers salute the banner of the Pioneers and/or the national flag, and are given their scarves and badges (usually inscribed with some variant of "Be Prepared") after making a "solemn Promise" before the assembled company. This one is from Rumania, and very close to the Soviet original: "I, a Young Pioneer of the Rumanian People's Republic, in the presence of my comrades, solemnly promise to love passionately my motherland, the Rumanian People's Republic, and to live, learn and struggle as the Rumanian Workers' Party teaches us."[93] Speeches of welcome are made by the leaders, and everything is done to make the ceremony as impressive as possible. In many cases, Pioneers are also required to go through grades or tests, lest the seriousness of their commitment should decline into habit; in Hungary there are three of them, for 10–11-year-olds, 11–13, and 13–15, as well as special tests to qualify as office-bearers.[94] Once again, comparisons with the Scouts spring to mind—Tenderfoot tests, second-and first-class badges, Queen's Scouts tests, and so forth.

Obvious though they are, comparisons with Scout-type organizations should not be pushed too far. They too, of course, have a moral and social, even political aim ("do my duty to God and the Queen", etc.) behind all the ritual and uniforms and the activities, but it is doubtful if they make as much of such objectives as the Pioneers do. The Rules of the East German Young Pioneers illustrate at once the similarities and the differences:

> We Young Pioneers help to protect peace.
> We Young Pioneers love our Homeland and Nature.
> We Young Pioneers maintain friendship with children throughout the world.

[93] *Angajamentul solemn al pionierului*, from a plaque in a Pioneer room in a Bucharest school. The name of the country was changed in 1965 to the Socialist Republic of Rumania, and the Worker's Party was renamed the Rumanian Communist Party. The UTM became the Union of Communist Youth. Nevertheless, recent publications still use the older nomenclature, and plaques take time to replace.

[94] Ferenc Ábent, *op. cit.*, p. 571.

We Young Pioneers learn well at School.
We Young Pioneers help with work.
We Young Pioneers love our parents.
We Young Pioneers speak the truth.
We Young Pioneers love to sing, dance and play.
We Young Pioneers are good friends and help each other.
We Young Pioneers wear our blue scarves.[95]

The emphasis here is mainly on desirable kinds of personal and social conduct, appropriate to children between 6 and 10. These maxims, of course, are constantly elaborated and, as we have seen, a political gloss can be given not only to patriotism and love of peace, but affection for parents, working well at school, helping one another, etc. In the Pioneer group as in the classroom, moral, social and political education are inseparable. The political aims are clearly stated often enough; according to one Rumanian source: "The essential mission of the Pioneer Organization is to educate the children in communist morality."[96] Or again, in Bulgaria:

> The Youth League and the Pioneer Organization are the best helpers of the school in its responsible task of instructing youth in true Marxism–Leninism and awakening in them a love of knowledge, work and culture. The ... organizations help the pupils ... to develop noble characteristics such as modesty, truthfulness, comradeship, industriousness and other valuable qualities of the New Man.[97]

These social and political aims are pursued in many ways. The very flavour is, or course, communist—the banners, the badges, the red scarves, all the available symbolism. The promises and the rules likewise have political content. So do the mottoes—"For the Motherland, with Tito, forward!" or "In the struggle for the task of the Rumanian Communist Party, be prepared!" Some of

---

[95] *Vocational Training in the German Democratic Republic*, p. 38. (German Institute for Vocational Training, n.d.)

[96] "Rolul şi activitatea organizaţiei de pionieri şi a organizaţiei UTM în şcoală", p. 354. In: A. Dancsuly, A. Chircev and A. Manolache, *Pedagogia*. (Editura Didactică şi Pedagogică, Bucharest, 1964.)

[97] Naiden Čakarov et al., *Das Schulwesen in der Volksrepublik Bulgarien*, p. 170. In: DPZI, *op. cit.*

the activities are political too—youth festivals, meetings, discussions, parades. There is less specifically political activity than in the senior organizations, but politics are never far away. The study of Marxist–Leninist theory, for instance, does not figure prominently, but the general atmosphere, and the way in which other activities can be given a political relevance, lays the basis for more intensive ideological work later on.

Connected with this is the aim of encouraging "positive attitudes towards work", an essential component of communist moral education. "Pioneers", say the Rumanian regulations, "should consider work as an honour, respect the work of others, defend and protect with care the property of the people, take an active part in socially useful work, and help their parents and grown-ups."[98]

This is not done by preaching—not, at least, principally. Some of the children's activities are organized to make them familiar with different kinds of work, to get used to working together, and to appreciate its value to others. In Hungary there is a "Pioneer Town" on a hill-top at Csillebérc. Not only does it have the usual camping facilities for summer holidays, but its own post-office, kitchen, theatre and newspaper office, all run by the children with a minimum of adult help. It can be reached by the Pioneer Railway, a 7-mile miniature track complete with stations and trains, all named by the children themselves, dressed in the uniform of the Hungarian State Railways—"a garb of romanticism lent to practical knowledge".[99] On a less ambitious scale, excursions of all sorts are organized to factories and farms, especially to the groups's "patron" enterprise. As a Hungarian author comments on children visiting "their" steel factory: "Almost without knowing it they become familiar with the factory atmosphere, the various crafts, and this knowledge may later be a deciding factor in the children's choice of a vocation."[100]

---

[98] *Regulamentul organizaţiei de pionieri din RPR*, p. 14. Quoted in *Pedagogia*, p. 355.
[99] Ernő Bajor Nagy, *A Country at School*, p. 23. (Pannonia, Budapest, 1962.)
[100] *Ibid.*, p. 24.

Play and excursions are not enough, however; work must not only be useful but must be seen to be useful. Young children could not, of course, be expected to undertake major tasks, and in any case the time that even adolescents can spend on productive work, and the kind of work they can do, is severely limited by law. But they are encouraged to undertake useful jobs in the school and out—tidying classrooms, weeding school plots and cleaning up playgrounds, helping to keep public parks neat, helping invalids with shopping and housework, etc. Some tasks are more ambitious, such as decorating the Pioneer room in the school, even building a club-house with some adult help or supervision. Sometimes the scale is greater; in Bulgaria hundreds of children in larger teams have taken part in a programme of "Pioneer work for the Five-Year Plan", helping adults where needed, cleaning up villages, towns and schools, helping to lay out parks and gardens, planting trees, and so on.[101] Economically, the contribution may have been minor. but if they came to understand the relevance of their own work to the well-being of the community at large, the main objective was achieved. This attitude to work as a social good applies to school work as well. It is the Pioneer group that frequently mobilizes the opinion of the class on the teacher's side in matters of discipline, and puts collective pressure on the slackers who let the class down. This may take negative forms, such as preaching at the wayward pupil at meetings, satirizing him on wall newspapers, even suspending him from membership and taking away his scarf to make this fall from grace clear for all to see. On the more positive side, they frequently hold meetings at the end of term to discuss class reports, and if some pupils are blotting the class record by producing bad marks, they may arrange for them to be coached by some of their own number if they seem to be having genuine difficulty. "Help your comrade" is a frequent exhortation in the classroom, but not only teachers say it. Children are encouraged to feel responsible for each other's work, to be their brothers' keepers, and it is in the class

[101] Naiden Čakarov et al., op. cit., p. 171.
[102] *Pedagogia*, p. 357.

Pioneer groups that such general principles are translated into action.

But the work of the Pioneers is not all politics and good works, important though these are. Attending to "active leisure, amusements, cultural pursuits and physical recreation"[102] may normally appear as secondary objectives, but this is how most of the activity is spent, and the zest with which it is carried on—for Pioneers are in no way averse to having fun—balances that rather solemn tone of the official pronouncements. In the schools, the Pioneer organizations run an enormous variety of circles, clubs and societies—arts and crafts, hobbies, nature study, choirs and orchestras, aeromodelling, stamp collecting, amateur dramatics, radio, photography, school newspapers and magazines, gymnastics clubs and sports teams, literary societies, etc.—and circles where children who so desire can add to their normal curriculum by more science or art, music or an extra language or almost anything else. Not only does Pioneer activity cover the functions of youth movements elsewhere, but a great deal of it covers the work of schools societies as well.

This side of Pioneer work in the school can be limited by overcrowding. Ideally, children attend school in the mornings only, and in the afternoons both they and the school premises are free for clubs and circles. But there is still a severe shortage of school buildings in most countries, especially in the cities, making it necessary for most schools to operate a shift system, with the younger pupils attending in the morning and the older ones in the afternoon. As a result, the space available for extra-curricular pursuits may be limited to the Pioneer room and little else. This makes the facilities of the Pioneer House and Palaces all the more welcome. These are to be found in all major population centres, and often in suburbs and smaller towns as well. In Czechoslovakia there are 138 Pioneer and Youth Houses and 18 independent Pioneer stations; Bulgaria has 74 of them, East Germany 216, Rumania 110, Poland has 95 Children's and Youth Houses of Culture (DKDiM) and 19 Youth Houses of Culture (MDK), and so on.[103] Children's club-houses and the like are even more numerous. These centres vary enormously in size and quality. Many are modest and limited in facilities, often rather seedy in appearance. Others are palaces and mansions of the old régimes converted, others again are new and massive. Most of the big cities have at least one grand-scale Pioneer Palace, where the word "palace" seems far from pretentious—for example, the Palace of Pioneers in Bucharest, the Palace of Youth in Warsaw, the "Julius Fučik" House of Youth in Prague, the Klement Gottwald House in Bratislava, the "Walter Ulbricht" Palace of Pioneers in Dresden, etc. These have been described as the showplaces of the Pioneers, and certainly they seem to devote considerable space to displays, banners, ceremonial halls, and the like. But they are primarily for use; the great variety of facilities, the theatres and clubrooms, gymnasia and workshops, may be more lavish than usual, but they indicate the range of activities that come within the organizations' compass. There are also holiday camps in the mountains or by the sea, young naturalists' stations, young technicians' stations, etc. In the schools and out, during term and in holiday time, every kind of sparetime activity is catered for. Small wonder that the authorities regard the Pioneer Organization as an educational medium second only to the school in importance.

The organization of the Pioneers is linked closely with the school. There are many variations in names and subdivisions, but the basic unit is the class group (*Pioniergruppe* in East Germany, *detaşament* in Rumania, etc.), sometimes further divided into "links", "circles" and other smaller groupings of half a dozen to a dozen members. The Pioneers of the whole school make up the "Troop", "Unity", or "Friendship", and there may be intermediate "Family" groupings as well. Leaders are elected at class level, and the school as a whole has its council or committee to organize and co-ordinate activities, with the supervision of an

---

[103] Figures from DPZI, *op. cit.*, *loc. var.*
    DKDiM   *Domy Kultury Dzieci i Młodziezy:* Children's and Youth Houses of Culture.
    MDK   *Młodziezowe Domy Kultury*: Youth Houses of Culture.

adult Pioneer leader. The leader may be an adult specially trained for youth work, or a member of the senior organization, or a member of the teaching staff of the school. Significantly, Pioneer work is an important part of the teacher training programme,[104] and student teachers are normally required to put in some time during their courses at a Pioneer camp or centre, just as they have to practice the more academic side of their work in schools. Pioneer organizations are sometimes formally part of the youth organization, as in Czechoslovakia,[105] and sometimes independent, as in Poland; but either way, members of the senior organizations normally play their part in helping to run some of the activities, as do teachers, students, adults from the "patron" enterprises, members of "Friends of the Pioneers" organizations, interested parents, and so on. Help from people outside the school has obvious practical value, and is also welcomed as strengthening the links between the school and the community; but the work and organization of the Pioneers is firmly centred on the school itself.

The Senior Organizations

The Youth Leagues of the East European countries provide organizations for older adolescents and young adults from the mid-teens right up into the middle or late twenties. Generally, they start where the Pioneer organizations leave off. Thälmann Pioneers can join the FDJ (*Freie Deutsche Jugend* or Free German Youth) at 14; 15 is the entry age for the Rumanian UTM (*Uniunea Tineretului Muncitor*, Union of Working Youth), the Bulgarian DKMS, the Czechoslovak ČSM (*Československý Svaz Mládeže*, Czechoslovak Youth League). But in some cases there is an overlap; young people can stay in the Hungarian Pioneers (MUSZ) until they are 16, but it is possible to join the KISZ

[104] e.g. —"Rolul şi activitatea organizaţiei de pionieri şi a organizaţiei UTM în şcoală", *Pedagogia*, pp. 353–78. Or—Nikola Potkonjak, "Savez pionira Jugoslavije". In: Ljubomir Krneta, Milena Potkonjak and Nikola Potkonjak, *Pedagogija*, pp. 394–405. (Zavod za Izdavanje Udžbenika SR Srbije, Belgrade, 1965.)
[105] PO-ČSM—Pioneer Organization of the Czechoslovak Youth League.

(Communist Youth League) as early as 14, and in Poland one may be a senior scout till 18, or join the senior organizations at 16. The age limits are rarely precise, but generally the change-over to the senior bodies corresponds with the move from basic school to secondary education or employment. As a rule, the Youth Leagues present the same pattern as the Soviet Komsomol, a unitary organization covering the entire range of youth activities for senior pupils in schools, students in higher education, young workers and members of the armed forces, thus acting as a bridge between school and adult life. Poland provides an exception to the unitary pattern in having two youth leagues—the ZMS or Union of Socialist Youth (*Związek Młodieży Socjalistycznej*) for the towns and the ZMW, the Union of Rural Youth (*Związek Młodieży Wiejskiej*), for young people in the countryside. There used to be one organization as in other countries, the ZMP (Union of Polish Youth), but it was divided in 1956, when many other changes were made in the political and social life of Poland; apparently it was failing to make an adequate appeal to rural youth, and this seemed the best way of drawing them in.

Although much of the membership is adolescent and young adolescent at that, the tone of the Youth Leagues is carefully adult. While still relying on what one author calls "the romanticism of youth",[106] most of the ritual is dispensed with as more suitable for children. There are no "solemn promises" or sets of rules as in the Pioneers, no entry ceremonies, no red scarves, no uniform apart from the badge (except, in some cases, for a uniform worn on festive occasions, like the FDJ's blue outfit or the ČSM's dark trousers or skirt with blue shirts). In their activities, the political element is more prominent than in the Pioneers. "In the UTM", says the Rumanian programme, "the work of the pupils' ideologico-political education is intensified."[107]

The Youth Leagues are also mass organizations, but the mass is smaller than that of the Pioneers. Although less exclusive than the Communist or Workers' Parties, they are less all-embracing

[106] E. B. Nagy, *op. cit.*, p. 49.
[107] *Pedagogia*, p. 356.

than the Pioneers. Firm figures are difficult to come by, but it appears that only a minority of those leaving the Pioneers enter the senior organizations, though the proportion is much higher among senior pupils and students. This is partly because many do not wish to join; members are supposed to set the pace in volunteering for "socially useful work", such as helping with the harvests and other public projects, and generally to be an example to youth, which strikes some as an unduly arduous role. But even so, the Youth Leagues do not accept all-comers; aspiring members must have a good record of school work, conduct and Pioneer activity, which restricts the entry further. Nor is admission necessarily final; "passengers" who constantly fail to help in the Leagues' tasks and take part in their activities, or whose behaviour is deemed to be reprehensible, are liable to be expelled. This does not always happen, either through tolerance or negligence on the part of the branches concerned, but the possibility exists and is often carried into effect.

The status and organization of the Youth Leagues vary considerably. Some of them are junior branches of the Party, such as the KISZ in Hungary; under the leadership of the Party, like the Rumanian UTM; or formally independent, like the Polish organizations. (These last—the ZHP, ZMS, ZMW, along with the Polish Union of Students—come under the All-Polish Co-ordinating Committee of Youth Organizations, known as OKWOM.[108]) This point, like the extent to which the Pioneers are part of the senior bodies, is possibly of organizational importance, but it has little effect on policy or activities. The basic unit is the branch or group, centred, like those of the Party, on the member's place of work—class, factory, farm, regiment, etc. Members elect their own committees and councils at branch and district level, and have their own Congresses at national level, complete with delegates, Central Committees and all the rest of the organizational apparatus of the Party. Broad decisions of policy are taken at Congress, practical ones locally; naturally,

---

[108] *Ogólpolski Komitet Współpracy Organizacji Młodzieżowych.*

whatever the formal relationship with the Party, contacts are close, as are lines of policy.

League members do not have rules of the Pioneer type, but rather statements of rights and duties laid down in charters and constitutions. The rights are concerned with such matters as election to committees, voting for delegates to Congress, etc. The duties are mainly social and political obligations, such as these from the Constitution of the FDJ:

> To support actively the work of the FDJ and to attend meetings of his local unit; to fight for the implementation of the resolutions of the FDJ, the SED and the Government of the DDR; to be an active fighter for a unified, democratic, peace-loving Germany; to show exemplary conduct in industry, agriculture, trade and commerce; to study and disseminate Marxism–Leninism; to work actively with unorganized youth in order to bring them into the FDJ; to develop fearless criticism and self-criticism in order to eliminate all shortcomings and mistakes, etc.[109]

They are also expected to cultivate assiduously their own and others' intellectual, physical and aesthetic as well as moral, social and political education.

Apart from political matters, the work of the Youth Leagues covers the normal range of activities undertaken by the Pioneers, but on a more ambitious scale. This is most noticeable in help on public projects. In Hungary,[110] for example, KISZ members planted 100 million trees in 1957 as part of a forestry programme. In the marshy Hanság region they organized summer work camps where volunteer brigades worked on a land-reclamation project, draining over 11,000 acres of land for agricultural use. The KISZ "adopted" the Danube Cement Works, playing a major part in the construction of the plant. Another important part of their work is in helping the Pioneers—providing leaders for school groups of summer camps, helping to build (and often to finance) clubhouses. For their own members, they organize the customary youth activities—sports clubs and centres, camps and hikes, sailing

---

[109] *Statut der Freien Deutschen Jugend*, quoted in Paul S. Bodenmeann, *Education in the Soviet Zone of Germany*, p. 111 (adapted). (U.S. Dept. of Health, Education and Welfare, Washington D.C., 1959.)

[110] E. B. Nagy, *op. cit.*, pp. 49–53.

clubs, arts and handicrafts, dances and discussion-groups, and so on, in schools, club-houses, independent centres and Youth Houses and Palaces. They have their own publishing houses, like "Mladá Fronta" (Young Front) in Czechoslovakia, which produce not only Youth League and Pioneer newspapers and magazines, but books of all kinds for children and young people. In the schools, they help to mobilize class opinion on the side of the teacher to ensure discipline and attention to work, organize (like the Pioneers) help for classmates in difficulty with their studies, co-operate with teachers and directors in the organization of school functions, discuss problems of discipline and moral education with the head, and generally act as a liaison body[111] between staff and pupils, which includes speaking up for pupils who have been unfairly punished for their behaviour, or even unfairly marked for their work—as many teachers expecting the Youth Leagues to play a "prefect" or "N.C.O." role have discovered with a shock. At the level of higher education, the Leagues play an important part in the running of the institutions. Not only do they arrange the usual clubs and social functions, but they usually have representatives on the college or faculty councils, and sit on the committees dealing with the admission of students and the payment of grants. Their role as the official channel of communication between students and staff, their political connections, and their involvement with the administrative machinery, make them a powerful element in the life of any institution of higher education.

The youth organizations afford a good example of the total nature of education in communist countries. Not only is great importance attached to out-of-school activities, whether in socially useful work or for personal recreation, but the youth movements are so organized that the division between education in school and

[111] In Yugoslavia the picture is complicated by the recognition of the class and school "collective" as a separate *ad hoc* entity, existing alongside the official Yugoslav Youth Federation. Contacts between staff and students are made primarily through the representatives of the "collective", and both they and branch officials of the Youth League take part in meetings and discussions. The same system operates in higher educational institutions.

out of school is reduced to a minimum. For those who stay on into the senior bodies, this side of education extends onwards into adult life, and thus diminishes the difference between school-days and adulthood. For the younger pupils, the work and organization of the Pioneers lessens the gap between formal curricular work and education in the broader sense, and ensures that the life of the children is touched at practically every point. The communist view of education, social and political, necessarily means that they cannot regard it only as something that happens in classrooms; and the attention paid to the youth organizations is one example of their attempts to make not only the school, but society as a whole, an educational environment for their future citizens.[112]

5. GIRLS AND WOMEN

Along with equality of races, nationalities, etc., all the East European régimes subscribe to the principle of equality of the sexes in education. Any form of discrimination against girls and women is forbidden by law, and the notion that they should be trained for a subsidiary role in life is rejected as a relic of an outworn social structure. "In the past", says one statement,[113] "women were in an inferior position to men in the field of education. More of them were illiterate. Under our régime, women have equal rights with men in all fields of social life." Pronouncements of this kind abound; they are written into every constitution and basic educational law, often several times.[114] As far as the position of the sexes is concerned, the official position is stated clearly enough: women are to be treated equally with men in all respects.

[112] The age-range of the youth organizations goes well beyond voting age (18 as a rule). This, and the fact that large numbers are involved in adult education, means that *present* citizens are involved to an extent not common elsewhere. Youth Leagues may even have distinct parliamentary groups, as does the FDJ in the East German Volkskammer.

[113] A. Dancsuly, A. Chircev and A. Manolache (eds.), *Pedagogia*, p. 83. (Editura Didactică şi Pedagogică, Bucharest, 1964.)

[114] e.g. "All citizens, regardless of nationality, sex, social origin or religion, shall enjoy equal rights to education under the same conditions." General Law on Education in Yugoslavia, 1959, Article 7.

Education Today: Some General Features

But it is one thing to state a principle, another to make it a reality. Indeed, there can be difficulties even in deciding what policies would serve the principle, assuming that they could be carried into effect. Does the principle of equality require that the sexes must be educated in the *same* way? After all, they are not entirely the same; does this mean that they should be treated differently *in order* to be equal? In any society, communist or not, there is some difference in their social roles and what one Polish writer[115] delicately calls their "biological function". Whether one favours common or separate schooling depends, in the last resort, on whether the similarities or the differences are thought to be more important.

Communist educationists have rejected the policy of "separate but equal" facilities—to borrow a phrase made notorious elsewhere[116]—and follow a policy of complete co-education. (Poland, with a very few surviving single-sex schools, is a slight exception.) Boys and girls, therefore, go to the same schools, sit in the same classes, join the same youth organizations, work together in their periods of practical training, study the same subjects, and have substantially the same range of possibilities open to them at every stage of their educational careers. Boarding schools, too, are mixed as a matter of policy, without giving rise to any undue alarm.[117] There are a few concessions to sexual differences in the general school curricula, but they are only a few. Older pupils are usually separated for physical education. There is some differentiation in the kind of practical work done; for example, girls in Czechoslovak basic schools spend an hour a week in the last two years on the nutrition and care of children, while boys do not; but even so, this accounts for only a third of the time spent on practical training in classes VIII and IX.[118] The rest is shared with the boys. Again, Czechoslovak agricultural schools offer "Family and

---

[115] *Poland 1944–1964*, p. 144. (Polonia, Warsaw, 1964.)

[116] In the Southern States of the U.S.A. before (and even after) the Supreme Court ruling on the racial integration of the schools.

[117] e.g. "Fót Children's Town: the Makarenko Approach" (*Times Educational Supplement*, 27 November 1964).

[118] Stanislav Vodinský, *Czechoslovakia: Education*, p. 21. (Orbis, Prague, 1963.)

Housekeeping" as an optional subject; this means metalwork, woodwork and saddlery for the boys, sewing and cookery for the girls.[119] Similar bias can be seen elsewhere. In Poland, the programme[120] of the basic school assigns, in some detail, different kinds of practical studies to boys and girls. Between classes V and VIII, girls put in 60 hours on homecraft and 76 hours on sewing and knitting, while boys do 50 hours of woodwork, 50 hours of metalwork, 20 hours of mechanics, etc. But the girls still have 18 hours of woodwork and 18 hours of metalwork—and the boys do 15 hours of homecraft and 10 hours of sewing. Other subjects are arranged more equably (see Fig. 3). For all the recognition that girls are more likely than boys to handle the domestic side, fundamentally the field of industrial and technical training is not treated as a male preserve. In the general educational curriculum, and in

Fig. 3. Poland: Study-plan for Practical and Technical Instruction in Classes V–VIII

Class:	V		VI		VII		VIII		Total in 4 years	
Sex:	B	G	B	G	B	G	B	G	B	G
1. Paper-work, etc.	16	16	–	–	–	–	–	–	16	16
2. Woodwork	32	18	18	–	–	–	–	–	50	18
3. Sewing and knitting	–	20	10	36	–	20	–	–	10	76
4. Metalwork	–	–	20	18	20	–	–	–	40	18
5. Glass and plastics	–	–	–	–	15	15	–	–	15	15
6. Electrotechnics	–	–	–	–	15	15	36	16	51	31
7. Home economics	–	–	–	–	15	15	–	45	15	60
8. Basic mechanics	–	–	–	–	–	–	20	–	20	–
9. Technical drawing	–	–	–	–	15	15	20	20	35	35
10. Additional techniques	16	10	16	10	16	16	20	15	68	51
Total hours per year	64	64	64	64	96	96	96	96	320	320

[119] Stanislav Vodinský, op. cit., p. 39.
[120] Siegfried Baske, "Polen: Neuer Lehrplan für die Grundschule." (Informationsdienst zum Bildungswesen in Osteuropa, Heft 8/9, p. 35. Osteuropa-Institut an der Freien Universität Berlin, 1964.)

other school activities, the mixing is complete. Even the tendency, common here, for boys and girls to sit on different sides of the classroom, does not normally appear.[121]

The reasons for the coeducational policy are to some extent practical; two parallel school systems for boys and girls are inclined to be wasteful in the towns and impracticable in the countryside, as they discovered in the U.S.S.R. when segregation was introduced (officially) between 1943 and 1954.[122] It also makes it more feasible to make all kinds of courses at secondary level available to both sexes without the headaches of planning that would be involved if they were in different schools. But there is a social reason too; it is argued that by getting boys and girls to work together from infancy they can be led to think of each other primarily as *people*, not merely as potential sexual partners. In other words, separation and social equality are incompatible. Significantly, one Yugoslav writer regards the co-educational principle as one of the important bases of moral education, a practical training in mutual understanding and respect.[123]

In technical and higher education the same policy is followed, with some modifications. Training for most trades is open to both sexes. Legislation often makes a special point of encouraging the entry of girls into skilled trades (as in the East German Labour Law, for example), [124] and one does in fact find girls as well as boys taking up mechanical engineering, electronics, agricultural mechanization, and so on. Sheer physical differences, of course, do set some limitation on this; Czech forestry schools[125] do not

[121] This has been observed in some parts of the Central Asian Republics of the U.S.S.R., and may well happen in some parts of Eastern Europe as well; but except in Poland I have never seen it, nor has any East European teacher I have asked about it.

[122] Nigel Grant, *Soviet Education*, pp. 40–41. (University of London Press, London, 1965; Penguin, 1968.)

[123] Nikola Potkonjak, *Moralno Vaspitanje : Vaspitanje pravilnog odnosa medju polovina.* In: Ljubomir Krneta, Milena Potkonjak and Nikola Potkonjak, *Pedagogija*, p. 203. (Zavod za Izdavanje Udžbenika SR Srbije, Belgrade, 1965.)

[124] Paras. 65, 123. See *Vocational Training in the German Democratic Republic*, p. 92. (German Institute for Vocational Training, n.d.)

[125] *Types of Secondary School, Czechoslovakia* 1963, p. 14. (Unpublished document.)

accept girl entrants, and there are other fields, such as mining, which only boys take up for obvious reasons. Even so, the sex bias is less than one might expect. Not only do engineering schools take girls, but frequently (e.g. in Czechoslovakia) vocational schools for nurses and health workers admit boys.[126] On the whole, one's sex makes only a marginal difference to the range of available occupations. The same is true of higher education. Although there is still a tendency for men to prefer technology and women to choose the humanities, this is not a requirement. There are no courses barred to women, nor are there quota systems for female entrants, as in some faculties here. Existing trends, too, are changing; the number of women entering higher institutions, absolute and relative, is rising, and the participation of women in the fields of technology and applied sciences is on the increase.

Declarations of equal rights, co-education in the schools and the opening of practically all courses to both sexes certainly help, but do not in themselves secure equality in fact. There is little point in making it possible for women to train for professions and trades unless it is made possible to pursue them. However attitudes may change towards working wives, the status of the breadwinner, and the whole range of marital relationships, nothing can alter the fact that it is the woman who becomes pregnant, bears the children, and is most immediately involved in their rearing, at least to begin with. Communist governments (in contrast to the Soviet government immediately after the Revolution) declared strongly in favour of the family as an institution—which is reflected, among other things, in the elaborate systems of parents' committees and school–family consultations. But, they argue, the family should be based on the partnership of equals, and this can not be more than an empty phrase if women are forced (or brainwashed) into spending the greater part of their adult lives housekeeping, bearing and rearing children, and having their horizons bound by the home. Social policy, therefore, aims at making it easier for women to be wives and mothers *and* follow some occupation. Labour legislation provides for periods of paid

[126] *Ibid.*, p. 18. More surprisingly, only girls are admitted to teachers' schools.

Education Today: Some General Features

maternity leave (twelve weeks on full pay in Poland, for example —two weeks before confinement, eight weeks after, and two more at either end as required),[127] and also sets limits on the kind of work they may do, the hours of work allowed, etc. The system of pre-school institutions, crèches and kindergartens, is at least partly organized, quite expressly, to make it possible for women to continue with their jobs;[128] significantly, many crèches are attached to and run by factories, farms and other enterprises. By encouraging family planning (though provisions for this are uneven as yet) and (with some limitations) allowing abortion, even in mainly Catholic countries, the governments try not to only keep their own local population problems in hand,[129] but make it possible to free women from the burden of a succession of unwanted pregnancies. Policies of this kind make it possible for women to work with the minimum of interruption; the kind of schooling they receive encourages them to work rather than seek *total* fulfilment in home-making and children; and, it should be added, the level of earnings, especially in the poorer countries, often makes it necessary—though few of the women who could afford to stay at home seem to do so. One way or another, there is no need for a girl to make the choice of marriage or a career. These are not regarded as alternatives—most women do both.

Nevertheless, it cannot yet be claimed that women have achieved complete equality. Whatever yardstick one adopts, it shows them still behind their menfolk. In the political field, few rise to the top. For instance, of 190 Federal Deputies in Yugoslavia in 1963, 33 were women. Of 43,158 local councillors, 7072 were women. They did better in some fields than others: although there were only 16 women out of 120 in the Organizational and Political Chamber, there were 34 out of 120 in the Chamber for Education and Culture, 36 out of 120 in the Chamber for Social

[127] *Poland 1944–1964*, p. 149. (Polonia, Warsaw, 1964.)
[128] "Nursery schools fulfil a double function: they aid in the bringing-up of children and prepare them for school. Moreover, by ensuring care to children during working hours, they make professional work possible for women." Zygmunt Parnowski, *Education in Poland*, p. 11. (Polonia, Warsaw, 1958.)
[129] It is reckoned that Poland has a surplus birth-rate of 500,000 per year.

Welfare and Public Health.[130] But this is still a small minority in the country where women fought beside their menfolk in the Partisan Army. Again, in Easy German (to pick at random) the State Commission on the new education law contained 56 men and 12 women.[131] The same holds good in the field of employment: women form a large minority in such fields as education, health, government and social organizations, but a much smaller one in the various branches of the national economy. Out of over 112,000 apprentices in the whole of Yugoslavia, 21,000 are girls; women account for little over one-fifth of the skilled workers, and about one-eleventh of the highly skilled. As one might expect, the proportions are highest in the more advanced republics like Slovenia, lowest in the more backward such as Bosnia.[132] Even in such professions as teaching where women have long been more easily accepted, one finds a concentration at the level of primary school teaching (where they usually outnumber the men) and a falling off in the number of women at the higher stages and in promoted posts. In Albania, women do not even predominate at the primary levels; even among teachers of classes I to IV men are in the majority. Women outnumber them in urban primary schools, but nowhere else; teaching is still largely a masculine occupation.[133]

The same can be observed, in different degrees, at practically all levels of the educational system. In some countries and in some fields, women make up a large proportion of the students in higher institutions, but generally they are still in a minority. In Albania, they account for just over a sixth of all students, and even in teacher-training institutes less than one-third are women.[134] In Bulgaria they make up about 40 per cent of the total, but a

---

[130] *Statistički Kalendar Jugoslavije 1965.* (Savezni zavod za statistiku, Belgrade, 1965.)

[131] *Education and Training in the German Democratic Republic*, pp. 120–4. (Staatsverlag der DDR, Berlin, 1966.)

[132] *Statistički Kalendar Jugoslavije 1965.*

[133] *Vjetari Statistikor i R.P.Sh. 1964*, p. 363. (Republika Popullore e Shqipërisë: Drejtoria e Statistikes, Tirana, 1964.)

[134] *Ibid.*, p. 372.

breakdown of the figures shows that they preponderate in the youngest age-groups—teachers' colleges and other shorter courses—while men are the great majority at the later stages.[135] In East Germany, less than a third of the students in higher institutions, and about a quarter in professional schools, are women.[136] Finally, in most countries[137] fewer girls than boys go on with further education of any kind beyond the stage of compulsory schooling; and in places where there seems to be difficulty in securing attendance, as in rural Albania, girls are less likely to be enrolled than boys. While there is a falling off for both sexes from one year to the next, it is greater for girls than boys.[138]

The reasons for this lag are not far to seek. It is unlikely that any amount of social provision—maternity leave, crèches and the rest, could do away with the differences in social roles between men and women; they can make it easier to enter fields of work that would be otherwise closed, but many practical difficulties remain. Further, social attitudes take a long time to change. We have already seen something of the effects of the ferociously patriarchal atmosphere in the more backward Muslim areas,[139] which goes a long way towards explaining the particularly wide gap between the sexes in Albania and parts of Yugoslavia, especially Bosnia. (It would also explain, incidentally, the rather odd contrast between the overwhelmingly male composition of the primary teaching force in rural Albania and the preponderance of women in similar posts in the towns. Traditional attitudes die harder in the villages, which would make women teachers less acceptable than in the towns. Also, girls who had managed to acquire secondary or higher education would be reluctant to return to the villages and the restrictions that village life in these parts still often puts on women—restrictions which, furthermore,

---

[135] *Statističeski Godišnik na NR Bŭlgarija 1963, p.* 347. (NRB Centralno Statističesko Upravlenie pri Ministerskiya Sŭvet, Sofia, 1933.)
[136] *Statistisches Jahrbuch der DDR 1964.* (Staatsverlag der DDR, Berlin, 1964.)
[137] Not in Czechoslovakia or Hungary, where girls are now in a majority in general secondary schools.
[138] *Vjetari Statistikor i R.P.Sh. 1964,* pp. 362, 364–9, and chap. XIII diagrams.
[139] See pp. 40–41.

they had been led by their education to reject.) But all this applies to other areas than the Muslim parts or the south in general. In the Catholic areas, the traditional view of virtuous womanhood (seen in essentially domestic terms) is still strong, and in particular some of the social measures to free women from excessive childbearing have run into opposition from the Church. Family planning is constantly under attack from the Church in Poland, Cardinal Wyszyński once described women who used contraceptives as "living tombs"[140]—a silly enough phrase, but telling, and delivered by one whose pronouncements still carry much weight, especially with women and especially in the country. Even in the most advanced areas, the idea that women should find their life's work in the home—or, as the Germans had it before and during the Third Reich,[141] *Kinder, Küche, Kirche* (Children, Kitchen and Church)—takes more than a generation to break down.

It must also be recognized that the proportion of women taking advantage of education at all levels is rising fast, and has been rising since the war.[142] Also, although women are in a minority in responsible positions in government, industry, education, etc., not only are there more of them than there used to be, but women professors, school directors, heads of departments and the like are more commonly met with than in the West. Considering the weight of tradition, it is notable how far women have come in what is, after all, a comparatively short time. If they still fall short of the declared objective of complete equality in fact, they have none the less come nearer to it than most peoples elsewhere, and one finds throughout the educational system the assumption that girls should be educated first and foremost as people, not just for domesticity and decoration.

---

[140] Eva Fournier, *Poland*, p. 112. (Vista, London, 1964.)

[141] The Nazis made great use of this phrase, but it was not their own invention, rather the summing-up of a deep-rooted tradition which they took up for their own use.

[142] See any statistical account where the numbers of pupils and students are given by sex in the post-war years.

6. ADMINISTRATION AND CONTROL

Education in Eastern Europe is state-provided and state-controlled throughout. This is an essential feature of the school systems, and has been written into the various constitutions and educational laws since the communist régimes came to power after the war. According to the Czechoslovak constitution, for example:

> All schools shall be state schools. Basic education shall be uniform. . . . National committees shall discharge within the territory for which they have been elected . . . the administration of education and culture.[143]

There are very few exceptions to this. Poland still has a small (and dwindling) number of private schools run by church and voluntary bodies, but nowhere else is this allowed. The provisions of the Rumanian constitution more typically represent the maximum concessions made to the churches in education:

> The school is separated from the church. No religious confession, congregation or community can open or maintain any other teaching establishment than special schools for the training of servants of the Church.[144]

It goes without saying that the few private schools that do exist are subject to supervision by the State. As in this country, control is exercised by central authorities and by organs of local government; unlike Britain, however (but not unlike France), most of the power is firmly in the hands of the central authorities. (Yugoslavia, by virtue of its federal structure and the application of the principle of "workers' self-management" to schools as to factories, is more decentralized than the other countries in its system of administration, and differs in other ways from the general pattern. It will therefore be considered separately in a later section.)

Similar though they are in function, the central authorities differ in structure from country to country. In some cases, as in Russia, control is split between two ministries. Poland has a

---

[143] Detailed provisions of the Constitution, Sections 13 and 124. Quoted in Kathryn G. Heath, *Ministries of Education, Their Function and Organization*, p. 238. (U.S. Office of Education, Washington D.C., 1961.)

[144] *Constitution of the Socialist Republic of Rumania*, Article 30, p. 13. (Meridiane, Bucharest, 1965.)

Ministry of Education (*Ministerstwo Oświaty*) for the schools, and a Ministry of Higher Education (*Ministerstwo Szkolnictwa Wyższego*) responsible for most of the higher institutions. Similarly, in East Germany the Ministry for Public Education (*Ministerium für Volksbildung*) is responsible for general schools, part-time trade schools and teacher training, while a separate state secretariat (*Staatsekretariat für Hochschulwesen*) deals with full-time trade schools, the universities, and other higher establishments, excluding teacher training colleges. Czechoslovakia also followed such a dual pattern at one time, but now has a single Ministry of Education and Culture (*Ministerstvo Školství a Kultury*) for the entire system. This is the pattern generally favoured; Albania, Bulgaria, Hungary and Rumania, as well as Czechoslovakia, all have single Ministries of Education (or of Culture—the titles vary) responsible for the provision and running of all public education from kindergarten to university.

This statement needs some modification, since other branches of of government are frequently concerned with some aspects of the system. This may take the form of occasional responsibility in restricted fields—for example, university professors in Czechoslovakia are appointed by the President of the Republic, not by the Minister or the universities themselves—or it may run to responsibility for whole sections of the system. In Czechoslovakia, the Ministries of Agriculture and Forestry and of Health run the vocational schools of agriculture, forestry, nursing, public health, etc. In Rumania, the Ministry of Health and Welfare, not Education, looks after the crèches and day nurseries, a common arrangement in Eastern Europe. In Poland, the list of governmental and public organizations responsible for schools of some kind or other is formidable indeed: the Ministries of Agriculture, Mines, Culture and Art, Forestry, Health, Heavy Industry, Navigation, Railways, etc.; and the Central Administration of Labour Co-operatives, the Central Office of *Samopomoc* (Agricultural Co-operatives for Peasants' Self-help), and the Central Committee for Physical Culture. The heads of the governmental agencies are, like the Ministries of Education (whether double or single), responsible to the Council of Ministers (the equivalent of the Cabinet) and, in turn, to the Parliament (*Sejm, Volkskammer,* Grand National Assembly, etc.). Since the Party to all intents and purposes is the government the running of the educational system, however responsibility is distributed among ministers, is under Party control. Since bureaucracies have a habit of developing an "apolitical" identity of their own, there is often a higher Party body as well (e.g. in Czechoslovakia, the Department of Schools, Science and Art under the Party Central Committee) to study policy and reinforce political influence on the running of the system.

The internal organization of the Ministries naturally differs a good deal, depending partly on how much of the system they are responsible for. One example of a unified Ministry, the Hungarian Ministry of Cultural Affairs, can serve to illustrate the general pattern.[145] The Minister has under him four Deputy Ministers, each responsible for a different field, namely: (1) School, (2) Universities, (3) Scientific and Technical Education and (4) Cultural Affairs—radio, television, films, theatre and so forth. These departments are in turn subdivided; in the case of the department responsible for schools, these divisions include finance, curriculum methods, child welfare, polytechnical education, youth organizations, adult education, etc. Through this network the Minister controls the running of education throughout the country, making and having implemented regulations on the number and types of schools to be provided by each local authority, the training and qualification of teachers, curricula, schemes of work, textbooks, teaching methods and so on.

This retention of most of the power at the centre, even in such matters as the textbooks and teaching methods to be used in the schools, is typical of the area as a whole. The local bodies have no power to alter the subjects taught, the number of hours to be spent on them, or the methods to be used in teaching them, let alone decide on such matter of policy as comprehensive schooling,

---

[145] W. Kenneth Richmond, "Educational Planning in Hungary" (*Comparative Education*, **2**, 2 (March 1966), pp. 93–105).

separation of courses, polytechnical education, political education, etc. By the same token, neither have the directors of the schools or their teachers. The work of the local authorities is to translate the policy of the central authority into practice, to administer rather than initiate.

The local authorities—Provincial People's Councils, Regional Committees, District People's Committees, etc.—are, like local authorities in Britain, responsible for the usual range of public services such as lighting, roads, housing, etc., and thus correspond roughly to county councils or city corporations.[146] Like their counterparts, they have specialist departments to administer their various functions, including education departments, with general supervisors, supervisors of different branches—primary and secondary schooling, for example—and supervisors concerned with particular school subjects. The departments are staffed partly by permanent officials, partly by practising teachers. The local authorities normally have the task of allocating funds for schools in their areas, providing and maintaining school buildings within the framework of the Ministry's plans, and are responsible for inspecting the schools, local as well as central authorities having their own teams of inspectors.

This is not to say that the local authorities are mere rubberstamps. Although their function is chiefly to implement policy, and although their powers to initiate policy are, by contrast with our own local authorities, severely limited, they do not *only* pass on decisions from the Ministry to the school. In some countries at least they can influence the shaping of policy by making representations to the Ministry on anything from the need for more money for primary schooling to matters of school organization,

---

[146] In some cases the picture is complicated by a two-tier structure of local government. East Germany, for instance, is divided into fifteen *Bezirke* (regions), which are in turn subdivided into *Kreise* (districts), whose councils are the equivalent of county or city councils. Responsibility for educational administration is shared by both levels and their own offices of public education (*Volksbildungsämter*). Schools, for example, are run by the *Kreis*, teacher training colleges by the *Bezirk*. Even when several layers exist, of course, the greater part of decision-making and control is still kept at the centre.

Education Today: Some General Features

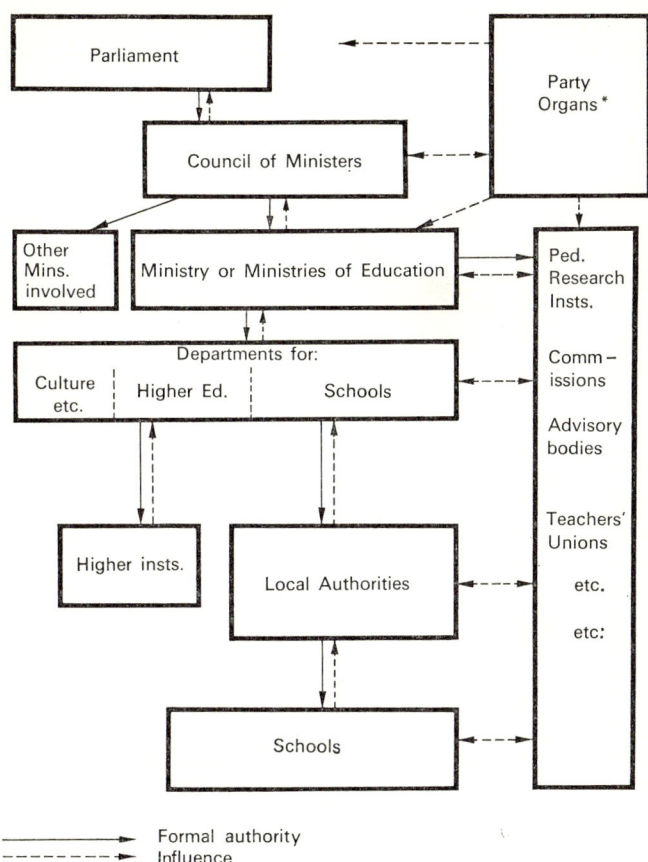

———▶ Formal authority
- - - - - -▶ Influence

*Lower Party Organs concern themselves with the running of the system at all levels

FIG. 4. Diagrammatic representation of control and administration of education in most Eastern European countries.

curriculum and teaching. During what one author calls the "glacial period",[147] local authorities were mainly concerned with doing what they were told, with little "feedback" working the other way. In recent years, however, most central authorities have been taking the trouble to consult with the local bodies continually, especially when policy is being formulated, and paying more attention to what they say. After all, not only do the regional and district councils know more about local needs and problems than a Ministry official sitting in an office in Bucharest or Sofia or Warsaw, but they are the people who have to make the policy work. The East European countries have all had experience of plans drawn up at the centre without adequate reference to realities on the spot, and find that consultation is not only more democratic, but more efficient. Further, there has been an increased tendency of late to leave certain areas of decision-making to the local authorities; even in such an important matter of policy as polytechnical education and production training, a surprising amount of local interpretation is possible. Individual teachers too, though they are not free to depart from the syllabus laid down, are not totally circumscribed. They are required to keep to the general methods approved by the Ministry and taught in the training institutions, but this does not make them necessarily uncritical followers of routine (though, of course, some of them are). The ministerial programmes do not always spell out the details of lesson presentation, and in practice teachers have more discretion in methods than one might expect from looking only at official documents. Also, the system of consultation is well developed in the schools; it is normal practice for the director to sit in on lessons taught by his staff—not just "to see that they are doing it properly", but also to discuss with them ways of improving techniques. It works the other way too; directors are watched in action by their colleagues, and hold group discussions with them afterwards—which according to some, can still be a daunting experience after doing it for twenty years.[148] The staff also have their own

[147] W. Kenneth Richmond, *op. cit.*, p. 93.
[148] Oral communications, 1965 and 1966.

methods circles and study groups, and although they normally need authorization before they can depart radically from approved practice, this is often done. Further, they often pass suggestions on "up the line" to the Ministry which may well become incorporated into normal practice. Heads of schools often regard as one of their chief duties acting as a link between the teachers and the education authorities.

Of particular importance is the work of the various advisory bodies and research institutes. These, at least, can temper the bureaucracy that can always arise in a centralized system; at best, they can be centres of experiment and power-houses of educational ideas. These bodies, and their relationship with the authorities, can differ considerably. In East Germany, for example, the Minister of Public Education has a council (*Kollegium*) to advise him on educational policy, and there are also *ad hoc* commissions, as elsewhere, to advise him and the Council of Ministers on the drafting of laws and regulations, as well as to study specific problems. The Minister is also helped by the German Pedagogical Central Institute or DPZI (*Deutsches Pädagogisches Zentralinstitut*), which concerns itself with a vast range of research and publication. General teaching methods, subject methods, programmed learning, textbook writing, the study of comparative education, relations with other educational bodies abroad, the running of examinations, and the publication of journals, research findings and books on educational theory—these are only some of the Institute's activities. All of the East European countries have institutes of this kind, all of which conduct research over a similarly wide field and publish a variety of books, reports and general and specialist educational journals; in some cases they are also responsible for the running of experimental schools, though most of the major research projects are conducted in a number of ordinary schools by arrangement with the Ministry. Sometimes these bodies are branches of the Academy of Sciences (as in Bulgaria), sometimes independent, like the Institute of Pedagogic Sciences in Rumania; sometimes, as in Poland and Czechoslovakia, both exist side by side.[149] They maintain close links with the university departments of education (often by the simple device of appointing a professor of pedagogy as director), with the administration, and with the schools. One way and another, the work of these institutes makes the classical picture of a simple one-way "chain of command" in the educational system something of an over-simplification.

But important (and often overlooked) though these modifying influences are, the fact remains that the administration of education is highly centralized by our standards. It is less of a rigid hierarchy than it looks on paper, and there is in most cases far more flexibility and room for discretion at local authority and school level than there used to be. But what divergencies there are exist with the knowledge and approval of the central authorities, and the basic principle remains that most of what happens in the school, and certainly all fundamental matters, are controlled by the Ministry, the Government and the Party in a nationally uniform and co-ordinated system.

[149] e.g. Bulgaria: Pedagogic Institute of the Bulgarian Academy of Sciences. Hungary: *Országos pedagógiai intézet* (National Institute of Pedagogy). Rumania: *Institutul de Ştiinţe Pedagogice* (Institute of Pedagogic Sciences). Yugoslavia: *Jugoslovenski Zavod za Proučavanje Školskih i Prosvetnih Pitanja* (Yugoslav Institute for Educational Research). East Germany: DPZI and *Deutsches Zentralinstitut für Lehrmittel* (German Central Institute for Educational Media). Czechoslovakia: *Výzkumný ústav pedagogický* (Educational Research Institute) and *Pedagogický ústav Jana Amosa Komenského ČSAV* (Jan Amos Komenský Pedagogical Institute of the Czechoslovak Academy of Sciences). Poland: *Instytut pedagogiki* (Pedagogical Institute) and *Komitet nauk pedagogicznych i psychologicznych PAN* (Committee for pedagogical and psychological sciences of the Polish Academy of Sciences).

CHAPTER 8

Eastern European Education Today: The Pattern of Schooling

THE countries of Eastern Europe share not only a basically similar philosophy and certain common characteristics in their approach to education, but also the general pattern of their school systems. The following chapters, recognizing the important differences, will deal separately with the various countries. First, however, this common pattern will be briefly described, stage by stage, to underline the shared rather than the distinctive, and to serve as a background against which to examine the national "case-studies".

1. PRE-SCHOOL INSTITUTIONS

Pre-school education is compulsory in none of the Eastern European countries, but a word must be said about it at this stage in view of its growing importance. Unlike the later stages of education, it is not generally free; fees are payable, but they are normally low, and can be wholly or partly remitted in case of need, as determined by the local authorities. Nor is it universally available for all children whose parents want them to go. The figures vary enormously (and are sometimes obscure or ambiguous), but cover a range from Albania, with under 20 per cent of eligible children attending, to East Germany with over half; most countries vary from about 20 to 40 per cent. In spite of the gap in most countries between supply and demand, it is clear that pre-school education plays a much bigger part in the system than in this country and, to point a further contrast, the proportion of the age-groups attending such institutions has grown many times since the war, and large further increases are planned in every case. The authorities, whatever proportion of money and material they actually allocate to it, regard pre-school education as valuable and worth expanding. Certainly, their motives are mixed; one of the declared purposes is, as we have seen, to release mothers for work. This is particularly true in the towns; in the countryside facilities are much more scarce, though the provision of seasonal nurseries at times of maximum activity (such as harvest or sowing) does help. But it would be a mistake to regard pre-school establishments as nothing but institutionalized baby-sitters. One often hears teachers, parents and officials make much of the importance of early training, not in academic skills, but in the formation of habits and attitudes. Care is taken that children should have a balanced diet, adequate rest, training in cleanliness and bodily care, and so forth. Further—and this is difficult to ensure in many homes, whatever their quality—they get used to living with other children, learn how to behave in a group, and have the chance to play with other children of their own age. Since one of the general aims of education is to accustom children to the discipline of the "collective", pre-school education is preparing the children for school proper, and thus answering a need of the child as well as the mother. As one teacher put it:

> Young children *need* to play with others—several others—and learn how to get on with them and do things together. There is no guarantee that they will have the chance for that in the neighbourhood. We don't try to make them all the same, but we do try to make them less egotistical. It's not good for a child to be with adults or one or two brothers and sisters all the time; he must be allowed to be a child, with other children.

Pre-school institutions are of two main types: *crèches* or nurseries for children under 3, and *kindergartens* for children between 3 and the start of compulsory schooling—6 or 7 as the case may be. Crèches are only marginally part of the educational system; they are frequently provided by, and located in, factories, office buildings, etc., though they may be organized to serve an area as well. They are ultimately responsible to the Ministries of Health, not Education, and the accent is on child welfare rather than on training—though, of course, attention is paid to instilling habits of personal cleanliness, regular routine for rest and meals, polite behaviour, and so forth.

Kindergartens come under Ministries of Education, and are more closely linked with the rest of the educational system. The programmes are worked out by the authorities, and the teachers trained, with a view to fostering the children's "moral, social, physical, aesthetic and intellectual growth", and preparing them for school work. This does not usually mean teaching in any formal sense, but rather continuing with welfare and habit-training as before, getting them to draw, sing, model with clay, paper, cloth, etc., and organizing games to develop their use of language and sense of number—acting-games, word-games, counting-games, and the like. Generally, what goes on in the kindergartens is not greatly different from our own, except that one sees less inclination to leave children to amuse themselves in different corners of the room. This is done sometimes, but the teachers are more concerned to direct the children's play so that it will teach as well as entertain.

2. BASIC SCHOOLS

The basic school, comprehensive and unified, from early childhood to middle adolescence, is the fundamental unit of every Eastern European educational system. The length of course varies from seven to ten years (eight years is the most common) and generally provides for the entire period of compulsory schooling from the age of 7 (or 6 in Hungary, Czechoslovakia and East Germany) up to 15 or 16. There are some deviations from this pattern; Albania still has compulsory schooling only till 14, as had Poland and Rumania until recently, and both Hungary and East Germany require some kind of schooling, even if only part-time, at the secondary stage as well. Also, there exists in every country a number of special schools for the mentally and physically handicapped, and for the specially gifted in the arts, physical education, etc., and these may take children from the very beginning of their school careers in some cases, or at some later stage (at the age of 11 or 12, for example) in others. But the vast majority of children attend this single school of eight or more classes for all their basic education, from the time they start school until they leave to take jobs or, more commonly, enter some kind of further course at the secondary stage.

Internally, there is some variation in the structure of these schools. In some countries (e.g. Yugoslavia and Rumania) it is declared policy to move away from the traditional division of the primary school into distinct primary and secondary stages, and attempts have often been made to blur the line of demarcation by introducing "secondary" subjects gradually over three years or so instead of bringing them all in at one point (usually about the age of 11). This "phasing in" happens in all countries to some extent, but in most cases, whether the division is officially recognized or not, the basic school has two clearly discernible levels—primary up to the age of 11 or thereabouts, and secondary thereafter. With few exceptions, children are taught by general teachers in the primary classes and by subject specialists in the secondary classes, with one teacher acting as class tutor to attend to their general welfare and maintain some cohesion. It should be emphasized, however, that even when most precisely drawn, the division between primary and secondary classes is purely an internal convenience. Children normally move to a different part of the building when they go into the secondary department, but they do so as a whole class. There is no wholesale redistribution among classes or selection of the "eleven-plus" type; the children simply move on from primary to secondary as they did from class II to class III.

Like the Soviet basic schools, on which they were frequently modelled, these schools are not only unified but comprehensive and unstreamed as well. There is no grading by ability, actual or innate; intelligence tests are not used, except in Yugoslavia, and even there they are not used to grade the children into classes of sheep and goats. Where the size of the school demands that there be several classes in one year, a number of devices can be resorted to—random selection, alphabetical order, or the use of medical and psychological tests to *mix* the groups as far as possible. Each class, then, is supposed to contain a complete cross-section of ability, and all children study the same subjects at the same pace, and aim at the same standard. Pupils are assessed regularly throughout the year on the basis of homework and classwork as well as tests. Those who fail to reach a satisfactory level have to repeat the year's work, and those who are on the borderline have to pass an extra examination at the beginning of the next session before being allowed to proceed. Firm and over-all figures are hard to come by. Individual schools report anything from under 5 to about 10 per cent of their pupils repeating at any given time; but even if one increases the figure by allowing for the fact that most of the assessment is oral (and therefore more open to leniency), and that there may be pressure on teachers from parents and directors not to have too many repeats in their classes, they do none the less seem to get the majority of their pupils up to a standard that in Western countries is (or was until recently) thought to be possible for only a minority.

This extreme interpretation of the comprehensive principle stems partly from ideological considerations, from emphasis on environment rather than heredity, from a general suspicion of the concept of immutable inborn ability, and from the emphasis on the value of sheer hard work by pupils and teachers alike. There was a time when, in Eastern Europe as in the U.S.S.R., it was often claimed that children were not so much bright or dull as hard-working or lazy, well or badly taught. Few teachers would make such a claim today. Most will quite readily admit that teaching children in completely unselected groups does raise problems, particularly for slow learners who have difficulty in keeping up the pace, and for the more gifted children who may be necessarily held back. But the point is often made that by having them mix together, avoiding segregation into "better" and "poorer" classes, and by getting them to help each other is, in spite of teaching difficulties, a useful social education for mutual responsiblity. The psychological and social dangers of typing children early as relative failures are appreciated in the

East as well as (now) in the West. One teacher put it like this:

> Of course we know that some children can achieve less than others, and that they could be more easily taught if they were put together to work at a slower pace. But if we give in to this too easily by putting them apart (as some of us want to do), they will feel that less is expected of them, and achieve even less than before. As it is, the brighter ones can stimulate them.

As for the problem of the abler children who want to push ahead all the time, there are some moves to provide special classes for them—in Rumania and Czechoslovakia, among others—on an experimental basis. But this idea is gingerly handled; the communist countries, committed as they are to the building of a classless society, are well aware of the social and political problems of fostering the growth of a meritocracy, and any move towards what looks like discrimination must give rise to political misgivings. But there are educational misgivings too, and there has been criticism of such proposals from teachers and educationists as well as party ideologues. Possibly, this may eventually resolve itself into some kind of modified system of "setting", with children in unselected groups for art, music, physical education, practical subjects and the like throughout the school, but with the older pupils in graded groups for such subjects as foreign languages, mathematics, natural sciences, etc., so organized that one pupil might be in the top section for Russian and the second for mathematics. But this is still mainly speculative; moves in this direction in the basic school are as yet experimental and tentative. Apart from these and other devices (extra subjects on an optional basis, for example), the great majority of the children in the basic school follow the same curriculum together until they leave.

There are other ways of trying to help the slower pupils and to provide more scope for the gifted. The emphasis in the class is on co-operation rather than competition; the "arm-round-the-book" mentality is discouraged, and since there are no class places for merit, a child's success in no way depends on another's relative lack of it. In most countries, the other children in the class, or the Pioneer organizations, are encouraged to help those of their classmates having difficulty with their work. Many schools have special study rooms, with a teacher permanently in attendance, where children can go for help and advice; there are also extra classes in particular subjects which pupils falling behind may be required to attend. In some experimental schemes, attempts are being made to organize the classwork so that children can work at their own pace instead of that of the class average. More generally, the atmosphere of the schools, and the presentation of learning as a social duty as well as of personal advantage, seems to keep many children working hard—often with surprising results —who might have given up in a more competitive system. As for the more able children, the schools normally adopt the idea of "enrichment" rather than streaming; that is, they provide opportunities for them to branch out into other fields, or to study some favoured subject more deeply, in the multiplicity of study-circles in the schools and Pioneer Houses and Palaces. It is not claimed that all the problems are thus solved, but there is a great reluctance in most countries to take over uncritically the system of selection and grading, especially if it is done early. There is little objection to the practice of selection and differentiation later on, when pupils go on to different types of secondary education, and higher education everywhere is rigorously selective. But many argue that that is quite soon enough, and that if a younger child is separated from others on the basis of his ability, real or apparent, at (say) 9 or 11, the chances are that he will settle into this level of ability for the rest of his time in school. One also hears the argument that although differentiation of courses and interests is reasonable after the middle 'teens, it should rest on an educational experience and body of knowledge shared by the entire community—on, in short, the basic school.

The curriculum of the basic schools differs from country to country, but again the general pattern is similar. Only in Yugoslavia has there been any radical departure, notably in trying to break down the barriers between subjects by devising a programme on "Study of Nature and Society" which gradually develops into its main branches and eventually into the more familiar disciplines of physics, chemistry, biology, history and geography. Otherwise, the curriculum for the primary classes concentrates chiefly on the mother tongue and mathematics, along with some music and singing, drawing and work study. History and geography appear a little later (about class II or III as a rule), and a foreign language—Russian in most countries—at the beginning of the secondary stage. Biology, physics, chemistry and polytechnical education come in at about the same time or a little later. Apart from schools where it is possible to elect for additional courses—a second foreign language, for example—the same curriculum is followed by all. In teaching methods, too, there is a general family resemblance. The typical pattern is rather formal in structure: the lesson begins with recapitulation of the work of the previous lesson, and the hearing of homework by the teacher—it is common practice for one pupil to be asked to put his work on the blackboard, or read it from the floor, while the teacher uses it as the basis for more general questioning of the class to make sure that the earlier materials has been understood and retained. Then comes the introduction of new material—the next passage in the reader, the next set of physical experiments, the next mathematical process—and the explanation by the teacher, often in lecture form, with further questioning and discussion to see that the major points have gone home. Finally, the teacher draws the threads of the whole lesson together with a brief summary (this is often put on the blackboard or dictated to the pupils) and gives out homework for the next time. Essentially, it is a one-way process, with the teacher imparting information by time-honoured "chalk and talk" methods according to a prescribed scheme of work and a standard lesson-plan.

As so often happens, this needs some further qualification to convey a more accurate picture of what actually goes on in the classrooms. For one thing, the atmosphere in lessons is frequently much less formal in fact than the outline of the scheme suggests. In the case of unimaginative teachers (of whom there are plenty) it can indeed be rigid and mechanical. But the general framework does leave room for improvisation and active involvement of the pupils, and this is much more in evidence than it used to be. It would be rash to assert that two-way discussion, jocular cross-talk and spur-of-the-moment digressions are universal, but they are certainly common. Formality of lesson-structure seems to allow for considerable informality of manner without leading to disintegration of discipline or concentration. Of course, this is noticeable in different degrees in different countries—rather more in Poland and Hungary than East Germany or Rumania, for instance—but nowhere does the picture of a teacher lecturing a passive class according to a stereotyped formula tell the whole story of Eastern European classrooms.

Further, there has been some move away from the formal and traditional pattern of classroom teaching. Something has already been said about the increased development of audio-visual aids, language laboratories, programmed learning and group-teaching methods in recent years. There is a school in Prague where the staff are experimenting with special science programmes for "machine-teaching"; four schools in Warsaw and one in the countryside nearby are trying out a method of teaching that combines the principle of programming with active working in groups: almost everywhere one finds schools experimenting with television teaching, language-learning with small groups of young children, improvement of language-learning by teaching other subjects in a foreign language, and so on. Many of the experiments come under heavy criticism from some educationists for *uncritical* borrowing, especially from the U.S.A., and often for lack of sufficiently precise criteria for assessing the results. But one of the most striking developments of the last few years has been the increase in experiment; and though the experimental schemes can often be faulted (and often are, scathingly) for lack of clarity and control, it has been noticed that experimental *attitudes* tend to spill over into other classes and schools not actually following new programmes at all—hence more flexibility than was thought possible a few years ago.

3. SECONDARY SCHOOLS

At the end of basic schooling, a number of possibilities are open to the pupils. In most countries, he can leave and go directly into employment. This is becoming rarer; already, in every country except Albania, a majority—often an overwhelming one—of basic school leavers carry on with some kind of secondary education, full- or part-time. There are many categories and subcategories of secondary schools, but for the sake of convenience they can be grouped as follows: (a) *General Secondary Schools*; (b) *Vocational Secondary Schools*; (c) *Trade Schools*. The courses offered in many of these, especially the general secondary schools, are also available for adults through evening or correspondence study, either in the ordinary schools or in special adult institutes.

(a) *General Secondary Schools*

These are the successors to the old selective academic *lycées* and *gymnasia* of pre-war days, whose lower forms have since been absorbed into the basic schools. In spite of the emphasis on polytechnical training, their main function is still to concentrate on academic studies, and pupils aiming at a university or college entrance will normally seek admission to one of these schools. The course lasts for three or four years (depending on the country), and culminates in the final school certificate. This is a prerequisite for (but not a guarantee of) admission to higher education. The degree of specialization is, by British standards, slight; it varies from place to place, but the student usually has to attain the required standard in a wide range of subjects. From this point of view, the certificate resembles the German *Abitur* or the French *baccalauréat* rather than the English GCE or even the broader Scottish Certificate of Education.

General secondary schools usually provide some degree of subject choice, though it it not possible to make any hard and fast generalizations about this. In some cases (e.g. Rumania and Yugoslavia) there are clearly defined courses with a bias towards the sciences or the humanities; in others (e.g. Poland, Hungary and Bulgaria) there is a common course for all, but with time left in the curriculum for optional subjects. The position here is continually being re-examined; Czechoslovakia recently changed from three courses to two, Hungary from two to one, with opportunities for options. Either way, this means specialization to some extent, but as a glance at the curricula of the individual countries will show, it does not go very far. While the principle of *some* differentiation is generally accepted, narrow specialization at school level is not. In every case, the "core" of the curriculum is much larger than the optional or specialized area.

In most cases there are more applicants for general secondary schools than there are places. This is relieved to some extent by the drift from general to vocational secondary schools in some countries (e.g. Poland), but the problem remains, and is likely to remain as the level of educational expectation rises. Methods of selection vary—sometimes reports from the basic schools are relied on, sometimes interviews, but in most cases there is an entrance examination as well, usually in the mother tongue and mathematics, though there may be other requirements, depending on the course desired by the pupil.

Sometimes, particularly in towns, basic and general secondary schools are organized in the same building as a single twelve-year school. In such a case, the pupils from the basic school do not move on automatically into the secondary school as they did from class to class. A good many of them do, but some leave to go to other kinds of secondary schools, others come in from other basic schools.

(b) *Vocational Secondary Schools*

Professional, vocational or technical secondary schools—the equivalent of the Soviet *tekhnikum*—have been growing in importance since the war. All the countries in question have schools of this sort at secondary level, except for East Germany and Rumania, where the arrangements for professional education are rather different. The function of these schools is twofold: principally, to train students for a particular occupation, and also to continue general education up to the level of the secondary school certificate. The general educational content is less than in the general secondary schools, and more limited in scope; but, as we have seen, it is still considerable, and the possession of the certificate entitles the students to apply for higher education on the same terms. They are not necessarily limited to the specialized institutions relevant to the particular vocation they have studied, such as technical institutes, agricultural colleges, and the like; but, in view of their interests and the more specialized nature of the courses, this is the line that most of them follow in practice. A wide range of professions is provided for—engineering, electronics, agriculture, nursing, kindergarten teaching, forestry, social work, librarianship, communications, computer programming, and so forth. The length of the course varies from three to four years; in some countries there are also short courses of two years, almost entirely devoted to vocational training, for the graduates of general secondary schools.

Some of the vocational schools are responsible to the educational authorities; it is usual, however, for the other appropriate ministries—health, agriculture, etc.—to supervise the schools concerned with their own particular fields.

(c) *Apprentice and Trade Schools*

For pupils leaving the basic school and seeking a qualification as skilled workers in particular trades, the apprentice or trade schools offer two- or three-year courses of instruction, theoretical nd practical, in the classroom and on the factory floor. Some time is spent on general educational subjects (usually the mother tongue, mathematics, civics, and sometimes a foreign language and natural sciences as well) but this accounts for only a small part of the teaching time, generally 20 per cent or less. The main emphasis is on trade qualification. These schools are voluntary in most countries, but in Hungary and East Germany, where compulsory schooling does not end with the basic school, they are obligatory for all who do not go on with some other kind of secondary education. In practice, they admit the great majority of basic school leavers who are not in full-time secondary schools—almost all in Czechoslovakia and Bulgaria, with Poland not far behind.

4. HIGHER EDUCATION

Whether the higher educational systems are of great antiquity, as in Poland and Czechoslovakia, or of more recent creation, they are distinguished from the system in Britain in several ways. Most obviously, they are all subject to direct state control in a way that Britain's are not. It is difficult to draw the hard and fast line, so familiar here, between the universities and the rest. There are some differences in status and prestige; a diploma from the University of Bucharest carries more weight, and involves a higher standard of work, than one from a three-year teacher's college in Tîrgu Mureş. But technical, medical, agricultural and similar institutions have the same status, standard and, usually, esteem as the universities. This is partly an historical development—compare the West German *Hochschulen*, for instance of which the same could be said. It is also due in part to the emphasis placed since the war on technology and the applied sciences; and it is also due to the fact that many areas of study dealt with in university faculties here—medicine, engineering, law, economics, etc.—are more usually studied in separate institutes in the East European countries. The mystique of "university standards", as something qualitatively different from any other kind of higher education, has therefore little currency.

Courses usually last for five years in institutions of university level, but they can range from four to six years, depending partly on the country but more often on the field of study. (In some teachers' colleges and technical colleges the courses are shorter—four, three or even two years.) The distinction between honours and ordinary or pass degrees is not usual; students opt for their speciality at the beginning of their courses, and at the end take their

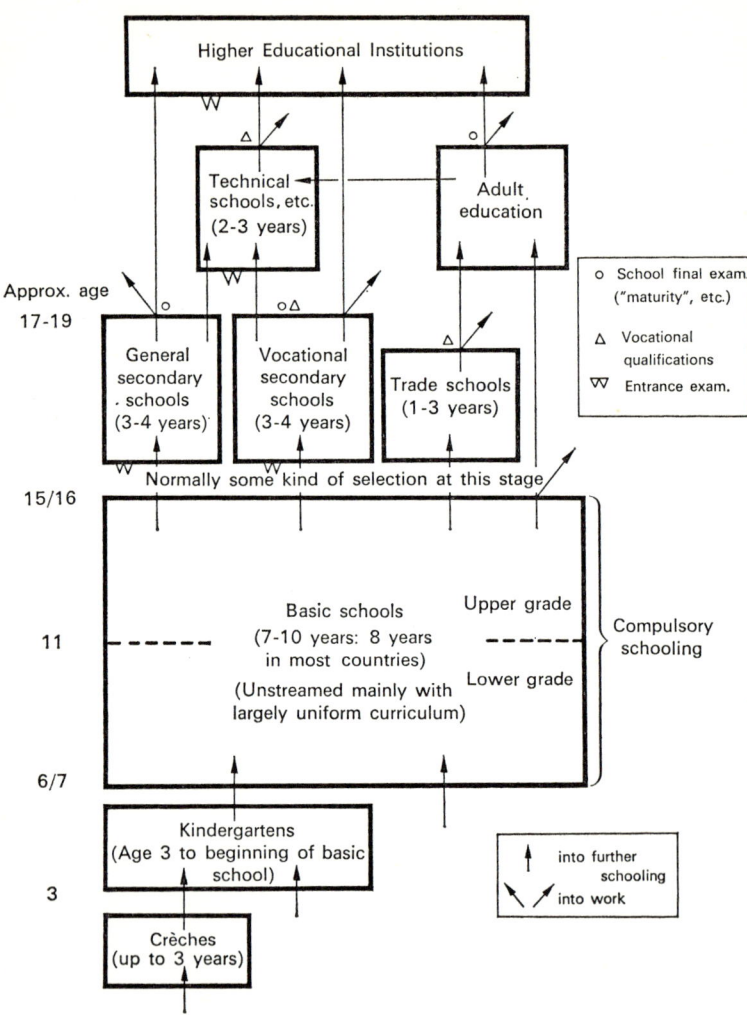

Fig. 5. Patterns of schooling in Eastern Europe: the typical system.

diplomas with or without grades of distinction. Most follow the Soviet pattern of post-graduate studies, with two kinds of degrees, Candidate and Doctor, roughly equivalent to our Ph.D. and D.Litt. or D.Sc. respectively.

Actual numbers of students, absolute and proportional, vary greatly, but general trends have been towards great expansion of the number of places; and, since the number of applicants (thanks to the growth of secondary education in past years) has expanded even faster, there is keen competition for places, with the attendant problems that have already been noted. There has also been a general trend for a greater proportion of students to follow part-time courses. The reasons for this, as we have seen, are partly economic (such a system is cheaper, and puts less strain on the supply of manpower), partly ideological, since this is one way of keeping the students in touch with the realities of working life; and partly because this seems the most feasible way of coping with at least some of the growing number of potential students clamouring at the gates.

5. TEACHER TRAINING

There is perhaps more local variation in this sector than in any other, but a number of common features stand out. One of the most obvious is that the distinction between the different levels of teachers is more sharply drawn than in Britain, a distinction usually reflected in a greater multiplicity of training institutions. Generally there are four levels of teaching recognized and separately trained: (a) kindergarten; (b) primary classes in the basic school—general subjects; (c) secondary classes in the basic school—special subjects; (d) secondary schools—special subjects. Kindergarten teachers may be trained in two-year colleges or teachers' secondary schools. Primary teachers are trained in teacher's schools or, more usually now, in colleges with courses of two or three years. Teachers for the secondary classes of the basic school normally come from three- or four-year colleges; and finally, teachers for the secondary schools are university graduates, who have taken the usual teacher-training subjects (education, psychology, teaching methods and teaching practice) as an integral part of the university course. This four-tier division is not always so precise, since there is often some overlapping. For instance, in Hungary the levels of training are quite distinct, from five-year university courses for secondary school teachers to two-year college courses for kindergarten teachers; there are no secondary teachers' schools. Such schools do exist in Poland and Czechoslovakia; but while they train only kindergarten teachers in Czechoslovakia, in Poland they produce primary teachers as well. There are other kinds of duplication too; in Poland, secondary school teachers have to have degree qualifications, but they can be obtained at higher pedagogical schools as well as universities. To complicate the picture further, teachers do not always teach at the level for which they were trained. In the countries of the "southern tier", where there are still acute teacher shortages in some places, especially in the country areas, underqualified teachers can be found at all levels; by contrast, there is often a problem of surplus in the major cities. Thus, in many Yugoslav rural schools the older classes may be taught by someone qualified only for the primary department, perhaps not even that, while in Belgrade there are schools where the primary classes are taught by university-trained subject specialists.

There has, in recent years, been some move to unify the training system to some extent. Secondary teachers' schools can be transformed into short-course colleges for secondary-school graduates, as is proposed in Yugoslavia, or teacher training colleges can be "levelled up" to university status, as seems likely to happen in Rumania. But such developments take time, and the multiple-level system of training seems likely to be the rule for some years yet.

There is also a widespread network of facilities for the further training of teachers already in service. The Institutes for the Improvement of Qualifications proved particularly useful in the post-war years when most countries had to make do with many under-qualified teachers; emergency and part-time courses helped to close the gap. In some countries, especially in the north, the problem is no longer so acute, but there is still considerable demand for the chance to take higher qualifications, and in any case there is the need to keep up to date with new teaching techniques and developments in particular subjects; in-service training and refresher courses remain, therefore, as an important part of the system, whatever the teacher supply situation may be. The official attitudes to teachers' qualifications vary; in Hungary they are valid for all time from the day of graduation, but in Rumania they are only provisional, and have to be confirmed after a period of teaching service by a further examination. But either way, much is made of the need for continual retraining, whether in the improvement institutes, in inter-schools methods circles, or in the schools themselves. As one headmaster has put it, "Teacher training ends with retirement", and variants of this sentiment are commonplace. The teachers' unions too, by organizing meetings and conferences and publishing papers, journals and reports, contribute in a less formal way to the same process.

So far, we have looked at the background—geographical, historical, social and political—of the East European area as a whole, and examined some of the general features of education in these countries. With this brief sketch of the pattern of the school systems, we now turn to individual examination of the Eastern European countries.

PART TWO

CHAPTER 1

Poland

1. BACKGROUND TO THE SYSTEM

Poland is the Poles. In 1966 both Church and State held their Millenium celebrations—a thousand years of Polish Catholicism in one case, a thousand of Polish nationhood in the other. During this long period, the country has expanded and contracted on the map like an amoeba, throwing out processes here and pulling them in there, keeping little constant but for a nucleus round Warsaw. At the point of greatest expansion, medieval Poland–Lithuania stretched from the Baltic to the Black Sea, taking in areas that were not Polish at all; in her turn, Poland has often suffered loss of territory to powerful neighbours, and from the Third Partition at the end of the eighteenth century until after the First World War, disappeared from the map altogether. Even in independence, Poland has had little experience of permanent frontiers. Disappointed in the West after the First World War, she compensated by acquiring large tracts in the East, where the population outside the major cities was largely Byelorussian and Ukrainian. Emerging again after the Second World War, she lost these areas back to the U.S.S.R., but gained German territory in the West up to the Oder–Neisse Line. Every change has brought all kinds of linguistic and national pressures to bear, since the population-patterns on the fringes of Poland have usually been even more mixed than in other parts of Eastern Europe. Small wonder that all Poles—the *szlachta* or nobility, the democrats of the Republic before 1926, the rulers of "Colonels' Poland" before the Second World War or the communists after it—have clung with such tenacity to their past history and present identity. Small wonder, too, that the national anthem of the People's Republic (the same as that of the pre-war régime) is an exile's song, and sees nationality as a matter of people, not soil: "Not yet has Poland perished while we are alive." This determination to "be Polish" cuts across social class and political alignment. Polish patriotism was the watchword of the communist and anti-communist resistance armies alike, even after they took to fighting each other; the Party and the Church, even when their quarrels were at their bitterest, have claimed to be acting in the interests of Poland, rather than Kremlin or Vatican. It is no accident that both the Communist State and the Catholic Church regarded the recent millenium as something particularly their own, and their own work as loyal to the traditions of a thousand years of Polish history.

This attitude, whether on the right or the left, has often been criticized (by Poles) as too romantic, sentimental, backward-looking, even obsessional; there are some, Communists and Catholics, who feel that this consciousness of the past and obsession with nationhood is holding them back from making real advances. But there do not seem to be very many of them; even the most determined internationalists and modernists have to concede that this awareness of continuous Polish identity has proved useful in stimulating the will to survive.

It was nearly not enough. Some countries, even where there was much damage and loss of life, now see the war rather dimly through the intervening twenty years. But in Poland the scars will remain for a long time. It has already been noted how great was the devastation and loss of life—about 20 per cent of the population—that the Poles suffered in the Second World War. What is sometimes overlooked (though never by the Poles) is that all this was not just the result of the fighting on their territory, destructive as that was; it was a systematic attempt by the Nazis to eradicate Poland and everything Polish, and one which nearly succeeded. After the German invasion, the western provinces were incorporated in the Reich, Polish schools were closed, the Polish language forbidden; the eastern areas, taken from the U.S.S.R.

after the First World War, were reoccupied under the German–Soviet Pact; and the core of the country, in German hands, was ruled as a colonial province, the "Government-General of Poland", to be Germanized later, after the western areas had been digested. In the meantime, only elementary and a few technical schools were allowed, secondary and higher education being strictly forbidden. Most of the wartime deaths in Poland were not due to battle, but to starvation, disease and massacre. Since there is a limit to the numbers that even the most determined of exterminators can shoot and dispose of in any given time, the Nazis adopted a system of priorities. Intellectuals, the aristocracy, the clergy and all Jews (regardless of social status) were to be killed first; the rest would have to wait. The breakthrough in the "final solution" policy came with the use of Cyclon B, large-scale gas chambers and more efficient cremation facilities in the concentration camps. As it was, the Nazis succeeded in killing one Pole in every five; if such methods of mass-slaughter had been developed earlier, or if the war had gone on for even a couple of years more, it is quite possible that most of the Polish people would have been wiped out. There is little doubt that this was the intention.

The fate of Warsaw is a good illustration of this. It is well known that over 80 per cent of the city was in ruins when the Germans were finally driven out; but though much of the damage was done at the taking of Warsaw in 1939 and during the risings of 1943 and 1944, most of it occurred after the rising collapsed; the Wehrmacht went through the city systematically, house by house and street by street, with explosives and flame-throwers, levelling everything to the ground. It was a massive, carefully planned and almost totally successful operation; only the arrival of the Red Army stopped it from being utterly complete. Even today, when the city has been rebuilt, with the entire Old Town painstakingly reconstructed, stone by stone, it is possible to pick out most of the buildings that were left standing—they are the ones pitted with bullet-holes or bearing the marks of repair and patching. There are not very many of them.

If it is painful to dwell on long-past sufferings and the more recent frightfulness of the war (though in all conscience any account must be woefully inadequate in face of the reality), it is necessary to bear it constantly in mind, for the continual struggle for survival has moulded not only the fierce national consciousness of the Poles, coupled with determination to avoid anything of the kind again, but also provides clues to some factors—even apparently contradictory ones—in politics, social life and education. Thus, Poland had made a reputation for "trail-blazing" in many fields, but also clings tenaciously to the past. For a long time after 1956 Poland's communist régime was the most liberal in Eastern Europe, most deeply committed to going her own way; at the same time she remained committed to the Soviet alliance, if only as a guarantee of the Oder–Neisse frontier against the possibility of German revanchism. (It was widely remarked in Eastern Europe in the late 1950's that "in Yugoslavia you can say anything against the Russians but nothing against the government; in Poland you can say anything against the government but nothing against the Russians.")

Relations between Church and State also bear the imprint of the past. Poland has lacked an effective political expression of nationhood for much of her recent history, and has been subjected to repeated attempts—rarely as frightful as that of the Third Reich, but determined for all that—to Germanize, Russianize or otherwise replace Polish language, culture and national identity. As often happens in such situations, the Church filled the gap in the absence of a State, and emerged from the Second World War with the traditional devotion of the Poles reinforced by its identification with patriotic resistance. The Stalinist régime dealt more warily with the Church than was the case in other countries; when the more liberal régime of Władysław Gomułka took over in October 1956 ("Spring in October", as the change was described at the time), the compromise with the Church, and the concessions made to it, were more far-reaching than elsewhere. Not only was the teaching of religion in the state schools permitted once more, but the Church was allowed to retain control of a number of schools. In the last two or three years, relations have deteriorated again, with the two sides constantly sniping at each other. Religion can no longer be taught in the schools, ministerial control over the few remaining Church schools is tighter, and there have been moves to emphasize the materialist side of political teaching. At the same time, parents who want their children to have religious teaching can arrange this with the priests, students can still study theology at the universities, and the Catholic University of Lublin still functions. Catholic publications continue to appear, and the hierarchy still feels able to be more forthright in its statements than was ever conceivable before Gomułka's return to power. It is no secret, of course, that the Party wants to weaken the power of the Church, or that the Church is anxious to retain its influence—any other view would be inconsistent with the principles of either organization. They are, it is often said, competitors for the soul of Poland; the Party doubtless hopes that the influence of the Church will decline anyway, with the advance of industrialization and education, as has happened in other countries. Meanwhile, it has to recognize the hold that the Church retains over most Poles, and refrain from pushing too hard.

The same influences are doubtless responsible for the fact that many features of communist education in Poland are either muted or take on a peculiarly Polish form. As we have seen, the structure and role of the Youth Organizations[1]—the ZHP, ZMS, ZMW—follow the general lines of the organizations in other East European countries; but we have seen some important differences too, especially in organization, and there are others that show up on closer examination. It may seem a small point, but the League of Polish Scouts (ZHP) retains not only the name but also the badge and much of the atmosphere of the old Baden-Powell version. In the schools, they concentrate more on hobbies, excursions and the like, and less on problems of schoolwork, discipline and moral education, than is usual in other East European countries. Their membership in a school may be as low

[1] See pp. 123–38.

as 60 or 50 per cent without anyone getting worried about it;[2] and their room in the school is more likely to be decorated as a forest hut than a committee-room.

The treatment of political education is another example. It is there, of course, and most of the ways of putting it across, already mentioned in relation to Eastern Europe as a whole, can be observed in Poland as well. But there are differences. The use of "visual aids" in political teaching—slogans, banners, posters and so forth—has dwindled practically to vanishing-point. Every classroom seems to display the Polish arms (the white eagle on a red shield, crownless since the war), and there are some schools where they put up pictures of Gomułka as well. There is also the occasional wall-newspaper display condemning the doings of the Americans in Vietnam, or history classroom exhibit on popular protest movements, but that is about all. As elsewhere, the teaching of history and other subjects carries political content, but the emphasis is more "national" than in most countries, much being made of Polish history as an age-old struggle for national liberation. As for subjects that could be called *directly* political, there are two courses in operation at the moment, both taught in the final year of secondary schools. On the theoretical side, there is "Introduction to Philosophy" (*Propedeutyka filozofii*),[3] dealing with logic, aims and tasks of philosophy, dialectical materialism, historical materialism—a fairly straightforward elementary course on Marxist theory. There is also the course on "Poland and the Modern World" (*Wiadomości o Polsce i świece współczesnym*),[4] which in practice is a civics course on the structure and working of Polish society, government, state organs, etc., based partly on straight lessons and partly on discussions of newspaper articles and the like. The treatment is undogmatic, discussion often lively. These two courses (lacking cohesion, according to some, as they stand) are now to be replaced by a new course of "Social Study"

[2] Oral communications, Warsaw, 1966.
[3] Zbigniew Sabiłło (ed.), *Program Nauczania Liceum Ogólnokształcącego*, pp. 170–4. (Państwowe Zakłady Wydawnictw Szkolnych, Warsaw, 1965.)
[4] *Ibid.*, pp. 168–9.

(*Nauka o Społczeństwie*)[5] which seeks to integrate basic philosophical, historical, economic and political theory with more specific teaching about the socio-political and economic structure of Poland and discussion of current affairs. What is notable here is not the political direction—that is expected—but the time and emphasis devoted, in the new course as in the old, to matters specifically Polish.

Post-war Poland inherited a twofold legacy in education—high standards and well-established traditions of excellence on the one hand, and much illiteracy and educational backwardness, especially in the countryside, on the other. Great pride is taken in a heritage of scholarship that can be traced from the foundation of the University of Kraków in 1364 (the second university in Central Europe) to the present day; among contributors to world learning, Copernicus and Maria Słodowska-Curie (Marie Curie) are the best known, but are not by any means isolated examples. The pre-war secondary schools were usually excellent, and selective though the system was, it contained at least the beginnings of a unified system, more open to the talents, after the reforms of 1932.[6] Nevertheless, its scope was narrow, there were too many blind alleys, especially on the technical side, and most glaring of all was the discrepancy between the town and countryside. As we have already seen, about a quarter of the population was illiterate. Nominally, seven years of schooling were compulsory, but enforcement was ineffective; and the classification of elementary schools into three grades of different levels of attainment, meant in effect that only children who went to grade III schools (which offered the full course) had much chance of going on to secondary education. The secondary schools, good though they were, drew on a restricted section of the population. Quite apart from war devastation, the gap between traditional education at its best and what most children in fact got was at the same time an obstacle and a challenge.

[5] *Ibid.*, pp. 158–67.
[6] Ferdynand Herok, "The Unified School" (*Polish Perspectives*, **6**, 2 (February 1963), p. 20).

2. THE OLD SYSTEM

(a) *Elementary Schooling*

The pre-war system, brought into effect by the School Reform of 1932, provided for compulsory education at the elementary or "common" schools from the age of 7 to 14. It has been reckoned,[7] however, that about 10 per cent did not attend, and the figure may in fact have been higher. The "common" schools were of three types: grade III covered the full seven-year course in seven years, and grades II and I took the same length of time, but covered only part of the work. Most of the grade III schools were in the town; in the countryside, 73 per cent of the schools were grade I in 1937–8.[8] They were also usually small and scattered; an elementary school had to provide for four times its present area before the war,[9] and over 50 per cent of all such schools were one-teacher establishments—more, of course, in the countryside. (The present figure is 21 per cent.)[10] In principle, pupils from any kind of common school could take an entrance examination for secondary schools—at the end of the sixth class from a grade III school, or at the end of the entire course from a grade I; but it must be obvious from the foregoing that grade II and I pupils had the slimmest of chances in practice.

(b) *Secondary Schools*

The general secondary school (*ogólnokształcąca szkoła średnia*) started after the sixth class of the common school. The total course lasted for six years, and fell into two stages: the gymnasium (*gimnazjum*) provided a four-year course; at the end of this, pupils could take the entrance examination for the lyceum (*liceum*),

---

[7] *Poland 1944–1964*, p. 153. (Polonia, Warsaw, 1964.)

[8] Mieczyslaw Pęcherski, *Das Schulwesen in Volkspolen*, p. 289. In: Deutsches Pädagogisches Zentralinstitut, *Das Schulwesen sozialistischer Länder in Europa*. (Volk und Wissen Volkeigener Verlag, Berlin, 1962.)

[9] Ferdynand Herok, *op. cit.*, p. 22.

[10] *Polska w Liczbach, 1944–1964*, p. 87. (Główny Urząd Statystyczny, Warsaw, 1964.)

which gave a two-year course. There were four types—classical, humanistic, mathematics and physics, and natural sciences. Fees were charged for secondary schooling; scholarships were available, but only to a fraction—1 per cent in 1936–7.[11] Since the lyceum was the road to higher education, it is perhaps hardly surprising that the proportion of university and college students who came from working-class or peasant families was under 1 per cent.[12]

Vocational secondary schools, though not greatly developed in the pre-war system, came in a wide variety of types. There were "lower-grade schools" (*szkoły stopnia niższego*), providing practical trade or agricultural courses. Entry was from grade I schools or the appropriate point in grade II and III schools. There were vocational schools corresponding to the two stages of the general schools (*gimnazja zawodowe* and *licea zawodowe*). There were also various one-year vocational courses for students who had completed the general schools, trade schools for master-craftsmen and foremen, etc.

Teachers for secondary schools were trained at the higher educational level; elementary school teachers could go either to a three-year pedagogical lyceum (*liceum pedagogiczne*) from the gymnasium, or to a two-year *pedagogium* on the completion of the general lyceum course. Entry to all universities and higher institutions was from schools of the lyceum type, whether general, vocational or pedagogical.

It should be pointed out that this system was a considerable advance on the one that existed before 1932. But the deficiencies were obvious—disparity of provision at primary level, over-examination, high selectivity with consequent wastage of talent, fragmentation of the school system and the existence of many "dead ends", to mention the most glaring. The system did not come to an end with the beginning of the Nazi occupation; although the schools were closed entirely in the annexed areas and partly in the "Government-General", they continued to function. The system went underground; programmes were

[11] Mieczyslaw Pęcherski, *op. cit.*, p. 290.
[12] *Ibid.*

drawn up, instructions passed on, pupils taught and examinations taken at every level from primary school to university. In the "Government-General", the permitted trade schools often provided a useful cover for secondary and even higher education; in the annexed areas, where the very language was forbidden, the Polish school system had to be totally secret—with the teachers frequently paying the price if they were caught, or even suspected.

3. POST-WAR DEVELOPMENTS

The reconstruction of the educational system after the war has already been touched on.[13] The most pressing problems were dealt with by crash programmes—adult education courses to wipe out illiteracy, building programmes to replace the ruined schools and fill the gaps that existed before the war. The anti-illiteracy campaign was a short-term measure, but the problems of school accommodation proved rather more intractable. Much has been done, but much remains, especially as many of the post-war schools had to be housed in temporary structures. Up to the present time, it has been necessary to mount special campaigns for "A thousand schools for the thousandth anniversary" (which in fact produced 1200 schools between 1959 and 1965),[14] and still it is necessary to use many old buildings and organize some schools on a shift system.

The most significant changes in the structure of the system were the abolition of the three-grade classification of elementary schools, the unification of secondary schooling, and the reorganization of the vocational schools. By extra building, co-ordination of the primary schools in given areas, and stricter enforcement of attendance, it proved possible to make the seven-year basic school effectively compulsory. It was increased to eight years in 1961, the change being gradually "phased in" until it became complete by 1966. The two-tier secondary school was replaced by a single four-year lyceum, and vocational courses arranged to run parallel,

---

[13] See pp. 82–83.

[14] *The Development of Education in the Polish People's Republic in the School Year 1965–1966*, p. 6. (PPR Ministry of Education, Warsaw, 1966.)

thus avoiding some of the gaps and overlaps that characterized the old system. A number of organizational drawbacks persisted, notably the gap between the age of leaving school (14) and the age for entering certain types of vocational schools or jobs (15 or 16). The raising of the school-leaving age to 15 was intended partly as a means of alleviating difficulties of this kind.[15]

4. THE PRESENT SYSTEM
(a) *Pre-school Education*

Pre-school education in Poland follows the usual two-stage pattern. Crèches (*złobki*) are for young children up to the age of three; they are normally provided by factories and similar enterprises, and are responsible, ultimately, to the Ministry of Health. For orphans of the same age there are the young children's homes (*domy małego dziecka*). There are about seventy of these, with 6000 children, out of about 1000 crèches with 50,000 children.[16]

Young children between 3 and 7 can enter the kindergarten (*przedskoła*). Some kindergartens are state-run, others organized by the Society of Children's Friends, Rural Housewives' Circles, and similar bodies. Most of them are state-run—nearly 8000 with 460,000 children out of a total of some 13,000 centres with 603,000 in attendance in 1966. The balance is changing, however. In 1965–6 the number of children in state and community-run kindergartens showed an increase over the preceding year of just over 1 per cent and 8 per cent respectively; but seasonal centres and pre-school children's circles increased by 12 and 24 per cent respectively.[17]

In spite of the expansion of facilities there are still not enough places to cope with the demand. The authorities, therefore, have adopted a system of priorities: preference is given to children whose parents are both working, and account is also taken of the

---

[15] Herok, *op. cit.*, pp. 23–25.
[16] Pęcherski, *op. cit.*, p. 307.
[17] *The Development of Education in the Polish People's Republic*, from which all figures are taken unless otherwise stated.

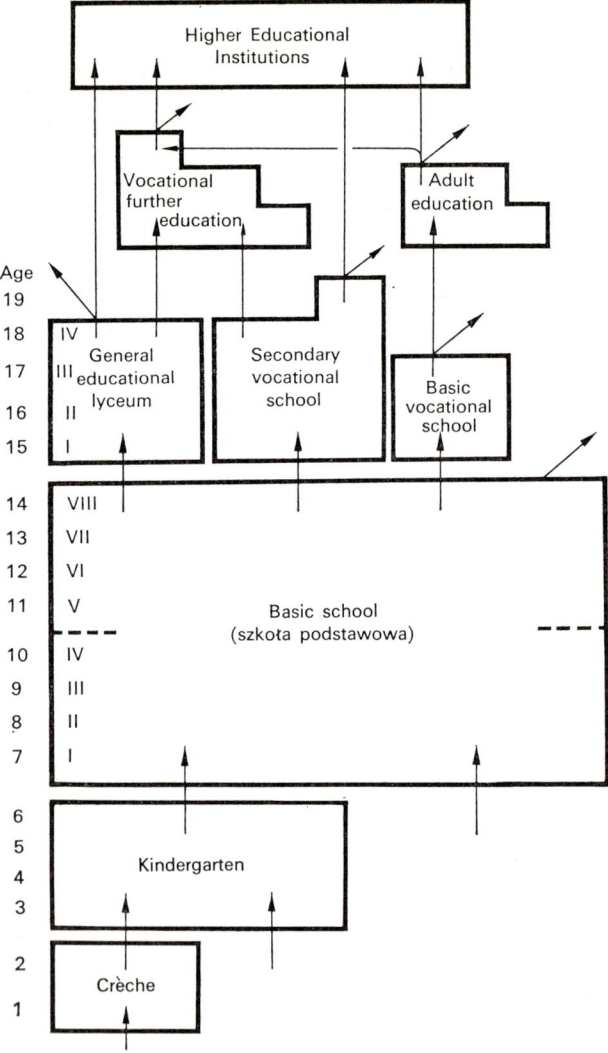

Fig. 6. The Polish educational system.

size of families, housing conditions, etc. A charge is made for the children's meals, according to the income of the parents.[18]

(b) *The Basic School*

Compulsory schooling now lasts from 7 to 14, and is provided in the basic eight-year school (*szkoła podstawowa*). It is divided into two stages: from classes I to IV the curriculum, consisting mainly of Polish and mathematics, with some music, physical training and combined art and practical work (see Fig. 7), is taken by general teachers. As usual, some subjects are introduced during this stage, such as nature study and geography, but the greatest change is in class V, when the teaching switches over to subject specialization. Russian enters at this point, as does history, and other "secondary" subjects like biology, physics, chemistry, etc., come on to the time-table at various points during the second stage, classes V to VIII. Time is found for the additional subjects partly at the expense of others (Polish dwindles from eight hours a week in the first year to five in the eighth), but mainly by the gradual increase in the number of teaching hours per week, from eighteen in class I to thirty-three in class VIII. In the second stage, too, it is possible for a pupil to add extra subjects to his curriculum, such as sports, instrumental music, school choir, or a second foreign language—a choice of English, French or German.

Shortage of space still makes it necessary for some basic schools to work two shifts in the towns, though every year there are more working the "long morning" only (six days a week). The problem of teacher shortage, so acute in some countries, is not serious in Poland. Even in the countryside it is possible to staff the schools adequately; the average size of basic school classes is down to twenty-six (thirty-five in the towns, twenty in the countryside), and is still falling. Nor has it been necessary to accept constant dilution of the profession. By increasing training-college places and facilities for improving the qualifications of serving teachers,

[18] Zygmunt Parnowski, *Education in Poland*, p. 11. (Polonia, Warsaw, 1958.)

Fig. 7. Poland: Eight-year School Curriculum.[19]

Class:	I	II	III	IV	V	VI	VII	VIII	Total
1. Polish language and literature	8	10	9	9	7	7	5	5	60
2. Russian	—	—	—	—	3	3	3	2	11
3. History	—	—	—	—	2	2	2	2	8
4. Citizenship	—	—	—	—	—	—	1	2	3
5. Nature study	—	—	2	2	—	—	—	—	6
6. Biology	1	—	1	—	2	2	2	2	6
7. Geography	—	—	—	2	2	2	2	2	10
8. Mathematics	5	6	6	6	6	6	5	5	45
9. Physics	—	—	—	—	—	2	3	3	8
10. Chemistry	—	—	—	—	—	—	2	2	4
11. Practical/technical instruction	2	2	2	2	2	2	3	3	16
12. Art	1	1	1	1	1	1	1	1	8
13. Music	1	1	1	1	1	1	1	1	8
14. Physical education	2	2	2	2	2	2	2	2	16
15. Class teacher's period	—	—	—	—	1	1	1	1	4
Total hours weekly	18	21	23	25	29	31	33	33	213
Additional subjects:									
1. Western European language	—	—	—	—	—	3	2	2	7
2. School choir							2		2
3. Music ensembles							2		2
4. Sports							2		2

[19] *The Development of Education*, p. 10.

the authorities have been able to increase the number of teachers in basic schools who have higher educational qualifications to 43 per cent; the figure is expected to rise to about 50 per cent by 1967. Where it is still proving difficult to develop such policies as dividing language and practical classes into half-sections, reduce the shift system, increase the amount of activity work, and so on, the obstacle is not lack of staff but of equipment and classroom space.[20]

The standard of buildings and equipment varies considerably. Some of the schools, especially the "Millenium Schools", are as modern, spacious and well equipped as one could wish; others are long overdue for renovation or replacement, and there are constant complaints about lack of money for audio-visual aids, laboratory apparatus, etc.; the authorities have declared in favour of the widespread use of television and tapes for the teaching of languages, science, geography and the like, but so far only 35 per cent of the schools have television sets, and tape-recorders are in shorter supply. But the authorities can sometimes be badgered into disgorging more money, and energetic school directors seem able to persuade "patron" organizations to help; the director of Zamenhof School No. 4 in Warsaw, for example, managed to get 20,000 *zloty* from the police department for classroom equipment, and similar sums from other sources. Many factories have established funds to help schools in their areas, and these can sometimes eke out the official grant. But even in the older and poorer schools great efforts are made to keep them bright. Bare walls and bleak corridors are no longer approved of; a little paint goes a long way, and in older schools the severity of design can be counteracted by the pictures and visual aids that festoon every classroom. Sometimes this is rather overdone; smaller classrooms easily acquire a cluttered look with maps, drawings, charts, portraits, cases of specimens, wall newspapers and so forth on every available square foot of wall; but at least they are rarely dull.

One of the items that can be seen on corridor walls is a list of rules for pupils' conduct, glazed and framed and helpfully

[20] Oral communications, Warsaw, 1966.

illustrated with pictures of children working hard in class, giving up their seats to old people on the bus, helping their parents with housework, and performing other laudable actions; and certainly the usual rules of formal behaviour in school are in force—standing up when the teacher enters the room or when asking or answering a question, greeting their elders with a slight bow, using formal language to address the teacher, and the like. (All this is felt to be particularly important in Poland, where formality of manner that would seem old-world in many other countries is regarded as normal—gentlemen kiss ladies' hands on every conceivable occasion, friends of years' standing address each other "Sir" and "Madam", and the use of even the second person plural is considered boorish.) But formal behaviour does not mean regimented discipline; classroom atmosphere is notably relaxed. Not only are there no uniforms, but the variety of dress tolerated (both for pupils and teachers) would give many a headmaster in Britain apoplexy—Alaska shirts, jeans, girls in trousers—anything, apparently, that they feel like wearing. To the observer used to more traditional pupil–teacher relations, the absence of any tension is quite striking; yet the teacher is clearly and unambiguously in control throughout. There are discipline problems (mostly, it is said, with adolescents from professional homes), but they are reported to be rare and, judging from a few concrete examples cited, fairly mild.

The same programme is in force for all basic schools, whether urban or rural, but there are some departures from this in practice. It would, of course, be inappropriate to insist on the same kind of work for handicapped children, and accordingly the curricula and schemes of work are modified in the special schools (which provide for nearly 70,000 children at this level). Experimental schools are on the increase. Some of them are mainly concerned with trying out new techniques, but others experiment with the curriculum too—Zamenhof School in Warsaw, for instance, is trying out a scheme whereby entire unselected classes learn to play instruments and form musical ensembles, with considerable success. Others are experimenting with new approaches to subject divisions, others (two in Warsaw and one in Kraków) are trying out self-government as a method of social and moral education. It is not easy to give firm figures, since there is some doubt about the definition of an experimental school (as distinct from a school where one or two classes are trying something different). One educationist's "experiment" is likely to be demolished as lacking in methodological guidance, and therefore not an experiment at all. Whatever doubts there may be about their scientific validity, however, experiments are usually popular with parents, since they feel some gratification at the extra interest shown by the visiting experts; the selection of a village school for an experiment in teaching methods (at Bikówek, in Warsaw province) had a marked effect on the amount of interest shown by the parents in what was happening in the school. One figure given by the Institute of Pedagogy, which is generally responsible for overseeing such schools, suggests that there are forty-one of them; but the figure may be larger or smaller, depending on one's criterion.[21] In addition to experimental schools and special schools for the handicapped, there are also special schools for children showing exceptional gifts in music (classes I to VIII) and ballet (IV to VIII). With these exceptions, the basic schools are run on the same lines throughout the country.

There are, of course, no fees for any kind of school, and books are also provided free. Enforcement is now virtually complete; some 27,000 did not attend in 1965–6, less than 1 per cent of school-age children. Of these, over 22,000 had reasonable cause (chronic illness, mental backwardness, etc.). Repeating of classes has been reduced to under 6 per cent, so that now nearly all pupils complete the course. The number of children finishing basic school is now nearly five times the pre-war figure[22]—an even more significant increase than it seems, as the present population of 30 million, in spite of the "baby boom" of recent years, is still

[21] This figure was given by one of the speakers at a conference on experimental schools in the Pedagogic Institute in Warsaw, 22 September 1966. The doubts and criticisms of experimental methodology, and some of the defences, were also expressed at this conference.

[22] *Polska w Liczbach*, p. 86.

less than it was before the war. All this, in view of the unsatisfactory position before the war and the devastation during it, represents an achievement of a high order, quite apart from the advances in the other sectors of the educational system.

(c) *Secondary Schools*

Compulsory education ends with basic school, and it is possible to enter employment at this point, though the labour laws restrict the occupations that can be taken up before the age of 16. This is comparatively uncommon; the great majority go on with some kind of further schooling—nearly 77 per cent in 1965. Of these about three-quarters entered vocational or technical schools, and a quarter general educational secondary schools.

The general educational lyceum (*liceum ogólnokształcące*) is now the single academic secondary school, with a four-year course leading up to the final certificate (*Matura*), which entitles the holder to apply for higher education. In some cases, basic schools and lyceums are organized together as twelve-year schools, though there is some change-over of pupils after class VIII (age 15). The reforms that lengthened the course have also taken the opportunity of revising the curricula and schemes of work—as they had to, since class VIII was the first year of the lyceum until this year. There have been many changes in the content of courses, mostly concerned with bringing material up to date (especially in natural and social sciences), strengthening the polytechnical content (though discontinuing pupils' work in factories), and making available further choices in the course. This last is done not so much by differentiating the school into separate arts and science "sides", as happens in other countries, as by making more time available to concentrate on chosen fields, while retaining the basic course for all pupils throughout (cf. Figs. 8 and 9). The curriculum is still new, and will be subject to further examination and possible change.

In secondary as in basic schools, pupils who fail to reach a satisfactory standard have to repeat the year's work. The pro-

FIG. 8. POLAND: GENERAL EDUCATIONAL LYCEUM, 1965–6[23]

Class:	VIII	IX	X	XI
1. Polish language	5	5	5	5
2. Russian language	3	2/3	3	3
3. Western language or Latin	3	3	3	3
4. History	2	3	3	4/3
5. Poland and the modern world	–	–	–	1/2
6. Introduction to philosophy	–	–	–	2
7. Biology	–	3/2	2	1
8. Hygiene	–	–	–	1
9. Geography	2	3	2	–
10. Mathematics	5	4	4	4
11. Astronomy	–	–	–	1
12. Physics	3	3	3	3
13. Chemistry	2	2	2	2/1
14. Technical training	2	2	2	–
15. Technical drawing	2	–	–	–
16. Physical training	2	2	2	2
17. Pre-military training	–	2	2	2/0
Total hours weekly	31	34	33	34/31
Class teacher's period	1	1	1	1
Additional subjects:				
School choir			2	
Musical ensembles			2	
Sports			2	

portions are higher than in the basic school, as one might expect; but 62 per cent of those enrolling at the beginning of the course successfully complete the final year. The remainder is made up of repeats (9 per cent), drop-outs (5·5 per cent), and those who stay on to the end but fail to gain the certificate. All these figures have shown a steady decrease from year to year.

Like the other schools, the lyceums are co-educational. There are a few—very few—single-sex schools still in existence, but the trend is towards mixing them. The Reytana lyceum in Warsaw,

[23] *Program nauczania liceum ogólnokształcącego*, p. 7.

FIG. 9. POLAND: GENERAL EDUCATIONAL LYCEUM, REFORMED CURRICULUM[24]

Class:	I	II	III	IV	Total
1. Polish language	4	4	4	4	16
2. Russian language	3	3	3	2	11
3. English, French or German	4	4	3	3	14
4. History	3	3	3	–	9
5. Social study	–	–	–	3	3
6. Biology	–	–	3	2	5
7. Hygiene	–	–	–	1	1
8. Geography	3	3	–	–	6
9. Mathematics	4	4	4	3	15
10. Physics	3	3	3	2	11
11. Astronomy	–	–	–	1	1
12. Chemistry	2	2	2	–	6
13. Technical education	3	3	3	3	12
14. Art and Music	2	1	1	–	4
15. Physical training	2	2	2	2	8
16. Pre-military training	1	2	2	–	5
17. Options	–	–	–	4	4
Total hours weekly	34	34	33	30	131
Additional subjects:					
Latin	2	2	2	2	
Choir or ensembles		2*			
Sports		2*			

* Activities are organized in inter-class groups from Classes I to IV.

for example, was a boys' school until recently, but now only the last year is made up of boys only, and next year they will all be mixed. If this school is at all typical in its reaction to the change, there is little evidence that the boys show any resentment at the encroachment—quite the contrary.[25]

Tuition and books are also free in the secondary schools. Meals normally are not, but they are comparatively cheap and can be provided free if family circumstances warrant it. As in the basic

[24] *Development of Education*, p. 16.
[25] Pupils' comments, Reytana Lyceum, September 1966.

school, a doctor and a nurse are in regular attendance (anything from two days a week to full-time), and concentrate on regular inspection and preventive medicine.

It can be seen from the curriculum that all pupils now study Russian and a Western language (English, French or German); Latin can be taken as an extra if desired. The days are gone when the main concern was with linguistic technicalities; teaching is mainly by the direct method, the emphasis is on speaking and understanding (language classes meet in groups of under twenty), and attention is paid to the life and culture of the country in question as well. There are no less than seventeen lyceums where the bulk of the teaching (except for Polish and other languages) is given in Russian, English, German or French. These schools are much sought after by parents, impressed with the splendid command of the language imparted, but though the demand is high the expansion of such schools is not as fast as most would like. This is due to lack of suitably qualified staff; Poland is better off for linguists than many other countries, but the number of teachers competent to teach chemistry in German or geography in French is still severely limited.

Lyceums follow the normal East European pattern of attendance—from 8 a.m. to lunch-time, six days a week. Unlike some basic schools, they do not work a shift system, but there are frequently parallel evening courses for adults in the same building but with a different staff. The Reytana Lyceum, for example, with over 800 pupils, also has an evening school for some 500 adults, including fifty women. The content of the courses and the examinations taken are substantially the same. While the enrolment of adults in basic school courses is falling (as the need for them declines), lyceum-level courses, evening or correspondence, are on the increase. Over 128,000 adults were taking such courses in 1965–6, an increase of over 10 per cent on the previous year.

Some graduates of the lyceum go into employment, but it is principally regarded as a channel to further education. Of the 18–19-year-olds leaving with the *Matura* in 1965, 63 per cent went on to some kind of further study; 28 per cent entered universities or equivalent institutions, the rest going to technical, commercial, agricultural or teacher training colleges.

(d) *Vocational Schools*

Vocational and technical schools are of many types, but may be classified broadly under two categories according to the level of instruction. Basic vocational schools (*zasadnicze szkoły zawodowe*) provide three-year courses of trade-training for pupils leaving the basic school at 15. Some general educational matter is included in the curriculum, but the emphasis is overwhelmingly on mastery of the theory and practice of a particular trade, augmented by practical work in factory and workshop (see Fig. 10). Agricultural schools, with two-year courses on average, could also be included in this category. More advanced vocational education is given in the equivalent of the lyceum, the vocational technical school (*technika zawodowa*). This provides a five-year course (though there are some variations) with a combination of general education and vocational training in over 100 special fields—engineering, agriculture, economics, administration, health service, communications and a host of others. The final examination covers both the vocational qualification and the *Matura*, and can lead on to higher or further education. There are also technical and vocational schools for students who have completed the lyceum or equivalent, with courses of from one to three years, depending on the special field. Unlike the vocational technical schools, they are solely concerned with vocational instruction.

This sector of the educational system has expanded more spectacularly than others since the war—there were over eight times as many students in schools of these types in 1966 as in 1938. Further, the expansion has been much greater in the vocational secondary schools than the basic trade schools. Students in the vocational secondary schools were outnumbered eighteen to one by those in the basic trade schools before the war, but have now overtaken them, a trend which seems likely to continue.[26]

[26] *Polska w Liczbach*, p. 86.

Fig. 10. Poland: Basic Vocational School—Electromechanic[27]

Class:	I	II	III	Total
A. Practical work study				
1. Mechanical	12	–	–	12
2. Electrical	–	12	24	36
Total A	12	12	24	48
B. Vocational subjects				
3. Electrical apparatus	–	2	4	6
4. Electrical machines	–	2	3	5
5. Principles of electrotechnics	4	4	–	8
6. Electrotechnical practice	–	–	3	3
7. Technology of metals	2	2	–	4
8. Machines	–	2	–	2
9. Technical drawing	4	2	–	6
10. Industrial economics	–	–	2	2
Total B	10	14	12	36
C. Auxiliary subjects				
11. Mathematics	4	2	2	8
12. Physics	3	–	–	3
13. Chemistry	–	1	–	1
Total C	7	3	2	12
D. General subjects				
14. Polish language	3	3	2	8
15. Poland and the modern world	–	–	2	2
16. Russian language	2	2	–	4
17. Physical education	2	2	–	4
Total D	7	7	4	18
Total A + B + C + D	36	36	42	114

[27] Ministerstwo Oświaty, *Plany Nauczania Zasadniczych Szkół Zawodowych*, p. 24. (Państwowe Zakłady Wydawnictw Szkolnych, Warsaw, 1964.) Nearly 100 different kinds of course are listed, some taught in the same school as others of the same group. The balance of trade and general subjects is similar, except that waiters' courses include a Western European language as well.

(e) *Higher Education*

There are seventy-four institutions of higher education in Poland. Eight of them are universities, ranging from the 600-year-old Jagiellonian University of Kraków to the post-war foundations of Łódź, Toruń and Lublin—the last existing alongside the Catholic University which deals mainly, but not entirely, with theology and canon law. The number of institutions has fluctuated over the years: thirty-two before the war, rising to a peak of eighty-four in 1954, and now, with the amalgamation of smaller institutions, apparently settling down at seventy-four, though this will doubtless not be final. The number of students has shown a more constant growth; there have been fluctuations here too, but minor ones. The current figure is in the region of 220,000, nearly five times the pre-war figure. Since 1949 there has been an increased accent on evening and external courses, from none until they accounted for nearly 40 per cent of all students in 1964.[28] Part-time students are entitled to time off for consultations with tutors, and special centres have been set up in towns with no university or college facilities; part-time students, however, still tend to take more than the standard five years to complete their courses, and drop out rather more readily.

The policy of broadening the social character of the student populations, and making higher education more readily available, has been helped by the provision of student hostels, and about 60 per cent now receive full scholarships. Nobody claims that this is adequate, and it is recognized generally that there are still not enough places to make higher education as open as most would like. The increase in part-time courses is one way of relieving the pressure, as is the expansion of professional schools. But still demand outstrips supply, and competition for entrance remains keen.

The universities are mainly concerned with the pure sciences and the humanities, and the other higher institutions—polytechnical institutes, art academies, medical colleges, etc.—with

[28] *Polska w Liczbach*, p. 91.

higher professional qualifications. The growth of the system, and the allocation of limited funds, is planned with an eye mainly to the needs of the economy for highly trained manpower. The need for this "social utility" yardstick is not questioned, but some educationists take a longer view. One study of the Polish universities ends thus:

> We must expect that with the spread of democracy, with the development of automation and shorter working days, an increasing number of people... will want to augment their knowledge of the world for personal reasons and not only for professional purposes. Will not the universities then be needed not only to train young people for a profession, but also as places where anyone could acquire knowledge in his free time? In undertaking this task, will not the universities revert to their historical tradition, to the great ideal—knowledge about everything for everybody? To undertake this task would undoubtedly mean fulfilling the dream of democratic universities, which at present they fulfill only within the limits of their function of training for a definite profession.[29]

It is true that Marxists (and others, for that matter) tend to emphasize the value of education, and higher education in particular, in producing people with the specific knowledge and skills required by society. But professional preparation is not the only kind of social utility; and the above passage is a useful reminder that Marxist thinking includes the long-term as well as short-term interpretations of what makes for social usefulness.

(f) *Teacher Training*

At the moment, the different categories of teacher training institutions are as follows:

(i) *Secondary teachers' schools with a five-year course.* These are of two kinds: lyceums for kindergarten teachers, and pedagogical lyceums (*liceum pedagogiczne*) for teachers of general primary subjects in classes I to IV of the basic schools. Students enter these schools direct from the basic school, and follow a course of teaching practice, educational theory, teaching methods, psychology, and general education up to the standard of the *Matura*. Most

---

[29] Zofia Skubała and Zbigniew Tokarski, *Polish Universities*, p. 175. (Polonia, Warsaw, 1959.)

graduates from the pedagogical lyceums take up their teaching appointments straight away, but it is possible to go on to higher education, full or part time, on the same terms as graduates of other types of secondary school. As recently as 1963[30] these schools seemed indispensable for the supply of primary teachers, but now that the position has improved they are being run down. No more students are to be admitted; when the last of the present ones has left, all primary teachers will be trained at the higher educational level, albeit of a shortened kind.[31]

(ii) *The teachers' college (studium nauczycielskie)*. This admits graduates of the general educational lyceum and provides a two-year course. As well as taking over from the pedagogical lyceums in training primary teachers, they train teachers of specialist subjects for classes V-VIII of the basic school. The main emphasis is on special subjects (teachers, especially in smaller schools in remote areas, have to be able to teach two subjects to make the schools viable), and on art, music and handwork (in which they are expected to have some competence, for the same reason), and on teaching practice and the usual theoretical subjects. There is a certain amount of controversy at present about the adequacy of a two-year course for teachers at this level.

(iii) Specialist teachers in secondary schools come from two sources, the universities and higher pedagogical schools (colleges of university status). These colleges were set up after the war to cope with the expansion of secondary education, which the universities by themselves could not do. Although technically on the same level, the two types of institution are recognized to have differences in standard. University students concentrate on a single specialization, and although their courses do include education, psychology, methods and teaching practice, these form a very minor part of the courses. Students in the higher pedagogical schools, on the other hand, have much greater attention paid to professional practice, a more extensive and thorough grounding

---

[30] Bogdan Suchodolski, *Education of Teachers in Poland*, p. 275. In: *The Year Book of Education 1963*.
[31] *Development of Education*, pp. 48–49.

in theory, and are expected to qualify in two cognate subjects—
e.g. mathematics and physics, chemistry and biology, Polish
language and history. It is said that they have greater professional
expertise than their university counterparts, but that university
graduates have a deeper knowledge of their subjects, and at least
one author feels that they have a higher intellectual standard
generally than teachers from the higher pedagogical schools.[32]
That this dualism raises problems is not denied; but since higher
pedagogical schools are easier to establish and staff than universities, and since it is felt that to gear the universities too closely to
the production of teachers would do them no good in the long
run, the division is accepted as preferable to any scheme for unification. They fulfil, it is argued, different functions and produce
different kinds of teachers; and there is ample room in the secondary schools for both kinds.

These, then, are the principal courses for the training of teachers
for general schools. Parallel to these are the various institutions
for the training of teachers in vocational and technical schools,
and there also exist facilities of the usual kind whereby teachers
can improve their professional qualifications while still in
service.

5. PROSPECTS

Prediction is always rash; nevertheless, it is a reasonable guess
that further major changes in the Polish system are unlikely in the
immediate future. The extension of basic schooling from seven to
eight years has only recently become effective, and it is clear that
this and other advances have been a severe strain on what is, after
all, not a rich country. It would be easy to pick faults—much of
the teacher training (not to mention teachers' salaries) is still
inadequate, there is still some lack of cohesion between the basic
schools and some kinds of vocational schooling; experiments and
new methods are sometimes embarked on with enthusiasm but
all too often without sufficient organization and control; ideas
and practices from the West are welcomed more than they used to

[32] Bogdan Suchodolski, *op. cit.*, p. 278.

be—John Dewey, still *persona non grata* in the U.S.S.R., is translated and read in Poland,[33] for instance—but some educationists have been as guilty of uncritical importation of Western ideas as their predecessors were of Soviet methods. Many promising advances, too, are held by lack of money, and others by bureaucratic machinery in the administrative system. These complaints, and many more, are frequently and loudly voiced by the Poles themselves, even by those involved in the running of the system. But against this one must set the great strides made in little over twenty years—the virtual elimination of illiteracy, the unifying and universalizing of basic schooling, and the expansion of secondary, vocational and higher education. The great demand for education at all levels, and the achievements to date, would be noteworthy in any circumstances; when it is remembered that the new system has not so much grown out of the old but has rather been built on its rubble, they become impressive indeed.

[33] *Democracy and Education* is on sale in the bookshops, and the ideas of Dewey and other Western educationists are examined in the standard textbook of educational theory: Bogdan Suchodolski (ed.), *Zarys Pedagogiki* (2 vols.). (Państwowe Wydawnictwo Naukowe, Warsaw, 1966.)

CHAPTER 2

East Germany

1. BACKGROUND TO THE SYSTEM

According to a story widely current in Eastern Europe in the late 1950's, Walter Ulbricht and Mao Tse-tung once met to discuss matters of mutual interest. As they talked about the relative political reliability of different sections of the population, Mao declared that the Chinese revolution owed its success to its strong base in the masses of the peasantry.

"I suppose," Ulbricht is said to have asked, a little wistfully, "you now have the support of all sections of the Chinese people?"

"Of course," Mao replied, "practically unanimous."

"But there must be *some* who are opposed to you," Ulbricht insisted.

"An insignificant number," Mao shrugged. "Any régime is bound to have a handful of malcontents. We have somewhere between 15 and 20 millions, no more."

"Ah," said Ulbricht, "what an extraordinary coincidence!"

The population of East Germany is approximately 17 million.

Apocryphal though it is, this tale highlights some of the peculiar problems of East Germany. Estimating the support enjoyed by any régime is largely a matter of guesswork, but if the stream of refugees,[1] stopped only by the building of the Berlin Wall, is anything to go by, it is probable that East Germany, with a higher living standard than any other communist country, has by far the lowest degree of support or even acceptance of its régime. This is not just because the régime is one of the most rigid in Eastern

[1] Until the building of the Berlin wall, an average of 30,000 refugees a year crossed from East to West Germany.

Europe, though this doubtless has something to do with it. Alone in the whole area, it is not a country in its own right, but only part of one, and a minor part at that—West Germany has a population of about 60 million as against East Germany's 17 million. It is the less prosperous part; and whether one attributes this to less efficiency in the East, or to the fact that the West has long been more highly industrialized and able to offer a higher standard of living, it is not surprising that many East Germans have tended to look westwards, quite apart from political considerations. Further, the régime is so obviously the product of Soviet occupation that it is hard to present this to East Germans as something of their own; the appeals to national sentiment that have proved so effective elsewhere are not practicable in this case. The frontier between East and West Germany is merely the demarcation line between military occupation zones, and in Berlin, where the whole position is reproduced in miniature, the wall, straggling across the city, blocking off streets in a quite irrational way, is an unlovely reminder of the artificiality of the division. From this point of view, East Germany is a political freak; and the fact that the authorities have felt it necessary to use a wall—and firearms—to keep the population in does nothing to make it less so.

It is impossible to get away from the division of Germany even in naming it. The East German régime insists on calling itself the DDR (*Deutsche Demokratische Republik*, German Democratic Republic), while West Germany insists on calling it the "Soviet Occupation Zone", and refuses to have any relations with any country according official recognition to the DDR. Even the comparatively neutral term "East Germany" is not acceptable in the West; since they do not recognize the Oder–Neisse frontier, they use the term "East Germany" for the territories now incorporated in Poland and the U.S.S.R.—Silesia, Pomerania and Prussia—and refer to the DDR as "Middle Germany". In a situation where even the names of countries become slogans, however, "East Germany" is the nearest thing to a neutral designation that one is likely to get.

The carving up of Germany into two states was not formalized until 1949. Before that time, it was intended that the country should be re-united, and that the British, French, American and Soviet zones should only be temporary administrative areas, co-ordinated for the time being by an Allied Control Council. In Berlin, also divided into four zones, a four-power Kommandatura was responsible for matters affecting the city as a whole. As it turned out, agreement was not forthcoming; conferences were held in London and Moscow in 1947, and as both sides continued to show a good deal of stubbornness, the Berlin Kommandatura ceased to function in 1948. In that year, a one-sided currency reform was countered by the Soviet authorities in the form of an attempt to blockade the city; this in turn was answered by the allied airlift of supplies to West Berlin, whereupon the two sides settled down to mutual irritants and a grudging acceptance of the existing state of affairs. In 1949 the Western powers set up the German Federal Republic in their zones, and the Soviet Union transformed their zone into the DDR, consisting of the five eastern *Länder* (states) of Saxony, Thuringia, Sachsen-Anhalt, Brandenburg and Mecklenburg. These were abolished in 1952, and reorganized into fifteen administrative regions under a centralized government in East Berlin. The sealing off of West Berlin completed the process. In this situation it is, perhaps, not altogether surprising that East Germany has been comparatively unaffected by the currents of reassessment and relaxation that have been making themselves felt in most of Eastern Europe. With most Germans living across the border in the Federal Republic, the East German authorities have little to gain from national feeling, and when faced with new problems have often fallen back on dogmatic responses. This is not only the way it looks from the West; in Eastern Europe too they have a reputation for inflexibility. Some of this may be due to more general anti-German sentiment, but it is politically significant for all that.

2. THE OLD SYSTEM

Education in Germany before the Nazis came to power, as in West Germany today, was the responsibility of the *Länder*, and therefore varied somewhat from place to place. Generally, though, it followed a standard pattern of early selection for high-standard secondary schools, with a terminal elementary school for those not so selected, and compulsory part-time trade-training for all young people up to the age of 18 who were not in full-time schooling. The main stages of schooling before the Third Reich were as follows:

(a) *Elementary schools (Grundschule or Volksschule)*. Children entered at the age of 6; a minority were selected for secondary education (*Oberschule*) at the age of 10, the rest staying on in the elementary school's upper grade (*Oberstufe*) until about the age of 14.

(b) *Secondary schools (Oberschulen)*. These were of various types: the *Gymnasium* gave a course emphasizing the classics from the age of 10 up to 19, ending with the *Abitur* examination (otherwise known as the *Reifeprüfung* or "test of maturity") which gave the right of entry to higher education. This was the secondary school which enjoyed the highest esteem, but there were also the *Realschulen* and *Oberrealschulen*, emphasizing modern languages and the sciences, and the *Deutsche Oberschule*, which concentrated on German language, literature, history and culture. For pupils who missed being selected at 10 (due to attending small country schools, for example) there was the "build-up school" (*Aufbauschule*), which provided a concentrated course from 12 to 19 up to *Abitur* standard. The standard of academic attainment in secondary schools was high, and selection severe. The middle school (*Mittelschule*) provided a less demanding secondary course, and did not aim for *Abitur* standard.

(c) *Vocational schools*. Trade or vocational schools (*Berufsschulen*) gave part-time courses up to the age of 18. Their main emphasis was on trade qualification, but there was also an element of general education. They were made compulsory for all elementary school leavers in 1919. At a higher level there were the *Fachschulen*, full-time technical schools.

(d) *Higher education.* This was given at universities and *Hochschulen* (more specialized colleges of university status). The organization of courses was extremely flexible; students with the *Abitur* could enter by right, and took whatever classes they pleased in what time they pleased. The only degree was the doctorate, which most students did not trouble to take. If they were seeking a professional qualification, they took a state (not university) examination whenever they felt ready.

Hitler came to power in 1933, and planned radical changes in the educational system. Most of them did not in fact come into operation until 1938, and thereafter the war held up many more. The principal changes were the centralization of the school system under the National Ministry of Education and Youth Welfare, and the nazification of the teaching profession and of the school curricula. The structure of the system changed little; the pattern of primary and secondary schooling inherited from the Weimar Republic was retained, with some shifts of emphasis; more attention was now paid at secondary level to the *Deutsche Oberschule* (as one might expect) which became the most prestigious of the *Oberschulen*, followed by the *Aufbauschule*. There were also the Nazi Party schools—the *Adolf Hitler Schule*, *Napola* (*Nationalpolitische Erziehungsamt*, national political education centre), and the *Ordensburgen* or "Castles of the Order", which were designed to provide a nine-year training for the Party élite. At the university level, a *Hochschule der Partei* (Party college) was projected, but never came to anything.

3. POST-WAR DEVELOPMENTS

The school system of the Nazi period came to an end with Germany's defeat and the temporary closing of the schools throughout the country. In every zone, the occupying powers issued orders for the reorganization of the schools—in the Soviet zone, the relevant decree was Order No. 40 of August 1945, signed by Marshall Koniev, Military Commander of the Zone and

Commander-in-Chief of the Soviet Forces in Germany. This Order required the eradication of all manifestations of Nazism, militarism and racialism, ordered the screening of all teachers to exclude Nazis and Nazi sympathizers, and provided for the reopening of the schools at the beginning of October 1945, with new textbooks and new curricula to be approved by the occupying authorities.[2] The East German school system, like the East German state, was thus the creation of the Soviet Union. It was not alone in this; the orders issued by the Western commanders were very similar to the Soviet Order No. 40, except that they did not ban private schools. Otherwise, they ran along much the same lines. While there still seemed a chance of organizing Germany as a single unit, the four powers took some joint decisions on education as on other matters. In 1947, for instance, Control Council Directive No. 54, adopted by the four powers, declared in favour of a unified system: "Schools for the compulsory period should form a comprehensive educational system. The terms 'elementary education' and 'secondary education' should mean two consecutive levels of instruction, not two types or qualities of instruction which overlap."[3] This had been proposed by the United States authorities; it had, however, been operated already in the Soviet zone for a year, and was not implemented in the other zones.

The new system was brought into force by the "Law for the Democratization of the German Schools",[4] passed by the five East German *Länder* (with identical texts) between 22 May and 6 June 1946. It declared that all children had an equal right to education; it made education the responsibility of the State (thus ruling out any private schools); and it provided the legal basis for the reconstructed school system. Broadly, this was based on a common comprehensive eight-year school, from 6 to 14 years of

---

[2] *Befehl* Nr. 40. *Betrifft: Die Vorbereitung der Schule zum Schulbetrieb.* In: Wilhelm Schneller, *Die deutsche demokratische Schule*, pp. 16–18. (Volk und Wissen Verlag, Berlin, 1955.)

[3] Control Council Directive No. 54: *Basic Principles of Education in Germany.* Quoted in Paul S. Bodenmann, *Education in the Soviet Zone of Germany*, p. 14. (U.S. Office of Education, Washington D.C., 1959.)

[4] *Gesetz zur demokratisierung der Deutschen Schulen. Ibid.*, pp. 12 ff.

age, followed by a four-year secondary school, or a two-year middle school plus a two-year secondary school, or by a variety of trade and technical schools. Since many of the technical and vocational schools provided courses equivalent in standard and qualification to the secondary schools, this kept open alternative routes to higher education.

On the foundation of the DDR in 1949, many features of the reformed school system were written into the Constitution.[5] These included not only the usual provisions about the right of all citizens to education, the purposes of education, the separation of school and church, and so forth, but also listed the types of schools, described their function and prescribed the length of compulsory schooling. Since that time there have been further enactments, dealing mainly with the extension of the system, increasing the attention paid to polytechnical and vocational education, and strengthening the political orientation of the system at all levels. The 1959 "Law on the Socialist Development of Education in the DDR"[6] was partly a piece of consolidating legislation, but it also made some major changes in the structure of the system. The most important of these was the extension of the basic school to ten years (6 to 16) for all pupils. It was divided into a lower grade (*Unterstufe*) from classes 1 to 4, and a higher grade (*Oberstufe*) from classes 5 to 10. For the time being, the four-year secondary school (age 14 to 18) was kept as it was, thus involving some degree of selection two years before the end of basic schooling (see Fig. 11). It was also possible to enter vocational schools (*Berfusschulen*) at this stage. For those leaving the basic school at 16, there were various types of *Berufsschulen*, some of which offered *Abitur* classes, thus providing another channel to higher education. From the ordinary *Berufsschulen* one could go into employment, or to higher vocational schools, evening secondary schools, adult courses, etc., and thence, again, to higher education.

[5] Constitution, Articles 34–40. *Ibid.*, pp. 7–8.
[6] *Gesetz über die sozialistische Entwicklung des Schulwesens in der Deutschen Demokratischen Republik, 1958.* In: Ministerium für Volksbildung, *Sozialistische Schule*, pp. 140–59. (Staatsverlag der DDR, Berlin, 1964.)

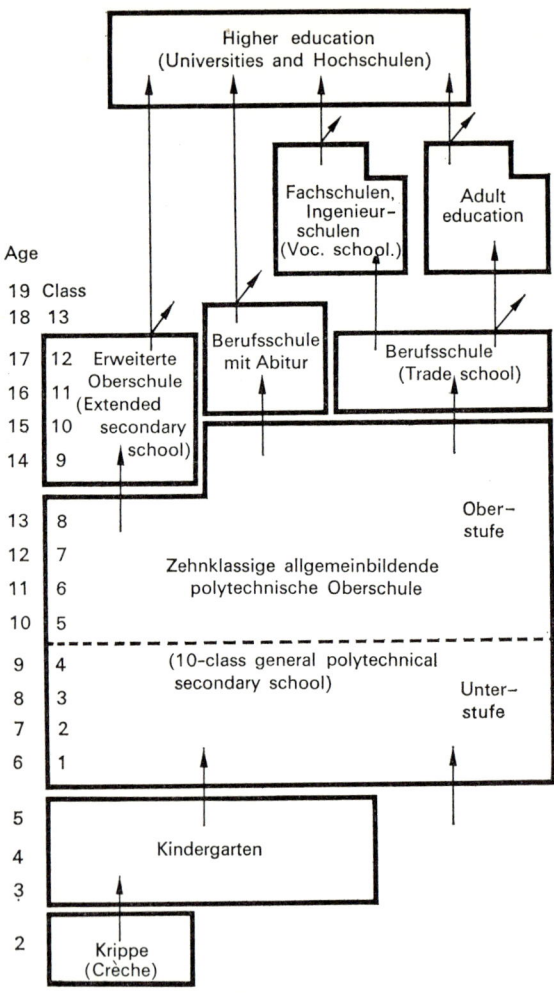

Fig. 11. East Germany: School system 1959–65.

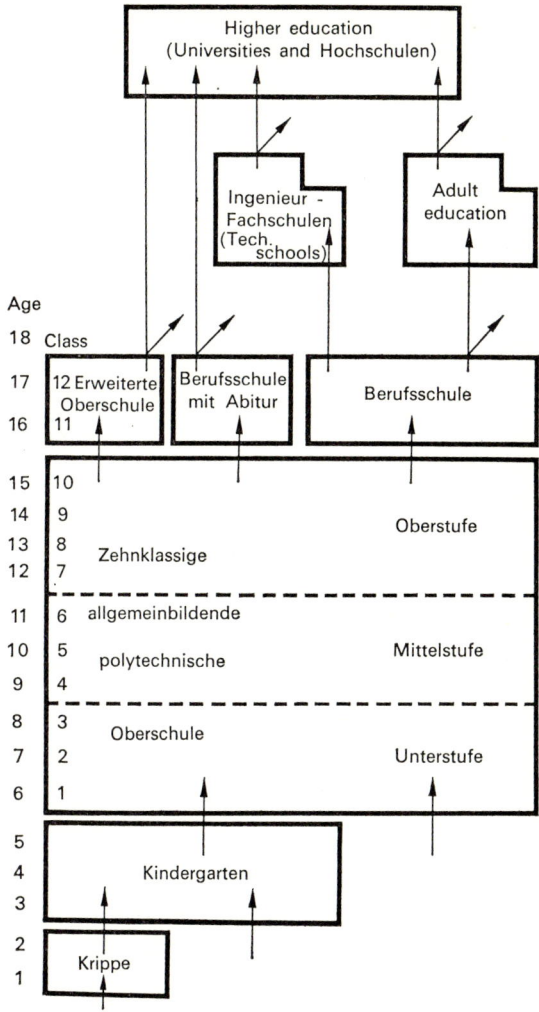

Fig. 12. East Germany: School system (1965).

To give some idea of the detail prescribed by this law and its supplements, it is worth noting in passing that various sections dealt thoroughly with the exact procedure for school discipline, rewards and punishments, the organization of teachers' councils and parents' committees, the professional titles that could be used by teachers, the programmes of polytechnical education, the work of the Youth organizations, and a host of other topics, no important aspect of the educational system, in school or out, being overlooked.[7]

Among other developments in the post-war period was the expansion of adult education courses, notably the evening secondary school (the part-time equivalent of the secondary school comprising classes 9 to 12) and the Workers' and Peasants' Faculties. These last, run by the universities and other higher institutions, were another device for keeping open more paths to higher education. They provided three-year preparatory classes for adults, usually those who had completed vocational training and who wanted to enter higher education after some time in productive work. In the field of higher education, the most marked developments were the increase in the number of specialized courses and the increased emphasis on part-time study.

4. THE PRESENT SYSTEM

The present school system in East Germany has been canvassed for some time. Some of its features were foreseen in the Law of 1959, others assumed in later writings from authoritative sources. In 1963 a State Commission was set up to examine the details of reorganizing and integrating the system, and it was brought into effect by the "Law on the Integrated Socialist Educational System" of 1965.[8] Like its predecessors, the Law reiterates the principles of state control, free instruction, compulsory basic schooling, and regulates the provisions for vocational, further and higher

---

[7] *Sozialistische Schule*, pp. 229 ff., 231, 232 ff., 234–5, 326 ff.
[8] *Gesetz über das einheitliche sozialistische Bildungssystem*, 1965. In: *Unser Bildungssystem—wichtiger Schritt auf dem Wege zur gebildeten Nation*, pp. 83–133. (Kanzlei des Staatrates der DDR, 1965.)

education. There is now to be a uniform basic system with some "differentiation in the education facilities in the upper levels according to social requirements and individual talents".[9] Naturally, there has to be a period of transition from the old system to the new, and some features of the 1959 system are likely to linger until the transformation is complete; this is recognized by the Law, which provides for the gradual implementation of the reforms. The principal types of schooling under the new system are as follows:

(a) *Pre-school Education*

Pre-school institutions are of the usual two main types, crèches for children up to the age of three, and kindergartens for children between 3 and 6. Crèches (*Kinderkrippen*) are principally for children whose mothers are working or studying, and are mainly concerned with health, welfare and habit training. "The daily course of the crèche is to be arranged so that the children are accustomed to order and regularity, and their independence promoted in accordance with their age."[10] Crèches can be organized by factories and co-operatives, and have to be licensed by the state. Their plans of organization and activity are drawn up by the Ministry of Health. About 12 per cent of children under 3 are in crèches, compared with 6 per cent in 1955 and 0·6 per cent in 1950, not counting the additional seasonal crèches.[11]

Kindergartens (*Kindergärten*) also give preference to children whose mothers are working or studying, but they are much more widely available—there are over four times as many kindergarten as crèche places.[12] The law provides for their supervision by the Ministry of Public Education, state licensing, co-operation with parents, and the recognition of play as the most important activity at this stage. Kindergartens are concerned with more than babyminding; children are prepared for school work by getting used to

[9] *Ibid.*, p. 88.
[10] *Statistisches Jahrbuch der DDR 1964.* (Staatsverlag der DDR, Berlin, 1964.)
[11] *Ibid.*
[12] *1965 Law* (in *op. cit.*), p. 93.

doing things together, by attention to their increased command of language, and through opportunities for painting, drawing, modelling, singing and dancing "to awaken their sense of the beautiful in nature and in our social life". At a simple level, their political and moral education is to be taken in hand too:

> The children are to be educated to love their socialist homeland and peace. Friendship among the children of all nations, mutual readiness to help, team spirit, truthfulness and love and respect for their parents and all other working people are to be developed. Firm habits are to be developed by means of a meaningfully planned day. The children are to be accustomed to taking over simple duties and helping themselves independently.[13]

Kindergartens are the responsibility of the local councils, and are also provided by co-operatives and industrial enterprises, especially those employing women. Kindergarten sections are also found in children's weekly homes (*Kinderwochenheime*), residential schools (age 3 to 12) where children are admitted at the request of their parents. Admission is limited to the children of working mothers, and account is also taken of such factors as housing conditions, family size, health and the like. There are also special kindergartens for children suffering from mental or physical handicaps.

(b) *The Basic School*

Basic schooling in East Germany is now provided by the single uniform *Ten-class general educational polytechnical secondary school* (*Zehnklassige allgemeinbildende polytechnische Oberschule*), from the age of 6 to 16. Like its counterparts elsewhere it is co-educational, unified and comprehensive, though this does not exclude some differentiation in the later classes. It is now divided into three stages: the lower grade (*Unterstufe*) from classes 1 to 3; the intermediate grade (*Mittelstufe*), classes 4 to 6; and the upper grade (*Oberstufe*), classes 7 to 10.

The lower grade concentrates on the basic skills and fundamental subjects—reading, writing, German language, mathematics—together with visual arts, music and physical education.

[13] *1965 Law*, p. 94.

FIG. 13. EAST GERMANY: CURRICULUM OF THE TEN-YEAR POLYTECHNIC SECONDARY SCHOOL[14] (BEFORE 1965)

Class:	Unterstufe				Oberstufe						Total hours
	1	2	3	4	5	6	7	8	9	10	
1. German language and literature	9	12	14	16	7	6	5	5	5	4	3154
2. Russian language	–	–	–	–	6	5	4	3	3	3	912
3. Mathematics	5	6	6	6	6	6	6	5	5	5	2128
4. Physics	–	–	–	–	–	3	2	3	3	4	570
5. Astronomy	–	–	–	–	–	–	–	–	–	1	38
6. Chemistry	–	–	–	–	–	–	2	3	3	4	456
7. Biology	–	–	–	–	3	2	2	2	2	2	494
8. Geography	–	–	–	–	2	2	2	2	2	1	418
9. Work training	1	1	1	2	2	2	–	–	–	–	342
10. Needlework	–	–	1	1	–	–	–	–	–	–	76
11. Technical drawing	–	–	–	–	–	–	1	1	1	1	152
12. Socialist production	–	–	–	–	–	–	3	4	4	4	570
13. History	–	–	–	–	–	2	2	2	2	2	418
14. Citizenship	–	–	–	–	–	–	–	–	1	2	114
15. Drawing	1	1	1	1	1	1	1	1	1	–	342
16. Music	1	1	1	1	1	1	1	1	1	1	380
17. Physical education	2	2	3	3	3	3	2	2	2	2	912
Total hours per week:	19	23	27	30	32	33	33	34	35	36	11,476
Optional subjects:											
Second foreign language	–	–	–	–	–	–	4	3	3	2	456
Needlework	–	–	–	–	1	1	–	–	–	–	

[14] Karl-Heinz Günther (ed.), *Die Schule in der Deutschen Demokratischen Republik*, p. 229. In: Deutsches Pädagogisches Zentralinstitut, *Das Schulwesen sozialistischer Länder in Europa*. (Volk und Wissen Volkseigener Verlag, Berlin, 1962.)

Work-training appears as a fundamental subject right from the start, and involves simple manual skills, modelling, and "a first survey of the economy of their home region". Direct political instruction does not appear until later, but already children are to be "made aware of their social surroundings" and "acquire the first knowledge and perceptions of nature, work and socialist society" through their general studies.[15]

All these subjects are continued and developed in the intermediate grade, and further studies are added—natural science, social science, foreign language. The natural science group, intended to lead children "to the perception of the laws of nature, their effectiveness and possibilities of application", comprises biology, chemistry, and physics. Social study embraces history and geography; citizenship and political theory are not yet taught directly, though as we have seen these studies can be used to convey political judgements. Indeed, this is declared to be one of their principal objectives.[16] Foreign language means, at this stage, Russian, compulsory for all pupils, with particular emphasis on the mastery of the spoken language. At this stage too work instruction is elaborated to familiarize pupils with some of the basic techniques of production in rather more detail than the elementary handwork of the lower grade. Further, children are acquainted through visits and excursions with the main occupations in their area, and some steps are taken to develop embryonic vocational interests, though vocational training is not attempted yet. In physical education, more attention is paid to teaching particular skills—swimming is part of the regular programme—sports competitions are organized, and pupils introduced to a wide range of sporting activities outside schools hours. In this, as in other fields (social education, work study, etc.), the role of the Ernst Thälmann Pioneer Organization is stressed both in the Law and in current practice.

The actual content of the curriculum changes little during the final upper grade. There are some innovations; civic education is

[15] *1965 Law*, p. 96.
[16] *1965 Law*, p. 98.

introduced in the last two years with the aim, as we have seen, of introducing the pupils to the study of Marxism–Leninism. In addition to Russian, a second foreign language is now compulsory for all pupils; this is usually English, though French and Spanish are sometimes taught. In literature, independent reading is especially encouraged, and the school course makes a particular point of introducing the pupils to socialist realism. The natural sciences (now defined as physics, astronomy, chemistry, biology and physical geography) concentrate on experiment and observation, the deduction of scientific laws, appreciation of the applied value of the sciences and the development of a "scientific picture of animate and inanimate nature".[17] In art and music, special attention is paid to practical activity as well as appreciation; in physical education, all are to take part in sports and reach the "sports badge" standard, a kind of basic attainment test, not a competitive award. The greatest change of emphasis at this stage is on the labour-polytechnical side. So far, this part of the course has consisted chiefly of basic instruction in handicrafts, woodwork, metalwork and horticulture, in school workshops and plots, with some visits to enterprises outside the school. In the upper grade, however, the course of polytechnical instruction becomes more intensive and can be differentiated according to the kind of area in which the school is situated and the pupils' vocational interests. In the industrial areas the pupils are taught engineering and electrotechnics, and also have a basic course in agricultural production; in the country there are basic courses in engineering and electrotechnics, and much more extensive studies in animal husbandry and plant cultivation.[18] Unlike some other countries (e.g. Poland) East Germany has kept up, and even developed, the practice of carrying on polytechnical instruction in factories and farms. As the authorities see it, this has political as well as practical value. "The Socialist attitude towards labour is to be especially developed through close contacts between the

[17] *1965 Law*, p. 99.
[18] *Polytechnische Bildung und Erziehung in der DDR*, pp. 52–53, 60–61. (Volk und Wissen Volkseigener Verlag, Berlin, 1962.)

pupils and the teams of working people, and through independent, responsible execution of production tasks."[19] Instruction is not only polytechnical, furthermore; it can be vocational as well. Provisions are made whereby some pupils can undergo the bases of vocational training in classes 9 and 10, while still attending the ten-year school. Other pupils who receive what is described as "pre-vocational polytechnical training"—that is, a wider course with some reference to a number of occupations—will have vocational training proper after leaving the basic school. In either case, of course, the greater part of teaching time is concerned with general educational subjects.

Pupils in the East German basic schools are promoted from one class to the next in the same way as in other Eastern European countries—continuous assessment (on a marking scale of 1 down to 5, exactly the reverse of the Soviet system) of classwork and homework, with those who fail to make the grade repeating the year's work. As in other countries, the number repeating is reported to be low; the great majority go on with the same programme from class to class. One clear departure from this comprehensive principle is the system of special schools for the highly gifted, which cover a wider range than is usual in Eastern European countries—sport, technical studies, art, music, languages, mathematics, natural sciences, etc. These schools either take children from the beginning of their school careers or at later stages, and are meant specifically for the development of corps of specialists in the appropriate fields. The courses are the same as in the general schools, apart from a massive addition of the special subjects, and lead on to the relevant higher educational institutttions. There are also special classes, run on exactly the same lines, located in ordinary schools. Classes are notably smaller than in the ordinary schools—fifteen pupils per class as against a national average of twenty-eight.[20] These schools are supervised directly by the Minister, who is empowered to determine their number and the special subjects that will be provided. At the moment, children

---

[19] *1965 Law, loc. cit.*
[20] *Statistisches Jahrbuch der DDR 1964.*

in special schools and classes make up less than 3 per cent of the total,[21] and it is clear that the numbers are to be kept strictly limited.[22] Presumably it is felt that as long as they deal with specific areas of talent, and involve only a few pupils anyway, they are not likely to assume the proportions of a privileged sector of the school system or disrupt the comprehensive principle too far. Also separate from the uniform system are the schools for the handicapped (*Sonderschulen*). Children enrolled in these schools follow programmes modified according to their disabilities, with vocational training if possible. They are run by the Ministry of Public Education, in close co-operation with the Ministry of Health.

(c) *Secondary and Vocational Schooling*

If it is difficult in Eastern European countries to draw a definite line between general secondary education and vocational training, in East Germany it is impossible. Even when the four-year secondary school started two years before the end of the ten-year school and taught to the *Abitur* standard throughout, the official view was that the basic school followed by vocational training should be "the chief way for the development of technical school and university cadres".[23] There are differences of emphasis, but general secondary and vocational schools overlap so much that they are best dealt with together. For the pupil leaving the ten-year school, the following possibilities exist.

(i) *The extended polytechnical secondary school* (*Erweiterte polytechnische Oberschule*). Formerly of four classes (the 9th to the 12th), this type of school now offers a two-year course (classes 11 and 12) leading to the *Abitur* and the chance of entry to higher education. At the same time, vocational training is given. This has given rise to a number of problems and some criticism; some feel that polytechnical education is all very well, but that to insist on vocational training at this stage as well is too expensive and wasteful,

[21] *Ibid.*
[22] *1965 Law*, p. 102.
[23] Paul S. Bodenmann, *op. cit.*, p. 27.

Fig. 14. East Germany: Extended Secondary School Curriculum before 1965[24]

Class:	9 A	9 B	9 C	10 A	10 B	10 C	11 A	11 B	11 C	12 A	12 B	12 C	Total A	Total B	Total C
1. German	4	4	5	4	4	4	4	4	3	4	4	4	608	608	608
2. Russian	5	3	3	3	3	3	3	3	3	3	3	3	532	456	456
3. Second foreign language	5	3	6	4	3	4	4	3	4	4	3	4	646	456	684
4. Third foreign language	—	—	—	4	—	6	5	—	6	5	4	7	532	—	722
5. Mathematics	3	5	3	3	5	3	3	5	3	3	4	3	456	722	456
6. Physics	2	3	2	2	3	2	2	3	2	1	3	1	266	456	266
7. Chemistry	2	2	2	2	3	2	2	3	2	1	3	1	266	418	228
8. Biology	1	2	2	1	2	1	1	3	1	2	2	—	190	342	152
9. Geography	2	2	2	1	1	1	1	1	1	1	1	1	152	190	152
10. Astronomy	—	—	—	—	—	—	—	—	—	1	1	1	38	38	38
11. Technical drawing	1	1	1	1	1	1	—	—	—	—	—	—	76	76	76
12. Socialist production	4	4	3	4	4	3	4	4	4	4	4	4	608	608	532
13. History	2	2	2	2	2	2	2	2	2	3	3	3	342	342	342
14. Citizenship	1	1	1	1	1	1	1	1	1	1	1	1	152	152	152
15. Drawing	1	1	1	1	1	1	1	1	1	1	1	1	152	152	152
16. Music	1	1	1	1	1	1	1	1	1	1	1	1	152	152	152
17. Physical education	2	2	2	2	2	2	2	2	2	2	2	2	304	304	304
Total hours weekly:	36	36	36	36	36	36	36	36	36	36	36	36			

[24] Karl-Heinz Günther, *op. cit*, p. 239.

both of money and the students' time.[25] The majority of students in these schools are mainly concerned with going on to higher education—this, indeed, is clearly expected in the school law of 1965[26]—and although these schools have declined in importance relative to other kinds of secondary schooling, they are still an important source of students for the universities, medical colleges, law courses, teachers' training institutes, and the like. To expect them to qualify as lorry-drivers or post-office technicians, when none of them is likely to pursue these occupations, is an over-generous interpretation of the principle of "linking the school with life". There is, in fact, evidence that the disproportionate amount of time spent on practical work has been having a bad effect on *Abitur* examination performance.[27]

(ii) Growing in importance are the *Abitur* classes in establishments of vocational training (*Abiturklassen in den Einrichtungen der Berufsausbildung* or, more simply, *Berufsschulen mit Abitur*, vocational schools with *Abitur*). These now offer two-year courses of combined vocational training and general education, and lead to a double qualification—the *Abitur*, and the skilled worker's qualification (*Facharbeiter-prüfung*). Students from these schools can either go into employment at 18, or go to higher or further education, usually in a field closely related to their vocational study. About 20 per cent of school-leavers entering vocational schools follow courses of this kind, and the number is likely to rise.[28] The content of the courses of both types mentioned is the concern of the Ministry of Public Education, in close co-operation with the State Secretariat for Higher and Technical Education and the State Planning Commission.

(iii) *Vocational schools* (*Berufsschulen*) provide the equivalent of an apprentice training. They are of two main types. Factory vocational schools (*Betriebsberufsschulen*) are attached to publicly owned enterprises, and give general and theoretical instruction as

[25] Oral communications, various.
[26] *1965 Law*, p. 104.
[27] Siegfried Baske, "Abiturientenzahlen" (*Informationsdienst zum Bildungswesen in Osteuropa*, **10/11**, pp. 73–74).
[28] Günther, *op. cit.*, p. 235.

Fig. 15. East Germany: Curriculum for *Abitur* Class in Machine Construction,[29] *Berufsschule* (before 1965)

Class:	1	2	3	Total
Natural Science subjects:				
1. Mathematics	3	3	3	369
2. Physics	1	2	2	205
3. Chemistry	1	1	2	164
4. Biology	1	2	2	205
5. Geography	1	1	—	82
"Arts" subjects:				
6. German	2	2	3	287
7. Russian	2	2	2	246
8. Second foreign language	2	4	4	410
9. History	1	2	1	164
10. Citizenship	1	1	1	123
11. Physical education	2	2	2	246
Trade theory:				
12. Technology	1	1	2	164
13. Technical drawing	1	1	1	123
14. Materials	1	1	—	82
15. Organization and economics	—	1	1	82
16. Trade practice	3 days per week	2 days per week	2 days per week	2828
		+ 5 weeks per year		
17. Excursions, etc.		90 hours per year		270

[29] Günther, *op. cit.*, p. 238.

well as vocational practice, which is carried out in the factories concerned. General vocational schools are run by local councils, and provide training for apprentices from privately owned industries, as well as from nationally owned industries without schools of their own. These in turn can be further subdivided: there are separate agricultural, retail trade and craft schools, and "all-purpose" schools which provide several kinds of training in the same institution. There are also central vocational schools for comparatively unusual occupations with a limited demand—bee-keeping, roofing, etc. These generally take students for concentrated courses of four weeks in the year, the rest of the courses being taken at other vocational schools nearer the students' homes.

The content of the courses is strongly biased towards vocational subjects—general and special vocational theory and practice— but general educational studies continue as well—mathematics, physics, chemistry, civics, German, Russian, and sport (see Fig. 16). Practical work in industry is considered important not only for the obvious reasons, but also for social and political development. Indeed much is made of the moral and social, as well as the

FIG. 16. EAST GERMANY: CURRICULUM FOR TWO-YEAR VOCATIONAL SCHOOLS (*Berufsschulen*)[30]

Class:	1	2	Total
1. German language and literature	1	1	84
2. Civics	1	1	84
3. Russian language	1	1	84
4. Mathematics	1	1	84
5. Physics	1	1	84
6. Chemistry	1	1	84
7. Sport	2	2	168
8. Factory economics	1	1	84
9. Theoretical vocational instruction	5	5	420
10. Practical vocational instruction	30	30	3060
Total hours	44	44	4236

[30] *Ibid.*, p. 258 (adapted).

vocational, aspects of the whole course.³¹ At the end of the two years, the passing of the examination gives the students their vocational qualification (*Facharbeiterprüfung*) and a lower version of the *Abitur* (*Fachschulreife*), which qualifies them for admission to a technical school.

Selection for *Abitur* classes of any kind is made largely on academic attainment, but that is not the only criterion. According to the Law of 1965: "The best and ablest applicants are admitted to educational institutions leading to the *Abitur*, taking into consideration the social structure of the population."³² This additional qualification means in effect that some preference is given to students of working-class or peasant origin. There used to be quite elaborate regulations for this in the 1950's, but the position is now more vague. It is made clear, however, that apart from good school attainment, "active social participation and exemplary conduct" must also carry weight. Exemplary conduct is self-explanatory; "active social participation" is taken to mean a good record of activity in the youth organizations, socially useful work, etc.—in effect, a political criterion.³³ Whatever the reasons, East Germany admits fewer pupils *directly* to leaving certificate courses than any other Eastern European country. Precise figures are not readily available, since the system is in transition at the moment, but the proportion of pupils leaving the ten-year schools who enter *Abitur* classes of any kind appears to be less than 30 per cent.³⁴

But this is not the only way to higher education. For pupils taking the ordinary vocational school course, there are two further ways: (1) They can go to a technical school (*Fachschule*), of which more presently, and it is possible to go on from there to higher education. (2) They can continue general and vocational education in the various kinds of adult education centres—evening

[31] *1965 Law*, p. 111.
[32] *1965 Law*, p. 104.
[33] Bodenmann, *op. cit.*, pp. 28 ff.
[34] Rudolf Weissner, Helmut Brauer, Willy Mann, "Das Bildungswesen der zweiten Stufe in einigen sozialistischen Ländern: Eine vergleichende Studie", *Vergleichende Pädagogik*, **10** (June 1964), pp. 19–24. Extrapolated.

and factory schools (*Abendoberschulen* and *Betriebsoberschulen*), Workers' and Peasants' Faculties (*Arbeiter-und-Bauern-Fakultäten*) and similar establishments. Some of these courses are in individual subjects, others are general school courses, and others are special courses for particular qualifications, including entrance examinations to higher education. Judging from official statements, this particular sector is likely to see even greater expansion in the future.[35]

(d) Technical Schools

Engineering and technical schools (*Ingenieur- und Fachschulen*) provide three-year courses leading to higher professional qualifications, though on a lower level than the university and college qualifications. Among the professions that can be studied there are engineering, metallurgy, transport, telecommunications, mining, agriculture, horticulture, forestry, librarianship, nursing, food science, economics, business management, graphic and fine arts, acting, kindergarten teaching, social work and a host of others. Assessment is based on regular tests throughout the course, and is concluded by a state examination, which provides both a professional qualification and the *Abitur*. Those accepted for higher education may be allowed to take their degrees in a shorter time if studying in the same or related fields; the others go directly into employment, to which they can be virtually directed—at least, the Law states that "students are to be encouraged to begin their activity at a place where the interests of society require after the completion of their study".[36]

There are rather more students in the *Fachschulen* than in higher education (140,000 as against 115,000 in 1963),[37] and it is interesting to note that the social class composition is more biased towards students of working-class and peasant origin than is the case in universities and colleges.[38] Courses can be taken full-time,

[35] Günther, *op. cit.*, pp 262–4.
[36] *1965 Law*, p. 119.
[37] *Statistisches Jahrbuch der DDR 1964*.
[38] *Ibid.*

through evening classes, or by correspondence; nearly two-thirds take part-time courses, the numbers of correspondence and evening students being roughly equal.[39]

(e) *Higher Education*

There are forty-four universities and other higher institutions (*Hochschulen*) in East Germany. Aming the universities, the largest are the Humboldt University in Berlin and the Karl Marx University of Leipzig, with over 10,000 full-time students each; the Martin Luther University in Halle, the Friedrich Schiller University in Jena, the University of Rostock and the Ernst Moritz Arndt University of Greifswald are smaller, with between 5000 and 2000 full-time students each. The number and organization of faculties vary; the Humboldt University has eleven—philosophy, mathematics and science, law, agriculture, forestry, medicine, veterinary medicine, economics, education, theology and a Workers' and Peasants' Faculty; Greifswald, on the other hand, has only philosophy, mathematics and science, medicine, theology and a Workers' and Peasants' Faculty. The others are intermediate, but generally follow the same pattern , providing for the humanities, the pure sciences, and some of the older "liberal" professions which are also taught in the more specialized *Hochschulen*. Most *Hochschulen* are relatively small, with under 2000 full-time students; some, like the Medical Colleges of Magdeburg and Dresden, the Building College of Leipzig, and some of the pedagogical institutes, number their students in hundreds rather than in thousands. Others are of university scale as well as standard, notably the Technical College (*Technische Hochschule*) in Dresden, which is the second largest higher institution in the country, with over 10,000 full-time students.[40]

The main types of *Hochschulen* are: (1) *Technical colleges*. These may cover many subjects—the Technical College in Dresden, for example, has eleven faculties (mathematics and science, civil engineering, mechanical engineering, technology, electrical en-

[39] *Statistisches Jahrbuch der DDR 1964.*
[40] *Ibid.*

gineering, engineering economics, forestry, vocational teacher training, aeronautics, atomic technology and a Workers' and Peasants' Faculty). Others are more specialized, dealing with one subject or group of subjects—for example, mining in Freiberg, electrotechnology in Ilmenau, industrial chemistry in Leuna-Merseburg or machine construction in Karl-Marx-Stadt. (2) *Agricultural colleges*, with different specializations. The Institute of Agronomy at Neugattersleben trains agricultural scientists, the Institute at Barnberg concentrates on agricultural economics, the Central College of Agricultural Production Co-operatives at Meissen trains leaders and managers of farming co-operatives, and so forth. (3) *Economics, Law and Business colleges*. The best known of these is the College of Economics in Berlin–Karlhorst, which trains statisticians, industrial economists, and specialists in economic planning, banking, state finance and similar fields. There are also colleges for internal and foreign trade in Leipzig and Staaken. In this category one might also include the Walter Ulbricht Academy of Political Science and Law in Potsdam-Babelsberg. (4) *Medical colleges* fulfil the same functions as university medical faculties. (5) *Art colleges*. These include institutions for the study of fine arts (theatre in Leipzig, visual arts in Dresden, film in Potsdam-Babelsberg, music in Berlin, Weimar, Leipzig, Dresden) and the applied arts—graphics and book production in Leipzig, applied design and plastic arts in Berlin, architecture and building in Weimar. (6) *Pedagogical institutes* (*Pädagogische Hochschulen*). (7) Others—e.g. the Institute of Archives in Potsdam or the College of Physical Culture in Leipzig.

Courses in higher education vary in length from three to six years, depending on the field of study. The content of instruction is related to the special field throughout—there are no courses equivalent to an ordinary or general degree—but there is also a compulsory element of non-specialist studies, namely physical education, Russian and another foreign language, and the study of Marxism–Leninism, described officially as "an essential part of a college education".[41] Study may be full-time, through evening

[41] *1965 Law*, p. 121.

classes or by correspondence; part-time students are given lighter working-loads to enable them to pursue their courses, although part-time study takes longer than full-time. Part-time students in higher institutions (in contrast to the *Fachschulen*) make up less than half the total number.[42] Application can be made by anyone with the entrance qualifications, and admission is decided by the institutions on merit and performance, with regard to the manpower needs of the national plan, and once again, "taking into account the social structure of the population". Although students from the intelligentsia form a greater proportion of the student body than in the *Fachschulen*, they are heavily concentrated in the part-time courses; for admission to full-time study, preference seems to be given to applicants of working- and peasant-class origin.[43]

Higher education is controlled by the State Secretariat for Higher and Technical Education, working closely with the State Planning Commission. Apart from basic policy, it controls all senior staff appointments, approves courses and teaching programmes, co-ordinates research, supervises examinations and the award of scholarships, and determines quotas for the various institutions and fields of study. At the level of the colleges themselves, each institution has its own Senate of senior staff, which elects the Rector. The Rector, as head of the college or university, is responsible for its whole administration, and is helped by four deputies (Prorectors) responsible for particular fields, and by a business manager. Each faculty, similarly, is headed by its faculty council, dean and assistant dean.[44]

The number of students in higher education has grown by about four times since 1951. This has involved a large expansion in courses of all kinds, but most spectacularly in part-time courses; correspondence courses have increased nearly ten times, and evening courses nearly seventeen times.[45]

---

[42] *Statistisches Jahrbuch der DDR 1964.*
[43] *Ibid.*
[44] Paul S. Bodenmann, *op. cit.*, pp. 78–82.
[45] *Statistisches Jahrbuch der DDR 1964.*

(f) *Teacher Training*

The training of teachers is the responsibility of the Minister of Public Education, in consultation with the other principal state organs, and is carried out in various institutions according to the level of the class taught.

(i) Kindergarten teachers are trained in pedagogical schools (*Pädagogische Schulen*). There are sixteen of these, with a two-year course of instruction.

(ii) Teachers of the lower grade of the ten-year school (*Unterstufenlehrer*) are trained in thirty-six teacher-training institutes (*Instituten für Lehrerbildung*), the equivalent in standard of the *Fachschulen*. Students enter these institutes from the 10th class of the ten-year school and take a three-year course, consisting of general subjects (German, mathematics, physics, chemistry, biology, geography, history, Russian, drawing, music and physical education), Marxism–Leninism, professional subjects (educational theory, history of education, psychology and methods) and teaching practice—four weeks in the first year of a Pioneer or school holiday camp, six weeks in a school in the second, and twenty hours a week in the third.

(iii) Teachers of the middle and upper grade (*Oberstufenlehrer*) are trained at the universities, the pedagogical institutes (*Pädagogische Hochschulen*) in Potsdam and elsewhere, or in specialized colleges of physical education, music, etc. Students enter with the *Abitur* and study for four years. Qualification is in two cognate subjects—German and history, German and Russian, mathematics and physics, physics and fundamentals of production, and so forth. Polytechnical studies are taken in the first year, and music, physical education and a foreign language throughout. Special subjects take up about 57 per cent of the time, professional subjects about 21 per cent. Teaching practice consists of one day a week in school in the second and third years, four weeks in Pioneer or holiday camps, and thirteen weeks of practice—eight of them making up a continuous period in the final year.

(iv) Teachers of *Abitur* classes are trained at the same institutions, but take a five-year specialist course.

(v) Teachers of technical and vocational subjects take either a five-year course at a suitably equipped university or technical college, or qualify at a *Fachschule*, following this with a special training course of about a year's duration.

(vi) Pioneer leaders take four-year courses in teacher-training institutes. In the first two years they follow the same programmes as intending primary teachers, but in the last two they specialize more in youth work. The state examination at the end of the course qualifies the student either as a primary teacher or as a Pioneer leader.[46]

5. PROSPECT

The present system came into effect at the beginning of the 1965–6 school year, and will naturally take some time to replace the previous one. Even where they have not yet been fully realized, however, the changes do provide some pointers to the way the school system is going. In the first place, the unified basic school has been taken further than in other East European countries, but seems unlikely to extend to later age-groups at the moment. Unlike some other countries, East Germany has pressed further with the integration of polytechnical and vocational training with general education, and although, as we have seen, there are some doubts about the wisdom of pushing it so far, it still seems likely that this trend will continue. There may be some modifications of the vocational rquirements in the extended secondary school, especially if (as seems probable) this is interfering with the efficiency of the *Abitur* examination. However, the authorities are so heavily committed to the principle of the "unity of education and work", and to increasing the shift of emphasis to the "second way" to higher education through vocational and adult education, that any move back to the older system would not only mean a complete reversal of present trends, but would be difficult to work in

[46] Günther, *op. cit.*, pp. 276 ff.

practice. This development has meant an extension of specialization down into the school system, as some commentators have been quick to point out;[47] on the other hand, the building up of the ten-year school has meant an increase of general education for the majority, as compared with the pre-war selective system.

As for the rationale and content of the East German system, it appears that, for all the declarations on the need to develop "independence of thinking" in pupils, the general tone is more rigid and dogmatic than is now usual in Eastern Europe. It is only fair to point out that this does not necessarily mean regimentation in the classroom; the absence of uniform is often paralleled by absence of rigidity in pupil–teacher relationships, as has been observed elsewhere. Classroom formality is greater than, say, in Poland, but is far less fearsome than the regulations seem to suggest. Nevertheless, there is no denying that the political pressures on teachers and students are stronger and more readily applied than, for instance, in Poland or Hungary. This has changed to varying degrees in different countries; but in this case the anomalous political situation, and the tensions that it engenders, have so far held back the progress of the "thaw" in East Germany.

[47] Bodenmann, *op. cit.*, p. 28.

CHAPTER 3

Czechoslovakia

1. BACKGROUND TO THE SYSTEM

Czechoslovakia is a modern creation, and in some ways an artificial one. The population of 14 million is made up almost entirely of nearly 10 million Czechs and 4 million Slovaks, two peoples closely related, linguistically at least—they can converse in their respective languages as easily as a Scot and a Yorkshireman. But there are differences of geography, history and tradition, which go deeper than the Czech love of beer and the Slovak preference for wine. Both peoples have spent the last few centuries, up to 1919, as subjects of the ramshackle Austro-Hungarian Empire. Since the Habsburg Emperor was King of Bohemia as well as Archduke of Austria and King of Hungary, the Czechs could feel (sometimes) that they had at least some kind of identity in their own right; Slovakia, however, had not even nominal identity, being administered simply as part of the Kingdom of Hungary. Not that the Czechs were really much better off; although Bohemia was renowned in the Middle Ages as a centre of learning—Charles University in Prague is the oldest in Central Europe—and of reformist inquiry, typified in the movement led by Jan Hus, the Thirty Years' War put an end to all that. Bohemia was subjected to counter-Reformation (even today, many Czechs dislike their Baroque churches as symbols of this) and to a process of Germanization. The Czech language was discouraged, and large numbers of Germans moved into the country, till they made up most of the population in many of the principal towns and in the area surrounding Bohemia on three sides, the Sudetenland; their descendants were to be the cause of much trouble centuries later. Many Czechs must have wished that they really had the sea-coast that Shakespeare once wished on them.

National awareness never really died out, but it was firmly damped down. Under the Dual Monarchy (not, notice, the Triune Monarchy—the Habsburgs did not take the crown of Bohemia very seriously), any stirrings of nationalist or pan-Slavic aspirations were suppressed with a ruthlessness tempered only by an almost incredible inefficiency. To many Czechs, the best reaction seemed to be the apparently passive one of Jaroslav Hašek's Good Soldier Schweik, "Maul halten und weiter dienen" (Shut up and get on with it). Others lacked Schweik's patience; during the First World War, thousands of Czechs defected to the Russians and re-formed in the Czech Legion to fight against the Austrians, in spite of the certainty of being shot out of hand if they were recaptured.

The creation of the Czechoslovak Republic after the First World War freed the Czechs and Slovaks from foreign rule, and enabled them to push ahead with political and economic development until the country was one of the most politically stable and industrially advanced in Central Europe. But it left some problems that were to grow in time, notably the presence of large numbers of Hungarians in Slovakia, about 3 million Germans in Bohemia, and some remaining tensions between the more advanced Czechs and the poorer and less numerous Slovaks, many of whom felt that they had exchanged Habsburg for Czech domination. All of these problems were later exploited to the full by Hitler, providing the occasion first for absorbing the German-speaking Sudeten areas, then turning Bohemia and Moravia into "protectorates", while Slovakia, trimmed of part of its territory by Hungary, was transformed into a puppet "republic"—all on the classic principle of divide and rule.

During the occupation, resistance flared up from time to time, and was repressed with the ruthlessness that the Nazis showed in special degree when occupying Slav countries. It did not reach the scale of similar activities in Poland and Yugoslavia; the shooting of student demonstrators in Prague and the destruction of Lidice were not isolated incidents, but when the Soviet Army finally drove the Germans out, the country had at least been spared devastation of the kind that faced other post-war governments. Czechoslovakia, as we have seen, came late into the communist camp. The restored Republic, under Beneš and Masaryk, tried for a time to steer a middle course between East and West, but the communist *coup* of 1948, after the Soviet armies had withdrawn, brought Czechoslovakia politically into line with the rest of Eastern Europe.

The educational and social problems inherited by the communist régime thus differed in many ways from those in other countries. Nationalism, then as now, was less strident, and was in any case directed more against the Germans than the Russians. Czechoslovakia has had only a minor nationality problem since the end of the Second World War and the expulsion of the Sudeten Germans. Over 94 per cent of the population are now Czechs or Slovaks, with Hungarians, Poles and Germans forming tiny minorities.[1] Nationalism has taken the form of pride in educational and cultural achievements; perhaps it is for this reason, and because the Czechoslovak revolution was home-made, that the régime has been closer to the Soviet Union, even in externals, than is the case now in Poland, Hungary or Rumania. Further, Czechoslovakia has long been more industrialized than the other countries—over 80 per cent of the population is urban[2] —and has thus been spared many of the problems of educational backwardness and low living standards that have so sorely tried the resources of Poland or Yugoslavia. For all its shortcomings, the pre-war system was one of the most broadly based in Eastern Europe, spread more widely the high standards of the academic

[1] Hungarians 3·1 per cent, Poles 0·6 per cent, Ukrainians 0·6 per cent, Germans 1·2 per cent, others 0·3 per cent. (Mojmir Dýma and Jaroslav Kojzar, *Das Schulwesen in der Tschechoslowakischen Sozialistischen Republik*, p. 449. In: Deutsches Pädagogisches Zentral-institut, *Das Schulwesen sozialistischer Länder in Europa*, Berlin, Volk und Wissen Volkseigener Verlag, 1962.) In addition, some of the Slovaks who returned to Czechoslovakia in the exchange with Hungary after the war had become so Magyarized that they preferred Hungarian schools for their children.

[2] *Ibid.*

secondary and higher schools, and left only a tiny fraction of the population illiterate. But there were problems. Even in the most advanced countries, the traditional school systems have tended to be too narrowly based on one social class, and the Czechoslovak system was no exception. Some rural areas in Bohemia and Moravia, and most of Slovakia, lagged behind the rest of the country. In 1938 there were 1560 schools with courses beyond the fifth class in Bohemia and Moravia; in Slovakia, with nearly half as many inhabitants, there were only 284. In higher education, the discrepancy was even greater—just over 2000 students in Slovakia out of a total of 19,000 for the whole country.[3] (It was not until the early 1950's that the distribution became more equitable.) Clearly, special efforts were needed in Slovakia; but in the rest of the country too there was need for expansion of education at all levels, especially in the technical sector.

2. THE OLD SYSTEM AND POST-WAR DEVELOPMENTS

The pre-war system in Czechoslovakia, and the changes that took place after the communist government came to power, have already been described (see pp. 75–77, 83–84). The present system was brought into being by the school reform of 1960, which was to be implemented by stages between 1960 and 1965. The most important changes were the lengthening of the basic school course to nine years, the further expansion of vocational and technical education, the increased emphasis on polytechnical and technical studies in the schools, and the introduction of new types of schools for adults.

3. THE PRESENT SYSTEM

(a) *Pre-school Education*

As usual, pre-school institutions exist at two levels, the crèche (*jesle*) for children up to the age of 3, and the kindergarten

[3] Alena Gregorova (ed.), *Educación e Instrucción en Checoslovaquia*, pp. 28, 102. (Statní pedagogické nakladatelství; Prague, 1958.)

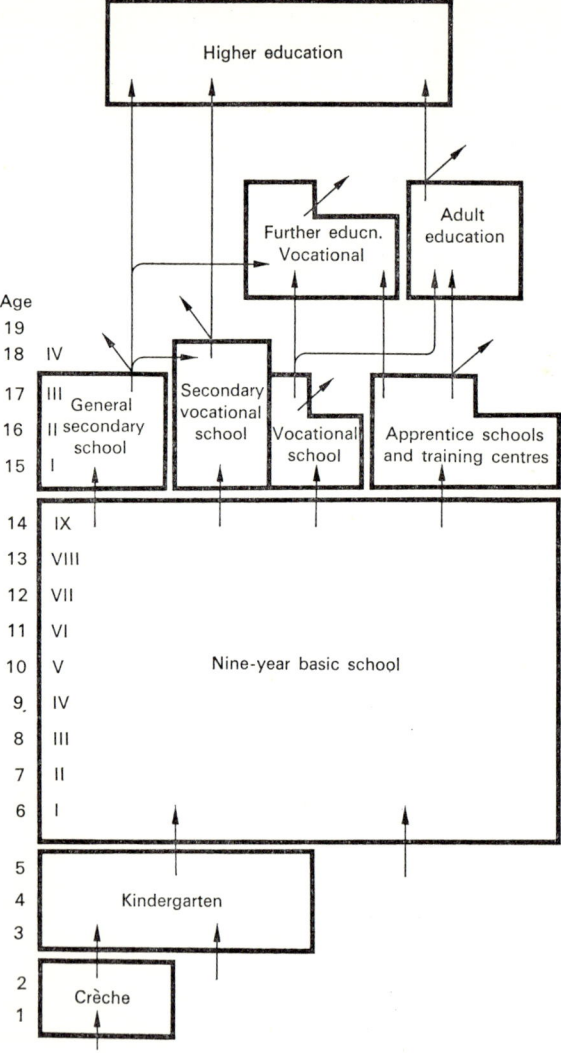

Fig. 17. Czechoslovakia: School system.

(*mateřská škola*) for children from 3 to 6 years of age. Crèches are sometimes provided by factories and farms, though most are organized by the national committees (the local government councils) under the supervision of the Ministry of Health. Most are day nurseries, but there are some where children can board during the week, going home at week-ends, and some with continuous boarding. Children are looked after by nurses specially trained for this kind of work, assisted by less qualified helpers, and doctors visit daily. The children are divided into groups (not classes) for games and other activities, according to age—up to 10 months, 10 to 18 months, and 18 months to 3 years. The emphasis of the programme is on play, rest, hygiene, habit training, welfare; the children are not taught in any formal sense, though the communal activity of the crèche is regarded as helpful in developing the necessary skills, attitudes and the ability to get on with others. Daytime meals are taken there, and for this the parents are expected to contribute between one and eight crowns a day (roughly, from 6*d*. to 4*s*.). This can be reduced or waived according to the number of children in the family or size of parental income. Crèche places have risen to nearly five times the pre-war figure.[4]

Kindergartens are run on the principle of Comenius that "children should learn by tiny steps, without being aware of it, as if playing". This does not, of course, mean formal lessons for 3 to 6-year-olds, nor yet completely random activity. There seems to be more direction of activity than in our own nursery schools; toys "are not just for whiling away the time", but are picked for their educational value, as are other activities—games, drawing, painting, modelling, puppetry, and so on. Children are also accustomed to the rudiments of "socially useful work" by tidying their toy cupboards, looking after flowers, and generally helping in so far as their age and stage of development allows. The daily programme is arranged not only for convenience, but to accustom the children to the discipline of regularity in living. The times of

[4] Stanislav Vodinský, *Schools in Czechoslovakia*, p. 13. Dýma and Kojzar, *op. cit.*, p. 472.

starting and ending the day are kept flexible to fit parents' working-hours, and it is also possible to attend for half-days as well as whole days. With these reservations, this is a typical daily programme:

Up to	8.45 a.m.	Play and free activity.
	8.50 a.m.	Exercises.
	9.00 a.m.	Wash, mid-morning snack.
	9.30 a.m.	Activities.
	10.00 a.m.	Walks, playing in garden.
	12.15 p.m.	Wash, lunch.
	1.00 p.m.	Rest.
	2.30 p.m.	Games and open-air activities for older children until 4 p.m.
	3.00 p.m.	Games and open-air activities for younger children until 4 p.m.
	4.00 p.m.	Wash, afternoon snack.
	4.30 p.m.	Play and free activity until departure.[5]

Typically, children are divided into three groups: 3–4 years, 4–5, 5–6. In smaller kindergartens (in country areas, for example) there may be only one or two groups. Again, parents are required to contribute (0·50 to 4 crowns daily) towards the children's meals, the amount depending on size of family and parental income. The number of children in kindergartens has more than trebled since before the war, from 104,000 in 1937 to 317,000 in 1964.[6] Already it is possible for all 5-year-olds whose mothers so wish to enter kindergarten, and it is hoped to make full kindergarten education available for all who want it, irrespective of whether the mothers are working or not; this, however, will take rather longer.

(b) *Basic Schools*

The compulsory stage of education, from 6 to 15, is provided at the basic nine-year school (*zakladní devítiletá škola*). Like its

[5] Stanislav Vodinský, *op. cit.*, p. 14.
[6] *Ibid.*, p. 122.

counterparts elsewhere, it is comprehensive, co-educational and unified. Formally, there is a break between the lower and upper grades, but in practice this means no more than switching over from general to specialist teaching. The curriculum in the first years concentrates heavily on the mother tongue (Czech or Slovak) and mathematics, with smaller allotments of time to physical education, art, music and work practice. By the end of the course it has broadened to take in Russian, civics, history, geography, physics, chemistry, natural sciences, geometric drawing and some extra subjects. Most of the "secondary" subjects are introduced gradually from the fourth to the sixth class. Over the nine years, the curriculum (see Fig. 18) devotes about 33 per cent of the time to language, 10 per cent to the social sciences, 31 per cent to mathematics and natural sciences, 18 per cent to physical education and music and 8 per cent to work training.[7]

Czech and Slovak are taught in the respective parts of the Republic. Children are taught one or the other; since the languages are mutually comprehensible, this does not give rise to any great problems. Czech works are, however, sometimes included in the Slovak scheme, and vice versa. In recent years there has been more stress on mastery of the spoken language and on creative writing, although drilling in correct grammar (spelling is not a matter of much difficulty) continues to claim a prominent place. In the teaching of foreign languages—Russian at this stage—there has again been an increased emphasis on the use of the spoken language.

Homeland and nature study, like "Study of Nature and Society" in Yugoslavia, is a subject intended to lead on to more specific disciplines. In practice, it forms part of the curriculum in the mother tongue during the first two years, and is taught separately in the next three. Its purpose is to give a general introduction to the whole social and natural environment, not unlike the "environmental studies" nearer home. In the sixth class and later, it branches out into the sciences—chemistry, physics and "natural sciences"—and the social studies, history and geography.

[7] *Ibid.*, p. 22.

Fig. 18. Czechoslovakia: Basic Nine-year School Curriculum

Class:	I	II	III	IV	V	VI	VI	VIII	IX	Total
1. Czech/Slovak language and literature	11	13	10	8	8	6	6	5	5	72
2. Russian language	—	—	—	2	2	2	3	3	3	15
3. Civics	—	—	—	—	—	1	1	1	1	4
4. History	—	—	—	—	—	1	2	2	2	7
5. Geography	—	—	—	—	—	3	2	2	—	7
6. Mathematics	4	5	5	5	5	6	5	5	5	45
7. Homeland—nature study	—	—	3	3	4	—	—	—	—	10
8. Physics	—	—	—	—	—	—	2	2	3	7
9. Chemistry	—	—	—	—	—	—	—	2	3	5
10. Natural science	—	—	—	—	—	3	2	2	2	9
11. Physical education	3	3	3	2	2	2	2	2	2	21
12. Art	1	1	1	2	2	2	2	2	—	13
13. Technical drawing	—	—	—	—	—	—	—	—	2	2
14. Writing	—	—	1	1	1	—	—	—	—	2
15. Music	1	1	1	1	1	1	1	1	1	9
16. Practical training	1	1	1	2	2	3	3	3	3	19
Total	21	24	24	26	27	30	31	32	32	247
17. Optional subjects	—	—	—	—	—	2	2	2	2	8
18. Hobby groups	—	—	2	2	2	2	2	2	2	14

Note: Practical subjects include 1 hour per week on child care for girls in classes VIII and IX. Optional subjects: English, German, French, choral singing, art.

History, as elsewhere, emphasizes the history of the motherland against a background of world history, with a marked political inclination. Whereas Poland emphasizes the national aspect and East Germany the political, Czechoslovakia is roughly in between. In the sixth year ancient history is taught—a series of topics more than a continuous chronology, rather like the "patch" method now gaining vogue in Britain; in the seventh, Czechoslovak history in its world context up to the rise of capitalism; in the eighth, the development of capitalism and imperialism; and in the ninth, world history from 1917 to the present day. The same approach can be seen in the geography programme—the World excluding Europe in the sixth year, Europe and the Soviet Union in the seventh, and Czechoslovakia in the eighth, with "stress on economic and political aspects" throughout. Civics is more directly political in content. Its purpose is "to provide instruction about the most important aspects of political and economic institutions in Czechoslovakia, make the pupils familiar with all the essentials of the scientific world outlook of Marxism–Leninism, and to bring home to them the principles of communist morality".[8] Apart from elementary political theory, the subject seeks to do this through study of the constitution, the system of government and government bodies, the work of the mass organizations (the Communist Party, the trade unions, the ČSM, etc.) and the organization of the country's economy. Unlike most other subjects, it is not marked for the pupil's record.

The other subjects follow the familiar pattern, though it is worth noting that "Natural Sciences" cover not only biology but hygiene, geology and mineralogy as well. Work study takes the form of handwork in classes 1 to 5, and practical work in school plots and workshops thereafter. The emphasis is not on vocational training, but on acquainting the pupils with tools, materials, basic skills, work habits, and "the correct attitudes towards physical work". Wherever possible, the teaching of the sciences is linked to this subject in an attempt to show the connection between theoretical sciences and their practical

[8] Stanislav Vodinský, *Czechoslovakia: Education*, p. 22. (Orbis, Prague, 1963.)

application. Time is also set aside for visits to factories and farms.

From the sixth year onwards, two hours a week are set aside for a choice of extra subjects. These include games, sewing and cookery, art and choral singing, or more "academic" subjects such as extra biology, chemistry or physics (laboratory work) or an additional foreign language. Two hours a week are also available for hobby circles from the third year onwards.

The nine-year school, like its equivalents elsewhere, is comprehensive, pupils being promoted from one year to the next on the basis of their assessment on the five-point scale. In this assessment, physical education, civics, art and music are not counted, and a pupil may still go on with one or two subjects in the "unsatisfactory" grade, provided one of them is not the mother tongue or mathematics. But he will be expected to take extra classes to improve his performance, and in any case the school's pedagogic council (consisting of the director and his staff and representatives of the parents) have to approve promotion in such cases. Generally, all children at the same stage follow the same course, but in some schools there has been introduced a system of "setting" in the last year, with experimental "special classes" of the more able in Czech or Slovak, foreign languages and mathematics. This is welcomed by many teachers, who find selected groups easier to teach; others are more critical, watch carefully in case this turns into a system of "streaming", and want to know more about the criteria for judging the success of the experiment, which do seem rather vaguely conceived by the authorities.[9] There does appear to be general agreement, however, on the need to provide outlets for the more able older pupils. The optional classes are one way of doing this. Extra-mural competitions, like the "mathematical Olympiad" with about 25,000 competitors every year, provide another. So do the People's Schools of Art and Languages, after-school centres, and the various circles run by the ČSM Pioneers in the Pioneer Houses. These are, as a rule, provided along with the recreational activities that make up so much of the

[9] Oral communications, Prague, September 1966.

organization's work. But even here there is a mild degree of specialization, at least in Prague, where the House of Czechoslovak Children (*Dům Československých dětí*) concentrates on hobbies and recreational facilities, allowing the Julius Fučík Central Pioneer and Youth House (*Ústřední dům pionýrů a mládeže Julii Fučíka*) across the city to devote more of its facilities to subjects study groups.

In spite of recent building programmes, about 14 per cent of the children, especially in the first five classes in the major towns, attend school in shifts.[10] In the countryside other problems arise due to lack of classroom space—some small villages cannot support a full nine-year school, only the first five classes. In such cases, the older children are taken by special buses or trains to central schools in the nearest town or large village. Remaining shortages in the towns can be met, in time, by more building; but in the country, where the population is dropping as more drift to the towns, even five-year schools become less viable. The trend is now to concentrate on providing more central nine-year schools, with a transport system for the children in the surrounding areas. This necessarily involves some dislocation and waste of the pupils' time, but it is hard to see what else could be done in the circumstances.

(c) *Secondary Schools*

Compulsory schooling ends with the ninth class of the basic school, but it is claimed that practically all pupils go on with some kind of schooling beyond this stage. Each nine-year school has a commission of teachers, in constant touch with the national committees and employment offices, which is charged with giving guidance to pupils and their parents, and also to the directors of the secondary schools. Selection of applicants is made by an admission board of the secondary school, headed by the director, on the basis of the applicant's past school record and an interview. The main choices available beyond the nine-year school are.

[10] Vodinský, *Schools in Czechoslovakia*, p. 30.

(i) *The general educational secondary school (střední všeobecně vzdělávací škola)*. This type of school admits about 20 per cent of the 15-year-olds from the nine-year schools, and provides a three-year course leading to the leaving certificate (*Matura*). This is the course preferred by those intending to go on to pure science or arts courses at the universities.

FIG. 19. CZECHOSLOVAKIA: GENERAL SECONDARY SCHOOL CURRICULUM (1965–6)[11]

Class:	I	II	III	Total
1. Czech/Slovak lang. and lit.	4	3/4	3/4	10/12
2. Russian	2/3	2/3	2	6/8
3. Second foreign language	3/4	3/4	3/4	9/12
4. Social sciences	–	2	2	4
5. History	2	2	2/3	6/7
6. Geography	2	2	1	5
7. Mathematics	5/4	5/4	5/4	15/12
8. Descriptive geometry	–	2/–	2/–	4/–
9. Physics	5/3	5/3	6/4	16/12
10. Chemistry	5/3	4/2	3/2	12/7
11. Biology and geology	4/2	4/3	5/3	13/8
12. Fundamentals of production	4	–	–	4
13. Physical education	3	3	3	9
14. Elective subjects	–	2	2	4
Total	36	36	36	108
Optional subjects	2	2	2	6

Alternative entries thus: 2/3 = 2 hours in the science course, 3 in the arts course.
Social sciences: philosophy, psychology, logic, sociology.
Second foreign language: English, French or German.
Elective subjects: Science course—Latin, art, technical drawing.
               Arts course—third foreign language, art, descriptive geometry.
Optional subjects: Foreign language conversation, music, sport.

---

[11] This curriculum replaces the three-course scheme in force until 1964. Vodinský, *Czechoslovakia: Education*, pp. 42–43.

Until recently, there were three types of course, emphasizing the humanities, physics and mathematics, and chemistry and biology, with a large common core of the humanities, sciences, physical education and work training. Work study was intended to provide basic vocational qualifications, but this was found not to be a success; since few students actually took up the trades they learned, the time allotted to them was hard to justify, particularly when the standard of work in general education began to drop. Some changes were made in 1964–5, reducing the amount of time spent on work training, and treating it as general polytechnical education, not as vocational preparation. Pupils are now introduced to modern technology, mechanization and automation, and repetitive work has been cut out. Further, the whole subject is now more flexibly organized; only the maximum number of hours and the broad outlines are laid down, the details being left to be arranged at school level according to local conditions and the pupils' interests.[12]

The general secondary schools now offer two main courses, biased towards mathematics and the sciences on one hand, languages and social sciences on the other. There is also a greater degree of choice of subjects within the courses. Once again, there is a large common core, so as to avoid excessive specialization; more language teaching has been brought into both courses. Among other changes, geology is now a compulsory subject on the science side, and in the arts course Latin is now one of the elective languages, instead of being merely a possible extra as formerly[13] (see Fig. 19).

(ii) *The vocational school (odborná škola)* or *secondary vocational school (střední odborná škola)*.

Secondary vocational schools provide four-year courses for pupils from the nine-year schools, giving a combination of vocational training and general education leading to a professional

---

[12] Johannes Faensen, "Verkürzung des Produktionsunterrichts" (*Informationsdienst zum Bildungswesen in Osteuropa*, **8/9**, pp. 44–45. Osteuropa-Institut an der Freien Universität Berlin, 1964.)

[13] *Times Educational Supplement*, 29 October 1965.

qualification and the *matura*. After completing these courses, students can either enter employment or go on to higher education. There are also two-year courses, without the general subjects, for students who already have the *matura*.

FIG. 20. CZECHOSLOVAKIA: TECHNICAL SCHOOL CURRICULUM[14]
MECHANICAL ENGINEERING: SPECIAL SUBJECT—ENGINEERING TECHNOLOGY

Class:	I	II	III	IV	Total
1. Czech/Slovak language and literature	3	2	2	2	9
2. Russian language	2	2	2	2	8
3. History	2	2	–	–	4
4. Economic geography	–	–	2	–	2
5. Civics	1	1	1	1	4
6. Mathematics	5	3	3	–	11
7. Physics	4	–	–	–	4
8. Chemistry	4	–	–	–	4
9. Political economy	–	–	2	–	2
10. Electrical technology	–	3	2	–	5
11. Technical drawing	4	2	–	–	6
12. Mechanics	–	5	3	–	8
13. Machine parts	–	6	5	–	11
14. Machinery	–	–	4	8	12
15. Technology	3	3	3	8	17
16. Organization and economics	–	–	–	4	4
17. Laboratory work	–	–	–	4	4
18. Workshop training	5	4	4	4	17
19. Operational training	–	–	–	1	1
20. Physical education	3	3	3	2	11
Total hours weekly:	36	36	36	36	144
Optional subjects:					
Second foreign language	2	2	2	2	8
Mathematics	–	–	–	2	2
Physics	–	–	2	–	2
Sport and games	2	2	2	2	8

Also: three weeks' workshop and operational training at end of classes I, II, III.

[14] Vodinský, *Czechoslovakia: Education*, pp. 46–47.

FIG. 21. CZECHOSLOVAKIA: AGRICULTURAL SCHOOL CURRICULUM. SPECIAL SUBJECTS—PLANT CULTIVATION AND ANIMAL HUSBANDRY

Class:	I	II	III	IV	Total
1. Czech/Slovak language and literature	3	2	2	2	9
2. Russian language	2	2	2	2	8
3. History	2	2	–	–	4
4. Economic geography	–	2	–	–	2
5. Civics	1	1	1	1	4
6. Mathematics	5	4	–	–	9
7. Physics	4	–	–	–	4
8. Chemistry	5	4	–	–	9
9. Biology	6	–	–	–	6
10. Crop production	–	4	7	7	18
11. Plant protection	–	–	–	4	4
12. Horticulture	–	–	2	–	2
13. Animal husbandry	–	4	7	7	18
14. Veterinary science	–	–	–	3	3
15. Mechanization	2	5	3	–	10
16. Economics and organization	–	–	5	5	10
17. Practical training	3	3	–	–	6
18. Physical education	3	3	3	2	11
19. Psychology and hygiene	–	–	–	1	1
20. Geodesy	–	–	2	–	2
21. Processing of agricultural products	–	–	2	–	2
22. Accounting	–	–	–	2	2
Total hours weekly:	36	36	36	36	144
Optional subjects:					
Second foreign language	2	2	2	2	8
Sport and games	2	2	2	2	8
Typing	–	–	2	–	2
Mathematics	–	–	–	2	2
Driving	–	–	1	–	1

Also: six weeks' practical training in 1st year, nine weeks' operational training in class II, eight weeks' in class III.

Vocational schools provide two- or three-year courses for pupils from the nine-year school, with less general education. These courses give only the professional qualification, not the *matura*. Students who want to go on to higher education can still do so, but not directly; they have to attain the general education standard through the adult educational system. Some professions are taught in four-year secondary vocational schools only, but in many (e.g. agriculture, economics and management, some branches of industry) there are both types of course.

The 647 secondary vocational schools, with their 180,000 students, are grouped according the the area of specialization: industry, transport and communications; agriculture; forestry; economics; catering and hotel management; social work; nursing and public health; teaching; librarianship; applied arts, crafts, graphic and industrial design; and the conservatories. Each group embraces further specializations. Schools of the first category, for instance, give courses in technical and nuclear physics, geology and prospecting, metallurgy, mechanical engineering, electrical engineering, applied chemistry, food technology, light industry, building and surveying, transport and communications. Agricultural schools have foremen's courses, and courses in plant cultivation, animal husbandry, horticulture, winemaking, poultry keeping, agricultural improvement, agricultural mechanization, agricultural economics, veterinary medicine, bee-keeping and co-operative management. Economics schools train personnel for foreign trade, telecommunications, economic administration, communal catering, hotel management, and so forth. These, with the nursing and medical schools, form the great majority of schools of this type—industrial schools alone account for about half the total. The others are more limited in number, but still train for a wide range of occupations. The secondary applied art school at Brno, for example, offers seven courses, including furniture design, interior decoration, plastics and photography; so does the one at Uherské Hradiště, including ceramics, machine and tool design and "reproduction sculpture"; there is a school of this kind in Karlovy Vary specialising in ceramics, another in

Železný Brod for glass technology, textiles in Brno, jewellery in Turnov, etc. Finally, conservatories train artists and musicians; they are highly selective, requiring demonstration of special talent as well as general educational competence.[15]

At present, about 40 per cent of pupils leaving the nine-year school go to some kind of secondary school, general or vocational. By 1970, according to current plans, this figure should rise to about 60 per cent or more.[16]

(iii) *Apprenticeship.* About 60 per cent of the basic school leavers enter apprenticeship; they are trained at any apprentice training centre (*odborné učiliště*) or apprentice school (*učnovská škola*). These give three-year courses; it is possible for apprentices who already have the *matura* to have the courses reduced to one and a half years or less, but this is comparatively uncommon. The apprenticeship courses are usually entered straight from the basic school. Apprentice training centres are situated in and run by major industrial concerns, while apprentice schools are run by national committees, and give training in trades where the numbers are so small that factory centres would not be an economical proposition. In either case, the apprentice is bound by contract for the entire course. Since the object is to train qualified workers, about 80 per cent of curricular time is spent on vocational training, both theory and practice, the rest being devoted to general education (see Figs. 22, 23 and 24).[17]

The courses fall into fifteen categories: mining; foundry work; chemical industries; engineering and metalwork; electrotechnology; building; ceramics and glass-making; woodwork and musical-instrument making; film, photography and polygraphy; textiles; leatherwork and shoemaking; food industries; agriculture and forestry; transport and communication; commerce, catering and non-productive services. To give some idea of the variety of trades included within these categories, these are some of the branches that come under the engineering and metalwork group:

[15] *Types of Secondary Schools, Czechoslovakia 1963.* (Prague, unpublished.)
[16] Vodinský, *Schools in Czechoslovakia*, p. 58.
[17] Vodinský, *op. cit.*, pp. 37–39.

Fig. 22. Czechoslovakia: Apprentice School Curriculum (for Mechanics)

Class:	I	II	III	Total
1. Czech/Slovak language and literature	2	2	1	200
2. Russian language	1	1	1	120
3. Civics	1	1	1	120
4. Mathematics	2	2	1	200
5. Physics	2	2	1	200
6. Technical drawing	3	2	1	240
7. Materials	1	1	–	80
8. Technology	3	3	2	320
9. Machinery and plant	–	2	2	160
10. Organization and planning	–	–	2	80
11. Technical training	18	21	28	3400
12. Physical education	3	2	2	280
Total:	36	39	42	5400
Optional subjects:				
Second foreign language	2	2	2	240
Laboratory work	–	2	2	160
Sport and games	2	2	2	240

form-maker, smith, tube-maker, fitter, boiler-maker, tool-maker, ship mechanic, locksmith (machine, maintenance, building, vehicle or artistic), refrigerator mechanic, gun-maker, plumber, car-body maker, airframe maker, metal-turner, metal-grinder, car mechanic, aircraft mechanic, watchmaker, galvanizer, goldsmith, silversmith, knife-maker, surgical-instrument maker, sewing-machine mechanic, calculating-machine mechanic—forty-five trades in all. For the first half of the course, the students are paid at apprenticeship rates (not very much—the equivalent of a few pounds a month); later according to the work done, they earn 60–100 per cent of the normal wage. Apprentices are entitled to three to four weeks' paid leave a year. Boarding, where applicable, is free in the "preferential trades" (mining, foundry work, chemical industry, transport, agriculture, building, etc.); in other

Fig. 23. Czechoslovakia: Apprentice School Curriculum (for Weavers)

Class:	I	II	Total
1. Czech/Slovak language and literature	2	2	160
2. Russian language	1	1	80
3. Civics	1	1	80
4. Mathematics	2	1	120
5. Physics	2	1	120
6. Specialized drawing	–	2	80
7. Texture and analysis of fabrics	3	3	240
8. Materials	2	1	120
9. Technology	2	3	200
10. Organization and economics	–	1	40
11. Technical training	18	21	2028
12. Physical education	3	2	200
Total:	36	39	3468
Optional subjects:			
Second foreign language	2	2	160
Laboratory work	–	2	80
Sport and games	2	2	160

trades the apprentice pays from 20 per cent up to the full cost, depending on parental income; non-boarders are entitled to free or cheap travel. (Czechoslovakia has an acute labour-shortage problem; the concessions given to apprentices in the "preferential trades" are intended to tempt trainees into the most essential sectors of the economy.) The course ends with an examination in theory and practice, and the award of the Certificate of Apprenticeship, the skilled-worker's qualification.

(d) *Special Schools*

Over 40,000 children are in special schools for the handicapped. These are grouped according to the pupils' defects—schools for the mentally backward, the deaf and hard of hearing, the dumb and those with speech defects, the blind and partially sighted, the

FIG. 24. CZECHOSLOVAKIA: APPRENTICE SCHOOL CURRICULUM (AGRICULTURAL MECHANIZATION)

	Class:	I	II
1.	Czech/Slovak language and literature	2	2
2.	Russian language	1	1
3.	Civics	1	1
4.	Mathematics	2	1
5.	Physics	2	1
6.	Chemistry	1	1
7.	Physical education	3	2
8.	Crop production	3	2
9.	Livestock production	3	2
10.	Engineering	1	3
11.	Organization and economics	–	2
12.	Workshop training	3	2
13.	Technical training	15	18
	Total	37	38
	Optional subjects:		
	Family and housekeeping*	3	3
	Mathematics	2	2
	Sport and games	2	2

*Family and housekeeping—metalwork, woodwork and saddlery for boys; sewing and cookery for girls.

physically handicapped, and maladjusted children. Most of these categories include kindergartens and basic schools, and in some of them there are secondary, vocational and apprentice schools as well. Schools for maladjusted children (only very exceptionally accepting children under the age of 11) are generally boarding; so, less commonly, are some of the other types. Others are attached to hospitals, children's convalescent homes or sanatoria.

At the other end of the scale are special schools for the highly gifted. These are not greatly developed in Czechoslovakia as yet, being confined to a few experimental projects for children with special talent in mathematics or languages, started in 1963 and under review until 1970. A little older are the People's Schools of

Art (*lidové školy umění*), which provide instruction in visual arts, music, singing, dancing and drama. Children are enrolled in these on the recommendation of their teachers in the nine-year schools; they attend in their spare time, continuing with their other studies in the ordinary school. Adult students can attend as well. The same system is operated in the People's Schools of Languages (*lidové školy jazyků*).

(e) *Adult Education*

The secondary school for workers (*střední škola pro pracující*) is a comparatively new development. In 1959 thirty classes were set up on an experimental basis in some of the major industrial plants, attended by students who had already taken their apprenticeships. Since then the numbers have grown speedily. These schools give courses leading to the *matura*, and thus provide another route to higher education.

Since the schools are attended by workers of varying ages and educational standards, the length of course also varies. The maximum is three years; but students who have completed both the nine-year school and apprenticeship can be admitted to the second year. Indeed, if they pass a supplementary examination they may go straight into the third year. Students from the short-course vocational schools, likewise, can join in the third year subject to the same requirement. In some cases, schools of this type are organized together with apprenticeship centres to form uninterrupted five-year courses leading to the skilled worker's qualification and the *matura*.

Some of the secondary schools for workers are run by large industrial concerns for their own employees, but taking some from the smaller plants as well. Others are run by national committees, and draw their pupils from smaller industries, agriculture and other sources. There are three types of course specializing to some degrees in physics, chemistry or biology, and a fourth of a more general nature (see Fig. 25).[18] The curriculum is somewhat

[18] Vodinský, *Schools in Czechoslovakia*, p. 72.

Fig. 25. CZECHOSLOVAKIA: SECONDARY SCHOOLS FOR WORKERS

Course:	Physics			Chemistry			Biology			Gen. Ed.		
Class:	1	2	3	1	2	3	1	2	3	1	2	3
1. Czech/Slovak language and literature	2	2	2									
2. Russian language	2	2	1									
3. Civics	1	—	1		Subjects 1–6: same curriculum for all courses							
4. History	—	—	1									
5. Geography	—	3	1									
6. Mathematics	4	—	4									
7. Descriptive geometry	—	2	—	—	—	—	—	—	—	—	—	—
8. Physics	2	3	3	2	2	2	2	2	2	2	2	2
9. Chemistry	1	1	1	1	3	2	1	1	1	1	1	1
10. Biology	—	—	1	—	1	1	—	3	2	—	3	1
11. Technical instruction	3	4	4	3	4	4	3	4	4	3	4	4
12. Optional subject	—	—	—	—	—	—	—	—	—	—	—	—
Total hours weekly	15	18	18	15	18	18	15	18	18	15	18	18
13. Additional subjects:	2	2	2	2	2	2	2	2	2	2	2	2

Note: Optional subject—second foreign language, art, descriptive geometry.
Additional subjects—foreign language, descriptive geometry, art, music, Latin.

narrower, and the time more limited, than in the general secondary school. Workers attending these schools are given half the time off from their work, and have to find the rest themselves. Originally, it was planned to make 15,000 places available by 1965, but before long it was clear that expansion was going to outrun the plan. In 1961–2 the figure had already risen to over 14,000, a rapid growth from the starting figure of 1000 in 1959.[19]

On the more directly vocational side, there are several kinds of courses in factories for the further development of trade qualifications, and a number of two-year schools that provide vocational qualifications for students who have already completed general secondary education.

(f) *Higher Education*

There are over forty higher educational institutions (*vysoké školy*) as against nine before the war. They are of four kinds:

(i) *Universities*. There are eight universities, ranging in size from the ancient Charles University of Prague, with eleven faculties (law, arts, mathematics and physics, natural sciences, general medicine, paediatrics, hygiene and public health, the Institute of Adult Education and Journalism, the Institute of Physical Training and Sport, and two additional faculties of medicine in other towns, Plzen and Hradec Králové) to the Palacký University of Olomouc or the Šafařík University of Košice, with three each (medicine, philosophy and science). In between comes the Comenius University of Bratislava, with six faculties (medicine, pharmacy, law, philosophy, science, physical education and sport), the chief university of Slovakia. The Schools of Economics of Prague and Bratislava are normally included in the same category as the universities. In a class by itself is the 17th November University in Prague, named after International Students' Day, the anniversary of the execution of student leaders by the Nazis in 1939. Like the Patrice Lumumba University in Moscow, it

[19] *Czechoslovakia: Education*, pp. 40–43.

specializes in the training of overseas students, especially those from the Afro-Asian and Latin-American countries. The Faculty of Language and Specialized Preparation, as the name suggests, is chiefly concerned with providing preparatory courses in Czech and filling some of the gaps in the students' schooling. The Faculty of Natural and Technical Sciences concentrates on training engineers, scientists and technologists, while the Faculty of Social Sciences provides courses for secondary school teachers in the humanities.[20]

The universities deal principally with the humanities, pure sciences, economics and the older professions such as medicine and law. The normal length of course is five years, and six in medicine.

(ii) *Technical universities and colleges.* There are fourteen of these, mostly modern foundations, though the Czech Technical University of Prague dates from 1707. Some give courses in many branches of technology, such as the Prague Technical University, the Technical University of Brno, or the Slovak Technical University in Bratislava, all of which have faculties of architecture and building, engineering and electrical engineering; Prague also has a faculty of technical and nuclear physics, Bratislava of chemical engineering. Others are more specialized—agriculture at Brno, Prague and Nitra, chemical technology at Prague and Pordubice, mining and metallurgy at Ostrava, forestry and wood processing at Zvolen, and so forth. Most courses last for five years, though five and a half are required for engineering, electrical engineering and building, and six for architecture. The technical universities and colleges have rather more than half the total number of students in higher education—over 42,000 full-time and 17,000 part-time students in 1963.[21]

(iii) *Schools of fine arts.* There are six of these: the Academy of Fine Arts in Prague and the College of Fine Arts in Bratislava concentrate on drawing, painting, sculpture, design, etc. Prague, Bratislava and Brno have colleges of music and dramatic arts;

[20] Luděk Holubec, *University Education in Czechoslovakia*, pp. 37 ff.
[21] Vodinský, *Schools in Czechoslovakia*, p. 80.

they cover much the same ground, except that Prague also has a faculty of film and television. There is also a college of applied arts, again in Prague. Courses in the fine arts colleges last for six years, and four or five years in the colleges of music and drama.

(iv) *Teachers' training colleges.* These give three-year courses for teachers in the basic nine-year schools, both for general subjects in the early classes and subject specializations in the later ones. After completing the course and passing the state examination, students teach under supervision for a further year, at the end of which they take a proficiency examination to confirm their qualification.

Each higher educational institution is headed by a Rector, assisted by Prorectors, and each faculty, similarly, is run by a Dean and sub-Deans. Among the staff, lecturers and senior lectures are appointed by the Rectors, and docents (readers) are appointed from their ranks by the Minister of Education and Culture. Professors, however, are appointed by the President of the Republic, though presumably he relies on ministerial advice. The number of students has risen from about 20,000 before the war to over 130,000 in 1964, some 40,000 of whom followed part-time courses.[22]

(g) *Teacher Training*

Training is given at three kinds of institution, according to the level of class to be taught. Kindergarten teachers are trained at pedagogic schools, with four-year courses for students direct from the nine-year schools, or two-year courses for those who hold the *matura*. These are now being converted to post-*matura* courses only, and the four-year courses are being run down.[23] All other teachers must have some kind of higher educational qualification— teachers' training colleges for the nine-year schools, university degrees (the teacher-training subjects forming part of the normal

[22] *Ibid.*
[23] Oral communications, Prague, September 1966. Ministerstvo školství a kultury, Čj. 21 069/65–I/3 (1965). (Ministerial instruction.)

course) for secondary schools,[24] and one-year training courses after the completion of technical colleges studies for teachers of vocational subjects. Further, every major city has an institute for the organization of refresher courses and courses leading to higher qualifications, and each of the 108 districts has a pedagogical centre for the exchange of information, dissemination of literature, etc. These, and other specialist advisory bodies (the State Commission for Higher Schools, the Central Commission for Vocational Guidance, the research institutes, the Central Cultural Council for Adult Education, the Teaching Aids Centre, the State Pedagogical Publishing House and others), work under the general supervision of the single Ministry of Education and Culture.

The educational system of Czechoslovakia, spared some of the worst drawbacks common in other countries, did not have to devote so much of the available energies and resources to basic education, dealing with illiteracy, and filling essential gaps. But expansion there has been, and the rural areas, especially Slovakia, have benefited from this. Since 1948 there have been several major reforms, and in the last two or three years there have been still more changes, more noticeably in the expansion of adult education and the reassessment of the place of labour and polytechnical studies in general education. More generally, there has been some change of tone in the recent past. Political content, though still prominent, is less dogmatic in treatment and less stridently expressed. There is a greater willingness to experiment with new methods, curricula, aids and textbooks; admittedly, much of the planning that accompanies this is rather random, and some of the innovations are received too uncritically, as were the innovations from Soviet practice at an earlier stage. Nevertheless, there does seem to be an increased readiness to reassess what is being done, and a determination to continue building up a system that can reconcile the need for a common basic educational experience for all with differentiation to suit various needs and talents in the later stages.

[24] Luděk Holubec, *op. cit.*, pp. 37 ff. Prospective teachers at university study a combination of two subjects, others specialize in one only.

CHAPTER 4

Hungary

1. BACKGROUND TO THE SYSTEM

Hungary is vulnerable. Lying at the crossroads of migration routes, the plains of the Danube and the Tisza have been open to invasion and conquest throughout recorded history. The Magyars themselves were invaders, sweeping in from Asia and settling in the area at the end of the ninth century A.D. They were not the first; Thracians, Illyrians, Celts, Teutons, Slavs, Huns, Avars and others had passed before them. Nor were they the last; the Mongols devastated the territory in the thirteenth century and the Turks, after some reverses, took most of it by the middle of the sixteenth. The rump of Hungary passed under the dominion of the Habsburgs, who used it as a springboard for their drive against the Turks. But this turned out to be little more than a change of masters. When the Turks were finally driven out in 1686, Hungary became in effect a conquered province, and for centuries afterwards was run as a semi-colonial dependency of the Austrian Empire.

Revolts as well as wars have punctuated Hungarian history. The Habsburgs pursued, there as elsewhere, a policy of Germanization, even under the comparatively enlightened despotism of Maria Theresa and Joseph II. There was a serious national uprising under Prince Rákóczy at the beginning of the eighteenth century, a Jacobin movement at the end, and Hungary, under Lajos Kossuth, took part in the wave of revolutions that swept Europe in 1848. The revolution was put down with the aid of foreign troops—a pattern that was to be repeated more than once —but it did at least force some concessions from the Austrians. Under the Dual Monarchy compromise of 1867, Hungary became, nominally at least, a kingdom in her own right with her own parliamentary institutions. Serfdom (again, nominally at least) was abolished. The concessions did not, however, extend to the Slovenes, Croats, Slovaks and Rumanians who made up the bulk of the population of the kingdom. They had to wait until the Austro-Hungarian Empire fell apart at the end of the First World War.

Independence did not bring security. In Hungary itself, a republican government was set up, resigned, and was replaced by the communist government of Béla Kún. This was in turn overthrown, by foreign troops, after 133 days, and the counter-revolution brought to power Admiral (!) Miklós Horthy as "Regent" of Hungary. He was to remain in power until the end of the Second World War.

Horthy was an old-fashioned reactionary, greatly given to banging the nationalist drum and demanding the return of the territories ceded in 1920 to Czechoslovakia, Rumania and Yugoslavia. The best chance of having these demands met seemed to lie in alliance with the Axis powers whose policy, especially in its anti-Semitic and anti-Communist aspects, appealed to Horthy's régime in any case. Anti-Jewish laws were formalized in 1938, the Vienna Awards gave Horthy much of the territory he demanded, and finally Hungary completed the process of joining the Nazi camp by entering the war on Hitler's side. Little was gained from it. The temporary reoccupation of parts of Slovakia, Yugoslavia and Rumania was paid for at a heavy price; the German and Soviet armies fought it out across the whole of Hungary, with enormous damage and the loss of probably half a million (out of $8\frac{1}{2}$ million) Hungarian lives.

The agonies were not over yet. The expulsion of the Germans by the Soviet Army in 1945 got rid of Horthy, but the Stalinist rule of Mátyás Rákosi became increasingly repressive until even Party circles had to recognize that the population had become quite alienated from the régime. Rákosi was removed from office, but it was too late. In October 1956 yet another uprising broke out (started by Communists, whoever else may have joined later) and was put down by Soviet troops. Loss of life has been estimated at some 200,000.

Wars and revolts have been only part of Hungary's tribulations. Even in times of peace and relative stability, under the House of Árpád in the Middle Ages or the Angevin dynasty that succeeded it, there were constant clashes between king and nobility, nobility and peasantry. The failure of the Peasant Revolt under György Dózsa in 1514 marked the consolidation of serfdom and the power of the aristocracy; from that time on, throughout the period of Habsburg rule, Hungary became the granary of Austria, underdeveloped and stagnant economically. There was some development of light industry under Horthy, but not enough to make for much improvement; between the wars, Hungary was known, with some justice, as the "land of three million beggars". Before the Second World War, 14 in every 10,000 were dying of tuberculosis annually;[1] infant mortality was high, unemployment rife. Illiteracy was over 8 per cent,[2] and 20 per cent did not even complete four years of primary school, let alone go any further.[3] Secondary and university education had been developed to a high standard, but reached only a small section of the population. Among the pupils of secondary grammar schools—then the only way to higher education—only about 4 per cent were the children of workers or peasants.[4]

The legacy of the past, distant and recent, has profoundly affected the development of education in Hungary. The low living standards, backward agriculture and the undeveloped state of industry, added to the damage caused by the war, made economic growth urgently necessary. Hungary could no longer afford to be an agrarian country, but had to industrialize; and

[1] *Language and History of the Hungarian People*, p. 12. (Pannonia, Budapest, 1964.)

[2] Márton Horváth, "Public and Higher Education", p. 81. In: János Veres (ed.), *The Experiences of Building a New Society*. (Pannonia, Budapest, 1964.) The rate is higher if younger children are excluded from the reckoning. Thus, in 1941 over 12 per cent of people over the age of 8 were illiterate. (Census of 1941.)

[3] *Language and History of the Hungarian People*, p. 11.
[4] *Ibid.*

for this, planning and economic investment were not enough. Educational expansion at all levels, and particularly in the technical and vocational sectors, was necessary for the success of such a policy. None of this, of course, could guarantee economic success, as was to become abundantly clear in the 1950's, but it was an essential development none the less. Further, on grounds of sheer efficiency, quite apart from political and ideological considerations, the narrowly based traditional educational system could not be adequate to meet new needs. The mould, as one observer has put it,[5] had to be broken.

Hungary's chequered and violent history has also left its mark. Hungarians are intensely proud of being Hungarian; this fierce national pride was submerged somewhat during the Stalin era, but boiled over in the rising of 1956. The suppression of the rising (officially, of the counter-revolution) set a limit to Hungarian nationalist aspirations, but at the same time it made abundantly clear the dangers of limiting them too far. There was no reversion to the cruder methods of the Rákosi period, but an increased liberalization and flexibility that has made itself felt during the last decade in education as in other things. In its present form, national pride is reflected not only in an increasing tendency to go their own way in solving their own problems, but in an ever-growing interest in world issues and international contacts. The educational system, appropriately in a country of 10 million surrounded by quite different peoples, has become outward-looking.

2. THE OLD SYSTEM AND POST-WAR DEVELOPMENTS

Education in Hungary traces its beginnings from the founding of the first schools in the eleventh century and the first universities in the fourteenth and fifteenth. Throughout the intervening centuries there have been many attempts to reform the schools and build up a national educational system. János Apáczai-Csere, a

[5] W. Kenneth Richmond, *Educational Planning in Hungary*, p. 99 (*Comparative Education*, **2**, 2 (March 1966), pp. 93–105).

contemporary of Comenius, was a notable advocate of educational reform, as was, in a different way, Tessedik in the eighteenth century. Many prominent nineteenth-century leaders of the national revival, among them Kossuth, Kölcsey and Széchenyi, pressed for national education as a way of achieving their aims, and József Eötvös, the first Minister of Education, tried to carry these ideas into practice. Development was slow, however, and, as we have seen, limited in extent. Educational expansion figured largely in the programme of the 1919 Hungarian Soviet Republic, but it did not remain in power long enough to do much about it. By the end of the Horthy period, there was still only a six-year basic school, from which a minority went on after four years to four-year intermediate or eight-year secondary schools. Most children, however, did not even complete the six-year elementary school. Many of the schools were private or run by church organizations, and nearly all were fee-paying.

Changes since the war have already been touched on (see p. 83). The first piece of legislation—the most fundamental—was the Law of 1945, which nationalized the private and church schools and instituted a compulsory basic school from 6 to 14. Of the measures taken shortly afterwards, the anti-illiteracy campaign of 1948 was a clearing-up operation, and the 1949 Constitution, by writing in the right to free and compulsory basic education, laid the formal ground for later development. Among other changes in the post-war period were the expansion of technical and vocational as well as the more traditional forms of secondary schooling, and the absorbtion of apprentice training into the educational system.

3. THE PRESENT SYSTEM

The present school system is laid down in the Education Law of 1961. Like its counterparts in other countries, the 1961 Law brought in an increased emphasis on polytechnical education in the general schools, and pressed on with expansion in the whole system—in this case, more specifically, extending compulsory

264   *Society, Schools and Progress in Eastern Europe*

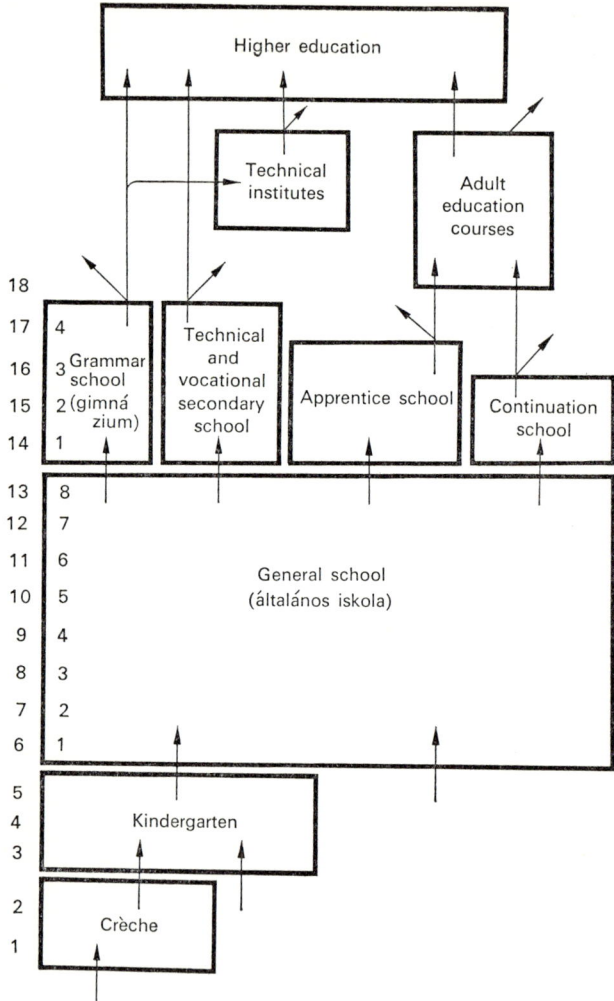

Fig. 26. Hungary: Educational system

Fig. 27. Hungary: Eight-year School Curriculum[6]

Class:	I	II	III	IV	V	VI	VII	VIII	Total
1. Hungarian language and literature	11	12	12	12	8	6	5	4	2310
2. Mathematics	6	6	6	6	5	5	4	4	1386
3. Russian language	—	—	—	—	3	3	3	3	396
4. Knowledge of the homeland	—	—	1	—	—	—	—	—	33
5. Geography	—	—	—	2	2	—	2	2	363
6. History	—	—	—	—	2	3	3	2	264
7. Physics	—	—	—	—	—	3	3	2	165
8. Chemistry	—	—	—	—	—	—	—	3	99
9. Biology	—	1	—	—	2	2	2	2	264
10. Drawing	—	2	2	2	2	2	2	2	429
11. Singing	2	2	2	2	2	2	2	2	528
12. Physical education	2	2	2	2	2	2	2	2	528
13. Work study	1	1	1	1	2	2	2	2	396
14. Class teacher's period	—	—	—	—	1	1	1	1	132
Total hours weekly	22	24	26	27	29	31	31	31	7293
15. Optional foreign language	—	—	—	—	2	2	2	2	264

Work study—"handwork" in classes I–IV, "practical work" in V–VIII.
Optional foreign language—English, French or German.

[6] Márton Horváth, *op. cit.* p. 85.

education to the age of 16. This was done, however, not by extending the basic school (as in other countries), but by making other arrangements at secondary level. There have been some modifications since then—reappraisal of the role of polytechnical education, reorganization of secondary schools, increased experimentation and the introduction of new curricula, programmes and textbooks. The main stages are as follows:

(a) *Pre-school Education*

As usual, the pre-school institutions are on two levels: crèches (*bölcsődek*) for children up to the age of 3, and kindergartens (*óvodák*) for children from 3 to 6. Both are voluntary, and may make a charge for maintenance, depending on parental income.

Crèches may be day- or boarding-nurseries, run by local authorities or factories and other enterprises. There are still not enough places for all who want them (about 10 per cent of the age-group) but the expansion has been dramatic, over forty times the admittedly low pre-war figure.[7] They are supervised by the Ministry of Health.

Kindergartens may also be run by economic organizations as well as local authorities, subject to the supervision of the Ministry of Cultural Affairs. They are of various types, the full-day kindergarten being the commonest, over half the total number. There are also seasonal, half-day, and weekly or permanent boarding kindergartens. Expansion has been slower in this field than in others. There were under 190,000 children in kindergartens in 1965–6, an increase of just over 1 per cent on the previous year.[8] This is not much over 30 per cent of the age-group, as compared with just under 24 per cent in 1938.[9] Certainly, it is a high pro-

[7] *Education, Social Conditions and Public Health*, p. 7. (Pannonia, Budapest, 1964.)

[8] Ministry of Cultural Affairs, *Report on Educational Progress in 1965–1966*, p. 6. (Report to the XXIX Session of the International Conference on Public Education, Geneva, July 1966.)

[9] Ferenc Ábent et al., *Das Schulwesen in der Ungarischen Volksrepublik*, p. 551. In: Deutsches Pädagogisches Zentralinstitut, *Das Schulwesen Sozialistischer Länder in Europa*. (Volk und Wissen Volkeigener Verlag, Berlin, 1962.)

portion by our standards, but the Hungarians feel that it is not good enough and calls for more attention.

(b) *The Basic School*

The basic unit of the Hungarian educational system is the general school (*általános iskola*), with a course of eight years from 6 to 14. The curriculum follows the general pattern of similar schools in other East European countries, starting with the main emphasis on Hungarian language and mathematics (together with art, handwork, music, physical education) in the earlier classes, and introducing other subjects—history, geography, languages, the sciences—about half-way through the course. The curriculum and schemes of work were revised in 1963, and since then have been introduced gradually to replace the older plans of 1959. The process of transisition was completed in the current school year (1966–7), and is now in force for all general schools throughout the country.[10]

But there are some departures from the uniform scheme. In the last few years there have been moves to provide more scope for special talents, and to take advantage of the greater flexibility of younger children for certain kinds of learning, by developing a system of special classes in music and foreign languages (Russian, English, French and German). In 1965–6 over 10 per cent of the general schools ran special classes of this kind; in 1966–7 the figure was 12 per cent, and further expansion is planned. There are 762 music classes and 679 language classes at the moment.[11] Children in special language classes begin studying the language in the third year, about the age of 8. This development is popular with parents; the Hungarians are in any case eager linguists—they have to be—and seize keenly on opportunities to learn at any stage. (Ernő Nagy tells of a private teacher in Budapest who offered lessons in Bushman and Bantu languages and was swamped with applications.)[12] The level of language-teaching

[10] *Report on Educational Progress*, p. 11.
[11] *Report on Educational Progress*, p. 9.
[12] Ernő Bajor Nagy, *A Country at School*, pp. 111–12.

in Hungarian schools is high enough, but really excellent in the special classes, giving the children a high degree of competence in the spoken and written language and, incidentally, familiarity with the life and culture of the country in question. One gets used to linguistic competence among East European children, and comes to assume that they will know immeasurably more about our country than we do about theirs; nevertheless, it can still be startling to be knowledgeably cross-examined by 10-year-olds, in reasonably good English, on the relative merits of historic buildings in Edinburgh or football teams in Glasgow.

There is the usual system of assessment (5 *down to* 1 this time) and promotion from class to class. Children who fail more than two subjects have to repeat the year; if they fail two only, they have a second chance at a supplementary examination after the summer holidays.

Practical training was introduced in the basic schools in 1963. There is not very much of it—one hour a week in the first two years, two hours thereafter. The programme begins with elementary handwork, and develops into a coverage of more complex skills. The approach is polytechnical, not vocational, and the teaching is done in school workshops. The aim is not only to acquaint the children with the elements of production, but is social and moral as well. According to one writer:

> Systematic, careful and precise work trains the children to be neat, gives them individual initiative, and helps to instil in them a respect for labour. ... Our experience indicates that practical training has a good influence on the whole range of educational and teaching work, and the children are better able to master and assimilate theoretical subjects. During the debate on the curriculum there were some people who opposed the introduction of manual instruction, but today both teachers and parents know that it makes the whole school work more productive, and the time devoted to it is repaid many times over.[13]

Some teachers are not so sure about this particular line of argument, which begs a number of questions, and it is said that some parents, particularly those in white-collar occupations, are less than enthusiastic about "dirty hands". Teachers prefer to argue

[13] Márton Horváth, *op. cit.*, p. 86.

on general educational grounds for the spending of some time on practical work—provided it is not too much—and many parents, especially workers, seem to approve the idea that their children's schooling should not be exclusively bookish or too far removed from their own experience.[14]

Rural general schools still present something of a problem. Although the development of agricultural co-operatives has helped to some extent in collecting the rural population into larger and more viable groups, there are still remote areas where the population is thinly spread. In some cases it is possible to arrange transport so that children can travel to central schools for the upper class courses; alternatively, weekly boarding schools for children between 10 and 14 can be used if the distances are great. So far, however, the "cultural differences" between town and country have still to be smoothed out.[15] In the towns, there remains some shortage of building space. Some of the existing schools are overcrowded or overdue for renewal, and some general schools still have to work on a shift system. This, however, is being reduced steadily every year.

(c) *Secondary Schools*

General schooling ends at 14, compulsory schooling at 16. Consequently, all must go on to some kind of further schooling. The secondary system is under going some changes at present, but the main categories are as follows:

(i) *Grammar school (gimnázium)*. The grammar school gives a four-year general course leading to the leaving certificate (*érettségeri*). The curriculum was until recently entirely academic, specializing to some extent either in the humanities or the sciences (see Fig. 28).[16] This, however, had been heavily critized for some time. In 1958 experiments were begun with what has become known as the "5 + 1" system—five days of general education and

[14] Various conversations, Budapest, September 1966.
[15] Horváth, *op. cit.*, p. 87.
[16] Ábent, *op. cit.*, p. 559.

FIG. 28. HUNGARY: SECONDARY GENERAL SCHOOL (*gimnázium*) CURRICULUM 1965 ("5+1")[17]

Class:	I	II	III	IV	Total
1. Hungarian language	2	1	1	1	5
2. Hungarian literature	2	3	3	3	11
3. History	2	3	3	3	11
4. Basis of our ideology	–	–	–	3	3
5. Russian language	3	3	3	3	12
6. Second foreign language	2	2	2	2	8
7. Mathematics	4	4	4	4	16
8. Physics	–	2	4	4	10
9. Chemistry	2	2	2	–	6
10. Biology	2	2	2/0	2	7
11. Psychology	–	–	0/2	–	1
12. Geography	2	2	2	–	6
13. Art	2	–	–	1	3
14. Singing and music	2	1	–	–	3
15. Physical education	2	2	2	2	8
16. Practical work	5	5	5	5	20
17. Class teacher's period	1	1	1	1	4
Total	33	33	34	34	134

Note: This is the basic "5+1" curriculum. There are many variants with only two hours per week devoted to practical work; these include curricula in which the extra time is given to foreign languages, mathematics, mathematics and physics, physics and chemistry, chemistry and biology, art or music. The time allocation for the other subjects remains substantially the same.

one of practical vocational training (see Fig. 28).[17a] The system was expanded gradually, until by 1964 it was said that the vast majority of grammar schools were working under this scheme.[18] The day of production training consists of two hours of technical theory and technical drawing, and three hours of in school or factory instruction workshops in the second and third years, and work alongside skilled workers in the fourth year. The final examination gives the student a preliminary vocational qualification, but he still needs up to a year of further training before

[17] Muvelődésügyi Minisztérium, *Tanterv és Utasítás a gimnáziumok számára: Óratervek*, pp. 7–15 (Tankönyvkiadó, Budapest, 1965.)

[17a] Ábent, *op. cit.*, p. 559.

[18] Horváth, *op. cit.*, p. 89.

becoming a fully qualified skilled worker. This much in theory. In practice, the scheme has run into the kinds of difficulty experienced elsewhere—lack of adequate facilities in many places, lack of interest on the part of both pupils and staff in taking the principle of practical training as far as that, much time spent on time-consuming and repetitive work, and so forth. Even where there were suitable factories nearby, their facilities have often failed to cope with the numbers—there have been too few instructors, and many managers, glad though they are to welcome groups of students, do not relish having them under their feet in large numbers every week. There is still considerable controversy about the system; it is not dogmatically enforced, and one observer at least notes that it is often not enforced at all. In 1966 only 43 per cent of the grammar schools were operating it fully, the rest contenting themselves with the two hours of theoretical technical instruction.[19] The details of the programme are in any case left to the local authorities or even individual schools to work out. Clearly, the question is not yet closed, but it seems unlikely that *vocational*, as opposed to *polytechnical*, training will become a central feature of the curriculum.

The two-course division of the curriculum is on the way out. In 1965 a new uniform curriculum was drawn up; this was introduced in the first class immediately, and should be universally in force by 1968. It is not completely uniform, however. Room has been made for a wider choice of subjects within the framework of the common course, and it is now possible to concentrate more on languages (Russian, English, French, German, Italian, Spanish), music, fine arts, the sciences, mathematics, etc.[20] This has been generally welcomed, oddly at first sight, by the advocates both of more and less specialization. It is, perhaps, a viable compromise; the common core of humanities and sciences is retained for all pupils, but at the same time they can pay more attention to the particular areas that interest them. Provision for this modified specialization is still uneven, but increasing.

[19] Richmond, *op. cit.*, p. 102.
[20] *Report on Educational Progress*, pp. 9–10.

Among other innovations is a new subject called "The Basis of our World View", a course in civics and political theory of the type familiar elsewhere. It was tried out in a number of schools in 1965–6, and is to be introduced in the final year of all grammar schools in 1967. The principal themes to be dealt with are laid down in the Ministry's scheme,[21] and the textbook (as for other subjects) is centrally prescribed. It is emphasized, however, that the subject is to be taught through discussion, not preaching.[22]

Grammar schools are sometimes organized together with general schools as complete twelve-year schools. In such cases, however, some pupils go elsewhere at the end of class VIII, and others come into the first year of the grammar school from other general schools.

(ii) *Secondary vocational and technical schools.* The technical secondary school (*technikum*) was set up to give intermediate instruction in some fifty branches of industry and agriculture, with courses ranging from two to four years, depending on the speciality, 35 per cent of the time being given to general education, 35 per cent to vocational theory, and 30 per cent to vocational practice. These have been developing into full four-year courses of combined technical and general education, leading to both a trade qualification and the leaving certificate. Experiments with *secondary vocational schools* began in 1959. These now give four-year general and vocational courses, also with a double qualification. Curricular time is divided between theoretical and practical work on a 4:2 or 5:1 ratio, with four weeks' continuous work practice at the end of the school year. Nearly forty trades are taught, including those of fitter, toolmaker, motor mechanic, pharmacist, and various kinds of workers in hydraulics, poultry breeding, viticulture and fruit-growing, crop protection, commerce, foreign trade, economics, postal communications, etc.[23]

Secondary schools of this type are also being reorganized. Some

[21] József Gert Farkas, "Gymnasallehrplan 'Grundlagen unserer Weltanschauung'" (*Informationsdienst zum Bildungswesen in Osteuropa*, **10/11**, pp. 50–52. Osteuropa-Institut an der Freien Universität Berlin, 1965.)

[22] Oral communications, Budapest, September 1966.

[23] Ábent, *op. cit.*, p. 582.

of the more advanced and specialized trades are being moved from the secondary stage to higher technical schools (open to students who have completed secondary education); the rest of the technical and vocational schools are to be integrated, under an order of 1965, into a unified secondary vocational school. The transition should be complete by 1968. Curricula are still being prepared; in general, it is expected that the bias will be 2 to 1 in favour of theoretical subjects, subject to variations according to the vocation in question. The maximum number of hours per week is to be thirty-six and not more than six theoretical or eight practical lessons in one day.[24]

(iii) *Apprentice training schools* (*Ipari tanulók gyakorló iskoláják*). These are generally attached to industrial concerns or agricultural co-operatives; the courses, heavily biased to vocational training, lead to skilled-workers' qualifications but not the secondary school leaving certificate. Most courses last for three years, though in some trades they may be shorter, and can be reduced to one year for students who have completed secondary schooling. In a few trades only students holding the leaving certificate are accepted,[25] but this is unusual—the great majority of apprentices are between the ages of 14 and 17. At the end of the course, the newly qualified workers normally go straight into employment; they may, however, qualify for higher general or technical education by taking secondary qualifications, equivalent to the grammar school certificate, through the adult educational system.

(iv) *Continuation schools* (*továbbképző iskolák*). Pupils who leave the general school at 14 and do not continue with their studies in secondary or apprentice schools are required to attend *continuation schools* until they reach the age of 16. They must attend two days or the equivalent (ten hours) per week. Under 20,000 are enrolled in these schools, as against 172,000 in three-year apprentice training schools and over 230,000 in grammar, technical and vocational schools.[26]

---

[24] *Report on Educational Progress*, p. 12.
[25] Ábent, *op. cit.*, p. 579.
[26] *Report on Educational Progress*, pp. 7–8.

Selection for secondary schools is made by the schools themselves, based on reports from the general schools. Attempts are made to ease the process, however, by guidance at the general school stage, in conjunction with the local authorities and the National Council for Choice of Career. According to latest information, about half the age-group seem to go on with some kind of full-time secondary schooling up to the age of 18.[27]

(d) *Special Schools*

Special schools for children requiring special educational treatment (*gyógypedagógiai iskolák*) are classified according to the children's handicaps—schools for the deaf, hard of hearing, blind, partially-sighted, convalescents, the mentally retarded, children with speech defects, children with sensory-motor defects, etc. They include kindergartens, general schools, and secondary and apprentice schools. The children are given remedial and special training, and otherwise follow curricula as close to those of the ordinary schools as their handicaps permit. For orphans, the maladjusted and children from "problem" homes there are the "children's towns", self-contained communities with boarding facilities, workshops and plots, and schooling from kindergarten to secondary school stage. Fót Children's Town (*Fót Gyermekváros*), the largest of these, cares for over 900 pupils from the age of 3 to 18; there is a model farm, workshops and, of course, a Pioneer detachment, with the object of providing for social education and practical training as well as general schooling.[28]

For the specially gifted there are general schools with a musical bias, and secondary arts schools. The curriculum is substantially the same as in the ordinary schools, with a large additional element of instrumental music, singing, visual arts, or whatever special field is involved. The majority of children in

[27] There is some doubt about the exact figures, owing to uncertainty about the categories of "secondary schools" referred to in various sources. Estimates range from 45 to 60 per cent.

[28] "Fót Children's Town: the Makarenko Approach" (*Times Educational Supplement*, 27 November 1964).

these schools go on to the appropriate higher educational institutions.

(e) *Adult Education*

General schools for adults provide evening or correspondence courses on the same lines as the basic eight-year school, the length of course depending on the standard already reached. Secondary schools, both grammar and technical, also provide part-time courses to enable adults with only basic schooling to reach the leaving-certificate standard or improve their vocational qualifications.

Numbers are falling at both stages, but much more noticeably in the adult general schools. In 1965–6 there were over 61,000 students, about a third less than the previous year. In the adult secondary schools, there were over 60,000 in grammar and over 110,000 in technical courses, a drop of 6 and 9 per cent respectively from the previous year. This is only to be expected, as the spread of secondary schooling and the enforcement of compulsory basic schooling make these facilities less necessary.[29]

Apart from adult institutions giving formal qualifications, there are others which give courses for vocational improvement or general culture—the Peasant Academies, Youth Academies, Parents' Academies and, most popular of all, the "Free Universities" which are organized in all the major towns. The Free Universities offer courses between one and four years in length on almost every conceivable subject from electron physics and textile technology to logic or history of art and, of course, languages. The József Attila Free University, for example, teaches sixteen languages to over 7000 students, including not only the more usual European languages but other like Chinese, Hindi, Arabic and Turkish as well. No qualifications are given for these courses; they are being taken, for interest only, by about 20,000 students in their spare time—another example of the "learning disease" that Hungarians talk about.[30]

[29] *Report on Educational Progress*, p. 7.
[30] E. B. Nagy, *op. cit.*, pp. 112 ff.

(f) *Higher Education*

As it is currently used in Hungary, the term "higher education" applies not only to universities and colleges of equivalent standard, but to other institutions giving shorter courses of professional training to students who have completed secondary schooling—rather like the East German *Fachschulen*. There are now ninety-two institutions altogether, with 111 faculties. Some of them have been in existence for centuries; even in 1945 there were sixteen, a not inconsiderable number for a relatively underdeveloped country with a population (then) of $8\frac{1}{2}$ million. Most, however, are recent creations, notably the technical and agricultural schools; the newest so far is the Higher Building Institute at Debrecen, established in 1965.

The main categories are: (1) Universities—five of the classic type (humanities and pure sciences), four technical universities, three universities of agricultural science and five medical universities. (2) Fine art academies (four). (3) Pedagogical institutes —five of these. (4) Agricultural colleges (four). (5) One college of physical culture. These could be considered as of university standard; courses generally last for five years, though some are four-year courses, and medical courses take six years. (6) Fourteen teacher training colleges of various types. (7) Higher technical schools—twenty-five industrial, twenty agricultural, three professional. Courses in these are of two or three years' duration, and lead to qualifications below degree level.[31]

There are 94,000 students in higher educational institutions of all types at the moment. Over half are attending full time courses (51,000), the rest studying in the evenings or by correspondence.[32] The number of students is over eight times the prewar figure; even if allowance is made for the inclusion of students following shorter and less demanding courses, it is still a dramatic

---

[31] József Gert Farkas, "Statistische Angaben zur Entwicklung des Hochschulwesens (*Informationsdienst zum Bildungswesen in Osteuropa*, **10/11**, pp. 54–57, Berlin, 1965).

[32] *Report on Educational Progress*, p. 8.

increase. The change of emphasis, too, is striking. Before the war, nearly 40 per cent of all students were in the law faculties, compared with 10 per cent studying engineering.[33] Now, by way of contrast, students of technology outnumber law students by seven to one.[34]

Students concentrate on their special field from the first year of the course, but they are also obliged to continue with Russian (and sometimes another foreign language as well), physical education, and political subjects—political economy, Marxist-Leninist theory, and the like.

As elsewhere, competition for entry is keen, and is becoming keener with the spread of secondary education. In 1965 there were three times as many applicants for the universities as there were places. Obviously, the leaving certificate is not enough; entrance examinations have to be taken in subjects related to the proposed speciality—biology and physics for medicine, mathematics, chemistry and biology for agriculture, Hungarian and history for law, and so on. The number of places is being increased, but the number successfully completing the secondary schools is increasing faster. The building up of the technical schools is one way of taking up some of the extra numbers.

Over half the students live in hostels (due partly to the heavy concentration of cultural life and higher educational facilities in the capital), and all are entitled to scholarships if their marks are satisfactory (93 per cent of the total in 1964).[35] The actual amount varies according to family income. It does not amount to much more than pocket-money, but hostel accommodation and meals are heavily subsidized. Outstanding students in academic work and social activity can win special scholarships that come nearer the average working wage.[36]

Higher institutions are organized on the familiar pattern—a Rector and Prorectors and a council of senior staff at the head,

---

[33] Nagy, *op. cit.*, p. 55.
[34] Farkas, *op. cit.*, p. 56.
[35] *Ibid.*, p. 57.
[36] Horváth, *op. cit.*, pp. 96–97.

with an analogous system operating at faculty level. They work under the general supervision—which extends to textbooks and curricula—of the Universities and Scientific and Technical Departments of the Ministry of Cultural Affairs.

(g) *Teacher Training*

Teachers are trained in separate institutions according to the level of class taught. There are now no pedagogical secondary schools; all intending teachers must complete secondary education before embarking on professional training. (i) Kindergarten teachers are trained in two-year colleges (*Óvónőképző iskolák*); there are three of these in the whole country. (ii) Teachers of the first four classes of the general school take three-year courses in teacher-training colleges (*Tanár továbbképző kollégiumok*). The curriculum includes teaching methods for the general subjects that they will teach (Hungarian, mathematics, art, music, etc.), general science, hygiene, educational theory, Russian language and political subjects. Teaching practice begins in the third half-year in the school attached to the college, and ends with a term of continuous practice in another school. There are ten of these colleges at present. (iii) Teachers for the upper classes of the general school take four-year courses in the pedagogical institutes (*pedagógiai intézetek*), and are trained as subject specialists. The courses include, in addition to the special subjects, educational theory, psychology, teaching methods and teaching practice—one or two days a week from the sixth semester (half-year), and a continuous period of practice in the fourth year, in the school attached to the institute. (iv) Subject specialist teachers for the secondary schools come from the universities, where the five-year course in the humanities and the pure sciences includes (for all students, whether intending to be teachers or not) educational theory, methods, psychology, philosophy, logic and the usual additional courses in political subjects and one or two foreign languages. Teaching practice is carried out in "pilot schools" in the final year, under the supervision of the school staff. In the second to fourth years the students also come to observe lessons, increasingly (as in the Apáczai-Csere School, for example) through closed-circuit television, which makes it possible for relatively small numbers of schools to cope with the growing numbers of students. (v) Finally, teachers of handicapped children are trained in four-year courses in a special institute. Apart from the usual subjects, they have special courses in the care of backward or handicapped children.

In some specific fields, such as mathematics, physics and foreign languages, there is still some shortage of teachers;[37] but underpaid though teachers are (not only by Western standards but in comparison with many other professions in Hungary), there is no general shortage. Even in the country districts, where there was a supply problem until recently, it is usually possible to staff the schools adequately—where overcrowding exists, it is due to shortage of buildings, not of teachers. This has been accomplished partly by the payment of bonuses to rural teachers and the building of houses and even the provision of private plots, partly to "scholarships with strings"—students who have received a scholarship from a local authority are required to teach in that area if needed.

The qualification given by the various institutes is, unlike those in some other countries, final; but extensive use is made of in-service courses run by the training institutes and the National Institute of Pedagogy (*Országos Pedagógiai Intézet*), under the general supervision of the Ministry of Cultural Affairs. New summer courses have been organized in history, mathematics, geography, physical education and foreign languages, including courses in the U.S.S.R., East Germany, Britain, France and Italy. Further, all schools hold two conferences a year, led by the director, on general problems. For these, the National Institute prepares booklets and bibliographies as a basis for discussion. Recent

---

[37] These are fields where better-paid employment is more readily available. A language teacher, for example, earned 1100 forints a month until the recent increase (itself not very much—an average of 290 forints a month); but an interpreter can earn 130 forints *a day*. (Richmond, *op. cit.*, p. 105.)

examples of the themes discussed at such conferences are "Pupil–Teacher Relations" in 1963, "Unity of Teaching Staff and the Education of the Community" in 1965, "The Educational Work of the Yough Organizations" (also in 1965), "Education for Patriotism" in 1966. School directors attend additional two-week summer courses organized by the local authorities.[38]

The Hungarians themselves are the first to point out past mistakes and recognize the existence of many problems still to be solved. There are still some shortages of teachers of particular subjects; some rural schools still teach several age-groups in the same classroom, and there remain other problems of co-ordination in the remoter rural areas. There is still considerable uncertainty about the best form of curriculum for the schools, especially the secondary schools, and many feel that the most desirable balance between general education and specialization is still to be struck. The place of technical and polytechnical studies remains something of a problem. For all that, the quantitative development of education at all levels since the war has been impressive by any standard, all the more so considering the number of false starts during the Rákosi period.

More striking, though more difficult to pin down, is the atmosphere that pervades the system, especially since the climate became milder after the events of 1956. Centralized though the system is, its actual working is more flexible than a reading of the rules and regulations might suggest. The "learning disease" that Hungarians talk about, half-jocularly, is more than a figure of speech; it may be that an open educational system is still something of a novelty that has not worn off yet, but however that may be there is no denying the great keenness to take advantage of the educational facilities in practically every section of society and every age-group. Even more difficult to be specific about (since one has to rely on impressions) is the atmosphere in the classrooms. Quite apart from the quality of the teaching (usually

[38] Oral communications, National Institute of Pedagogy, Budapest, September 1966.

good, though not of course universally so), one can hardly escape the feeling that children enjoy school, and that the teachers, whatever their level of expertise and at whatever stage they teach, are motivated before all else by a genuine fondness of the children in their care.

CHAPTER 5

Rumania

1. BACKGROUND TO THE SYSTEM

Rumania is the most recent deviationist in Eastern Europe. Long considered one of the most docile of the communist countries—the events of 1956, for example, raised not a flicker of unrest in Bucharest—Rumania created something of a stir on the international stage by striking out on a line of her own in 1965 with a new economic plan, a new constitution, even a change of name from the Rumanian People's Republic to the Socialist Republic of Rumania—a formal but symbolically important step. The changes were not limited to internal matters, but applied to foreign policy as well. Rumania is now developing closer relations with the West, especially with West Germany (much to the annoyance of the East German authorities). Alone among all the communist countries of Europe, she even manages to remain neutral in the present quarrel between the Soviet Union and China.

These developments arose, as we have seen, from an economic dispute with the U.S.S.R.—the Soviet Union (supported by the East Germans) pressing for greater economic integration of the East European bloc, the Rumanians insisting on building up an independent national economy. Having won the economic argument, the Rumanians pursued the logic of their policy into the political sphere. The Rumanian Communist Party loudly proclaimed the independence and equality of all communist parties; the customary declarations of homage to the U.S.S.R. were dropped from all manner of official pronouncements; and the Party leader, Gheorghe Gheorghiu-Dej, once a classic Stalinist, came to be regarded primarily as a national leader, and one of the few men who found it expedient—and possible—to keep on good terms with Mao Tse-tung *and* Tito. In contrast to developments in Yugoslavia, Poland or Hungary, this had little to do with liberalization of the régime, though this has happened to some extent. The appeal of Gheorghiu-Dej (and, since his death in 1965, his successors Maurer and Ceauşescu) was to Rumanian national sentiment.

In Rumania, as elsewhere in Eastern Europe, appeals to national sentiment are readily heard. Like many other countries that spent centuries under Turkish domination, Rumania emerged into independence encumbered with a nationality problem (due to the demographic complexity of the area), and a surfeit of patriotism left over from the struggle to throw off foreign rule— an awkward inheritance, liable to lead to irredentist movements, outbursts of chauvinism, and interminable squabbles over territorial claims. Rumania did quite well out of the post-war settlements, but was left with two particularly sensitive issues: the Rumanian-speaking population of Bessarabia (the Moldavian SSR) remained outside, and the million and a half Hungarians of Transylvania (perforce) inside. Nothing much could be done about the first but, as has been already noted, the revival of Rumanian nationalism has tended to make life more difficult for the national minorities in general and the Hungarians in particular. The Constitution, of course, officially guarantees equality of rights to the non-Rumanian nationalities, including the right to schooling in their own language; but in the present atmosphere, pressures to assimilate are strong. The merging of the Hungarian Bolyai University in Cluj with the Rumanian Babeş University in the same city has already been mentioned as the most striking example of this process. Certainly, the programme of the "Babeş Bolyai" University includes a good deal of Hungarian language and literature, but the principal medium of instruction is Rumanian.[1] The only higher educational institutions with instruction

[1] C. Ionescu-Bujor, *Higher Education in Rumania*, p. 41. (Meridiane, Bucharest, 1964.)

in Hungarian are now the Szentgyörgy István Theatre Institute and a three-year Pedagogical Institute, both in Tîrgu Mureş, capital of the Magyar region.[2]

Assertions of independence from the U.S.S.R., and flirtations with Western countries or with China, should not be given too much political significance. Under the Maurer-Ceauşescu régime, Rumania stays communist, but in her own way. Dalliance with China does not mean that Rumania is going the way of Albania, any more than improved relations with West Germany mean joining the Western camp. In some ways, Rumania's stance is analogous with that of Gaullist France—basically aligned on one side, but insisting on maximum national independence at the same time. In this, too, Rumania is helped by the strength of her economy; potentially, at least, the country is rich, and even now is able to withstand economic pressures that might be applied for political reasons. Continued economic growth is, therefore, particularly important; and, since the educational system is a necessary factor in maintaining this, it remains high on the list of priorities for investment—over 20 per cent of the national budget.

Apart from the constant drive to expand the educational system, often with specific reference to strengthening the national economy, the new-found independence shows itself in a number of ways, notably in the move away from Soviet models. The Maxim Gorki Institute of Russian Language and Literature in Bucharest, long a centre of Soviet influence, is now an Institute of Foreign Languages, with Russian merely one language among many.[3] Russian is no longer compulsory in school; pupils choose one out of four in the fifth year, and another at secondary level, French being the usual first choice as it was under the old system. The content of the curriculum has been not only "de-Stalinized" but de-Russianized as well; there are far fewer laudatory references to the U.S.S.R. than formerly, and fewer than say, in Bulgaria or East Germany at present. There is more attention given to Western practice, less borrowing from the U.S.S.R., and less acknowledgement when this is done. The basic political

[2] C. Ionescu-Bujor, *op. cit.*, pp. 47, 55.

alignment is as before, but is couched in specifically Rumanian rather than Soviet terms.

2. THE OLD SYSTEM AND POST-WAR DEVELOPMENTS

Rumanians are proud of the origins, which they trace back to the Roman colonization of Dacia in Imperial times, and of the strength of their language and culture which enabled them to keep their identity through centuries of Turkish occupation. The beginnings of education are lost in the fragmentary records of monastic schools during the dark ages, but by the thirteenth century there were schools giving instruction in Rumanian. Expansion continued from the fifteenth century onwards, with the foundation of "princely schools" for the sons of the boyars. But progress was uneven, to say the least; in the latter half of the seventeenth century travellers were commenting on the boyars' sons' ability in Latin, but the population at large was left outside the expansion. There were not even any school books printed in Rumania until the turn of the seventeenth century.

Something like a national educational system began to take shape during the nineteenth century, even before the end of Turkish rule in 1878. The setting up of Rumanian-language high schools was helped along by the efforts of nationalist intellectuals such as Lazăr, Rădulescu, Kogălniceanu and many others. Universities were established in Jassy in 1861 and Bucharest in 1864; in the same year, Prince Alexandru Ioan Cuza issued a "Law on Education" that laid the foundations of an integrated national system. In the following years it was expanded and frequently reorganized, most radically by Spiru Haret in 1898. It remained, however, strictly academic and confined to a small élite, and was strongly criticized for this by many liberal philosophers and writers such as Eminescu, Caragiale and Babeș, major figures in the Rumanian cultural pantheon.[4] The reformers

[3] *Ibid.*, p. 39.
[4] A. Manolache, *General Education in Rumania*, pp. 9 ff. (Meridiane, Bucharest, 1965.)

met with only limited success; even by the end of the 1930's, as we have seen, elementary schooling was still not effectively compulsory, about a quarter of the population was illiterate, and only a small minority was ever in a position to benefit from the high standards of the secondary schools.[5]

The structure of the pre-war system has already been touched on. The aim of the 1948 school reform was to make basic education universal, free and compulsory, but the actual changes were more modest. At first the new system consisted of: (1) voluntary pre-school institutions, instead of *theoretically* compulsory ones as before; (2) a basic comprehensive seven-year school, compulsory from 7 to 11, voluntary from 11 to 14; (3) at secondary level, a three-year *lycée* and various types of technical school. Since then, however, the school system has been extended in length and expanded in number of places. A fourth year was added to the *lycée* in 1956.[6] In 1958–9 a start was made in extending compulsory education to seven years.[7] No sooner was this process complete (1961–2) than the seven-year school was extended to eight years, the change being introduced gradually until it became universal by 1964–5.[8] After the war, fee-paying was kept for a time in schools beyond the compulsory stage, but was progressively abolished; there is now no charge for education at any level, apart from the usual contribution to the cost of maintenance in kindergartens and boarding schools. The provision of free textbooks has spread upwards from the fourth year. This was apparently regarded by the government[9] as a necessary step to create favourable conditions for the children of workers and peasants, but this too had to be done step by step. By 1965 free books were provided in the secondary schools as well.

[5] Herta Haase and Seymour Rosen, *Education in Rumania*, p. 2. (U.S. Office of Education, Washington D.C., 1960.)
[6] Haase and Rosen, *op. cit.*, p. 6.
[7] A. Manolache, *op. cit.*, p. 14.
[8] Ministry of Education of the Rumanian People's Republic, *The Educational Movement in 1964–1965*, p. 21. (Meridiane, Bucharest, 1965.)
[9] Gheorghe Gheorghiu-Dej, *Raport la cel de-al III-lea Congres al Partidului Muncitoresc Român, 1960*. Quoted in A. Dancsuly, A. Chircev and A. Manolache (eds.), *Pedagogia*, p. 80. (Editura Didactică şi Pedagogică, Bucharest, 1964.)

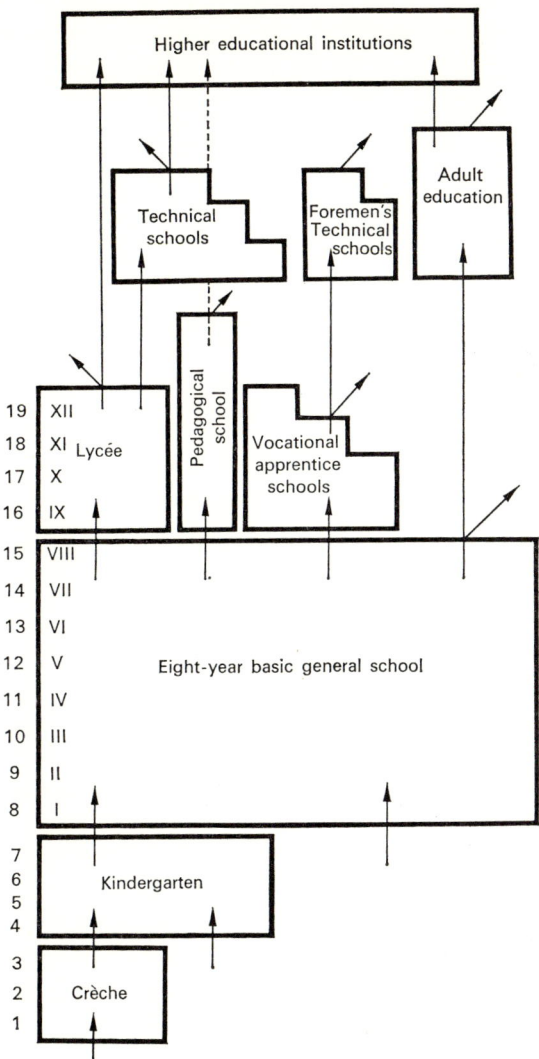

Fig. 29. Rumania: School system

3. THE PRESENT SYSTEM

(a) Pre-school Education

Crèches (*creşe*) take children up to the age of 3, kindergartens (*grădiniţe de copii*) from 3 to 7. In addition to normal kindergartens, there are some with reduced hours (open six hours a day instead of between nine and twelve) and seasonal kindergartens in the countryside, to fit in with specially busy times like the harvest. All pre-school institutions are voluntary. They now provide places for about a quarter of the age-group, a threefold increase since the war.[10]

(b) Basic Schools

The years of compulsory schooling, from 7 to 15, are spent in the basic eight-year school of general education (*Şcoala de bază de cultură generale de opt ani*). Like its counterparts, the Rumanian basic school is unstreamed, and promotes pupils from class to class on the basis of continual assessment, using a ten-point scale in this case. A mark of five or over is required (six for conduct), otherwise the pupil has to repeat the year. This happens to about 5 per cent on average.[11]

Although much is made of the "continuous process" in the basic school, the first four forms are still thought of as elementary, the next four as the first cycle of secondary education. For one thing, most of the "secondary" subjects are introduced about the fifth year (see Fig. 30);[12] for another, children are taught by general teachers in classes I to IV, and by specialists thereafter. But this is not unquestioned practice; recently there have been experiments with the use of specialist teachers in the earlier classes, which seem to have been favourably received.[13] There is

[10] *Anuarul Statistic al R.P.R. 1963*, pp. 418–19. (Direcţia Centrală de Statistică, Bucharest, 1964.)

[11] Oral communication, Bucharest, September 1965.

[12] *Pedagogia*, pp. 128–30 (adapted).

[13] Stanciu Stoian, "Cercetări privind experimentarea noului sistem de predare la clasele I-IV", *Revista de Pedagogie*, **5**, pp. 24–42 (1965). P. Popescu-Neveanu, "Particularităţile pedagogice ale sistemului profesor-obiect la clasele mici", *ibid.*, **8**, pp. 21–30 (1965).

1. R
2. F
3. H
4. C
5. T
   T

6. M
7. P
8. C
9. N
10. B
11. G
    T

12. D
13. C
14. M
15. P
    T

16. P
17. W
18. A
    T

T

V

also, apparently, some reassessment of the advisability of teaching some subjects (languages, for instance) earlier than at present—a development parallel to the spread of French, mathematics and science into the upper classes of our own primary schools.

Shortage of buildings and equipment, especially serious in view of the rapid expansion of basic schooling, makes the use of a shift system still necessary in some places. Arrangements vary, but the Ion Neculce School in Bucharest is fairly typical; classes I-IV attend from 7.30 to 1.30, V-VIII from 1.30 to 6.30, thus effectively doubling the use of the school building. The teachers change over with the pupils. In some towns, it has been found possible to have morning sessions only. This is preferred by the authorities, as well as by teachers, parents and the children themselves. But it will take some time before this is general, since further expansion of compulsory education has been given higher priority.

(c) *Secondary Schools*

From the eight-year basic school, some pupils go straight into employment, but the majority—just over half—go on to some kind of schooling beyond this stage.[14] For those who do go beyond 15, the main choice is between general and vocational secondary education.

(i) Middle school of general education (*Şcoala medie de cultură generale*), more popularly known as the *lycée* (*liceul*).[15] This is the normal route to higher education. Since it can take, as yet, only about a quarter of those leaving the basic school, selection is made by means of an examination in Rumanian and mathematics; about half the applicants are accepted, sometimes rather more.[16]

---

[14] *Educational Movement*, pp. 21–23. *Anuarul Statistic al R.P.R. 1963*, pp. 418–39.
[15] The Rumanian term for *lycée* has so many forms (indefinite *liceu*, pl. *licee*; definite *liceul*, pl. *liceele*) that the French original has been preferred here.
[16] Oral communications, Bucharest, September 1965.

Fig. 31. RUMANIA: MIDDLE GENERAL SCHOOL (*lycée*) CURRICULUM

Class:	IX	X	XI	XII	No. of hours in 4-year course Science	Hum.
1. Rumania literature	3	3/4	3/4	3/4	390	487
2. First modern language	3	3	3	3	390	390
3. Second modern language	3	3	3	3	390	390
4. Latin	2	-/2	-/2	-/2	66	260
5. History	2	2	2	2	260	260
6. History of world literature	—	—	-/1	—	—	33
7. Psychology	—	—	—	1	31	31
8. Logic	—	—	—	1	31	31
9. Political economy	—	—	2	—	66	66
10. Scientific socialism	—	—	—	2	62	62
Total hours for humanistic group:	13	11/14	13/17	15/18	1686	2010
11. Mathematics	4	5/3	6/3	5/2	650	393
12. Astronomy	—	—	—	1	31	31
13. Physics	3	4/3	4/3	3/2	456	359
14. Chemistry	2	2	2	2	260	260
15. Biology	2	2	2	1/2	229	260
16. Geography	2	2	—	2	194	194
Total hours for scientific group:	13	15/12	14/10	14/11	1820	1496

Rumania

16. Drawing	1	1	1/1	–	–	66	66	66
17. Music	1	1	1	1	–	99	99	99
18. Physical education	2	2	2	2	2	260	260	260
Total hours for PE/ aesthetic group:	4	4	4	3	2	425	425	425
19. Industry and agriculture	1	1		1		99	99	99
20. Industrial practice		Town: 3 days per term				135	135	135
21. Agricultural practice		Village: 12 days per term				180	180	180
Total hours for practical group:								
Town	1	1		1	–	234	234	234
Village	1	1		1	–	279	279	279
Tutorials	1	1	1	1	1		130	130
Total hours weekly:	32	32	32	32	32		4295	4295
							(Town)	
							4340	4340
							(Village)	
Weeks per year	35	35	35	35	31			

Alternative entries shown thus: 3/4 indicate three hours in the science course, four in the "humanistic" course.
Drawing in class X (1/1) indicates technical drawing in the science course, art in the "humanistic" course.

Once in, the pupils follow a common course for the first year, then specialize (mildly by our standards) in the "humanistic" or "scientific" courses for the next three (see Fig. 31)[17]. At the end of the four-year course comes the "maturity examination" (*examen de maturitate*), a combination of written and oral tests conducted by a commission appointed by the Ministry. A high pass rate is reported, and is usually attributed to the stringent selection at 15. Possession of the certificate entitles the holder to apply for admission to higher education, but is not in itself any guarantee—a stiff entrance examination must still be taken. Most pupils leaving the *lycées* do in fact go on with higher or further education of some kind; in 1963, for example, about 50,000 students finished at *lycées*. Of these, over 21,000 entered higher education, 19,000 went to technical schools, and the rest went straight into employment.[18]

(ii) *Vocational apprentice schools* (*Şcoli profesionale de ucenici*). These provide courses in a variety of trades in industry or agriculture, leading to a vocational qualification. They do not, however, give courses leading to the maturity examination; Rumania does not have the equivalent of the secondary vocational schools, with joint courses in general education and trade training, that have been described in other countries. The currently adumbrated industrial, agricultural and economic *lycées* will, however, eventually fill this gap.

(iii) *Six-year pedagogic schools* (*Şcoli pedagogice de şase ani*). With the addition of educational theory, psychology, teaching methods and teaching practice, these schools offer substantially the same course as the *lycées*, leading to the maturity examination and a teaching qualification. They train teachers for pre-school institutions (*educatoare*) and teachers of general subjects for classes I–IV of the basic school (*învăţători*). Subject specialists for classes V–VIII and the *lycées* (*profesori*) are trained at pedagogical institutes and universities respectively.

[17] A. Manolache, *General Education in Rumania*, pp. 36–39 (adapted).
[18] *Ibid.*, p. 21.

(d) *Special Schools*

There are both general and vocational schools for handicapped children. As in other Eastern European countries, they are divided according to the pupils' defects (deaf and dumb, blind and partially sighted, etc.). The special general schools work to special programmes, which follow the lines of the eight-year schools as far as possible, but in some cases they tend to pay more attention to vocational training from class IV.

Courses are organized regularly for the further training of teachers employed in the special schools. The faculty of defectology of the University of Cluj gives four-year courses for specialists. Regional logopaedic centres (there are twenty-seven of these, apart from those run by medical institutions) organize remedial work in the ordinary schools as well.

Schools for the specially gifted (art, music, dancing and physical education) correspond fairly closely to the ordinary schools in content, apart from the additional time spent on the special subjects. Some of the art schools take children from class I to VIII, others have the final four years, corresponding to the *lycée*, as well. The courses in physical education schools are from class V to XII. Schools of this type are developing, but affect only small numbers. There are forty-nine art schools, with about 20,000 pupils in the entire country, and 12 physical education schools with under 4000 pupils. All these schools are, naturally, highly selective. There are also art and sports schools which pupils who are enrolled in ordinary schools can attend in their spare time.[19]

(e) *Further Education*

General schooling at all levels is available for adults on a part-time basis. The more elementary courses have been run down as the need for them diminishes, though at one time they were an important part of the adult educational system. Literacy classes, for example, were attended by 870,000 adults in 1949–50 alone,

[19] *Ibid.*, pp. 22–24.

but they had ceased completely by 1956.[20] Adult courses covering the work of the first four classes of the basic school, likewise, have been run down, though courses dealing with the second stage (classes V–VIII) still function. The main emphasis is now on secondary courses, usually organized by the day schools; Ion Neculce School in Bucharest, with its 1500 day pupils, has 400 evening and 700 correspondence students. The proportion of part-time students is high in the country as a whole; in 1964–5, for instance, there were 180,000, as against 201,000 in full-time courses.[21] As in the day schools, part-time secondary courses lead to the certificate of maturity and the chance of entering higher education.

Further vocational training is provided in two main types of school. Workers who have attended apprentice schools may, after three to five years at work, enter foremen's technical schools (*şcoli tehnice de maistri*), which give two- or three-year courses leading to qualifications as foremen or technical instructors. Students who have completed the *lycée* can enter higher technical schools (*şcoli technice*). These offer courses of two or three years leading directly to a technical qualification, and provide a shorter and more immediately vocational alternative to institutions of higher education. In both function and standard they are not unlike the East German *Fachschulen*.

(f) *Higher Education*

There are forty-eight institutions of higher education in Rumania, compared with sixteen before the war.[22] The main types are as follows:

(i) *Universities*. There are five of these, counting the Babeş-Bolyai University of Cluj as one. They vary greatly in size and range of studies. Timişoara, for example, has three faculties

---

[20] A. Manolache, *op. cit.*, p. 26.
[21] *Educational Movement*, pp. 21–22.
[22] C. Ionescu-Bujor, *Higher Education in Rumania*, pp. 39 ff. Allowance has been made for the creation of a fifth university (in Craiova) in 1965.

(Mathematics-Mechanics, Physics, Philology), while Bucharest has nine (Mathematics-Mechanics, Physics, Chemistry, Biology, Geology-Geography, Law, Philosophy, History, Rumanian Language and Literature). Bucharest University also runs, as a separate entity, the Institute of Foreign Languages (formerly the Gorki Institute of Russian Literature and Language); it now has three faculties—Slavonic, Romance and Classical, and Germanic languages—and a separate department of oriental languages. The organization of faculties and departments varies from one university to another, but generally their function is to provide facilities for the study of the humanities and the theoretical sciences and, incidentally, to train teachers for the *lycées*; education, teaching methods and teaching practice form part of the normal course for all students. Full-time courses last for five years, part-time for a year longer.

(ii) *Technical institutes.* The ten technical institutes fall into two categories. *Polytechnical institutes* give courses in several different branches of technology. Some offer a great variety; the Bucharest Polytechnical Institute has faculties of Electroenergetics, Energetics, Electronics and Communications, Mechanics, Agricultural Mechanics, Machine-building Technology, Industrial Chemistry, Metallurgy, and Transport, with numerous specialist departments within each. Timișoara and Jassy, though less extensive, still offer considerable variety. The smaller ones, such as Cluj or Brașov, are much more limited, with three faculties each, while Galați has only two—Mechanics and Food Technology, with their subdivisions. *Specialist technical institutes* are concerned with single industries of fields of technology, such as the Mining Institute in Petroșeni. The others—the Construction Institute, the Institute of Oil, Gas and Geology, and the Institute of Architecture—are all in Bucharest. Courses in architecture and ship-building last for six years, others for five.

(iii) *Agricultural institutes.* There are five of these, giving five-year courses in agriculture, horticulture and veterinary medicine.

(iv) *Economics institute.* There is only one, the Lenin Institute of Economics and Planning in Bucharest. Courses are in various branches of economics, finance, accounting and commerce, and last for five years.

(v) *Institutes of medicine and pharmacy.* Courses in medicine last for six years, pharmacy for five. Four of these institutes have facilities for both branches, and a fifth (Timişoara) teaches medicine only. Medical students can either take their qualifications in general medicine, or specialize in paediatrics or stomatology.

(vi) *Art academies.* These include three music conservatories, two institutes of fine arts, the Hungarian Theatre Institute in Tîrgu Mureş, and the Caragiale Theatre and Cinema Institute in Bucharest. Courses in the Hungarian Theatre Institute last for four years, those in some of the branches of decorative and fine arts for six; all others are of five years' duration.

(vii) The *Institute of Physical Culture* gives four-year courses in sport and the teaching of physical education.

(viii) *Pedagogical institutes* give three-year courses for subject specialist teachers in the upper classes in the basic school. Most students are required to take two special subjects (e.g. French and Rumanian, history and geography, physics and chemistry, etc.). There are fourteen institutes, from Bucharest with its eight faculties to Suceava with two. Current policy is to build up the smaller pedagogical institutes in the provincial towns as one possible way of stemming the drift of students and teachers to the already overcrowded capital. (The final qualifications, incidentally—and this applies to teachers from the pedagogical schools and the universities as well—are not final, only provisional. New teachers must work under supervision for two or three years, then take a state examination under the auspices of the Ministry of Education, before they are regarded as finally qualified.)

Expansion in the field of higher education has been less spectacular than in general schooling—a fourfold as against a tenfold increase on pre-war figures.[23] Nevertheless, with over 123,000 students in a country of some 18 million (itself a rise of over 11,000 on the previous year)[24] the expansion is impressive enough;

[23] *Anuarul Statistic al R.P.R. 1963.*
[24] *Educational Movement,* p. 23.

28,000 of these are studying part-time, taking on average a year longer to reach their final qualifications.[25]

As in some other Eastern European countries, graduates can be directed to jobs anywhere in the country for up to three years. Health and personal considerations are taken into account by the Ministry commission responsible for assigning them (married couples must not be separated, for example), and part-time students have jobs already. Other things being equal, what counts is the standard attained by the students; in effect, they compete for first choice of vacancies. As elsewhere, it is not a popular system, either with students or with employers tired of getting the "leavings" every year. But the authorities see no way out. The capital acts as a powerful magnet in Rumania as in many other countries and, they argue, direction is the only way they can think of (sweetened with bonuses and provision of housing) to ensure that schools and industries in the outlying areas are properly staffed.

4. PROSPECTS

The eighth compulsory year of schooling is so recent a newcomer that the first *lycée* pupils to complete a twelve- instead of eleven-year course are doing so only in the current session. It might be reasonably expected that after this rapid expansion the chief concern would be to pause and consolidate the position. Consolidation there is to be, certainly, but already there is serious discussion of yet more changes in the structure of the system. Detailed schemes are not yet available, but ever since Ceauşescu called, at the ninth Congress of the Rumanian Communist Party in 1965, for a revision and further extension of secondary education, a number of innovations have been mooted.

1. There is to be a further increase in the length of compulsory schooling. In many quarters it is being seriously urged that it should be increased to *twelve* years within the next decade or so, though no one claims that this can be achieved either easily or

[25] C. Ionescu-Bujor, *op. cit.*, p. 13.

quickly. One scheme, outlined by Professor Stanciu Stoian,[26] seems likely to carry a great deal of weight. Pointing out the substantial proportion of 15-year-olds who are going on to secondary schooling at present, Stoian argues that the increase has, in effect, been partly achieved. "The problem", he says, "is no longer whether we can realize the extension of compulsory schooling, but *how*. Personally, we believe that it can include, right from the beginning, not one class but two, the ninth and the tenth.... If we extend by one year, then a little later by a further year, this must cause educational problems and difficulties—new curricula, new schemes of work, new textbooks."[27] He suggests that compulsory schooling begin at the age of 6, instead of 7 as at present; the basic school would thus take pupils up to the age of 16. The scheme, as the author points out, is only provisional and needs further discussion on many points, but in its present form it does not seem to mean simply a prolongation of the existing school to a ten-year school for all; it would still be possible, apparently, for some pupils to enter industrial or agricultural schools a year or two before the end of the ten-year course.

2. The present structure of secondary education is to be altered, with the introduction of new types of *lycée*. As Ceauşescu put it at the 1965 Congress: "In the coming years, there is going to be an extension of secondary education, which will include general educational *lycées* and specialized *lycées*. Industrial, agricultural, economic and pedagogical *lycées* will be set up."[28] Rumania is, in effect, falling into line (though that can hardly be the reason) with other Eastern European countries in providing a dual-purpose secondary school giving vocational qualifications and courses leading to the maturity certificate. It is also an attempt to minimize the division between academic secondary courses and the strictly vocational schools.

[26] Stanciu Stoian, "Un obiective important al politicii noastre", *Revista de Pedagogie*, **8** (1965), pp. 5–17.
[27] *Ibid.*, pp. 8–9.
[28] Nicolae Ceauşescu, *Raport la cel de-al IX-lea Congres al Partidului Comunist Român*, 1965. Quoted by Stanciu Stoian, *op. cit.*, p. 9.

3. With the extension of general schooling from eleven to twelve years, it is proposed to reduce some of the courses in higher education to four years.[29] At the same time, the present three-year pedagogical institutes can be extended to four years, and eventually absorbed fully into the university structure.[30] This is in line with current thinking on the desirability of removing some of the existing distinctions between different grades of the teaching profession—another aspect of the "unitary principle" in Rumanian education.

It is important to remember that this is still at the stage of proposal and discussion, and that there may be many alterations before the plans take their final form. But the decisions appear to have been taken in principle; the Rumanian authorities, having doubled the length of compulsory schooling since 1948, are committed to continuing the process, and at the same time to providing a greater variety at secondary level. If they can succeed in establishing universal schooling for ten years, let alone twelve, it will be a notable achievement; and if they can do it in such a way that the secondary schools can cope with the pupils' various needs, it will be more notable still.

[29] Stoian, *op. cit.*, p. 7.
[30] Oral communications, Bucharest, September 1965.

CHAPTER 6

Yugoslavia

1. BACKGROUND TO THE SYSTEM

There is a convenient (if rather slick) formula that can be used to convey some idea of the complexities of what is perhaps the most complex country in Europe. Thus, Yugoslavia is the country with *seven* frontiers (with Italy, Austria, Hungary, Rumania, Greece, Bulgaria and Albania); *six* republics (Slovania, Croatia, Bosnia, and Herzegovina, Serbia, Montenegro and Macedonia); *five* nationalities (Slovenes, Serbs, Croats Montenegrins and Macedonians);[1] *four* languages (Slovene, Croatian, Serbian, Macedonian); *three* religions (Orthodox, Catholic and Muslim); *two* alphabets Roman and Cyrillic); and *one* party (the Yugoslav League of Communists).

In one or two respects the catalogue is rather forced—Serbian and Croatian are practically the same language, albeit differently written[2]—but for the most part it is an understatement. The territorial divisions, for example, are even more complex; Serbia

[1] The population of Bosnia-Herzegovina is a mixture of nationalities, predominantly Serbian by language, distinguished from other groups mainly by religion; the common description of Bosnians as "Muslim Serbs" is an oversimplification, but has a point. Montenegrins are usually considered to be a distinct nationality on ground of history and cultural traditions. They are Serbian by language, but that does not make them Serbs, any more than speaking (almost) the same language makes the Scots English.

[2] Serbian uses the Cyrillic alphabet, Croatian the Roman. There are some other differences on vocabulary and pronounciation, but the dialectal differences within the two languages are almost as great as those which separate them.

contains within its boundaries the autonomous provinces of Vojvodina in the north and the Kosmet (Kosovo and Metohija) in the south. So is the composition of the population; apart from the main Yugoslav nationalities, there are over a dozen national minorities, from small groups (under 50,000) of Russians, Czechs and Italians to the Hungarians of Vojvodina and the Albanians of the Kosmet, numbering over half and three-quarters of a million respectively. Culturally, the country is split down the middle; the Croats and Slovenes, formerly under the Austrian Empire, are Catholic, more prosperous and culturally westward-looking, while the other peoples are Orthodox or Muslim, former subjects of the Sultan, poorer, and on the whole culturally oriented to the East. Yugoslavia's 19 millions present the problems and complexities—and the tensions—of the whole of Eastern Europe in miniature.

The country is as varied as its people. The contrast between fertile Slovenia and barren, mountainous Bosnia or the Kosmet could hardly be sharper, and this contrast is, inevitably, reflected in the peoples' living standards. Even crossing Serbia throws the contrasts into relief. North of Belgrade, the country rolls on to Vojvodina and the lush Pannonian plain; the name of the capital of the region, Novi Sad (New Garden), is not inappropriate. To the south-east, on the other hand, lies Montenegro, described by legend as the dumping-ground for all the rocks left over from the Creation. More of Yugoslavia is like Montenegro than like Slovenia or Vojvodina.

The backwardness of the country in general, and the differences between the parts, can be illustrated by the level of illiteracy. Even in 1961, 20 per cent of the entire population over the age of 10 were illiterate;[3] that in itself was bad enough, though a considerable improvement on the pre-war figure of 46 per cent.[4] More illuminating is the breakdown by republics: Slovenia was by far the lowest, with 1·8 per cent, Croatia coming rather a poor second with 12 per cent. At the other end of the scale, Bosnia

[3] 1961 Census.
[4] Stana Tomašević and Mustafa Begtić, *Vocational Training in Yugoslavia*, p. 37. (Belgrade, 1961.)

recorded 32 per cent, Macedonia 25 per cent, and Montenegro and Serbia 22 per cent—still over the national average.[5] The gulf between the northern and coastal regions and the rest illustrates plainly the cleavage in this country of uneasily coexisting peoples.

Centrifugal tendencies apart, the population patterns add their own quota to Yugoslavia's educational headaches. As in any country that suffered heavy loss of life during the war (over 10 per cent), there is a large population "dent" in the age-group now in the mid-forties (war deaths), a lesser one in the early twenties (loss of births), and a compensating population bulge of the kind familiar everywhere. In quantitative terms, 38 per cent of Yugoslavs are under 20 years of age, and over 30 per cent are under 14.[6] For an already backward country trying to build up a mass educational system, deal with illiteracy at all levels, and train badly needed personnel for industry, the serious implications of these figures must be obvious.

The damage done during the war, to school buildings as to much else, has already been mentioned. The Second World War was only the most recent episode in a bloodstained history, in which Kosovo Polje, and the slaughter of the First World War were outstandingly traumatic but by no means unique. On the positive side, the war was both a social revolution and a struggle for national liberation, and did a great deal to weld the nation together. Not that the welding was complete; the war also brought out the nationalist and fascist groups in Slovenia, Bosnia, Croatia and Serbia, who spent most of the time killing each other. The only thing that united them was a common detestation of the all-Yugoslav Partisan Army; it would be too much to expect that the forces that threw up the *ustaše* and the White Guards would vanish altogether with their defeat. Since the war, national tensions have been furtherest from the surface in times of crisis—during the quarrel with Stalin, for example—but they do still reappear from time to time. It has been pointed out that the Federal authorities are still careful to ensure that the composition of

[5] 1961 Census.
[6] 1961 Census, extrapolated.

committes and other government bodies on a national level reflect as wide a selection of nationalities as possible.[7]

Many Yugoslavs who have reservations about the communist régime none the less see it as the only force capable of holding the country together. This, and the fact that Tito's régime was one of the few to win power on its own account, is a source of strength; but at the same time concessions have had to be made to the country's diversity and the strength of Croat and Serbian (as distinct from Yugoslav) nationalism—hence the federal structure of government and a degree of decentralization, right down to the level of the local commune and even economic unit, that is quite unique in Eastern Europe. There is a central dilemma here; in the Yugoslav situation, a centralized unitary state is simply not feasible,[8] and in any case social self-government and workers' control fit the more flexible Yugoslav interpretation of communist theory. But at the same time, decentralization is likely to increase separatism by putting more responsibility on to the republics and their subdivisions. This in turn makes coherent planning on a national scale more difficult. In spite of difficulties, however, it seems that the arch-heretic of the communist world is determined to push further in the direction of decentralization and liberalization. The recent dismissal and arrest of Vice-President Ranković, a "hard-liner" and head of the security police, is only one indication of this. On the other hand, the continued imprisonment of Djilas and the recent trial of Mihajlo Mihajlov are reminders that the régime still feels it necessary to apply the brakes from

[7] This has been pointed out by D. Matko, of the Glasgow University Institute of Soviet and East European Studies.

[8] Apart from any other objections to such a policy, the domination of one nationality over the others would hardly be practicable. These figures are rounded off from the 1964 population estimates:

Yugoslavia	19 million
Bosnia-Herzegovina	$3\frac{1}{2}$,,
Montenegro	$\frac{1}{2}$,,
Croatia	$4\frac{1}{2}$,,
Macedonia	$1\frac{1}{2}$,,
Slovenia	$1\frac{1}{2}$,,
Serbia	$7\frac{3}{4}$,,

time to time. There is no denying, however, that there is more flexibility in political and social life at all levels than anywhere else in Eastern Europe.

One area where Yugoslavia is uniquely flexible is in the control and administration of the educational system; the standard pattern of centralized ministries does not apply here. The structure is conplex, but broadly the system works thus: education, like other things, is run on four levels—the Federation (i.e. the whole country), the Republic, the district and the commune. At each level there is an assembly, consisting of two parts—the political chamber (the rough equivalent of a parliament or council) [9] and a chamber or chambers of "working communities" elected by those involved in certain special fields. At the national level, for instance, the supreme organ of state is the Federal Assembly; its main component is the Federal Chamber, the nearest equivalent of the House of Commons. Alongside it work the Chamber of Nationalities and the specialist Chambers dealing with such matters as Health, Education, the Economy, etc. These cannot by themselves pass laws, but they draft them and give advice on matters within their province, so that in the farming of any educational law the Federal Chamber and the Chamber of Education and Culture are in effect running in double harness. Responsible to the Assembly is the Federal Executive Council (vaguely analogous to the Cabinet). It includes Federal Secretaries (the nearest thing to Ministers) who have under them secretariats responsible for particular fields, education being one of them. This pattern is repeated (more simply, of course, as one goes down the line) at Republic, district and commune level. To complete the picture, the principle of "workers' self-management" applies to schools as well as to factories. Each school has therefore a school council (*savet škole*), consisting of the teaching staff, parents' representatives, members of the pupils' "collective", and representatives of outside bodies—socio-political organizations,

---

[9] The analogy is not perfect, since only the assemblies at commune level are elected by direct vote. These, in turn, elect members (not necessarily from their own number) to the higher assemblies.

trade unions, etc. A smaller school-management board (*upravni odbor*) is elected by the teachers from among their own number; the staff as a whole form a council of teachers (*nastavničko veće*) to deal with general school problems, while the teachers of each class form a panel (*razredno veće*) to deal with the more specific problems of the class. Teachers of the same subject also organize their own subject panel (*stručni aktiv*) to discuss problems of content and methodology. A similar multiplicity of organizations exists in higher educational institutions. This kind of organization is not unknown elsewhere; but it must be emphasized that this is no mere pipeline for passing decisions down from the central authorities. At each stage, a considerable amount of discretion can be and is exercised. To cite only two examples, the school's finances are organized by the school council, and textbooks are chosen from a list approved by the republican authorities by the subject panel in the school.

This is not to say that the system is decentralized in the American sense, where the central bodies have practically no power, or even in the British sense of "partnership" between local and central authorities. Basic policy is decided at federal level and is more precisely intepreted by the republics, the districts, and so on down to the schools. How much discretion is left to the republics and their subdivisions, or to the schools themselves, varies from topic to topic. The length, of course, in basic schools and in most secondary schools is prescribed by federal law, but not in teachers' schools and some other institutions. The basic outlines of subject schemes of work are prescribed, but the details are not. Educational aims are formulated in federal enactments, but the classroom methods used to attain them are left to the school or the individual teacher. Skeleton curricula are drawn up at federal level, the details being decided by the republics (number of hours per subject per week). The system has some obvious advantages. Consultation is made easier at all levels, adjustment to local circumstances is also easier—no small matter in a country as varied as Yugoslavia. But there are drawbacks too, not the least of them being that local control tends to mean more local responsibility for finding the money, which can be felt acutely in the poorer areas. This is one reason, possibly, for the persistence of wide differences of standard between town and country, one republic and another, as another look at the literacy figures will confirm.

2. THE OLD SYSTEM AND POST-WAR DEVELOPMENTS

The pre-war system of education in Yugoslavia was of the traditional highly selective type already remarked on in other countries. Basic schooling was compulsory for four years, and was provided in the "national school" (*narodna škola*). This could be followed by the "higher national school" (*viša narodna škola*), a four-year terminal elementary course, or by secondary education. This was of three main types: (1) the general secondary school (*gimnazija*), with an eight-year course, sometimes divided into an upper and lower stage of four years each; (2) the "civic" school (*gradjanska škola*), designated by the law of 1931[10] as an incomplete secondary school, and comparable with the similarly-named schools in pre-war Czechoslovakia; (3) technical and vocational schools of various types. This sector was comparatively undeveloped, with 88,000 pupils in 1938–9 (as against 362,000 in 1964).[11] Not only was opportunity for secondary education severely limited, primary education was not effectively enforced outside Slovenia; but the illiteracy figures, again, are a fair indication of this, but the figure of 46 per cent for the whole of Yugoslavia does not tell the whole story. It was over 70 per cent in Macedonia, 72 per cent in Bosnia and Herzegovina.[12] Some groups were neglected altogether; the German minority had schools of their own, but the Bulgarians and Albanians did not. Nor, for that matter, did the Macedonians; what schools did exist in their part of the country gave instruction only in Serbo-Croat.

[10] Ljubomir Krneta, Milena Potkonjak and Nikola Potkonjak, *Pedagogija*, pp. 97 ff. (Zavod za Izdavanje Udžbenika SR Srbije, Belgrade, 1965.)

[11] *Statistički Kalendar Jugoslavije 1965*. (Savenzi zavod za statistiku, Belgrade, 1965.)

[12] Rodoljub Jemuović, *Education in Yugoslavia*, p. 4. (Mejunarodna Politika, Belgrade, 1964.)

The legacy of backwardness, compounded by the destruction of the war (14 per cent of school buildings destroyed, 36 per cent badly damaged, on average),[13] posed not only great obstacles but a dilemma. Given the need to expand the system, a choice had to be made between maintenance of standards or concentration on numbers. There was—and is—some controversy over this, but priority was given to expansion.[14] In 1945 compulsory education was increased to seven years (7–14), and in 1952 this was raised again to eight years, the increase to be introduced gradually. The General Law of Education of 1958 recast the whole system, adopting the eight-year school as the basic unit, expanding provision in secondary education (with a shift of emphasis from the *gimnazija* to vocational and technical schools, which were reorganized to provide alternative routes to higher education). To secure some degree of uniformity, basic curricula were drafted, leaving the detailed provisions to the republics.

By 1960 over 80 per cent of school age pupils were at basic school, 28 per cent at secondary school, nearly 6 per cent in higher education. The Social Plan for 1961–5 envisaged about 92 per cent in basic school, 35 per cent in secondary, 10 per cent in higher education. This was achieved, but with some shortcomings; although over 95 per cent of school children now attend basic school, not all of them stay on for the full eight-year course. In 1958 only 30 per cent of the age-group were enrolled in class VIII, in 1962–3 still only 46 per cent.[15] The proportion is rising but enforcement is not yet complete. Further, it seems that some pupils are still not attending at all, or lapsing into illiteracy after leaving; illiteracy is still a national problem,[16] the level being only marginally less than it was at the time of the 1961 Census.[17]

---

[13] *Ibid.*, pp. 5–6.
[14] Krste Crvenkovski, "Ability and Educational Opportunity in Present-day Yugoslavia" (*International Review of Education*, **7** (1962) 4).
[15] Crvenkovski, *op. cit.*, and Jemuović, *op. cit.*, pp. 14–15.
[16] "Osnovno obrazovanje i nepismenost u Srbiji", *Kulturni Život*, **8–9** (1965), pp. 963–9.
[17] Z. Židovec, "A.B.C... Svačija i Ničija Briga" (*Vjesnik u Srijedu*, p. 6, 16 February 1966).

The position is vastly better than it was at the end of the war, but the deficiencies are still obvious, and recognized by the Yugoslavs as serious.

3. THE PRESENT SYSTEM

Generalization is more difficult in the case of Yugoslavia than any other Eastern European country, owing to the federal structure of the country and the considerable regional variations. There are also, as we have seen, variations within the republics and even within smaller units, and many gaps between enactment and implementation in policy and organization. Exceptions to general statements, therefore, are likely to be commoner in Yugoslavia than elsewhere in the area under study.

(a) *Pre-school Education*

Pre-school education follows the usual two-tier pattern: crèches (*dečje jaslice*) for children up to the age of 3, and kindergartens (*dečji vrtići*) from 3 to 7. There are also residential pre-school institutions (*dečji domovi*) for orphans, deprived children, etc. The number of crèche places has soared since before the war (from 7000 in 1939 to 83,000 in 1964),[18] most of them being provided by factories and other enterprises. Kindergarten places have more than doubled, and are expected to reach two and a half times the present figure by 1970. But this will still be a modest proportion; even if the target is reached, there will only be places for 13 per cent of the age-group.[19]

(b) *The Basic School*

The period of compulsory education (7–15) is provided for in the basic or elementary school (*osnovna škola*). Like its counterparts, this school is comprehensive and unstreamed (though here, too, the possibility of "setting" in the senior classes is being looked

---
[18] *Statistički Kalendar Jugoslavije 1965.*
[19] Jemuović, *op. cit.*, p. 12.

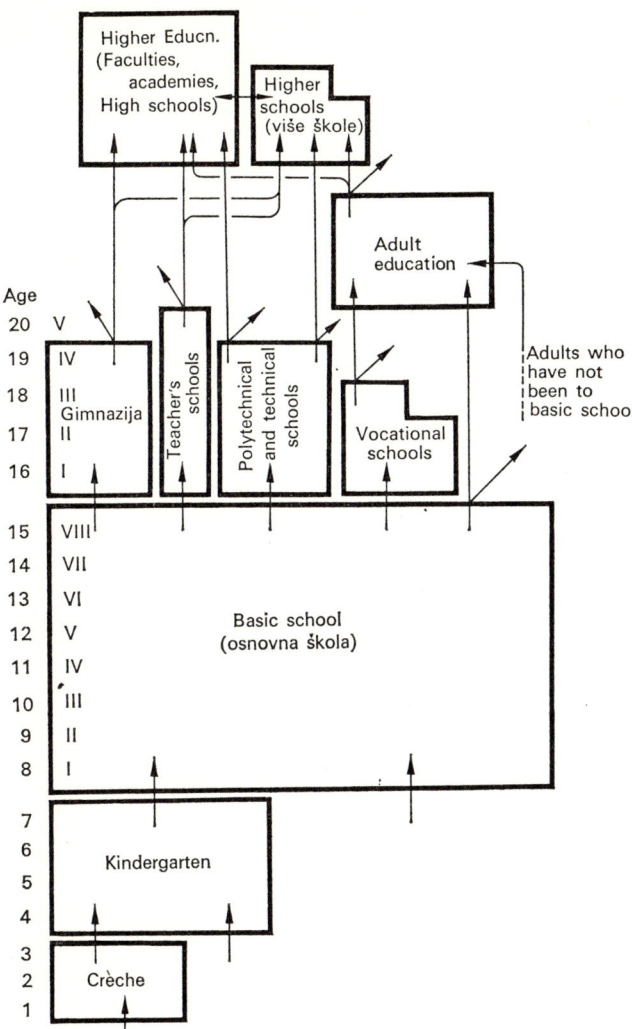

Fig. 32. Yugoslavia: School system

at). The usual system of continuous assessment is operated (with marks from 1 up to 5); a pupil failing in one or two subjects can sit an extra examination before the beginning of the next session, but if he fails more he repeats the year automatically. There is some regrouping of children in class V on the basis of previous results, but the aim is not to separate the pupils into streams; on the contrary, according to headmasters,[20] they attempt to ensure that each class contains a cross-section of ability.

The curriculum, as we have seen, varies from place to place, but the basic principles are observed throughout the country (see Figs. 33 and 34).[21] A clear-cut division at class V is, as far as possible, avoided, but there is still some difference between the lower grade (I–IV) and the upper grade (V–VIII), with a change from general teaching to teaching by subject specialists. The distribution of subjects follows much the same pattern as elsewhere, except that rather more is done than in most Eastern European countries to integrate the curriculum and break down the barriers between subjects. This is done mainly by retooling the curriculum so that the social and physical sciences are based on more elementary studies, and differentiate themselves only gradually through the school course. Thus, in the first three years, "Study of Nature and Society" appears on the time-table.[22] It is designed to introduce children to their total environment. Apart from elementary discussion of work and life at home and school, the children study, through lessons and excursions, their home region—the topography, natural environment, the kind of work people do—and use this as the setting for a closer look at the seasons, agriculture and industry, landscape, social organization, transport and communications, etc. Generalizations are drawn for specific observations; according to the programme, the main themes thus dealt with are the dependence of life on water, air and heat, the natural causes of weather, and man-made devices for controlling the natural environment. Finally, the past of the home region is

[20] Oral communications, Belgrade, 1965.
[21] Ljubomir Krneta (ed.), *The Elementary School in Yugoslavia*, pp. 31–32, 45.
[22] *Ibid.*, pp. 83–99.

Fig. 33. Yugoslavia: Eight-year Basic School—Draft Curriculum (1960)

Class:	I	II	III	IV	V	VI	VII	VIII
1. Serbo-Croat language and literature	6	6	6	5	5	5	4	4
2. Study of nature and society	4	4	4	—	—	—	—	—
3. Study of nature	—	—	—	3	3	3	—	—
(a) Physics	—	—	—	—	—	—	3	3
(b) Chemistry	—	—	—	—	—	—	2	2
(c) Biology	—	—	—	—	—	—	2	2
4. Mathematics	5	5	5	5	4	4	3	3
5. Principles of polytechnical education	—	—	—	2	2	2	2	2
6. Study of society	—	—	—	3	3	—	—	—
(a) Geography	—	—	—	—	—	2	2	2
(b) History	—	—	—	—	—	2	2	2
7. Foreign language	—	—	—	—	3	3	3	3
8. Socialist morals	—	—	—	—	—	—	1	1
9. Physical and health education	3	3	3	3	3	3	3	3
10. Art	2	2	2	2	2	1	1	1
11. Music	1	1	2	2	2	2	1	1
12. Domestic science	—	—	—	—	—	1	1	1
Total hours weekly:	21	21	22	25	27	28	30	30

Fig. 34. Yugoslavia: Basic Eight-year School Curriculum (Serbia)

Class:	I	II	III	IV	V	VI	VII	VIII
1. Serbo-Croat language and literature	6	6	6	6	6	5	4	4
2. Study of nature and society	2	2	3	—	—	—	—	—
3. Study of nature	—	—	—	2	2	3	—	—
(a) Physics	—	—	—	—	—	—	3	3
(b) Chemistry	—	—	—	—	—	—	2	2
(c) Biology	—	—	—	—	—	—	2	2
4. Mathematics	6	6	6	6	5	5	4	4
5. Principles of polytechnical education	—	—	—	2	2	2	2	2
6. Study of society	—	—	—	2	2	—	—	—
(a) Geography	—	—	—	—	—	2	2	2
(b) History	—	—	—	—	—	2	2	2
7. Foreign language	—	—	—	3	3	3	3	3
8. Physical and health education	3	3	3	2	3	3	3	3
9. Art	2	2	2	2	2	1	1	1
10. Music	1	1	2	—	2	2	1	1
11. Domestic science	—	—	—	—	—	1	1	1
Total hours weekly:	20	20	22	25	27	29	30	30

treated by means of stories, investigations into the significance of such things as street-names, visits to sites of archaeological interest, and especially "events and heroes of the period of the People's Liberation War". Only the broadest outlines are drawn at this stage in the programme—the details are left to the teachers.

In class IV the subject divides into "Study of Nature" and "Study of Society". The latter has been touched on elsewhere, as has its later bifurcation into more conventional history and geography. In "Study of Nature", the class IV programme deals with (1) the study of soil (types, formation, etc.); (2) water, air and weather—taking up and developing some points from the earlier course; (3) the development of life in the soil; and (4) "man as part of nature". This last deals with the comparison of man with plant and animal organisms; disease and protective medicine; and "man as an intelligent animal, and his role in changing nature". In class V the principal themes are: (1) "Man studies and uses the forces and wealth of nature"; this covers the development of sources of power from wind and water to electricity, the role of these in the development of transport, the use of metals, etc. (2) "Man changes and uses plant and animal life", a study of the growth of agriculture in relation to natural provision and human need. (3) "Plants and animals as sources of food", which treats on elementary dietetics and, among other related topics, "the dangers of excessive use of alcohol". In class VI the themes become more elaborate: (1) "Soil, water and light—conditions necessary for life". This covers (or at least introduces) the porosity of bodies, mass, capillarity, osmosis, weight and specific gravity, the principle of Archimedes, change of state, the water cycle in nature, the movement of air, the behaviour of light, bleaching and photosynthesis, etc. (2) "Organisms adapted to aquatic life". (3) "Organisms adapted to terrestrial life". (4) "Organisms adapted to life in water and on land". (5) "Some animal and plant communities"—forest, meadow, karst, and their appropriate flora and fauna. So far, the aim has been to work up from everyday things to the basic concepts and vocabulary of the sciences, and at the same time to emphasize constantly the interrelation of social man and his natural environment. Thereafter, the demarcation lines begin to appear, and the subject branches out into physics, chemistry and biology. Even in later stages, of course, the divisions between subjects are often arbitrary, but necessary to make systematic study possible. By means of this approach, however, it is hoped that the relationships between the disciplines will be clearer than they would be if they had been treated separately from the start. The idea is not new, of course; it has much in common with the principle of *Gesamtunterricht* (unified instruction) in German elementary schools, or the "environmental studies" nearer home, to mention only two out of many such approaches to subject teaching. But it has been thoroughly worked out in such a way as to combine a nation-wide basic syllabus with a considerable degree of local and personal initiative.

In view of the material difficulties that have already been mentioned, it is only to be expected that Jugoslav basic schools still tend to be severely overcrowded. Classes are often large, ancillary premises in schools in short supply, and the shift system is wellnigh universal. The Stefan Sindjelić School in Belgrade, for example, has 1200 day pupils, half of whom attend from 8 a.m. to 1 p.m., half from 1 to 5.30 p.m. In the evening, an elementary school for adults takes over. The shortages apply to books and equipment as well. School books are not free, though special funds, special school shops and book-exchange schemes help to minimize the burden; science equipment is often improvised by the teachers or, where feasible, made in school workshops; shortages of sports equipment are often met by donations from factories or other organizations in the area of the school.

(c) *Secondary Schools*

Schools of the second stage (*škole drugog stupnja*) differ somewhat from one republic to another in type, curriculum and methods of organization. There are also moves being discussed at present to integrate the existing secondary system into a common general

Fig. 35. Yugoslavia: Curriculum for Eight-year Schools (Serbia, 1952)

Class:	I	II	III	IV	V	VI	VII	VIII
1. Serbo-Croat language and literature	9	10	7	6	5	4	4	4
2. History	—	—	2	2	—	3	3	3
3. Geography	—	—	2	3	3	2	2	2
4. Foreign language	—	—	—	—	3	3	3	3
5. Nature study	—	—	2	3	—	—	—	—
6. Biology	—	—	—	—	3	3	2	3
7. Physics	—	—	—	—	—	—	3	3
8. Chemistry	—	—	—	—	—	—	—	4
9. Mathematics	6	6	6	5	5	4	4	—
10. Handwork	—	—	1	1	2	2	—	2
11. Economics and domestic science	—	—	—	—	—	—	2	2
12. Drawing	1	1	1	1	2	2	2	2
13. Writing	1	1	1	1	1	1	—	—
14. Singing	1	1	1	1	1	2	—	—
15. Physical education	1	1	1	1	2	2	2	2
Total hours weekly:	18	20	24	24	27	28	27	30

and pre-vocational two-year course, to be followed by more specialized types of school.[23] As yet, however, the principal choice for the youth leaving the basic school is between general secondary schools and more practical vocational or technical courses. The main categories are as follows:

(i) *General secondary school (gimnazija)*. With the gradual extension of basic schooling from four to eight years, the *gimnazija* has become a four-year secondary school (age 15 to 19) leading to the final examination and the possibility of entering higher education. Except for a small element of polytechnical education, the content of the course is highly academic. In some republics (e.g. Serbia and Croatia) there are two parallel courses, the "scientific-mathematical branch" (*prirodno-matematički smer*) and the "social-linguistic branch" (*društveno-jezički smer*). Differentiation takes place in the second year; it is a shift of emphasis, not complete specialization (see Fig. 36).[24] Like so many other issues, the question of specialization is subject to much controversy. Some want it to be more intensive and to begin in the first year; others feel that the second year is too early, and that the third year would be soon enough; others again are against specialization at all at school level, and argue that the higher educational stage is soon enough. (All these points of view were vigorously advocated by teachers and pupils in the principal's room of one school, the Ivo Lola Ribar Gimnazija in Belgrade, but they are typical of the main trends of thought outside. The present proposals to extend the common school, in effect, to ten year, will not settle this dispute, except that they will (if adopted) make earlier specialization highly unlikely; the rest of the dispute remains open.)

At first glance, the *gimnazija* appears to have stood almost still since before the war (125,000 students in 1939 compared with 168,000 in 1965; in Montenegro and Slovenia there has actually been a fall in numbers).[25] But the pre-war *gimnazija* was an eight-

[23] *Yugoslav Survey*, **6**, 23 (1965). pp. 3379–80.
[24] *World Survey of Education, III.* (UNESCO, Paris, 1963.)
[25] *Statistički Kalendar Jugoslavije 1965. Škole I i II Stepena, Početak 1964/65.* (Statistički Bilten 355, Belgrade, 1965.) Figures for school enrolments come from these two sources unless otherwise stated.

Fig. 36. Yugoslavia: *Gimnazija* Curriculum

Class:	I	II	III	IV
1. Serbo-Croat language and literature	4	4/3	4/3	4/3
2. History	3	3/2	3/2	3/0
3. Foreign language(s)	3	4/3	4/3	5/2
4. Latin	2	2	–	–
5. Sociology—political economy	–	–	2/0	3/2
6. Social organization in Yugoslavia	2	1	–	–
7. Logic and psychology	–	–	2	–
8. Philosophy	–	–	–	3/1
9. Drawing	2	1	1/0	2/0
10. Mathematics	4	3/4	2/4	2/5
11. Physics	2	2/3	2/3	0/3
12. Chemistry	–	2	2/3	0/2
13. Biology	2	2	2	0/2
14. Geography	3	2	–	2
15. Plane geometry	–	0/2	0/2	0/2
16. General technical education	1	2/1	2	2
17. Pre-military training	–	–	2	2
18. Physical education	3	3	3	3
Total hours weekly:	31	31	31	31

Alternative entries thus: 4/3 indicates four hours in the "humanistic" course, three in the science course.

year school, the new one a four-year school; on this basis, class for class, there has been a substantial increase. But it is true that the *gimnazija* has not expanded in proportion to secondary education in general. High though its prestige remains, the *gimnazija* no longer occupies quite so high a pinnacle in the Yugoslav system; more attention has been paid to developing the other kinds of secondary schools, especially those which teach to the level of the leaving certificate *and* provide vocational training. The number of students in vocational schools has more than quadrupled since 1939.

Perhaps for this reason, there is not quite the pressure on available places reported elsewhere. The *gimnazija* is selective, but does not always have to apply this in practice. When there are too many applicants, they are weeded out by means of an examination in Serbo-Croat (or other mother tongue) and mathematics—not a very stringent one by all accounts.

(ii) *Polytechnical and technical schools*. These are now referred to officially as technical and other vocational schools for the economy and public services (*tehničke i druge stručne škole za privredu i javne službe*). The other term, however, is still in use, and has the advantage of brevity. These schools give four-year courses leading to the school-leaving certificate as well as vocational qualifications. Currently, about a third of all students in higher educational institutions are coming through schools of this type first.

The industrial and agricultural technical schools train technicians for various branches of industry, including machine-building, industrial chemistry, electrical engineering, civil engineering, transport and communications, mechanical engineering, mining and, in agriculture, cattle-breeding, horticulture, viticulture, arable farming. These are only some of the available courses. On the non-industrial side there are medical, veterinary, economic, administrative, library and similar schools. Some schools specialize in one type of course, others have several specialities grouped together. Most agricultural schools, for example, offer a range of special qualifications. Among the industrial schools, the Nikola Tesla Electrotechnical School in Belgrade is fairly specialized, but nevertheless gives courses in three main departments—electroenergetics, electronics and telecommunications—with subspecialities within each. Whatever the special study, a considerable proportion of time is devoted to general education and general technical education (see Figs. 37 and 38).[26] The general educational programme applies to all schools of this type within each republic, while the general technical programme is worked out for all the schools in the republic working in the same field (e.g. agriculture or mechanical engineering).

In contrast with the general secondary schools, expansion in this sector has been dramatic (nearly eighteen times the pre-war

[26] Tomašević and Begtić, *op. cit.*, p. 80.

FIG. 37. YUGOSLAVIA: TECHNICAL SCHOOL CURRICULUM: ELECTROENERGETICS BRANCH

Class:	I	II	III	IV	Total hours
(a) *General educational subjects*					
1. Serbo-Croat language and literature	3	3	3	3	405
2. Foreign language	2	2	2	2	270
3. History and civics	2	2	–	–	140
4. Basis of political economy and economy of the S.F.R.J.	–	–	3	–	105
5. Organization of enterprises and production	–	–	–	3	90
6. Mathematics	6	5	4	–	525
7. Physics	3	–	–	–	105
8. Chemistry	3	–	–	–	105
9. Physical education	2	2	2	2	270
10. Pre-military training	–	–	2	2	130
Total	21	14	16	12	2245
(b) *General professional subjects*					
11. Technology of electrotechnical material	–	2	–	–	70
12. Technical drawing	5	–	–	–	175
13. Mechanics	3	3	–	–	210
14. Principles of electrotechnics	6	4	–	–	350
15. Machines	3	–	–	–	105
Total	17	9	–	–	910
(c) *Professional subjects*					
16. General machines	–	2	2	–	140
17. Electrical techniques	–	3	–	–	105
18. Electrical measurement	–	2	2	–	140
19. Training in electrical measurement	–	2	3	–	175
20. Electric lighting and installations	–	5	–	–	175
21. Electrical circuits and wiring	–	–	4	3	230
22. Electrical machines	–	–	6	5	360
23. Wiring of electrical machines	–	–	1	1	65
24. Testing of electrical machines	–	–	–	2	60
25. Training in electrical machine testing	–	–	–	3	90

continued on next page

Fig. 37 (*continued*)

Class:	I	II	III	IV	Total hours
26. Electrical power in industry and communications	–	–	–	3	90
27. Uses of electricity	–	–	3	3	195
28. Electrical plants	–	–	–	5	150
Total	–	14	21	25	1975
Total hours weekly	38	37	37	37	5130
29. Vacation practice: 24 days during I, II and III years					576
30. Health education					30
Total hours for entire week					5735

figure). Demand is rising too, but appears to fluctuate according to area and type of school. As usual, there is a discrepancy between town and country. In the towns it is usually possible to find room in *some* kind of technical school for most applicants, but some schools, more popular than others, have to select. In Belgrade, for instance, it is not too difficult to get into a mechanical engineering school, but electrical engineering schools have twice as many applicants as places. When this happens, the school sets an examination in mathematics and the mother tongue, and also have a close look at the applicant's mark record for the last couple of years at the basic school.[27]

(iii) *Vocational schools (škole za kvalifikovane radnike)*. These are of two types. Schools with practical instruction (*škole sa praktičnom obukom*) give three-year courses of training in certain specific trades such as machine construction, woodwork, metalwork, electrical trades, etc. Instruction is both theoretical and practical, with a bias to the practical; there is some co-ordination with interested industrial organizations, but most of the practical work

[27] Oral communication, Belgrade, 1965.

FIG. 38. YUGOSLAVIA: AGRICULTURAL TECHNOLOGICAL SCHOOL CURRICULUM (ARABLE FARMING)

Class:	I	II	III	IV
1. Serbo-Croat language and literature	4	3	3	3
2. Foreign language	2	2	2	2
3. History with civics	2	2	–	–
4. Mathematics	3	3	2	–
5. Chemistry and agro-chemistry	3	3	–	–
6. Biology	3	–	–	–
7. Pedology	–	3	–	–
8. Agricultural machinery	2	3	–	–
9. Arable-farming	–	–	4	5
10. Plant protection	–	–	2	–
11. Land improvement	–	–	2	–
12. Essentials of political economy and economy of Yugoslavia	–	–	3	–
13. System of co-operatives with economic policy in agriculture	–	–	–	2
14. Organization of production in agriculture	–	–	2	2
15. Physical education	2	2	2	2
16. Pre-military training	–	–	2	2
Total for theoretical subjects:	21	21	24	18
17. Practical work in production	14	14	13	16
Total hours weekly:	35	35	37	34

takes place in the school workshops. Apprentice schools (*škole učenika u privredi*) give two- to three-year courses, with theoretical instruction in the school and practical work in the enterprise with which the apprentice has made his contract. The final examination qualifies the student as a skilled worker. It is possible for students from these schools to proceed to higher education through the adult education network, but as a rule these schools are entered by those more interested in taking a trade qualification directly. The number of students is double the pre-war figure (88,000 in 1939), but has been surpassed by the expansion of technical and polytechnical schools.

Fig. 39. Yugoslavia: Technical School with Practical Instruction (Metalwork)

Class:	I	II	III
1. Serbo-Croat	2	2	2
2. Mathematics	3	2	2
3. Civics	–	2	–
4. Yugoslav economy and work organization	–	–	3
5. Physical education	2	2	2
6. Pre-military education	–	2	2
7. Mechanical technology	2	2	2
8. Technical drawing	3	2	2
9. Mechanical engineering	3	2	2
10. Elements of machinery	–	2	3
11. Encyclopedia of machinery	–	2	–
12. Elements of electrical engineering	2	–	–
Total for theoretical subjects weekly:	17	18	18
13. Practical instruction	24	24	24
Total hours weekly:	41	42	42

(d) *Special Schools*

There are 282 special schools (*specijalne škole*) with over 14,000 handicapped children from pre-school age upwards. Most of them (250) are basic schools, working to programmes as near as possible to those of the ordinary schools; there are also some special vocational schools, one special technical school (in Serbia) and three special schools for adults.

Over 5000 pupils attend special art schools (*umetničke škole*). There are forty-seven of these, giving special courses for gifted children in music, ballet and applied arts.

(e) *Adult Education*

Adult education is an important part of the Yugoslav educational system, largely because of the demand from people who missed the chance of ordinary schooling before, during and immediately after the war. It operates in two main areas: workers' universities and people's universities are extra-mural institutions for the provision of lectures, seminars, day and evening courses, dealing with a wide range of technical, scientific, political and economic and general subjects, the aim being to provide facilities for "self-improvement" on a national scale. Workers' universities also run preparatory courses for adults seeking to enter higher educational institutions. Parallel to the day-school courses are the schools for adult education (*škole za obrazovanje odraslih*). There are 575 of them throughout the country, with nearly 55,000 students, 12,000 of them women. They provide courses of every kind from the basic school to the full range of secondary schools, and the certificates awarded are accepted as the equivalent of the day-school qualifications. As elsewhere, the basic schools are regarded as a temporary expedient which will disappear as the need dwindles, but this will take some time. The need for adult secondary schools is expected to last longer. The tendency is certainly to phase these schools out; numbers have fallen from 105,000 to 54,000 since 1961. The courses are compressed, especially at elementary level; one such school in Belgrade (the Palilula Basic Adult Educational School) concentrates on giving the essentials of the work of classes V to VIII in a two-year course. This, even allowing for some cutting and splicing of material, means an intensive course of study, especially for an older man trying to keep his job going during the day. Not surprisingly, there is a high drop-out rate, about 12 per cent on average, mostly during the first year. Those who survive the first year have a good chance of completing the course. There seems to be no common policy (or at any rate practice) concerning the relations between adult schools and places of employment. Some factories make attendance compulsory, some do not; some make it a condition of promotion, some do not; more to the point, perhaps, some give time off for study, some do not. Public services and government departments are more thorough-going than most industries in giving co-operation, which is one possible explanation of the surprisingly large numbers of policemen, revolvers on hip, struggling with primary geography or Serbo-Croat composition.

(f) *Higher Education*[28]

The higher educational system in Yugoslavia was reformed in 1960, and now operates on three levels of approximately two years each. Graduates of the first level are trained with a view to providing specialists for various professions, with the emphasis on the practical side; the standard may be compared with that of a German *Fachschule*. The second level, with more accent on theory, corresponds to the more familiar university degree standard while the third level approximates to the standard of post-graduate study and research. Each stage is marked by the award of a diploma and the appropriate academic title (e.g. in engineering: I—engineer, II—master, III—specialist), and can either be regarded as self-sufficient or as a step to further study. In some fields the first and second level are run together as uninterrupted courses, usually of four years.

The main types of institutions are: (1) Higher schools (*više škole*); (2) High schools (*visoke škole*), which, confusingly enough, are higher than the higher schools; (3) Art academies (*umetničke akademije*); (4) Faculties (*fakulteti*). Of these, the higher schools give first-level qualifications only; the other types teach to the second and third levels as well.

The faculty, rather than the university, is the institutional unit. There are six university centres (Belgrade, Zagreb, Ljubljana, Sarajevo, Skopje and Novi Sad), but they are federal centres for faculties spread over twenty towns. Thus, the University of Belgrade has twenty-six faculties, mostly in the capital, but also including faculties of law, medicine and engineering in Niš, arts and law in Priština, economics and engineering in Titograd, mining and metallurgy in Bor, and two extra-mural departments

---

[28] Figures from: *Statistički Kalendar Jugoslavije 1965. Visoke Škole 1963/1964.* (Statistički Bilten 364, Belgrade, 1965.) Marijan Filipović, *Higher Education in Yugoslavia*. (Medjunarodna Politika, Belgrade, 1965.)

in Kragujevac. Similarly, the University of Zagreb has faculties in Rijeka, Zadar, Split and other towns in Croatia; Sarajevo has faculties all over Bosnia and Herzegovina, and so on. Faculties generally concentrate on the humanities and the pure sciences, but law, economics, technology, medicine, agriculture and forestry, stomatology and pharmacy also come under the university umbrella.

The high schools are academically the equivalent of the faculties (indeed, some of them are affiliated to the universities), but tend to be more specialized and more precisely geared to vocational preparation. There are seventeen of them altogether, including high schools of mechanical engineering, agriculture, government administration, political science, physical culture. In this category too come the pedagogical high schools—the Pedagogical Academy in Maribor, the High School of Defectology, specializing in the education of handicapped children, in Zagreb, and the High School of Industrial Pedagogy in Rijeka, which trains teachers for certain types of technical school.

Outside the state system, but of equivalent standard, are the faculties of theology—Orthodox in Belgrade, Roman Catholic in Ljubljana and Zagreb, and six other Catholic high schools. They are run by the respective churches for the training of priests. There were 751 students attending theological faculties in 1964.

Art academies give courses in fine and applied arts, music, drama, film, radio and television. There are fourteen of these with about 2000 students, over half of them in music academies. As with other institutions of this level, departments are distributed over several centres; the Music Academy of Belgrade, for example, looks after extra-mural departments in Niš and Novi Sad.

Higher schools (*više škole*) have expanded more than any other type of higher educational institution, from two teacher training colleges with 259 students in 1939 to 137 with over 53,000 in 1965. Courses are normally of two years' duration, and are available in a wide range of specialities, including teacher training, domestic science, social work, statistics, hotel management and catering, book-keeping and finance, agriculture, dentistry, surveying, textile technology, printing, industrial chemistry, railway engineering, mechanical engineering, economics, foreign trade, building technology and a host of others. The qualifications given in these schools are also available, in most cases, in the first-level courses in other higher educational institutes.

Places in higher education have increased almost tenfold since before the war, most of this growth being accounted for by the expansion of the higher schools. Attempts have been made, with some success, to spread the facilities rather more evenly over the country; Macedonia had one institute in 1939, with a few hundred students, and now has fifteen with over 9000 students. Bosnia-Herzegovina, with thirty-five institutes and 20,000 students, and Montenegro, with four institutes and 2000 students, had none at all before the war.

In spite of the growth, however, there are still not enough places to accept all qualified applicants. The development of part-time courses in most fields has helped to some extent, but the pressure on places is still strong. Students leaving school with outstanding marks used to be admitted without having to take the entrance examination; but since there has been some doubt expressed (there as here) about the predictive value of school-leaving examinations, all applicants are now required, where their number exceeds the number of places, to take the entrance examination irrespective of their attainments at school.

(g) *Teacher Training*

The teacher training system in Yugoslavia is complicated, like so much else, by the variations from one republic to another, and the gradual implementation of reforms. At the moment, the principal types of institution are:

(i) The teachers' school (*učiteljska škola*) admits pupils from the basic school and gives a five-year course (four in Bosnia) of combined general education and teacher training. Students completing the course are qualified to teach general subjects in classes I to IV of the basic school. Variants of this type include physical education schools, schools for kindergarten teachers (*škole za vaspitače*), etc. In Slovenia, Macedonia and the Kosmet one also finds teacher training departments in general secondary schools; there are not many of these, and most of them are concerned with training teachers for the national minority schools.[29]

(ii) The higher pedagogical school (*viša pedagoška škola*) admits students who have completed the *gimnazija* (or teachers' school), and gives a two-year course for teachers of special subjects in classes V to VIII of the basic school. Students specialize in two cognate subjects as a rule.

(iii) The pedagogical academy (*pedagoška akademija*), also a "higher school" on much the same lines, gives two types of course: two years for graduates of the *gimnazija*, six years for pupils from the basic school. The latter consists of a four-year *gimnazija* course with a slight bias to teacher training after the second year, followed by a two-year professional course. Students may train either as general or specialist teachers for any level of the basic school. Essentially, the pedagogical academy is a combination of the two types previously mentioned.

(iv) Specialist teachers for secondary schools come from the faculties. Training courses are provided concurrently with the main body of university studies, but in contrast to the practice in other Eastern European countries, they are not required. It is possible (and common) for secondary teachers to be completely untrained (as in some English schools, except that no one tries to make a virtue of it). A post-graduate training year has been suggested, but has not been favourably received. There are also four-year university courses in education, but these are taken mainly by intending specialists—lecturers in education, administrators, etc.

Present policy is to run down the teachers' schools, since it is

[29] Hans-Jürgen Drengenberg, "Der Stand der jugoslawischen Lehrerbildung zu Beginn des Schuljahres 1963/64" (*Informationsdienst zum Bildungwesen in Osteuropa*, **7**, pp. 42–47. Osteuropa-Institut an der Freien Universität Berlin, 1964.)

generally felt that they provide inadequate training, and to go over to a single type of institution, a pedagogical academy not unlike the kind already in existence, for all basic school teachers. The change-over is already almost complete in Slovenia and Croatia; eventually, all basic school teachers will have the equivalent of four years in the *gimnazija* and two years of training.[30] Nobody claims that this is enough; about 30 per cent of the students in Serbian two-year training courses fail the final examination, and this is usually attributed to the insufficiency of the course.[31] Three years is frequently mentioned as a much more reasonable length of course, but in the present circumstances this is more of a pipe-dream than a policy objective. The rather sparse training of university graduates is also liable to frequent criticism, not least from those actually involved in it. Proposals for further improvement, however, especially if they involve any lengthening of the course, founder on the hard facts of the situation. Yugoslavia is critically short of teachers; in some remote areas the deficiency is as high as 40 per cent, while in other places it is small—Belgrade even has a surplus of some 400. The national average is about 25 per cent below requirements.[32] Direction is not used, and inducements such as bonus payments, the provision of housing, and the like, have had limited success. Some students are reluctant to teach in rural areas, more still are reluctant to teach at all, since the salaries compare poorly with those in other professions.

It is not surprising, therefore, that the schools themselves pay more attention than in many other countries to their function as teacher-training institutions. No teacher is regarded as fully qualified as soon as he finishes his training, whatever its level. He is a probationer (*suplent*) for five years. During this time he is visited regularly by tutors from the appropriate institution, and eventually he takes a state examination (*državni ispit*) which gives

[30] Hans-Jürgen Drengenberg, *op. cit.*; confirmed Belgrade, 1965.
[31] Oral communication, Belgrade Higher Pedagogical School, September 1965.
[32] Figures orally from Jugoslovenski Zavod za Proučavanje Školskih i Prosvetnih Pitanja, Belgrade, September 1965.

the final qualification. But this is not the end of the process; teachers are expected to take frequent refresher courses (some of them carrying an additional qualification and additional salary); school directors regard it as one of their main tasks to visit teachers in their classes, discuss lessons with them, and give advice —although, since there are no prescribed methods, the teachers are under no compulsion to accept it. The work of the subject panel (*stručni aktiv*) is in a sense a perpetual internal refresher course. Quite apart from the requirements of the state examination and the bait of extra qualifications, continual retraining is accepted in any case; indeed, the idea that anyone can be regarded as qualified for all time is looked on as rather quaint. As one school director[33] has put it: "The training of a teacher ends when his life ends—and that applies to me no less than to my youngest colleague."

Yugoslavs are perfectly frank about the shortcomings of their system. Illiteracy, though reduced, remains far too high; pre-school education is underdeveloped by Eastern European standards. The eighth year of compulsory schooling, introduced in 1952 and written into the law of 1958, has still not become universal. There are criticisms of the overburdening of pupils in the basic and secondary schools, complaints that the two stages are insufficiently co-ordinated. Many economic organizations are unenthusiastic about the level of technical training, and often prefer to recruit unskilled workers and train them themselves. Drop-out rates are too high in higher education, and courses are taking, on average, two years longer than they should. Discrepancies between town and country, and between republic, though far less glaring than they were, are still there in large measure. Teacher shortage is holding back the expansion programmes at almost every level, and almost nobody is satisfied with the present standard of the professional training of teachers. Educational planning is all too often piecemeal and confused.

It has to be remembered, before invidious comparisons are

[33] Director of the Stefan Sindjelić Basic School, Belgrade.

drawn, that Yugoslavia has had a worse combination of handicaps to cope with than any other East European country. Among the eight countries with which we are dealing, only Albania had a higher level of illiteracy. In loss of life and destruction of property during the war, Yugoslavia suffered worse than any except for Poland. Economically and industrially, Yugoslavia was one of the most underdeveloped and poorest in resources. Most of the countries in the area have nationality problems to some extent, but in Yugoslavia they have always been much greater. By virtue of the early break with the Cominform, Yugoslavia escaped the worst excesses of the Stalin era with its obscurantist bureaucracy and pedantic planning, but it has to be conceded that the policy of decentralization of the educational system (as of the economy), whatever its virtues, does make coherent and effective planning more difficult.

History and geography have conspired to give Yugoslavia a particularly hard row to hoe in a generally stony field, and it is as well to take notes of what has been achieved. The quantitative expansion of education at all levels, compared with the unpromising start after the war, has been impressive by any standards. Basic education is practically universal, though not always the full course. Illiteracy is down to well below half the pre-war level —even less, if the pre-war figures are more realistically interpreted. Secondary schooling, if uneven in quality, has more than doubled, places in higher education have rocketed. Vocational and technical education have developed from poor beginnings, and the system of adult education, built up from practically nothing to the present extensive network of courses, has done much to eliminate the "dead ends" of the old system. There is, furthermore, a greater degree of open-mindedness and flexibility in tackling problems than in most parts of Eastern Europe. The unsolved problems are clear enough, and there is ample evidence that the Yugoslavs are by no means blind to them. This, and the efforts that have converted one of the most backward countries in Europe to one where every fifth Yugoslav is a student, cannot go for nothing.

CHAPTER 7

Bulgaria

1. BACKGROUND TO THE SYSTEM

At a time when most of the Eastern European countries have, in their own ways, been asserting their independence or at least individuality, Bulgaria clings closest of all to the U.S.S.R. This can be partly ascribed to a long-standing Russophile tradition; during the Turkish occupation (1396–1878), Russia often appeared in the role of liberator, and in spite of periods of disenchantment (as during the late nineteenth century, when Russia's primary concern with her own interests was particularly obvious), pan-Slavic ideas have tended to gain a readier hearing in Bulgaria than in most other Slav countries. The present régime, too, has never tried to play down its indebtedness to the Soviet Union for its very existence. Monarchist Bulgaria, certainly, fought on the Axis side during the Second World War, but neither the régime not its policy were popular, especially when the "Greater Bulgaria" gains turned sour as the tide of war ran against the Nazis. The fall of the old régime in 1944 was mainly the work of the invading Soviet army, but a broadly based armed uprising played some part as well.

The new régime under Georgi Dimitrov, an almost legendary figure in the communist world, tried, as we have seen, to bolster its independence by fostering some kind of Eastern European federation. This came to nothing, and the expulsion of Yugoslavia from the Cominform signalled the clamping-down of the Stalin régime all over the rest of Eastern Europe. Whether Dimitrov would have been able, or willing, to play the part of Tito (or even Gomułka) is beyond speculation, as he died in 1949, and was succeeded by Vulko Chervenkov, a "Muscovite" Communist and strict-line Stalinist. Chervenkov established himself firmly in power during the early 1950's; even the de-Stalinization drive after 1956 failed to dislodge him completely, though he did suffer some demotion. It was not until 1961 that the "Khrushchovite" Todor Zhivkov managed to muster enough support in the Party to dismiss him altogether, and it took another year to remove from office another Stalinist, Anton Yugov. On both occasions Zhivkov relied openly on Soviet support; though this proved effective, it did emphasize his weakness within the Bulgarian Communist Party.

Bulgaria is still mainly agricultural, though there has been some industrialization since the war. There was an attempt in 1958 to quicken the pace—almost a "great leap forward" on the Chinese pattern. Some successes were attained, but nowhere near the targets that had been set; these had to be revised, which gave rise to an economic crisis and a good deal of political uncertainty. The U.S.S.R. (perhaps to forestall the possible growth of Chinese influence) gave massive economic aid and received (presumably as a *quid pro quo*) total support from Bulgaria in the dispute with China. It is perhaps significant that although Zhivkov was clearly Khrushchov's protégé, his party was the only one in Eastern Europe not to protest at the manner of Khrushchov's dismissal in 1964.

Bulgaria is perhaps the most cautious of the Eastern European countries. The dependence of her economy on the U.S.S.R. makes independent policy initiatives unlikely. At the same time, Zhivkov appears to lack enough support in his own party to pursue the de-Stalinization policy, which has slowed down (after a spurt in 1962 and 1963) to a pace well short of Czechoslovakia or Hungary. This caution affects education as other areas of social life; the system is not a copy of the Soviet system, nor does it stand still, but it is hard to escape the conclusion that changes and reorganizations are made more with an eye on what is happening in the Soviet Union than can now be said for any other Eastern European country.

2. THE OLD SYSTEM AND POST-WAR DEVELOPMENTS

Bulgaria made a promising début on the European cultural scene with the invention of the Slav alphabet by the brothers Cyril and Methodius in the ninth century, and the beginnings of a national literature on into the eleventh. Development stagnated, however, during the period of Byzantine rule (1018–1186), and again under the Ottoman Empire. The "National Revival", however, did not have to wait for the end of Turkish rule, which was largely ineffective by 1878 anyway, but gathered force early in the nineteenth century. In addition to literary revival, the movement made itself felt in an increased interest in schooling as a means of modernizing the nation. The first high school was opened in Gabrovo in 1831, and development continued intermittently throughout the nineteenth and early twentieth centuries. By 1944 every medium-sized village could claim at least a four-year elementary school, some of the larger ones seven-year schools, and every town a secondary school of some sort. As one Bulgarian commentator[1] concedes, this was "a fairly extensive system" for a backward agrarian country.

Favourable though the position was compared with, say, Yugoslavia, it was still insufficient by any reasonable standards. The system was organized on three levels, with four-year elementary schools (age 7–11), followed by three-year "pro-gymnasia" and four-year gymnasia, which provided the only preparation for higher education. The four-year school was nominally compulsory, but was not available in about 2000 smaller villages; about 100,000 children of school age did not attend.[2] Of those who did, about half went on to the pro-gymnasium after the age of 11; about a third of their number went on to the gymnasium. Technical education, in particular, was poorly developed, accounting for less than a fifth of the total number in secondary

[1] Nevena Geliazkova (ed.), *Prosperity and Culture in Bulgaria*, p. 100. (Foreign Languages Press, Sofia, 1964.)
[2] *Ibid.*

schools;[3] the level of instruction did not make it possible for students from these schools to enter further or higher education. Adult education was virtually nonexistent. As a general index of the educational level of the country, 31 per cent of the population were illiterate.[4]

Between 1944 and 1950 a series of enactments set up external schools, provided for expansion of places at all levels, transformed and expanded the technical schools, and merged the courses of the elementary schools and the progymnasium into a basic seven-year school. In 1959 the "Law on the closer relationship of the school with life, and the further development of education in the Bulgarian People's Republic" (corresponding closely to the Soviet model of 1958 in title as in much of its content) increased polytechnical training in the general schools and extended basic schooling from seven to eight years. Since then there have been further modifications, paralleled elsewhere: polytechnical education has been pruned, vocational training for pupils in general secondary schools has been dropped, and the basic school and gymnasium courses have been reorganized to form a continuous eleven-year course.

3. THE PRESENT SYSTEM

(a) *Pre-school Education*

This follows the usual pattern of crèches (*jasli*) up to the age of 3, and kindergartens (*detski gradini*) from 3 to 7. Attendance is voluntary, and a charge may be made for maintenance. There are about twenty-five times as many places in kindergartens as there were before the war. At present, they are attended by over 60 per cent of children of pre-school age.[5]

---

[3] *Statističeski Godišnik na Narodna Republika Bŭlgarija 1963*, pp. 337–50 (N.R. Bulgarija Centralno Statističesko Upravlenie pri Ministerskija Sŭvet, Sofia, 1963), from which all figures are taken unless otherwise stated.

[4] Mihajlo Juhas, "Općeobrazovna škola i produženi boravak učenika u SR Bugarskoj", *Revija Školstva i prosvetna dokumentacija*, **1** (1965), pp. 23–29, Belgrade.

[5] Oral communication, 1966.

Bulgaria 335

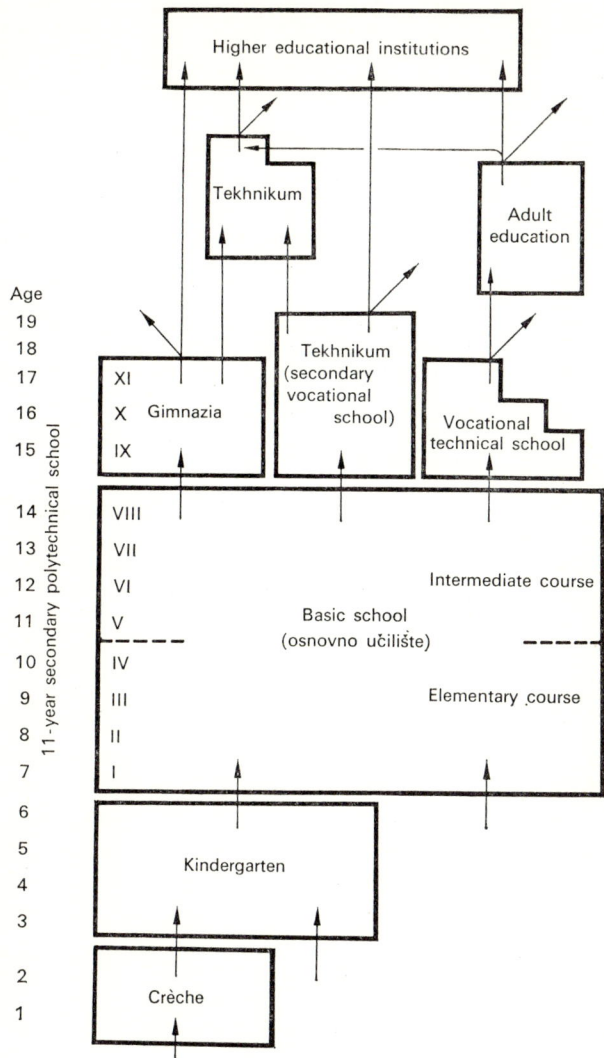

Fig. 40. Bulgaria: School system

Fig. 41. Bulgaria: Eleven-year General School Curriculum

Class:	I	II	III	IV	V	VI	VII	VIII	IX	X	XI	Total week-hours
I.												
1. Bulgarian language and literature	11	11	11	7	6	6	5	5	3	3	4	72
2. Russian language	–	–	–	–	3	3	3	2	2	1	1	15
3. Western language	–	–	–	–	–	–	–	2	3	3	2	10
4. Mathematics	5	5	5	5	6	5	5	4	5	4	5	54
5. Physics-astronomy	–	–	–	–	–	1	2	2	3	3	4	15
6. Chemistry	–	–	–	–	–	–	2	2	2	3	2	11
7. Biology	–	–	–	½	2	2	2	2	2	2	–	11·5
8. Geography	–	–	–	½	2	2	2	2	–	2	–	11·5
9. History	–	–	–	2	2	2	2	2	2	2	2	16
10. Bases of communism	–	–	–	–	–	–	–	–	–	–	2	2
11. Physical education	2	2	3	3	2	2	2	2	2	2	2	25
12. Drawing	1	1	1	1	2	2	2	–	–	–	–	10
13. Singing	1	2	2	2	2	2	1	1	1	–	–	14
Total:	20	21	22	23	26	27	28	25	25	25	24	
II. Work Training	2	2	3	3	3	3	2	2	–	–	–	20

Bulgaria

											Total
Polytechnical subjects:											
1. Principles of agriculture	—	—	—	—	—	—	2	—	—	—	2
2. Principles of industrial production:											
(a) Principles of mechanics and technical drawing	—	—	—	—	—	—	—	—	3	—	3
(b) Electrotechnics	—	2	3	3	3	3	2	4	3	—	1
Total	—	2	3	3	3	3	2	4	—	3	6	—	15
III. *Production training (theory and practice)*	—	—	—	—	—	—	—	3	6	6	15
IV. *Optional subjects*											
1. Stenography	—	—	—	—	—	—	—	2	2	—	4
2. Russian language	—	—	—	2	2	2	2	2	2	2	14
3. Western language	—	—	—	2	—	—	2	2	2	—	8
4. Latin	—	—	—	—	—	—	—	2	2	—	4
5. Turkish language	—	—	—	—	—	—	2	2	2	2	8
6. Music	—	—	—	—	—	2	—	2	2	—	6
7. Drawing	—	—	—	—	—	—	2	2	2	2	8
8. Car and tractor	—	—	—	—	—	—	—	2	2	—	4
Weeks per year	31	31	31	33	33	33	29	32	32	30	

(b) *The Basic School*

The basic school (*osnovno učilište*) takes children from 7 to 15, and provides the first two stages of what is now known as the eleven-year secondary polytechnical school (*sredno politekhničesko učilište*). The elementary course (*načalen kurs*) comprises classes I to IV, and is principally concerned with the basic subjects—Bulgarian and mathematics, with some music, art, physical education, handwork. The secondary course (*sreden kurs*) includes classes V to VIII; it is during this stage that such subjects as foreign languages and the sciences appear on the curriculum (see Fig. 41).[6] As a rule, the two stages run together in the same school, with the children moving on from class to class in the usual manner. (They are assessed for this purpose on a marking scale from 6 down to 2; between 6 and 7 per cent repeat the year's work.) In many smaller villages there is only an elementary school (*načalno učilište*); for the second stage, the children have to go either to the nearest complete basic school, or to one of the second-stage schools, with classes V to VIII only, that have been set up at central points in some country districts.

(c) *Secondary Schools*

Compulsory education ends with the completion of the basic school at 15, and it is possible for pupils to leave and go into full-time work. Very few in fact do so; currently, about 95 per cent go on with some kind of schooling beyond this stage. Some types of school are more popular than others. General secondary schools and technical schools are preferred to trade schools, and even within one type there are degrees of popularity; technical schools of radio-engineering, electronics and the like are more sought after than schools of building or agriculture. Selection is based on the pupil's marks in the final year of the basic school. The main types of secondary school are as follows:

(i) General secondary school (*Gimnazia*). This is the third stage

[6] Juhas, *op. cit.*, pp. 24–25.

of the eleven-year school, known officially as the higher course (*goren kurs*), comprising classes IX to XI and ending with the final school examination (*matura*), which entitles the holder to apply for entry to higher education. The course (see Fig. 41) is not divided into separate "sides" as in Yugoslavia or Rumania, but allows for some degree of specialization by making time available for optional subjects, mainly in the arts and foreign languages. Pre-vocational training in factories has now been replaced by a reduced element of general technical education, for the reasons that have been observed elsewhere.

The *gimnazia* takes about a third of the pupils leaving the basic school. Numbers have doubled since before the war, but in the last few years have declined slightly as the emphasis shifts to various types of technical or vocational secondary schooling.

(ii) *Tekhnikum*. The full title of the *tekhnikum* is the vocational secondary school (*sredno profesionalno učilište*). It gives a four-year course leading to vocational qualifications in various branches of industry (electrotechnology, computer programming, telecommunications, mechanical engineering, building, transport, machine construction, etc.), agriculture, and "non-productive" services, such as administration, economics, etc. At the same time, general studies are continued. The range is rather narrower than the *gimnazia* course, but includes Bulgarian language and literature, Russian and a Western European language, mathematics, physics, chemistry, history, geography, physical education, and in some schools art and music. These are taken to the level of the *matura*, and can lead to higher education, usually on the technological side. Curricular subjects are divided into three main groups: (1) general education, (2) general technical education, (3) theory and practice of special vocational subjects. About a third of the time is devoted to each group.[7]

It is also possible to enter a *tekhnikum* after taking the *matura*. Some types of *tekhnikum* operate only on this level, such as schools

---

[7] Naiden Čakarov *et al.*, *Das Schulwesen in der Volksrepublik Bulgarien*, pp. 176–80. (In Deutsches Pädagogisches Zentralinstitut, *Das Schulwesen sozialistischer Länder in Europa*, Volk und Wissen Volkseigener Verlag, Berlin, 1962.)

of mining, medicine, veterinary medicine, industrial chemistry, rubber technology and others. Students with the *matura* have a shortened course (two to three years), which does not include the general educational subjects, since they have been taken already. It does, however, include Marxism–Leninism, higher mathematics and physical education, as well as general technical and special vocational subjects.

The *tekhnikum* has expanded far more than the *gimnazia*, from about 10,000 students before the war (and 21,000 after it) to over 134,000 in 1962. The growth continues as the *tekhnikum* comes to dominate the secondary system as the *gimnazia* used to. At present it is enrolling about 40 per cent of the pupils leaving the basic school.

(iii) *Vocational technical school (profesionalno tekhničesko učilište).* These schools are analogous to the trade or apprentice schools in other countries, and train skilled workers in courses ranging from one to three years, according to trade—three years, for example, for metalwork and electrical trades, two for agricultural mechanization, one for building, etc. The curricula include Bulgarian, Russian, physics, mathematics, history and physical education, but such subjects play a more modest part than in the secondary vocational schools. Together with general technical subjects and vocational theory, they account for about half of the time, the rest being taken up with practical work, usually in factories or on farms. Numbers have doubled since 1944; vocational technical schools now enrol about 20 per cent of pupils leaving the basic school.

(d) *Special Schools*

The pre-war system in Bulgaria was particularly lacking in special facilities for handicapped children. Fewer than 400 children were cared for in five special schools (one for blind children, three for deaf mutes and one for the mentally backward) run by charitable organizations. In 1944 there were even fewer—four schools with just over 200 children. The handicapped, by and large, simply did not go to school. One of the provisions of the first enactments in 1944 was to set up such schools within the national system; development was slow at first, but by the early 1960's there were seventy special schools with over 8000 children. Apart from basic schools with a suitably modified programme, the main emphasis is on providing vocational training.

Separate schools for the specially gifted include music, art and ballet schools, some of them operating at secondary level, others providing the entire eleven-year course. There are also four-year foreign language secondary schools, where instruction is given through the medium of a foreign language. Apart from Russian, French is the favourite language, with German lagging behind and English bringing up the rear.[8] Some 2500 pupils attend schools of this type. Selection is made on the basis of their performance in foreign languages in the basic school.

(e) *Adult Education*

After 1944 one of the chief concerns in adult education was the provision of courses for illiterates and semi-literates. Illiteracy courses functioned until 1950;[9] for those who had been to school for one or two years, the need remained for elementary school courses for a few years longer. Beyond this stage, the network of part-time courses is still functioning. Part-time courses for the second stage (classes V–VIII) will presumably cease to be required in time, but at the level of the secondary schools (whether general or vocational) they remain a regular feature of the system. As well as providing a second chance for older students, they keep open the possibility of higher education for people whose secondary schooling has been confined to vocational technical courses. Part-time courses did not exist at all in 1944. They have developed

---

[8] The same order of preference is found in the ordinary secondary schools. Apart from Russian, which is compulsory, French is overwhelmingly the first choice; students of French in secondary schools outnumber students of German by nearly four to one; German has the advantage over English by roughly the same ratio. A tiny number (less than 100) study Italian.

[9] Juhas, *op. cit.*, p. 23.

slowly but steadily; at present, external students in general secondary schools, for example, account for one-eighth of the total number. There are also special preparatory courses, mainly on the technical side, for older intending students at higher educational institutions.

(f) *Higher Education*

The higher institutions in Bulgaria may be divided into two main categories, each giving a different level of course:

(1) The so-called "semi-higher" institutes (*poluvisši instituti*). This, for all practical purposes, means teacher training colleges (*učitelski instituti*), with three-year courses for primary school teachers (classes I–IV). There are also one or two other colleges in this category, including one for librarians.

(2) Higher educational institutions (*visši učebni zavedenija*), colleges of university standard. These include universities, technical institutes, agricultural institutes, medical colleges, higher schools of economics, art academies, etc.—twenty-two altogether. Six of them are in provincial towns (Plovdiv, Varna, Svishtov and Russe), the rest being situated in Sofia.[10] The length of course varies from four to six years, five years being the average.

Expansion has been rapid up to the present. Before the war there were just over 10,000 students; now there are 85,000 in the higher institutions and 16,000 in the teacher training colleges[11]—a large number for a country of 8 million people, making Bulgaria fourth (after the U.S.A., U.S.S.R. and Japan) in proportion of the population pursuing higher education. About a third of these are studying part-time, but this proportion is now declining slightly. Competition for admission is keen; the position varies from one institution to another, but on average there are four applicants for every place, nor is there any sign of the demand slackening. Nevertheless, there is not likely to be much more expansion over

[10] Čakarov, *op. cit.*, p. 184.
[11] Recent figures from Bulgarian Vice-Minister of Education, Edinburgh, 1966.

the next few years; not surprisingly, the pace of growth has strained resources (there is a shortage of adequate university teachers), and the authorities feel it is time to pause and consolidate. There will, therefore, be little increase until 1970 at least.[12]

(g) *Teacher Training*

Bulgaria used to have secondary teachers' schools (*pedagogičeski učilišta*) for the training of elementary school teachers. These have now been run down. Since the passing of the 1959 law, all elementary teachers (classes I–IV) are trained in teacher training colleges, and all secondary teachers (classes V up to XI) in higher educational institutions. As in many other countries, teacher training is a normal part of most higher educational courses; this, coupled with the fact that the Bulgarian authorities make full use of the powers to direct graduates to any job anywhere in the country for three years, keeps the problem of teacher shortage at bay (though presumably at the cost of an inconveniently high rate of turn-over in rural districts). What shortages do exist are at the higher level, not primary or secondary.

The Bulgarian system seems to have settled down to a period of consolidation. In some ways, the "tone" is rather unadventurous, compared with many other Eastern European countries. Experiment, though it does go on, is more limited and policy appears to be orthodox, as does the style of teaching. Quantitatively, however, the advances have been astonishing. The existing network of schools was more extensive than anywhere else in the "Southern Tier", but it was still backward, and Bulgaria is not a rich country. According to Bulgarian sources, there are now no illiterates under the age of 50.[12] With eight-year schooling compulsory and over 90 per cent going beyond 15, virtually all the 7 to 16 age-group are now attending schools,[13] and about 75 per cent follow full

[12] *Ibid.*
[13] Johannes Faensen, "Bulgarien: Statistische Angaben", *Informationsdienst zum Bildungswesen in Osteuropa*, **7**, pp. 40–41. (Osteuropa-Institut an der Freien Universität Berlin, 1964.)

secondary courses up to the age of 18. In higher education, the problem is not a shortage of qualified personnel, but the saturation of the professional labour force (in a still predominantly agrarian country) with graduates.

According to many observers, Bulgaria has been less successful than most of her neighbours in the policial and economic fields, dependent as she is on Soviet tutelage and subject to economic crises. The development of education, however, must be counted one of the major successes in Eastern Europe in the last twenty years.

CHAPTER 8

Albania

ALBANIA's claim to attention in recent years has little to do with the country or its people, but arises from the preliminary skirmishing that went on before the Sino-Soviet dispute broke out into the open. Mao did not, at first, attack the Soviet leadership as such, but rather the vague concept of "revisionism" or, when an actual illustration was required, Yugoslavia. Khrushchov and his allies, similarly, hesitated to anathematize as revered a figure as Mao, but directed their polemics against "dogmatism" and, as its main identifiable exponent, Albania. Everyone knew what was really meant, but for a time the public side of the dispute was kept on the edges of the communist world and not its centre. The need for pretence finally vanished when the chances of settling the quarrel dwindled to vanishing-point. Albania became Albania again instead of a code-word for China.

Albania's own quarrel with the Soviet Union went back to Khrushchov's *rapprochement* with Yugoslavia—no friend of Tito could possibly be a friend of Hoxha—and led to a complete rupture in diplomatic relations, the closing of the Soviet base at Vlonë, and the end of Soviet aid. Since the Sino-Soviet split became public, Albania is now chiefly noted as China's only ally in Europe. Recently, there have been signs that the Albanian leadership is less enthusiastic than it was, if the extremely lukewarm response to the "great cultural revolution" of 1966 is anything to go by. The Albanian Communist Party's "hard-line" positions of the last few years, however, have left very little room for manoeuvre, which makes a return to the fold highly unlikely.

In an Eastern Europe already far from monolithic, Albania is well out on a limb of her own.

Apart from her role in international Communist Party controversies, Albania is the least important of the Eastern European countries, with the smallest population (1¾ millions) and the most backward economy (there is little industry, and about 70 per cent of the population are still rural). Politically, Albania, has been quite unaffected by the events since 1956, at least as far as internal policy is concerned; one of the most independent countries in Eastern Europe, and one of the few with a home-made revolution, Albania now maintains her independence as the last bastion of classic Stalinism.

Perhaps for this reason, reliable information on education is not readily come by, apart from statistical returns. Enough is known, however, to note that the most backward country educationally in Europe before the war (with an illiteracy level of over 80 per cent) is still, in spite of advances over the last twenty years, the most backward in the entire area.

(a) *Pre-school Education*

Kindergartens (*kopshte*) take children from 3 to 7. There are ten times as many places as before the war, making room for about 20 per cent of the age-group.

(b) *Basic Schools*

Basic schooling is in two stages: (1) Elementary schools (*shkollat fillore*) provide four-year schooling from the age of 7 to 11, and concentrate, as elsewhere, on the basic subjects. (2) Seven-year schools (*shkollat 7-vjeçare*) comprise classes V–VIII. The course takes children approximately to the age of 14, though in practice there is a good deal of variation. There is a relatively steady falling-off from one year to the next; at present, this second stage is taken by about half the number enrolled in elementary schools. Some of the discrepancy can be accounted for by rising

Fig. 42. Albania: General Secondary School Curriculum[1]

Class:	V	VI	VII	VIII	IX	X	XI
1. Albanian language and literature	9	7	6	6	6	5	4
2. Mathematics	6	6	6	6	5	5	5
3. History	2	3	2	2	2	2	2
4. Study of the constitution	—	—	—	—	—	—	2
5. Geography	3	2	2	2	1	—	—
6. Biology and geology	2	3	2	2	2	2	—
7. Hygiene	1	—	—	—	—	—	—
8. Physics	—	—	3	—	3	4	4
9. Astronomy	—	—	—	—	—	—	2
10. Chemistry	—	—	2	2	2	2	3
11. Psychology	—	—	—	—	—	—	2
12. Russian	3	3	3	4	4	3	3
13. Second foreign language	—	—	—	2	2	2	2
14. Physical education	2	2	2	2	2	2	2
15. Drawing	1	1	1	—	—	—	—
16. Technical drawing	—	—	—	1	1	1	—
17. Singing and music	1	1	1	1	—	—	—
18. Practical work	2	2	2	2	2	2	2
Total hours weekly	32	32	32	32	32	32	34

[1] All figures are taken from *Vjetari Statistikor i R.P.Sh. 1964*, pp. 357–81. (Republika Popullore e Shqipërisë, Drejtoria e Statistikës, Tirana, 1964.)

birth-rate, but it is clear that a large proportion of children do not as yet go to school for more than four years.

(c) *Secondary Schools (shkollat e mesme)*

Secondary schools are attended by slightly less than half the number of pupils from seven-year schools. The main types available are:

(1) Eleven-year schools (*shkollat 11-vjeçare*) give four-year courses (classes VIII to XI) leading to the final examination and the chance of entering higher institutions. About half the number of all secondary school pupils are in courses of this kind.

(2) Secondary technical-professional schools (*shkollat e mesme tekniko-profesionale*) combine vocational courses with general education to the level of the final certificate. Technical schools (*teknikume*) specialize in such fields as mechanics, electrical engineering, metallurgy, agriculture, forestry, building, etc., and pedagogical schools (*shkollat pedagogjike*) train teachers for elementary schools. There are also schools of this type specializing in administration, music, art and physical education. Courses last for four or five years, and are attended by some 23,000 students, slightly less than the enrolment of the eleven-year schools.

(3) Lower vocational schools (*shkollat e ulte profesionale*) train skilled workers in such trades as agriculture, commerce, mechanics and other branches of industry. These are the least numerous of the secondary schools, and are attended by about 3500 students.

(d) *Higher Education*

There are eight higher educational instutitions (*shkollat e larta*) in Albania. The most important of these is the State University of Tirana, with seven faculties (law, economics, history and philology, engineering, geology, medicine, natural sciences, combining the functions of the universities and many of the specialized institutes in other Eastern European countries). In addition, there are small institutes of agriculture, art, physical culture and drama, and three larger pedagogical institutes for the training of secondary school teachers. Courses are normally of five years' duration, though there is some variation according to subject; the pedagogical institutes give two-year courses.

There were no higher educational institutions at all until 1950; in 1964 there were over 12,000 students, including over 3000 in the pedagogical institutes. Half of them are following part-time courses—by correspondence for the most part, though a few hundred attend evening classes. There is much variation in this pattern from one field of study to another; in the pedagogical institutes, for example, the majority are studying externally.

Set beside the other countries of Eastern Europe, Albania does not show up well in the present level of educational development; this is hardly a fair comparison, considering the backwardness of the country in practically every field before the war, and considering also the poverty which makes even Yugoslavia look quite well off by contrast. Set beside the pre-war picture, the system presents a spectacle of massive advance—pre-school places have increased ten times, general school places seven times; there are thirteen times as many students in pedagogic schools, seventy times as many in secondary vocational schools, while higher education has developed from scratch. But this is perhaps an unduly complimentary picture; any growth at all from zero is likely to look enormous. Developments to date, seen against the background of enormous disadvantages and the rigid atmosphere that has continued to the present time, represent a considerable advance; but the large numbers of children who still cannot expect more than minimal schooling are a reminder of how much still remains to be achieved.

Glossary

Abitur (Ger.). Final leaving certificate from secondary schools; entitles holder to apply for admission to higher education.
Abiturklassen in den Einrichtungen der Berufsausbildung (Ger.). Classes leading to *Abitur* in vocational schools. Also known as *Berufsschulen mit Abitur* (q.v.).
Aktiv (Yug.). Active group (e.g. of teachers) who concern themselves with problems relevant to their own field.
általános iskola (Hung.). General school; the eight-year basic school (age 6–14).
Arbeiter-und-Bauern Fakultät (Ger.). Workers' and Peasants' Faculty; adult education institute run by a university, where older students can take entrance qualifications to higher education.

Berufsschule (Ger.). Vocational school; part-time trade training for young people who have completed full-time basic schooling.
Berufsschulen mit Abitur (Ger.). Vocational schools with classes leading to the *Abitur* (q.v.) as well as a vocational qualification.
Betriebsberufsschule (Ger.). Factory *Berufsschule*.
bölcsődek (Hung.). Crèches for young children under age 3.

creşe (Rum.). Crèches for young children under age 3.
ČSM (Československý Svaz Mládeže) (Czech.). Czechoslovak Youth League; the senior youth organisation.

dečje domovi (Yug.). Children's homes; boarding kindergartens.
dečje jaslice (Yug.). Crèches for children under age 3.
dečje vrtić (Yug.). Kindergarten (for children age 3–7).
detski gradini (Bulg.). Kindergartens (children age 3–7).
DKMS (Dimitrovski Komunističeski Mladežki Săjuz) (Bulg.). Dimitrov Communist League of Youth; the senior youth organization.
domy małego dziecka (Pol.). Infant homes; boarding kindergartens.
DPO (Dimitrovska Pionerska Organisacia "Septemvrijče") (Bulg.). Septembrist Dimitrov Pioneer Organization; the junior youth organization.
DPZI (Deutsches Pädagogisches Zentralinstitut) (Ger.). German pedagogical central institute; the chief East German body for educational research.
društveni-jezički smer (Yug.). Social-linguistic branch; the arts course in classes II–IV in a *gimnazija* (q.v.).
državni ispit (Yug.). State examination; the final qualifying examination for teachers after a period of practical teaching as a *suplent* (q.v.).

educatoare (Rum.). Kindergarten teachers.

érettségeri (Hung.). Final school-leaving certificate; cf. *Abitur*.
erweiterte polytechnische Oberschule (Ger.). Extended polytechnical secondary school; a two-year course following completion of the ten-year polytechnical secondary school, and leading to the *Abitur* (q.v.).
examen de maturitate (Rum.). Examination of maturity; the final school-leaving certificate.

Facherbeiterprüfung (Ger.). Skilled worker's examination; vocational qualification given at the end of the course in a *Berufsschule* (q.v.).
Fachschule (Ger.). Vocational or technical school (two to three year course), giving vocational qualifications on a level above that of the secondary schools, but lower than higher educational institutions.
Fachschulreife (Ger.). Qualification (lower than *Abitur*, q.v.) to enter a *Fachschule*.
fakultet (Yug.). Faculty; the organizational unit of a university.
FDJ (Freie Deutsche Jugend) (Ger.). Free German Youth; the senior youth organisation.

Gesamtunterricht (Ger.). Unified instruction: general teaching without division into separate subjects.
gimnazija (Yug. & Bulg.). General secondary school. In Yugoslavia, a four-year course following the basic school, leading to the final certificate. In Bulgaria, a three-year course, the "higher course" *(goren kurs)* of the eleven-year secondary polytechnical school.
gimnázium (Hung.). General secondary school; a four-year course after the basic school, leading to the *érettségeri* (q.v.).
goren kurs (Bulg.). Higher course; last three years of the eleven-year secondary polytechnical school. Otherwise known as *gimnazija* (q.v.).
grădiniţa de copii (Rum.). Kindergarten (children age 3–7).
gyermekváros (Hung.). Children's town; residential school community for delinquent, orphan or problem children.
gyógypedagógiai iskola (Hung.). Special school for handicapped children.

Hochschule (Ger.). High school; higher educational institution of university standard.

învăţător (Rum.). Primary school teacher (as distinct from *professor* in secondary classes).
Institut für Lehrerbildung (Ger.). Teacher-training college for primary school teachers.
instytut pedagogiki (Pol.). Institute of pedagogy; the chief Polish centre for educational research.
ipari tanulók gyakorló iskolája (Hung.). Apprentice-training school.

jasli (Bulg.). Crèche for children under age 3.
jesle (Czech.). Crèche for children under age 3.
jiskry (Czech.). Sparks; organization for younger children, a preparatory stage to joining the pioneers.

Jugoslovenski Zavod za Proučavanje Školskih i Prosvetnih Pitanja (Yug.). Yugoslav foundation for educational research.

Jungpionieren (Ger.). Young Pioneers; members of the junior branch of the Thälmann Pioneer Organization.

Kindergarten (Ger.). Pre-school institution (voluntary) for children between the ages of 3 and (in East Germany) 6.

Kinderkrippe (Ger.). Crèche for children under age 3.

Kinderwochenheim (Ger.). Children's weekly home; boarding kindergarten.

KISZ (*Kommunista Ifjusági Szövetszége*) (Hung.). Communist Youth League; the senior south organization.

Komosomol (*VLKSM—Vsesoyuznyi Leninskii Kommunisticheskii Soyuz Molodyozhi*). All-Union Leninist Communist League of Youth; the Soviet senior youth organization, and prototype of similar bodies in Eastern European countries.

kopshte (Alb.). Kindergartens.

liceu (Rum.) (pl. *licee*; def. *liceul*, pl. *liceele*). *Lycée*; general secondary school, with a four-year course leading to *examen de maturitate* (q.v.).

liceum ogólnokształcące (Pol.). General educational lyceum; four-year course after basic school, leading to *matura* (q.v.).

liceum pedagogiczne (Pol.). Pedagogical lyceum; secondary school with general course leading to *matura* (q.v.) and primary teaching qualification.

lidové školy jazyků (Czech.). People's schools of languages; special language schools providing courses for adults and schools pupils.

lidové školy umění (Czech.). People's schools of art; schools providing courses for adults and school pupils.

mateřská škola (Czech.). Kindergarten for children aged 3–6.

matura (Bulg., Czech., Pol.). Secondary-school-leaving certificate; entitles holder to apply for admission to higher educational institutions (cf. *Abitur*).

měšťanské školy (Czech.). Civic schools; advanced elementary or lower secondary schools in pre-war system.

młodsi harcerze (Pol.). Junior scouts; younger members of the ZHP (q.v.).

MUSZ (*Magyar Uttörők Szövetszege*) (Hung.). Hungarian Pioneer League; the junior youth organization.

načalen kurs (Bulg.). Elementary course; the first stage (classes I–IV, ages 7–11) of the eleven-year secondary polytechnical school.

načalno učilište (Bulg.). Elementary school; a school giving the elementary course (*nacalen kurs*) only.

Narkompros (Russ.) (*Narodnyi Kommisariat Prosveshcheniya*). People's Commissariat for Education; the governmental body responsible for education in post-revolutionary Russia.

nastavničko veće (Yug.). Teachers' Council.

nauka o społczeństwie (Pol.). Social science; the new course in civics and political theory for final classes in secondary schools.

Oberschule (Ger.). Secondary school; in East Germany, the ten-year general educational polytechnical secondary school (*Zehnklassige allgemeinbildende polytechnische Oberschule*, q.v.), age 6–16.
Oberstufe (Ger.). The upper grade (classes 7–10) of the *Oberschule* (q.v.).
odborná škola (Czech.). Vocational school.
odborné učilište (Czech.). Apprentice training centre.
OKWOM (*Ogólpolski Komitet Współpracy Organizacji Młodzieżowych*) (Pol.). All-Polish Committee for Co-ordination of Youth Organizations.
organizaţia de pionieri (Rum.). Pioneer organization; the junior youth organization.
Országos Pedagógiai Intézet (Hung.). National Pedagogical Institute; the chief centre for educational research.
osnovna škola (Yug.). Basic school; general eight-year school, age 7–15.
osnovno učilište (Bulg.). Basic school; general eight-year school (7–15), comprising first two stages (*načalen kurs* and *sreden kurs*, qq.v.) of the eleven-year general polytechnical secondary school.
óvoda (Hung.). Kindergarten; for young children aged 3–6.
ovónoképző iskola (Hung.). School for kindergarten teachers.

pedagógiai intézet (Hung.). Pedagogical institute; four-year institutes for the training of subject specialist teachers for the upper classes of the basic school.
Pädagogische Hochschule (Ger.). Pedagogical high school; institute for higher pedagogical training.
pedagogičesko učilište (Bulg.). Teachers' school; a secondary school for the training of primary teachers, now replaced by three-year teacher-training colleges (*učitelski instituti*, q.v.).
pädagogische Schule (Ger.). Two-year school for the training of kindergarten teachers.
pedagoška akademija (Yug.). Pedagogical academy; six-year secondary or two-year post-secondary course of teacher training.
poluvisši institut (Bulg.). "Semi-higher" institute; higher colleges of less than university standard. (In practice, teacher-training colleges.)
prirodno-matematički smer (Yug.). Scientific-mathematical branch; the science course (classes II–IV) in a *gimnazija* (q.v.).
profesionalno tekhničesko učilište (Bulg.). Vocational technical school, providing trade training for pupils who have completed the basic school.
propedeutyka filozofii (Pol.). Introduction to philosophy; essentially a course in Marxist theory, now replaced by social study (*nauka o społczeństwie*, q.v.).
przedszkoła (Pol.). Kindergarten; for young children age 3–7.

razredno veće (Yug.). A panel of teachers of a single class, meeting for exchange of information and discussion of class problems.
Reifeprüfung (Ger.). Test of maturity; another name for the *Abitur* (q.v.).

savet škole (Yug.). School council; managing body of a school, consisting of teaching staff, parents' representatives, pupils' representatives, etc.

şcoală de bază de cultură generale de opt ani (Rum.). Eight-year general educational basic school; basic comprehensive school for pupils from 7–15.
şcoală medie (Rum.). Secondary school.
şcoală medie de cultură generale (Rum.). General secondary school, with four-year academic course (see *liceu*).
şcoală profesional de ucenici (Rum.). Vocational apprentice school, with courses leading to trade qualifications.
şcoală tehnică (Rum.). Technical school; two- or three-year courses for holders of the *maturitate* (q.v.).
şcoală tehnică de maistri (Rum.). Foreman's technical school; advanced courses for workers after some years at work.
shkollat e larta (Alb.). Higher educational institutions.
shkollat e mesme (Alb.). Secondary schools.
shkollat e mesme tekniko-profesionale (Alb.). Secondary technical-professional schools; combined vocational and general education to leaving-certificate level.
shkollat e ulte profesionale (Alb.). Lower vocational schools; secondary courses for the training of skilled workers.
shkollat fillore (Alb.). Elementary schools; four-year schools for children from age 7–11.
shkollat pedagogjike (Alb.). Pedagogical schools; secondary schools for the training of primary school teachers.
shkollat 7-vjeçare (Alb.). Seven-year schools; incomplete secondary schools, from age 7–14.
shkollat 11-vjeçare (Alb.). Eleven-year schools; complete secondary schools leading to leaving certificate.
škola drugog stupnja (Yug.). Second-stage school; secondary course following on basic school.
škola sa praktičnom obukom (Yug.). School with practical instruction; three-year courses in trade training.
škola učenika u privredi (Yug.). Apprentice school.
škole za kvalifikovane radnike (Yug.). Vocational schools; a term used to cover the previous two types.
škola za osnovno obrazovanje odraslih (Yug.). Basic school for adults.
škola za vaspitače (Yug.). School for kindergarten teachers.
škole za obrazovanje odraslih (Yug.). Schools for adult education.
Sonderschule (Ger.). Special school for handicapped children.
specijalne škole (Yug.). Special schools for handicapped children.
SPJ (*Savez Pionira Jugoslavije*) (Yug.). League of Pioneers of Yugoslavia; the junior youth organization.
sreden kurs (Bulg.). Secondary course; classes V–VIII of the eleven-year general polytechnical school.
sredno politekhničesko učilište (Bulg.). Secondary polytechnical school; the entire eleven-year school course.
sredno profesionalno učilište (Bulg.). Vocational secondary school; four-year course leading to vocational qualification and school leaving certificate. Also known as *tekhnikum* (q.v.).
Staatsbürgerkunde (Ger.). Civic or political studies.

starsi harcerze (Pol.). Senior scouts; older members of the ZHP (q.v.).
střední škola pro pracující (Czech.). Secondary school for workers.
střední všeobecně vzdělávací škola (Czech.). General educational secondary school; three-year course following the basic school, leading to the *matura* (q.v.).
stručni aktiv (Yug.). Subject panel; a group of teachers of the same subject meeting to examine methods and developments in that subject.
studium nauczycielskie (Pol.). Teachers' college; two-year course for the training of teachers for the basic schools.
suplent (Yug.). Probationer; a teacher who has not yet taken his final qualifying state examination (*držanvi ispit*, q.v.).
szkoła podstawowa (Pol.). Basic school, for pupils from age 7–15.

tanár továbbképző kollégium (Hung.). Teachers' training colleges.
technika zawodowa (Pol.). Vocational technical school; five-year course leading to vocational qualification and the *matura* (q.v.).
technikum (Hung.). Secondary vocational school.
tehničke i druge stručne škole za privredu i javne službe (Yug.). Technical and other vocational schools for the economy and public services; four-year schools leading to vocational qualifications and school-leaving certificate.
tekhnikum (Bulg., Russ.). Secondary vocational school.
technische Hochschule (Ger.). Technical college (of university standard).
teknikume (Alb.). Secondary vocational schools.
Thälmannpionieren (Ger.). Older members of the Thälmann Pioneer Organization.
továbbképző iskola (Hung.). Continuation school; two-year courses for pupils who leave basic school at 14 but do not go on with other kinds of secondary schooling.

učiteljska škola (Yug.). Teachers' school; secondary school for the training of primary teachers.
učitelski instituti (Bulg.). Teachers' institutes; three-year course for training primary teachers (classes I–IV).
učnovská škola (Czech.). Apprentice school.
umetnička akademija (Yug.). Art academy.
umetnička škola (Yug.). Art school; secondary school for the highly gifted in art.
upravni odbor (Yug.). School management board, elected by teachers from among their own number.
UTM (*Uniunea Tineretului Muncitor*) (Rum.). Union of Working Youth; the senior youth organization.

vaspitač (Yug.). Kindergarten teacher.
veće škole (Yug.). School council.
viša pedagoška škola (Yug.). Higher pedagogical school; two-year course for students who have completed the *gimnazija* (q.v.) or equivalent, qualifying them to teach classes V–VIII.
viša škola (Yug.). Higher school; two-year courses of post-secondary education, usually vocational. Equivalent to the first level of university-standard courses.

visoka škola (Yug.). High school: an educational institution of university standard.
visši učebni zavedenija (Bulg.). Higher educational institutions; colleges of university standard.
vysoké školy (Czech.). High schools; institutions of university standard.
výzkumný ústav pedagogický (Czech.). Pedagogical institute; the main centre for educational research.

zakladní devítiletá škola (Czech.). Basic nine-year school (6–15).
zehnklassige allgemeinbildende polytechnische Oberschule (Ger.). Ten-year general educational polytechnical secondary school; the East German basic school, for pupils aged 6–16.
ZHP (*Związek Harcerstwa Polskiego*) (Pol.). Union of Polish Scouts; the junior youth organization.
ZMS (*Związek Młodieży Socjalistycznej*) (Pol.). Union of Socialist Youth; the senior youth organization in urban areas.
ZMW (*Związek Młodieży Wiejskiej*) (Pol.). Union of Rural Youth; the senior youth organization in country areas.

Index

Administration *see* Local authorities; Ministries of Education
Adult education   17. In: Bulg. 341–2; Cz. 253–5; E. Ger. 212; Hung. 275; Pol. 195; Rum. 293–4; U.S.S.R. 69–70; Yug. 322–4
Agricultural schools   14–15, 196
Antonescu, General   42
Apprentices, apprentice schools. In: Cz. 120–1, 249–51; E. Ger. 166; Hung. 166, 273; Rum. 292; Yug. 144
Apáczai-Csere, János   262
Art academies   227, 256–7, 276, 296, 324
Assessment   158–60, 217–18, 225, 242, 268, 288, 310
Attendance, enforcement of   76, 78, 81, 181, 191, 307, 343
Audio-visual aids   87–88, 163, 189–90

Babeş-Bolyai University, Cluj   29, 283, 294
Babeş, Victor   285
Baden-Powell, Lord   106, 179
Bălcescu lycée   74
Balzac, Honoré de   122
Banja Luka *gimnazija*   110
Basic schools   157–63; length of course in, 157; organization of, 158; special classes in, 160. In: Alb. 157, 346–7; Bulg. 338; Cz. 157, 235, 238–43; E. Ger. 157, 209, 214–19; Hung. 83, 157, 263, 267–9; Pol. 82, 157, 184, 187–92; Rum. 82, 157, 158, 288–9; U.S.S.R. 67; Yug. 84, 158, 308–14

Belgrade, Music Academy of   325
Belgrade, University of   324
Beneš, Edvard   52, 234
Beria, Lavrenty   53
Bikówek School   191
Boarding schools   214, 269; and sex, 139
Braşov, Polytechnic Institute of   295
Bratislava, Comenius University of   255
Brno Applied Art Secondary School   248
Bucharest Institute of Architecture   295
Bucharest Palace of Pioneers   132
Bucharest Pedagogic Institute   296
Bucharest Polytechnical Institute   295
Bucharest, University of   167, 294, 295

Caragiale   101, 295
Caragiale Theatre and Cinema Institute   296
Ceauşescu, Nicolae   15, 56, 101, 283, 284, 297, 298
Četnik   44, 49
Chamberlain, Neville   45
Chervenkov, Vulko   332
Churches *see* Religion
Churchill, Winston   49, 40
Class, socio-economic: in pre-war schools, 78–79, 261; communist policy towards, 224–5, 261
Classics   75, 85, 245, 285
Cluj Polytechnical Institute   295

Co-education 139–42; and moral education, 14. In: Cz. 139–40; Pol. 140–1, 193–4; U.S.S.R. 141. *See also* Women and girls.
"Collective leadership" 52
Collective, Makarenko and 62, 108, 111; in pre-school education, 156; in youth orgs. 137
Colleges *see* Higher education
COMECON 4, 19, 52
Cominform 4
Communist Party 48–50, 51–57, 154; mergers of, 50; purges in, 52; national deviations in, 51; "thaw" in, 53; 20th Congress of Soviet, 53; and youth orgs. 123, 126, 135. In: Alb. 52; Bulg. 50, 51; Cz. 50, 52, 126, 241; E. Ger. 50; Hung. 50, 52; Pol. 50–52; Rum. 50–52, 282, 300; U.S.S.R. 65; Yug. 50–51, 300. *See also* Political changes
Comprehensive education: in basic schools, 157–61; and streaming, 66, 161. In: Cz. 239; E. Ger. 208–9; U.S.S.R. 66–67; Yug. 308–10.
Constitutional provisions: on education, 80–81, 209, 263; on national minorities, 27, 80–81; on sex, 138; on control of schools, 147, 209
Copernicus, Nicholas 181
Crèches 155–7. In: Bulg. 334; Cz. 235–7; E. Ger. 213; Hung. 266; Pol. 185; Rum. 288; Yug. 308
Csillebérc Pioneer Town 129
Cuza, Prince Alexander Ioan 285
Cyril and Methodius 37, 333

Darwin, Charles 101
Degrees *see* Higher education
Deutscher, Isaac 49
Dewey, John 61, 108, 202
Dimitrov, Georgi 51, 331
Discipline 102–12, 189–90; and youth orgs. 130–1; pre-school, 156; in Yug. 110–11. *See also* Moral education
Djilas, Milovan 303

Dózsa, György 261
Dresden, Medical College of 226
Dresden, Technical College of 226

ELAS 49
Elementary school *see* Basic school; Primary school
Engels, Friedrich 93
Eötvös, József 263
Examinations 164. In: Bulg. 339; E. Ger. 206, 224, 225; Pol. 192, 196; Rum. 292
Expansion 82, 85–86

Fót Children's Village 109, 274
Further education *see* Adult education

Galaţi, Polytechnical Institute of 295
General secondary schools 164–5. In: Alb. 348; Bulg. 338–9; Cz. 243–5; E. Ger. 219–21; Hung. 77–79, 269–72; Pol. 192–6; Rum. 289–92; U.S.S.R. 67; Yug. 316–18
Geography 93, 96, 97, 187, 216, 239
Gheorghiu-Dej, Gheorghe 282
Girls *see* Women and girls
Goethe, Wolfgang 121
Gomułka, Władysław 38, 39, 51, 52, 54, 178, 180, 331
Gorki, Maksim 121, 122
Grammar school *see* General secondary school
Greifswald, Ernst Moritz Arndt University of 226
Gubrovo High School 74, 333
Gymnasium *see* General secondary school

Habsburgs 32, 232, 233, 259
Halle, Martin Luther University of 226

Handicapped children, education of *see* Special schools
Hans, Nicholas 8
Haret, Spiru 285
Hašek, Jaroslav 233
Havemann, Prof. 56
Hemingway, Ernest 122
Higher education 167-9; pre-war, 74, 79; women in, 142, 144; expansion of, 69-70; higher degrees in, 169; Higher education in: Alb. 348-9; Bulg. 342-3; Cz. 167, 255-7; E. Ger. 167, 226-9; Hung. 276-8; Pol. 167, 198-9; Rum. 294-7; U.S.S.R. 69; Yug. 324-6
History 93, 97-100, 216, 229, 239, 241
Hitler, Adolf 24, 25, 26, 31, 207
Horthy, Admiral Miklos 35, 42, 260, 261, 263
House of Czechoslovak Children 243
Hoxha, Enver 23, 115
Humboldt University, Berlin 59
Hungarian Theatre Institute 296
Hus, Jan 232

Ideology *see* Political education; Religion
Illiteracy 6, 13, 17-18, 73; of women, 41, 138; "liquidation" of, 61-62, 81, 184, 263, 343. In: Alb. 346; Bulg. 73; Cz. 73; Hung. 73, 261; Pol. 73, 181; Rum. 73; Yug. 41, 73, 301-23, 306, 307
Industrial production 16-17, 19-20, 114-15
Industrialization 234, 261-2, 282-3, 332, 346
Ion Neculce School 294

Jassy Polytechnical Institute 295
Jena, Schiller University of 226
Joseph II, Emperor 259
József Attila Free University 275

Julius Fučík House of Youth 132, 243
Junior schools *see* Basic schools

Kádár, János 38, 54, 55
Karl Marx University, Leipzig 226
Karlovy Vary Ceramics School 248
Khrushchov, Nikita Sergeievich 5, 52, 53, 54, 57, 67, 68, 332, 343
Kindergartens 155-7. In: Alb. 346; Bulg. 334; Cz. 237-8; E. Ger. 213-14; Hung. 266-7; Pol. 185-7; Rum. 288; Yug. 309
King, Edmund 96
Klement Gottwald House 132
Kogălniceanu 285
Komenský, Jan Amos 102, 237, 263
Koniev, Marshall 207
Košice, Šafařík University of 255
Kosovo Polje, Battle of 33, 303
Kossuth, Lajos 259, 263
Kostov 52
Kraków, University of 36, 74, 181, 198
Krupskaya, Nadezhda 61
Kún, Béla 35, 260

Land use 12, 14
Language, foreign 95-96, 162, 163, 187, 195, 216, 229, 239, 245, 267-9, 271, 275, 284, 289, 339
Languages, minority 28. *See also* Minorities, national
Legislation *see* Reforms
Leipzig, Building College of 226
Leipzig, College of Physical Education of 227
Lenin, V. I. 61, 64, 93, 101, 105
Lenin Institute of Economics and Planning 296
Literacy *see* Illiteracy
Local authorities 149-50, 152, 154, 305-7
Łódź, University of 198
Lublin, Catholic University of 179, 198

Lublin, University of 198
Lycée *see* General secondary schools

Magdeburg, Medical College of 226
Makarenko, Anton Semyonovich 62, 108
Mao Tse-tung 203, 283, 345
Maria Theresa, Empress 259
Maribor, Pedagogical Academy of 325
Marx, Karl 59, 61, 62, 93
Marxism and Marxism-Leninism 5, 26–27, 51, 57; and educational theory, 59–60, 61, 65; and moral education, 104, 105; teaching of, 91, 92, 94–95, 99–100, 129, 217, 227, 229, 241; and science, 115–17
Masarýk, Jan 234
Maurer, Ion Gheorghe 101, 283, 284
Maxim Gorki Institute of Russian Language and Literature 284, 295
Methods 87–89, 162–3
Michurin 101
Mihajlov, Mihajlo 303
Mihajlović, Draža 49
Mindszenty, Cardinal 38, 39
Ministries of Education 147–54, 166, 156–7. In: Alb. 148; Bulg. 148; Cz. 148, 149, 153; E. Ger. 148, 153, 213, 221; Hung. 148, 149, 279; Pol. 147–8, 153; Rum. 65, 148, 153; U.S.S.R. 65, 147; Yug. 147
Minorities, national 20–29; Albanians, 40–41; Germans, 23–24; Transylvanian Hungarians, 25–26, 29, 283–4; schools for, 28–29. In: Cz. 23–24, 234; E. Ger. 23–24; Rum. 25–26, 29, 23–24, 283–4; Yug. 40–41, 301
Moral education 102–12; and youth orgs. 127–9; and sex, 141. In: E. Ger. 214, 217; Hung. 109; Pol. 105; Rum. 106, 107; Yug. 103, 106, 108–9, 110–11, 141. *See also* Collective, Makorenko and; Political education
Mother tongue 214, 229, 239, 267, 300

Nagy, Ernő Bajor 77, 78, 267
Nagy, Imre 54
Napoleon 32
Nationalism 25–29, 31, 33–36, 44, 50, 55–56; cf. patriotism, 106, 109. In: Cz. 234; Hung. 260, 262; Pol. 56; Rum. 55, 285; Yug. 44, 50, 302–3
Nature study 161, 187, 239, 310–14
Neugattersleben, Institute of Agronomy of 227
Nikola Tesla Electro-Technical School, Belgrade 122, 318
Novotný, Antonín 101
Nursery schools *see* Pre-school education

Olomouc, Palacký University of 255
Owen, Robert 62

Parents 212
Pătrăşcanu, Titel 52
Pedagogical schools, pedagogical institutes *see* Teacher training
Petroşeni Mining Institute 296
Physical education 214, 227, 229; and sex, 139
Physical environment 11, 29–30, 301
Piłsudski, Marshall 42
Pioneers *see* Youth organizations
Planning *see* Ministries of Education
Political changes 6–7, 41–48, 50–58, 80. In: Alb. 345–6; Bulg. 331–2; Cz. 51–52, 234; Hung. 54–55, 260–1; Pol. 55, 178–9; Rum. 282–5; Yug. 56. *See also* Communist Party
Political education 90–102; introduction of, 84–85; in curriculum, 91–92; in other subjects, 93; in civics, 64, 91, 92, 93, 217; in posters

Political education—*cont.*
  and slogans, 64, 100–1. In: Alb. 93, 100; Bulg. 93, 100; Cz. 93, 100, 241; E. Ger. 90, 101, 217, 229; Hung. 94–95, 272; Pol. 99–100, 101, 180–1; Rum. 100–1; U.S.S.R. 63–65; Yug. 90. *See also* Geography; History; Moral education; Social studies; Youth organizations

Polytechnical education 8, 61–62, 113–23; and youth orgs. 128–30, 136; East European adoption of, 68, 84; theoretical basis of, 61–62; practical difficulties of, 117–18, 122–3; and sex, 139, 140–1. In: Bulg. 115–16, 118; Cz. 116, 118, 241–2, 245; E. Ger. 113, 117, 211, 216, 217–19, 221, 229, 230; Hung. 113, 117, 263, 268–9, 269–71; Pol. 192; Rum. 318–20; U.S.S.R. 61–62, 68–69

Population complexities of, 23–25, 300–2; expansion of, 192; urban/rural, 12, 13–14, 234

Potsdam Institute of Archives 227

Potsdam-Babelsberg, Walter Ulbricht Academy of Political Science of 227

Prague, Charles University of 36, 74, 232

Prague, Czech Technical University of 256

Pre-school education 155–7; rural, 156. In: Alb. 155, 346; Bulg. 334; Cz. 235–7; E. Ger. 155; Hung. 266–7: Pol. 185–7, 213–14; Rum. 288; Yug. 308

Primary schools: pre-war, 43, 74, 78, 181, 182; specialist teachers in, 87. In: Alb. 346; Bulg. 333

Pushkin, Aleksandr S. 101, 122

Rădulescu 285
Rájk, lászlo 52
Rákóczy, Prince 259
Rákosi, Mátyás 39, 54, 55, 260, 262, 280

Ranković, Alexander 303

Reforms, educational 113; post-war, 81–84, 84–86, 183–5. In: Bulg. 82, 334, 343; Cz. 83–84; E. Ger. 207–12; Hung. 83, 263; Pol. 82–83, 183–5; Rum. 81–82, 285–6, 297–9; Yug. 84

Religion 22, 37–41; and the Communist Party, 38–40; and moral education, 104–5; religious instruction, 38, 177, 178–9; abolition of R.I. 85; Muslim, 22, 40–41, 145; Orthodox, 22, 37, 38; Roman Catholic, 22, 37, 38–40, 143, 146, 177–9. In: Alb. 145; Cz. 39, 232; E. Ger. 209; Hung. 37, 39, 263; Pol. 37, 39, 146, 177, 178–9; Yug. 39, 40–41, 302

Research 109–10, 190–1

Reytana Lyceum, Warsaw 193

Rijeka, High School of Industrial Pedagogy of 325

Rural schools 15, 28, 43, 76, 145, 170, 181, 182, 187, 243, 269, 343

Russian language 57, 71, 85, 95–96, 162, 187, 195, 216, 223, 227, 229, 239, 284

Sarajevo, University of 325
Sarpi, Paolo 45
Scholarships 77, 198, 277
Schweik, Josef 233
Science and technology, 112–23; in school curricula, 111–13, 161–2. In: Cz. 239, 241–2; E. Ger. 113, 216, 223, 229; Rum. 113; Yug. 122, 310

Secondary schools 164–7; pre-war, 74, 182, 206; post-war expansion of, 85–86; length of course in, 164; shift of emphasis in, 18–19. In: Alb. 348; Bulg. 165, 338–40; Cz. 75, 165, 243–53; E. Ger. 219–25; Hung. 165, 263, 269–74; Pol. 165, 182, 192–6; Rum. 74, 165, 243–53; Yug. 165, 263, 269–74

SED 50, 56
Selection pre-war in Hung. 77–78; for secondary schools, 78–79, 165, 224, 243, 289, 317; for higher education, 326, 342–3
Sex *see* Women and girls
Shakespeare, William 122
Shaw, Bernard 34
Slanský, Rudolf 52
Słodowska-Curie, Marie 181
Social studies. In: Bulg. 93; Cz. 241; E. Ger. 217, 223; Hung. 94–95, 272; Pol. 93–95, 272; Yug. 93, 310 ff. *See also* Geography; History; Marxism and Marxism-Leninism; Political education
Soviet education 59–72; influence of, 8, 10, 36, 57–58, 60, 63, 70, 71–72, 81–82, 84–85, 87, 158, 258, 343; "progressivism" in, 61; Russian tradition in, 8, 48–49, 62–63, 71; expansion of, 69–70
Special schools and classes 160. In: Bulg. 340–1; Cz. 160, 242, 251–3; E. Ger. 218–19; Hung. 268–9, 274–5; Rum. 160, 292; Yug. 322
Specialization 113, 122, 164–5, 192, 245, 288, 316, 339
Sport *see* Physical education; Youth organizations
Stalin, I. V. 5, 7, 22, 26, 27, 48, 49, 50, 52, 53, 54, 55, 56, 57, 61, 65, 68, 96, 100, 101, 178, 262, 331
Stefan Sindjelić School 314
Stepinac, Cardinal 38, 39
Stoian, Stanciu 299
Streaming 87, 242. *See also* Comprehensive education
Students 113–14, 198, 224–5, 276–7, 326, 342
Suceava Pedagogic Institute 296
Suchodolski, Bogdan 105, 106
Szentgyörgy István Theatre Institute 284

Tannenberg, Battle of 32

Teacher training 169–71; further training, 170–71. In: Alb. 348–9; Bulg. 343; Cz. 170, 257–8; E. Ger. 229–30; Hung. 171, 278–80; Pol. 170, 182, 187, 199–201; Rum. 171, 296; Yug. 170, 326–9
Teacher training colleges 169–71. In: Alb. 349; Bulg. 343; Cz. 258; E. Ger. 227, 229, 230; Hung. 170, 278; Pol. 200; Rum. 170, 296; Yug. 325, 327
Teacher training schools 169–71. In: Alb. 348–9; Bulg. 343; Cz. 170, 257; Hung. 278; Pol. 170, 182, 199–200; Rum. 75, 170, 292; Yug. 170, 326–7
Teachers, supply of 12, 144, 145. In: Bulg. 343; Hung. 279; Pol. 187–8; Rum. 12; Yug. 13, 328
Technical colleges. In: Bulg. 342; Cz. 256; E. Ger. 226–7; Hung. 276; Rum. 295; Yug. 327
Technical schools 18–19, 112–13, 119–22, 165–6; sex in, 140–3. In: Alb. 119–20, 348; Bulg. 333, 334, 339–40; Cz. 76, 120; E. Ger. 209, 225–6; Hung. 272–3; Pol. 196–7; U.S.S.R. 67; Yug. 122, 318–20
Tekhnikum *see* Technical schools
Terminal elementary schooling 74–75, 76, 78, 206
Testing, mental: Soviet rejection of, 66; East European rejection of, 158–9; Yugoslavia an exception, 87, 158
Thälmann, Ernst 216
Textbooks 87, 97–99, 106, 149, 258, 286, 305
Togliatti, Palmiro 7
Timişoara Polytechnical Institute 295
Timişoara, University of 294
Tîrgu Mureş, Pedagogic Institute of 117
Tito, Josip Broz 4, 27, 39, 40, 44, 50, 52, 53, 54, 55, 57, 93, 101, 128, 283, 303, 331, 345
Togliatti, Palmiro 7

Trade training *see* Vocational schools
Traditions: Russian, 8, 48–49, 60, 63, 70, 71–73; East European, 36, 73; traditional systems, 74–77; adaptation of, 81–84
Training colleges *see* Teacher training
Trotsky, Lev Davidovich 52
Turgenev 122

Uherské Hradiště Secondary School 248
Ulbricht, Walter 101, 203
Universities 167; pre-war, 74; control of, 149; teacher training in, 169. In: Alb. 348; Bulg. 342–3; Cz. 255–6; E. Ger. 226, 229; Hung. 276; Pol. 181, 198–9. 200–1; Rum. 294–5; Yug. 324–5, 327
University of 17th November 255
Ustaše 39, 44, 303

Vocational schools 17, 119, 165–6, 183. In: Alb. 348; Bulg. 340; Cz. 76, 245–9; E. Ger. 206–7, 209, 221–5, 230; Hung. 272–3; Pol. 182, 196–7; Rum. 119, 292; U.S.S.R. 67; Yug. 320–2

Walter Ulbricht Palace of Pioneers 132
War, Second World 31–34, 35, 43–44, 46, 80, 176–8, 233–4, 260, 302–3, 307
War, Thirty Years' 232
Warsaw Palace of Youth 132

Women and girls 40–41, 138–46; illiteracy of, 41, 138; and family planning, 146; and Islam, 40–41, 145–6; and technical education, 140–3; and pre-school education, 143; opportunities for, 40–41, 141–6. In: Alb. 144, 145; Cz. 139–40; E. Ger. 141–2; Pol. 139–40; Yug. 144
Work training *see* Polytechnical education
Workers' faculties 69, 212
Workers' Party *see* Communist Party
Wyszyński, Cardinal 38, 39, 146

Xoce, Koçi 23, 52

Youth organizations 123–38; organization of, 124–7, 132–3, 134, 136–7; activities of, 123–4, 125, 126, 129, 130, 131, 134, 136; in moral education, 111, 127–9; Pioneers, 70–71, 111, 124–33, 160, 216; youth leagues, 133–8; Palaces and houses of, 131–2. In: Bulg. 70–71, 123, 124, 128, 130; Cz. 125, 126, 133, 134, 242–3; E. Ger. 70, 125, 126, 187–8, 132, 134, 136, 212, 216, 229; Hung. 123, 124, 125, 129, 133, 135, 136; Pol. 71, 123, 124, 125, 133, 134, 135, 179–80; Rum. 71, 124, 127, 128, 132, 133, 134, 135; U.S.S.R. 70, 134; Yug. 70, 125, 128

Zagreb, University of 325
Zamenhof School, Warsaw 189, 190